Lecture Notes in Artificial Intelligence 11523

Subseries of Lecture Notes in Computer Science

Series Editors

Randy Goebel
University of Alberta, Edmonton, Canada
Yuzuru Tanaka
Hokkaido University, Sapporo, Japan
Wolfgang Wahlster
DFKI and Saarland University, Saarbrücken, Germany

Founding Editor

Jörg Siekmann
DFKI and Saarland University, Saarbrücken, Germany

More information about this series at http://www.springer.com/series/1244

Yves Demazeau · Eric Matson ·
Juan Manuel Corchado ·
Fernando De la Prieta (Eds.)

Advances in Practical Applications of Survivable Agents and Multi-Agent Systems

The PAAMS Collection

17th International Conference, PAAMS 2019
Ávila, Spain, June 26–28, 2019
Proceedings

 Springer

Editors
Yves Demazeau 🆔
Grenoble Computer Science Laboratory
Grenoble, France

Eric Matson
Purdue University
West Lafayette, IN, USA

Juan Manuel Corchado 🆔
University of Salamanca
Salamanca, Spain

Fernando De la Prieta 🆔
University of Salamanca
Salamanca, Spain

ISSN 0302-9743   ISSN 1611-3349   (electronic)
Lecture Notes in Artificial Intelligence
ISBN 978-3-030-24208-4   ISBN 978-3-030-24209-1   (eBook)
https://doi.org/10.1007/978-3-030-24209-1

LNCS Sublibrary: SL7 – Artificial Intelligence

This Springer imprint is published by the registered company Springer Nature Switzerland AG
The registered company address is: Gewerbestrasse 11, 6330 Cham, Switzerland

Preface

Research on Agents and Multi-Agent Systems has matured during the past decade and many effective applications of this technology are now deployed. An international forum to present and discuss the latest scientific developments and their effective applications, to assess the impact of the approach, and to facilitate technology transfer became a necessity and was created almost two decades ago.

PAAMS, the International Conference on Practical Applications of Agents and Multi-Agent Systems, is the international yearly tribune to present, to discuss, and to disseminate the latest developments and the most important outcomes related to real-world applications. It provides a unique opportunity to bring multi-disciplinary experts, academics and practitioners together to exchange their experience in the development and deployment of agents and multi-agent systems.

This volume presents the papers that were accepted for the 2019 edition of PAAMS. These articles report on the application and validation of agent-based models, methods, and technologies in a number of key application areas, including: agronomy and the Internet of Things, coordination and structure, finance and energy, function and autonomy, humans and societies, reasoning and optimization, traffic and routing. Each paper submitted to PAAMS went through a stringent peer review by three members of the Program Committee composed of 154 internationally renowned researchers from 29 countries. From the 54 submissions received, ten were selected for full presentation at the conference; another eight papers were accepted as short presentations. In addition, a demonstration track featuring innovative and emergent applications of agent and multi-agent systems and technologies in real-world domains was organized. In all, 14 demonstrations were shown, and this volume contains a description of each of them.

We would like to thank all the contributing authors, the members of the Program Committee, the sponsors (IEEE Systems Man and Cybernetics Society Spain Section Chapter and the IEEE Spain Section; Technical Co-Sponsor), IBM, Indra, Viewnext, Global exchange, AEPIA, AFIA, APPIA, PU, CNRS and AIR institute. We thank the funding supporting with the project *"Intelligent and sustainable mobility supported by multi-agent systems and edge computing"* (Id. RTI2018-095390-B-C32) and also the Organizing Committee for their hard and highly valuable work. Their work contributed to the success of the PAAMS 2019 event.

Thanks for your help – PAAMS 2019 would not exist without your contribution.

June 2019

Yves Demazeau
Eric Matson
Juan Manuel Corchado
Fernando De la Prieta

Organization

General Co-chairs

Yves Demazeau   Centre National de la Recherche Scientifique, France
Eric Matson   Purdue University, USA
Juan Manuel Corchado   University of Salamanca, Spain
Fernando De la Prieta   University of Salamanca, Spain

Advisory Board

Bo An   Nanyang Technological University, Singapore
Paul Davidsson   Malmö University, Sweden
Keith Decker   University of Delaware, USA
Frank Dignum   Utrecht University, The Netherlands
Toru Ishida   University of Kyoto, Japan
Takayuki Ito   Nagoya Institute of Technology, Japan
Jörg P. Müller   Technische Universität Clausthal, Germany
Juan Pavón   Universidad Complutense de Madrid, Spain
Michal Pěchouček   Czech Technical University in Prague, Czech Republic
Franco Zambonelli   University of Modena and Reggio Emilia, Italy

Program Committee

Emmanuel Adam   University of Valenciennes, France
Stéphane Airiau   University of Paris Dauphine, France
Analia Amandi   University of Tandil, Argentina
Frédéric Amblard   University of Toulouse, France
Francesco Amigoni   Politecnico di Milano, Italy
Bo An   Nanyang Technological University, Singapore
Luis Antunes   University of Lisbon, Portugal
Piotr Artiemjew   University of Warmia and Mazury, Poland
Matteo Baldoni   University of Turin, Italy
Joao Balsa   University of Lisbon, Portugal
Cristina Baroglio   University of Turin, Italy
Nick Bassiliades   University of Thessaloniki, Greece
Jeremy Baxter   QinetQ, UK
Michael Berger   DocuWare AG, Germany
Olivier Boissier   Ecole des Mines des Saint Etienne, France
Rafael Bordini   Pontifical University of Rio Grande do Sul, Brazil
Vicente Botti   Polytechnic University of Valencia, Spain
Anarosa Brandao   University of Sao Paulo, Brazil
Lars Braubach   Universität Hamburg, Germany

Sven Brueckner	Axon AI, USA
Bat-Erdene Byambasuren	University of Science and Technology, Mongolia
Javier Carbó	Carlos III University of Madrid, Spain
Luis Castillo	University of Caldas, Colombia
Sofia Ceppi	University of Edinburgh, UK
Helder Coelho	University of Lisbon, Portugal
Rafael Corchuelo	University of Seville, Spain
Luis Correia	University of Lisbon, Portugal
Daniela D'Auria	University of Naples Federico II, Italy
Paul Davidsson	Malmö University, Sweden
Keith Decker	University of Delaware, USA
Yves Demazeau (Co-chair)	Centre National de la Recherche Scientifique, France
Andres Diaz Pace	University of Tandil, Argentina
Frank Dignum	University of Utrecht, The Netherlands
Aldo Dragoni	Marche Polytechnic University, Italy
Ahmad Esmaeili	Purdue University, USA
Johannes Fähndrich	Technical University of Berlin, Germany
Rino Falcone	CNR, Italy
Klaus Fischer	DFKI, Germany
Ruben Fuentes	Universidad Complutense de Madrid, Spain
Katsuhide Fujita	Tokyo University of Agriculture and Technology, Japan
Naoki Fukuta	Shizuoka University, Japan
Stéphane Galland	Technical University of Belfort-Montbéliard, France
Qian Gao Qilu	University of Technology, China
Amineh Ghorbani	Delft University of Technology, The Netherlands
Sylvain Giroux	University of Sherbrooke, Canada
Marie-Pierre Gleizes	University of Toulouse, France
Daniela Godoy	University of Tandil, Argentina
Mauricio A. Gomez Morales	University of Texas at San Antonio, USA
Jorge J. Gómez-Sanz	Universidad Complutense de Madrid, Spain
Vladimir Gorodetski	University of Saint Petersbourg, Russia
Charles Gouin-Vallerand	Télé-Université du Québec, Canada
James Harland	Royal Melbourne Institute of Technology, Australia
Salima Hassas	University of Lyon, France
Hisashi Hayashi	Advanced Institute of Industrial Technology, Japan
Vincent Hilaire	University of Belfort-Montbeliard, France
Koen Hindrinks	University of Delft, The Netherlands
Benjamin Hirsch	Khalifa University, United Arab Emirates
Martin Hofmann	Lockheed Martin, USA
Tom Holvoet	Catholic University of Leuven, Belgium
Young-Dae Hong	Ajou University, South Korea
Jomi Hubner	Universidad Federale de Santa Catarina, Brazil
Toru Ishida	Kyoto University, Japan
Piotr Jedrzejowicz	Gdynia Maritime University, Poland

Yichuan Jiang	Southeast University of Nanjing, China
Vicente Julian	Polytechnic University of Valencia, Spain
Ozgur Kafali	Boğaziçi University, Turkey
Achilles Kameas	University of Patras, Greece
Ryo Kanamori	Nagoya University, Japan
Takahiro Kawamura	Toshiba, Japan
Yongho Kim	Argonne National Lab, USA
Stefan Kirn	Hohenheim University, Germany
Franziska Kluegl	University of Örebro, Sweden
Matthias Klusch	DFKI, Germany
Martin Kollingbaum	University of Aberdeen, UK
Ryszard Kowalczyk	Swinburne University of Technology, Australia
Jaroslaw Kozlak	University of Science and Technology in Krakow, Poland
Stesuya Kurahashi	Tsukuba University, Japan
Robin Lamarche-Perrin	University of Paris 6, France
Paulo Leitao	Polytechnic Institute of Bragança, Portugal
Brian Logan	University of Nottingham, UK
Henrique Lopes Cardoso	University of Porto, Portugal
Beatriz Lopez	University of Girona, Spain
Miguel Angel Lopez-Carmona	University of Alcala, Spain
Rene Mandiau	University of Valenciennes, France
Wenji Mao	Chinese Academy of Science, China
Viviana Mascardi	University of Genoa, Italy
Philippe Mathieu	University of Lille, France
Eric Matson (Co-chair)	Purdue University, USA
Shigeo Matsubara	Kyoto University, Japan
Toshihiro Matsui	Nagoya Institute of Technology, Japan
Byung-Cheol Min	Purdue University, USA
Tsunenori Mine	Kyushu University, Japan
José M. Molina	University Carlos III of Madrid, Spain
Mirko Morandini	University of Trento, Italy
Koichi Moriyama	Nagoya Institute of Technology, Japan
Bernard Moulin	University Laval, Canada
Jean-Pierre Muller	CIRAD, France
Joerg Mueller	Clausthal University of Technology, Germany
Aniello Murano	University of Naples, Italy
Ngoc Thanh Nguyen	Wroclaw University of Technology, Poland
Nariaki Nishino	Tokyo University, Japan
Itsuki Noda	Advanced Industrial Science and Technology, Japan
Paolo Novais	University of Minho, Portugal
Akihiko Ohsuga	University of Electro-Communications, Japan
Andrea Omicini	University of Bologna, Italy
Mehmet Orgun	Macquarie University, Australia
Ei-Ichi Osawa	Future University Hakodate, Japan

Yifeng Zeng	Teesside University, UK
Jinyu Zhang	University of Nanjing, China
Dengji Zhao	Shanghai Technological University, China

Organizing Committee

Juan Manuel Corchado Rodríguez	University of Salamanca, Spain and AIR Institute, Spain
Fernando De la Prieta	University of Salamanca, Spain
Sara Rodríguez González	University of Salamanca, Spain
Sonsoles Pérez Gómez	University of Salamanca, Spain
Benjamín Arias Pérez	University of Salamanca, Spain
Javier Prieto Tejedor	University of Salamanca, Spain and AIR Institute, Spain
Pablo Chamoso Santos	University of Salamanca, Spain
Amin Shokri Gazafroudi	University of Salamanca, Spain
Alfonso González Briones	University of Salamanca, Spain and AIR Institute, Spain
José Antonio Castellanos	University of Salamanca, Spain
Yeray Mezquita Martín	University of Salamanca, Spain
Enrique Goyenechea	University of Salamanca, Spain
Javier J. Martín Limorti	University of Salamanca, Spain
Alberto Rivas Camacho	University of Salamanca, Spain
Ines Sitton Candanedo	University of Salamanca, Spain
Daniel López Sánchez	University of Salamanca, Spain
Elena Hernández Nieves	University of Salamanca, Spain
Beatriz Bellido	University of Salamanca, Spain
María Alonso	University of Salamanca, Spain
Diego Valdeolmillos	University of Salamanca, Spain and AIR Institute, Spain
Roberto Casado Vara	University of Salamanca, Spain
Sergio Marquez	University of Salamanca, Spain
Guillermo Hernández González	University of Salamanca, Spain
Mehmet Ozturk	University of Salamanca, Spain
Luis Carlos Martínez de Iturrate	University of Salamanca, Spain and AIR Institute, Spain
Ricardo S. Alonso Rincón	University of Salamanca, Spain
Javier Parra	University of Salamanca, Spain
Niloufar Shoeibi	University of Salamanca, Spain
Zakieh Alizadeh-Sani	University of Salamanca, Spain
Jesús Ángel Román Gallego	University of Salamanca, Spain
Angélica González Arrieta	University of Salamanca, Spain
José Rafael García-Bermejo Giner	University of Salamanca, Spain
Belén Pérez Lancho	University of Salamanca, Spain

Ana Belén Gil González   University of Salamanca, Spain
Ana De Luis Reboredo   University of Salamanca, Spain
Emilio Santiago Corchado   University of Salamanca, Spain
    Rodríguez

Contents

Regular Papers

Massive Multi-agent Data-Driven Simulations of the GitHub Ecosystem   3
  Jim Blythe, John Bollenbacher, Di Huang, Pik-Mai Hui, Rachel Krohn,
  Diogo Pacheco, Goran Muric, Anna Sapienza, Alexey Tregubov,
  Yong-Yeol Ahn, Alessandro Flammini, Kristina Lerman,
  Filippo Menczer, Tim Weninger, and Emilio Ferrara

Towards Profile and Domain Modelling in Agent-Based Applications
for Behavior Change   16
  Jean-Paul Calbimonte, Davide Calvaresi, Fabien Dubosson,
  and Michael Schumacher

Towards Agent-Oriented Blockchains: Autonomous Smart Contracts   29
  Giovanni Ciatto, Alfredo Maffi, Stefano Mariani, and Andrea Omicini

Towards Topological Analysis of Networked Holonic Multi-agent Systems. . . .   42
  Ahmad Esmaeili, Nasser Mozayani, Mohammad Reza Jahed-Motlagh,
  and Eric T. Matson

Selecting Trustworthy Partners by the Means of Untrustworthy
Recommenders in Digitally Empowered Societies   55
  Rino Falcone and Alessandro Sapienza

Identifying Knowledge from the Application of Natural Deduction Rules
in Propositional Logic   66
  Fabiane F. P. Galafassi, Cristiano Galafassi, Rosa Maria Vicari,
  and João Carlos Gluz

Network Effects in an Agent-Based Model of Tax Evasion
with Social Influence.   78
  Fernando Garcia Alvarado

A New Deep Hierarchical Neural Network Applied in Human
Activity Recognition (HAR) Using Wearable Sensors   90
  Zahra Ghorrati and Eric T. Matson

Approximating Multi-attribute Resource Allocations Using
GAI Utility Functions   103
  Charles Harold, Mohan Baruwal Chhetri, and Ryszard Kowalczyk

Multiagent Reinforcement Learning Applied to Traffic Light Signal Control . . .   115
Carolina Higuera, Fernando Lozano, Edgar Camilo Camacho,
and Carlos Hernando Higuera

QoS-Aware Agent Capabilities Composition in HARMS Multi-agent
Systems.   127
Mohamed Essaid Khanouche, Nawel Atmani, Asma Cherifi,
Abdelghani Chibani, Eric T. Matson, and Yacine Amirat

MASS CUDA: A General GPU Parallelization Framework
for Agent-Based Models   139
Lisa Kosiachenko, Nathaniel Hart, and Munehiro Fukuda

Multi-agent Coordination for On-Demand Data Gathering with Periodic
Information Upload.   153
Yaroslav Marchukov and Luis Montano

Practical Applications of Multiagent Shepherding for Human-Machine
Interaction   168
Patrick Nalepka, Rachel W. Kallen, Anthony Chemero, Elliot Saltzman,
and Michael J. Richardson

Generating Real Context Data to Test User Dependent
Systems - Application to Multi-agent Systems   180
Pedro Oliveira, Paulo Novais, and Paulo Matos

Multimap Routing for Road Traffic Management   188
Alvaro Paricio Garcia and Miguel A. Lopez-Carmona

Financial Market Data Simulation Using Deep Intelligence Agents   200
Natraj Raman and Jochen L. Leidner

Smart Farming – Open Multi-agent Platform and Eco-System of Smart
Services for Precision Farming   212
Petr Skobelev, Vladimir Larukchin, Igor Mayorov, Elena Simonova,
and Olga Yalovenko

Demo Papers

SMACH: Multi-agent Simulation of Human Activity in the Household   227
Jérémy Albouys, Nicolas Sabouret, Yvon Haradji, Mathieu Schumann,
and Christian Inard

Giving Camel to Artifacts for Industry 4.0 Integration Challenges.   232
Cleber Jorge Amaral, Stephen Cranefield, Jomi Fred Hübner,
and Mario Lucio Roloff

AncientS-ABM: A Novel Tool for Simulating Ancient Societies   237
Angelos Chliaoutakis and Georgios Chalkiadakis

A Demonstration of Generative Policy Models in Coalition Environments . . .   242
Daniel Cunnington, Graham White, Mark Law, and Geeth de Mel

An Agent-Swarm Simulator for Dynamic Vehicle Routing Problem
Empirical Analysis   246
*Nicola Falcionelli, Paolo Sernani, Dagmawi Neway Mekuria,
and Aldo Franco Dragoni*

Heráclito: Intelligent Tutoring System for Logic   251
*Fabiane Flores Penteado Galafassi, Cristiano Galafassi,
Rosa Maria Vicari, and João Carlos Gluz*

Demonstration of Multiagent Reinforcement Learning Applied to Traffic
Light Signal Control   255
*Carolina Higuera, Fernando Lozano, Edgar Camilo Camacho,
and Carlos Hernando Higuera*

Modular and Self-organized Conveyor System Using Multi-agent Systems . . .   259
Paulo Leitão and José Barbosa

Multi-agent Coordination for Data Gathering with Periodic Requests
and Deliveries.   264
Yaroslav Marchukov and Luis Montano

Finding Fair Negotiation Algorithms to Reduce Peak Electricity
Consumption in Micro Grids   269
Simon T. Powers, Oscar Meanwell, and Zuansi Cai

EMiR 2.0: A Cognitive Assistant Robot for Elderly   273
*J. A. Rincon, J. Palanca, V. Botti, A. Costa, P. Novais, V. Julian,
and C. Carrascosa*

Agent Process Modelling: When Multiagent Systems Meet Process Models
and Microservices   277
Thiago R. P. M. Rúbio, Henrique Lopes Cardoso, and Eugénio Oliveira

Social Recommendations: Have We Done Something Wrong?   281
Alessandro Sapienza and Rino Falcone

An Agent Based Technique for Improving Multi-stakeholder
Optimisation Problems.   285
Neil Urquhart and Simon T. Powers

Author Index   291

Regular Papers

Massive Multi-agent Data-Driven Simulations of the GitHub Ecosystem

Jim Blythe[1(✉)], John Bollenbacher[2], Di Huang[1], Pik-Mai Hui[2],
Rachel Krohn[3], Diogo Pacheco[2], Goran Muric[1], Anna Sapienza[1],
Alexey Tregubov[1], Yong-Yeol Ahn[2], Alessandro Flammini[2],
Kristina Lerman[1], Filippo Menczer[2], Tim Weninger[3], and Emilio Ferrara[1]

[1] USC Information Sciences Institute, Marina del Rey, CA, USA
{blythe,dihuang,gmuric,annas,tregubov,lerman,ferrarae}@isi.edu
[2] Indiana University, Bloomington, IN, USA
{jmbollen,huip,pacheco,yyahn,aflammin,fil}@iu.edu
[3] University of Notre Dame, Notre Dame, IN, USA
{rkrohn,tweninger}@nd.edu

Abstract. Simulating and predicting planetary-scale techno-social systems poses heavy computational and modeling challenges. The DARPA SocialSim program set the challenge to model the evolution of GitHub, a large collaborative software-development ecosystem, using massive multi-agent simulations. We describe our best performing models and our agent-based simulation framework, which we are currently extending to allow simulating other planetary-scale techno-social systems. The challenge problem measured participant's ability, given 30 months of meta-data on user activity on GitHub, to predict the next months' activity as measured by a broad range of metrics applied to ground truth, using agent-based simulation. The challenge required scaling to a simulation of roughly 3 million agents producing a combined 30 million actions, acting on 6 million repositories with commodity hardware. It was also important to use the data optimally to predict the agent's next moves. We describe the agent framework and the data analysis employed by one of the winning teams in the challenge. Six different agent models were tested based on a variety of machine learning and statistical methods. While no single method proved the most accurate on every metric, the broadly most successful sampled from a stationary probability distribution of actions and repositories for each agent. Two reasons for the success of these agents were their use of a distinct characterization of each agent, and that GitHub users change their behavior relatively slowly.

Keywords: Massive scale simulations · Collaborative platforms · GitHub

1 Introduction

Two significant challenges on the way to realizing the promise of agent-based social simulation for policy evaluation and social science are making effective

© Springer Nature Switzerland AG 2019
Y. Demazeau et al. (Eds.): PAAMS 2019, LNAI 11523, pp. 3–15, 2019.
https://doi.org/10.1007/978-3-030-24209-1_1

use of available data and scaling to planetary-sized cognitive agent simulations. As a first step, the DARPA SocialSim challenge problem measured participant's ability, given 30 months of meta-data on user activity on GitHub, to predict the next months' activity as measured by a broad range of metrics applied to ground truth, using agent-based simulation. The challenge involved making predictions about roughly 3 million individuals taking a combined 30 million actions on 6 million repositories. We found that simulations of small subsamples of the population, on the order of tens or hundreds of thousands of agents, led to inconsistent and often misleading results, so a full-scale simulation was developed. It was also important to use the data optimally to predict the agent's next moves. We describe the agent framework and the data analysis employed by one of the top performers in the challenge. The team used a variety of learning methods contributing to six different kinds of agents that were tested against a wide range of metrics. While no single method proved the most accurate on every evaluation metric, the broadly most successful of those tried sampled from a stationary probability distribution of actions and target repositories for each agent. Two reasons for the success of this agent were that individuals on GitHub change their behavior relatively slowly and that distinct information was maintained for each agent without generalizing across agents. Our work that improves the performance achieved during the timeline of the challenge builds on these agents to incorporate novel behavior through further data analysis.

This paper makes the following contributions: First, we describe the agent-based simulator we developed to carry out massive-scale simulations of techno-social systems, which provides support for simulations of cognitive behavior and shared state across multiple compute nodes. Second, we present the inference methods that we employed to implement different agent-based models, based on statistical modeling of historical activity, graph embedding to infer future interactions, Bayesian models to capture activity processes, and methods to predict the emergence of new users and repositories that did not exist in the historical data. These are novel applications of existing analytical tools to derive agent models from available data. Third, we provide a rigorous evaluation of the performance of six different models, as measured by a wide range of metrics, in simulating different scenarios concerned with user and repository popularity and evolution, as well as multi-resolution accuracy at the level of individual agents, groups of agents (e.g., communities, or teams), and the whole system. We also describe the DARPA SocialSim GitHub Challenge, provide a characterization of its rules, and describe how our team tackled it. Our platform and models are general in scope, and have also been applied to large-scale agent simulations of behavior on the Twitter and Reddit social media platforms.

2   Challenge Problem Description

GitHub is a software social network where users interact with each other by contributing to repositories, following or becoming a member of specific projects, and interact with repositories through actions such as forking, committing, etc.

It is interesting to simulate since it combines aspects of social networks and collaborative work, and simulation may provide insights into team formation and productivity as well as aspects of widely-used code including the spread of vulnerabilities. The DARPA SocialSim Challenge aims at simulating specific types of interactions between users and repositories on GitHub over time. In particular, it focuses on the simulation of social structure and temporal dynamics of the system, as well as looking at individual, community and population behaviors.

There are ten event types in the model: create or delete either a repository, a tag, or a branch (respectively *Create* and *Delete*), create or comment a pull request (respectively *PullRequest* and *PullRequestReviewComment*), create an issue (*Issues*, *IssueComment*), and push (*Push*, *CommitComment*). Moreover, a user can *watch* and *fork* existing repositories. Note that in the GitHub API a *watch* event corresponds to starring a repository.

Given as an input the temporal information of users' actions on specific repositories, we aim at predicting future events of GitHub providing our simulation output in the following format: time, eventType, userID, repoID. Furthermore, the simulation aims at modeling not only the future events of existing users and repositories but also the creation/deletion of new repositories and users.

The training set we used for our simulation comprises all events of public users and repositories in the period spanning from 8/1/17–8/31/17 and 1/17/18–1/31/18, as well as metadata such as repository languages, user types etc. This includes a total of about $2.0M$ users and $3.3M$ repositories. For the challenge, we were asked to simulate the events, users, and repositories of GitHub from 2/1/18–2/28/18. As the training set included a gap of 4.5 months, additional information about the state of the system was provided, including all the profiles from users and repositories that were created during the gap.

3   Agent Framework and Domain Implementation

In this section we describe the simulation framework and the model of GitHub that was shared by all agents developed for the challenge. We also describe steps to scale the simulation efficiently to millions of agents and repositories.

To implement our agent models we used FARM—an agent-based simulation framework implemented in Python that supports large-scale distributed simulations [5]. FARM also keeps track of the repeated and systematic experimentation required to validate the results from multi-agent simulations. FARM supports agents developed with the DASH framework [4], although it may be used with any agent through an API. The DASH agent framework supports simulations of cognitive behavior, and includes support for dual-process models, reactive planning and spreading activation.

In our experiments, DASH agents represent GitHub users and implement GitHub events. Agents in FARM can communicate either directly or by taking actions that are sent to a shared state object, called a hub, that can be observed by other agents. In the GitHub simulation model, every action taken by a user acts on a repository, so communication is modeled indirectly by sending actions to a hub that maintains the state of a set of repositories and provides information to agents about their repositories of interest.

When all the agents and state relevant to a simulation reside in a single image, communication and action are efficiently implemented as method calls. However as we scale to millions of agents and repositories, some hardware cannot accommodate all the relevant state on a single host. FARM provides a multi-process infrastructure to divide agents and their state across multiple hosts as needed in a way that is transparent to the agent developer [5]. One hub is present on each image and shared state is managed with Apache ZooKeeper. Frequently interacting users and repositories can be allocated on the same compute node to minimize cross-host communications. Using a multi-level graph partitioning algorithm to minimize the amount of communication across partitions based on the user-repository links found in the training data, simulation time was reduced by 67% [5]. We further improved performance with demand-driven shared state, so that repositories were only synchronized between compute nodes when agents on different nodes began to interact with them. Finally, we modified DASH to reduce the space requirements of each agent so that the required simulations, with around 3 million agents taking a combined 30 million actions on 6 million repositories, run on a single host with 64 GB of memory in around 20 min.

4   Agent Models

4.1   Stationary Probabilistic Models

A stationary probabilistic model is a simple way to describe user behavior with a finite number of available actions. In the following models, each user's actions are determined by a stationary probability distribution built from the past history of events the user has initiated. Two aspects of each user's behavior are determined: their overall event rate and the probability of each action. Both of these parameters are computed individually for each user.

We implemented three variations of probabilistic simulation models. The first model selects an event type and independently selects the repository on which the selected action is to be applied. We refer to this as be *baseline model*.

The second model, called the *ground-event model*, selects an event type and repository simultaneously. As in the baseline model, in the ground-event model frequencies are computed from historical data but in this case the frequency is computed for each event and repository pair.

The third model, called the *preferential attachment model*, extends the baseline model by redefining user behaviour for *watch* and *fork* events. When a user agent decides to watch a new repository, it first selects a neighboring user, who also worked on a repository this user interacted with, and then selects a repository with which the selected neighbor previously interacted. The neighboring user and repository are selected based on their popularity.

In all models, the frequency of users' actions is determined by the event rate observed in the past for each user. The event rate remains constant for each user throughout the simulation. In all three models, the probabilities of choosing each event type, of selecting a repository, and of selecting a repository and an event as a pair are determined by frequencies computed from historical training data.

These stationary probabilistic agent-based simulation models compute probabilities for each user agent individually and thus capture individual characteristics of each user, creating a high resolution simulation. The approach is computationally simple enough to be scalable to millions of agents and repositories. Generally, this modeling approach is justified if users' future behavior tends to be similar to their past behavior. A limitation of these models is that they only predict users' interactions with repositories they have interacted in the past. That means that these models should be augmented with additional behavior rules to introduce previously unobserved user-repository interactions. The preferential attachment model is an example where such rules were introduced.

4.2   Link Prediction Through Embedding

One way of simulating user-repository interactions in GitHub is by predicting the likelihood that a user will perform an event of a certain type on a repository. We can formulate this problem as a link prediction task, by describing our system as a bipartite network in which each node is either a user or a repository and links in each network are specific events. By predicting such links, we can measure the probability of specific events between any given user-repository pair. Each network is built as follows. Nodes belong to either the group of users U or the group of repositories R, and a node $u \in U$ is linked to a node $r \in R$ if the user u performed an event on the repository r. We weight each link by computing the number of times the user performs that event. As a result, we generate a total of 12 bipartite networks, one for each event type with the exception of *create* and *delete* events. We can then represent each of the built networks as a weighted adjacency matrix $\mathbf{A}_e \in \mathbb{R}^{|U| \times |R|}$, where e is an event type. However, this link prediction problem does not take into account new users and repositories that have been added (or removed) by the system.

Table 1. Average MAP for links and weights prediction on GitHub event networks.

	Push	PullRequest	IssueComment	Fork	Watch
Random	0.01	0.03	0.02	0.03	0.03
LE	0.13	0.30	0.33	0.14	0.07
HOPE	0.13	0.25	0.26	**0.17**	**0.10**
GF	**0.25**	**0.42**	**0.48**	0.16	0.06

Given the matrix $\mathbf{A}_e$ for each event type e, we compare embedding methods against a random baseline: Graph Factorization (GF), Laplacian Eigenmaps

(LE), and Hybrid Orthogonal Projection and Estimation (HOPE). We test performance using the MeanAveragePrecision (MAP), which estimates a model precision for each node and computes the average over all nodes, as follows:

$$MAP = \frac{1}{|U|+|R|} \sum_{i}^{|U|+|R|} \frac{\sum_{k} Pr@k \mathcal{I}\{E_{pred,i}(k) \in E_{obs,i}\}}{|\{k : E_{pred,i} \in E_{obs,i}\}|}, \tag{1}$$

where, $Pr@k = \frac{|E_{pred,i}(1:k) \cap E_{obs,i}|}{k}$ is the precision at k, and $E_{pred,i}$ and $E_{obs,i}$ are respectively the predicted and observed edges for node i.

The results are shown in Table 1, where we consider the 5 main actions that users can perform on GitHub: contributions (*push* and *pull*), *issues*, and popularity (*fork* and *watch*). Here, we highlighted the highest performance obtained among the methods in each case. All the methods outperform our random baseline, which predicts links in a random fashion. Moreover, GF performs better than the non-linear models in the majority of cases. This is not true for popularity related events, where we find that HOPE is the best predictor. As discussed in Sect. 7, *forks* are more stable than *watches*. Thus, HOPE is able to capture non-linearity in the *watch* events better then GF. However, GF is comparable to HOPE in predicting *forks*, and it is also much more scalable. Thus, we decide to select GF and its link prediction to inform our agents.

4.3 Bayesian Model

The GitHub Challenge can be seen as finding relationships between the three governing entities: users, repositories, and events. We empirically measured the probabilities of these relationships to adjust the posterior probabilities of a generative model. In this section, we present exploratory findings and how they shaped the overall flow of our *Bayesian model*. Figure 1 shows one iteration of the Bayesian model, i.e., creating a tuple with a user, a repository, and an event type. In general terms, the model first chooses between to create a new user or to select an existing one. Then, it decides between a category of events. Finally, it selects a repository and an action to perform.

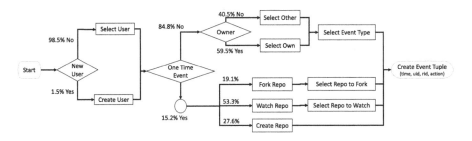

Fig. 1. Bayesian model from data inferred frequencies.

We investigated the trade-off between recency and history as driving forces to popularity [2]. The results showed that *less is more* in terms of the amount of data needed to predict users' activity level. For instance, the top-200 most active user rank of a particular month will intersect less with the rank from previous months as we aggregate more data; e.g., while +75% of the users in the rank remains when the rank is computed only from one month, the intersection drops to 72%, 59% and 56% if we aggregate data from the previous 3, 5, and 7 months, respectively. Recent users, i.e., the ones active in the previous month, represent more than 50% of the active users in the following month, and they are responsible for 4 out of 5 events being generated. The user selection implements a rank model [11] based on user's activity level, with past activity being less weighted using a 30-day half-life decay. From repository perspective, however, new ones are more likely to be active in the following month than old ones, in absolute numbers (68% *vs.* 10%) and in volume of events (38% *vs.* 5%). Yet, recent repositories account for almost 3 out of 5 events.

To address this imbalanced scenario, of increasing newcomers receiving little attention, the model splits between one-time or multiple-time events before choosing the repository. For instance, the same repository cannot be *created* twice and it is unlikely to be *watched* or *forked* more than once by the same user; conversely, users *push* and *create issues* multiple times on the same repository. The analysis of the event-specific bipartite networks of users and repositories reveals different mechanisms underling them. For instance, in the network formed by *watch* events, the degree distribution of repositories (i.e., the distribution of number of watches per repository), fits a steep power law ($\gamma = 1.81$ and $xmin = 3$); the *pull request* distribution, however, fits a longer tailed power law ($\gamma = 2.54$ and $xmin = 291$). There are two independent rank models [11] to select which repository to *watch* or to *fork*.

Users work more on their repositories (owners) than on other's (contributors). Moreover, they usually behave different depending on these roles. A owned-repository is selected with probability proportional to the amount of previous activity. Other's repositories are selected using a random walk with small length given by a geometric distribution (mean 2) capturing user's social vicinity. This mechanism assumes a user is more likely to work on repositories he/she already worked with or from previous collaborators. Nevertheless, 88% of the first action of users to a repository (repository discovery) is a one-time event: *watch* (64%), *fork* (20%), or *create* (4%). Hence, for multiple-time events the model first decides between working on a user's own repositories or not. Although *pushes* are the most prevalent action regardless repository's ownership, some events seemed to be over/under represented depending on ownership. For instance, *issue comment*, *commit comment*, and *watch* are more likely to be performed by contributors on others' repositories.

4.4 Modeling New Users and Repositories

GitHub grows quickly. Almost 50% of all user accounts that were active in 2017 were created in the same year and a significant fraction of repositories are also new, as mentioned in Sect. 4.3. Such a growth rate yields a system with high number of new active agents. Previously described stationary probabilistic models do not fully address the behaviour of the new agents, since they have no history of interactions. Here, we describe an extension of the models that focuses on predicting the actions of the new agents and newly created relations. Without a historical record of events between user and a repository, the most informative piece of data is missing. Still, both of the entities can be described by a set of their native features, such as: *age* or *number of followers*. We compiled a total list of 124 features extracted for a sample of user-repository pairs. Features include various statistics on user and repository activities for all event types.

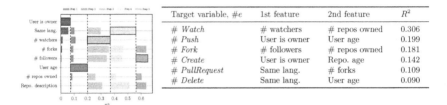

Target variable, #e	1st feature	2nd feature	R^2
# *Watch*	# watchers	# repos owned	0.306
# *Push*	User is owner	User age	0.199
# *Fork*	# followers	# repos owned	0.181
# *Create*	User is owner	Repo. age	0.142
# *PullRequest*	Same lang.	# forks	0.109
# *Delete*	Same lang.	User age	0.090

Fig. 2. On the left, the variation in the target variable *#PushEvents*, explained by each feature in each consecutive step of the S3D algorithm. On the right, the two most important features to predict the number of events for a new user-repository interaction. The R^2 column shows the total gain of the two features.

The aim is to build a parsimonious model, able to predict the frequency of a particular event type e performed by user u on a repository r, conditioned by non-existing history of interaction between u and r. The critical part of model creation is *feature selection*, as we are interested in minimizing the set of features by selecting only the most informative ones. For that purpose, we use Structured Sum of Squares Decomposition (S3D) algorithm [10]. The importance of features is quantified by a measure of variability R^2 of outcome variable Y the feature explains. A high value of R^2 suggests the strong predictive power. To prevent overfitting, we optimize an inter-model parameter λ.

For each event type e from the set of event types E we build the predictive model that for a given pair of user and repository $[u, r]$ estimates the number of events $\#e$ performed by the user u on the repository r. This way we create 14 different models, one for each event type. With each iteration we select the most informative feature which explains the largest amount of variation in the target variable $\#e$. Each successive feature explains the most of the remaining variation, conditioned on the previous one. The S3D algorithm allows the visual inspection of the selected important features. The iterative process of feature selection is illustrated in Fig. 2. To predict the number of *PushEvents*, a user u is going to perform on repository r, the most important feature is the information of the repository ownership. Other features such as *user age*, *# watchers* or *# user followers* become important in the following steps.

The rank of features differ among the models. Still, the most informative features for predicting the actions of a user to a repository, are derived from their mutual relation. Furthermore, many actions depend on the information of the repository ownership (Fig. 2). *User is owner* is a boolean variable indicating if the user is the owner of the repository. For some other events, the *Same lang.* variable becomes important. It indicates if the programming language assigned to a repository is the same as the programming language mostly used by a user. Even though the R^2 can not inform on a model accuracy, it can suggest the potential of a model's prediction performance.

5   Candidate Agents and Results

We developed GitHub user agents that implemented the following models described in the previous section: (1) the null model, (2) the probabilistic baseline model, (3) the probabilistic ground-event model, (4) the preferential attachment model, (5) link prediction via embedding (LPE), and (6) the Bayesian model.

The null model is just a shift of the past data to the future. In this case we used two weeks immediately preceding the test period and returned it, with dates adjusted, as the new prediction. Both baseline model and null model were used to compare relative performance of other agents. The LPE model was the best performing of a number of machine learning-based models that were explored.

The DARPA SocialSim Challenge design had multiple research questions in mind. There were five groups of research questions that covered user engagement, contributions, reputation, influence and popularity. To evaluate fidelity of the simulation a set of metrics was developed by PNNL. These metrics evaluate simulation fidelity on three levels: node-level, community-level and population-level. Although it is not feasible to discuss all metrics in the context of this paper, we selected the following five to discuss in detail, which cover user and repository metrics on individual, community and population levels.

User popularity - top 500 most popular users, measured as the total number of *watch* and *fork* events on repositories owned by user. Calculated as Rank-Biased Overlap (*RBO*) [21].

Repository popularity - top 500 popular repositories. Calculated as *RBO*.

Repository event count issues - the number of *issue* events by repository. Calculated as R^2.

Repository contributors - the number of daily unique contributors to a repository as a function of time. Calculated as Root Mean Square Error (*RMSE*).

Community contributing users - percentage of users who perform any contributing (e.g. *push, pull request* events) actions within the community.

To answer various research questions of the DARPA SocialSim Challenge more than a dozen metrics were used to evaluate our simulation results. Figure 3 on the left shows evaluation results for two bounded metrics: repository popularity, user popularity. All metrics are scaled to the [0, 1] interval, higher is better.

All simulation models except the link prediction via embedding model showed comparable results. Note that the popularity metric is not calculated for users and repositories that were created during the test period.

Predicting the 500 most popular users and repositories is difficult with a constant rate of events, due to high month to month turn out. On average about 30% of repositories in the top 500 change every month. Therefore, we can see that even the null model works better with respect to repository popularity metric.

The LPE model uses generalized rules to predict the user's action, which some cases leads to long-tail distributions of probabilities of repository selection. That process introduces noise and the model was also computationally intensive because it requires reconstruction of the *complete user × repository matrix*. To optimize memory usage when repository selection probabilities were computed we truncated long tails (repositories with small probabilities). We used a threshold of 100 repositories per user. The ground-event model showed slightly better results on popularity metrics than the baseline model and the preferential attachment model. All three models use the same approach to compute rate of users' activity but different ways to choose repositories. The preferential attachment model did not leverage much from explicitly modeling fork events and selecting repositories that also popular across user's neighbors.

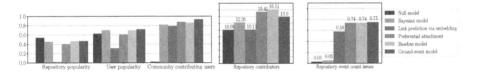

Fig. 3. Left: popularity metrics, RBO, and community contributing users, higher is better. Center: Repository contributors, $RMSE$, lower is better and right: event issue count, R^2, higher is better.

The LPE model generally showed poor results on repository-centered metrics. All models except the null model had a high percentage (more than 0.75) of community contributing users. The only two models that performed better than the baseline were the preferential attachment model and ground-event model. Figure 3 shows repository contributors - the number of daily unique contributors to a repository as a function of time. It is calculated as $RMSE$, lower is better. The null model and the link prediction model showed the lowest values here. Figure 3 also shows repository event count issues - the number of issue events by repository. It is calculated as R^2, higher is better. Both the null model and the bayesian model show much lower value compare to all other values. The stationary models capture user-repository interactions with better precision because they rely only on training data specific to that user-repository pair.

6   Related Work

Many groups have addressed large-scale agent simulations over the years. Tumer et al. consider simulations for air traffic flow management, handling more than 60,000 flights [20]. Distributed simulations have been developed [7,8,17], with agents typically partitioned by geographic location and migrated between compute hosts as they move in the simulated space. Noda describes a social simulation of tens of thousands of agents to help explore policies for urban traffic and disaster response [16]. Repast has been used to simulate up to 10^9 agents in a cascade simulation on supercomputers [7]. To our knowledge, the simulations in response to the SocialSim challenge are the first systematic experiments involving millions to tens of millions of agents with individual complex behavior.

Researchers have given an overview of the GitHub platform and user/repository statistics [9,12,13]. The amount of available data on GitHub allows observing group behaviour through the collaboration network structure [19] and studying the interaction patterns inside teams on public GitHub repositories [14,15,18]. Another line of research focuses on the success and popularity of open-source projects. Successful and popular repositories usually have consistent documentation [1,22], various growth patterns [6], and popular programming languages [3].

7   Discussion

We demonstrated novel agents built using six different learning principles to predict the future behavior of GitHub based on training data. The agents were tested in the same simulation environment with the same implementation of GitHub actions. Across a broad array of prediction metrics, no single approach dominated the others. The Bayesian model performed well on user popularity while the stationary per-agent action distributions performed better on predicting contributors and event counts. One interesting constant across all the models was that, since overall behavior is constantly changing, it was detrimental to use all available training data in building the agents. Instead, one month of data proved optimal across most of the agents, although this precise number is no doubt dependent on the social network in question.

The main contribution of this work is to develop a framework for massive-scale simulations in which agents embodying very different ideas about decision making and data use can be directly compared. Our approach is general, and has recently been applied to the Reddit and Twitter social networks. We are also considering ways to combine these agent models, both intra-agent, combining some of the best features of different approaches in a single agent, and inter-agent, with simulations with more than one type of agent.

Predicting new *user-repository* pairs requires the development of more general models that will be used to predict new pairings among different types of entities. While developing the probabilistic models, we were constantly faced with a particular chicken-egg problem: which pair to choose the first from the *user-repository-event* triad. The models implemented in the simulation make use of previously established links between users and repositories. We are developing a model to predict the number of events performed by a user both on old and new repositories. For a given user and type of event, the model will be able to identify a small subset of candidate repositories for the event, regardless of the previous interaction between the observed user and their repositories.

Addressing the new users and repositories is yet another challenge. Modeling the behaviour of entities never seen before can not rely on the historical records. Almost 20% of events in recent months have been performed by new users. Both new and old users continuously create new repositories. Even with such a high growth rate, GitHub is considered to be relatively slow-paced compared to some other systems, such as Twitter or Reddit. One way to address the newly created entities is to observe some latent features inferred from the user who created it or from the characteristics of the entity itself, avoiding the reference to the past. Therefore, we are continuing to develop the set of models explained in Sect. 4.4.

Acknowledgments. The authors are grateful to the Defense Advanced Research Projects Agency (DARPA), contract W911NF-17-C-0094, for their support.

References

1. Aggarwal, K., Hindle, A., Stroulia, E.: Co-evolution of project documentation and popularity within GitHub. In: Mining Software Repositories, MSR (2014)
2. Barbosa, H., de Lima-Neto, F.B., Evsukoff, A., Menezes, R.: The effect of recency to human mobility. EPJ Data Sci. **4**(1), 1–14 (2015)
3. Bissyand, T.F., Thung, F., Lo, D., Jiang, L., Rveillre, L.: Popularity, interoperability, and impact of programming languages in 100,000 open source projects. In: IEEE 37th Annual Computer Software and Applications Conference (2013)
4. Blythe, J.: A dual-process cognitive model for testing resilient control systems. In: 5th International Symposium on Resilient Control Systems, pp. 8–12, August 2012
5. Blythe, J., Tregubov, A.: Farm: Architecture for distributed agent-based social simulations. In: IJCAI/AAMAS Workshop on Massively Multi-agent Systems (2018)
6. Borges, H., Hora, A.C., Valente, M.T.: Predicting the popularity of GitHub repositories. In: PROMISE (2016)
7. Collier, N., North, M.: Parallel agent-based simulation with repast for high performance computing. Simulation **89**(10), 1215–1235 (2013)
8. Cosenza, B., Cordasco, G., De Chiara, R., Scarano, V.: Distributed load balancing for parallel agent-based simulations. In: 19th Euromicro International Conference on Parallel, Distributed and Network-Based Processing (PDP). IEEE (2011)
9. Dabbish, L.A., Stuart, H.C., Tsay, J., Herbsleb, J.D.: Social coding in GitHub: transparency and collaboration in an open software repository. In: CSCW (2012)
10. Fennell, P., Zuo, Z., Lerman, K.: Predicting and explaining behavioral data with structured feature space decomposition (2018). https://arxiv.org/abs/1810.09841
11. Fortunato, S., Flammini, A., Menczer, F.: Scale-free network growth by ranking. Phys. Rev. Lett. **96**(21), 218701 (2006)
12. Gousios, G., Spinellis, D.: Ghtorrent: GitHub's data from a firehose. In: 9th IEEE Working Conference on Mining Software Repositories (MSR), June 2012

13. Gousios, G.: The GHTorent dataset and tool suite. In: Proceedings of the 10th Working Conference on Mining Software Repositories, MSR 2013. IEEE Press (2013)
14. Klug, M., Bagrow, J.P.: Understanding the group dynamics and success of teams. R. Soc. Open Sci. **3**(4), 160007 (2016)
15. Lima, A., Rossi, L., Musolesi, M.: Coding together at scale: GitHub as a collaborative social network. CoRR abs/1407.2535 (2014)
16. Noda, I.: Multi-agent social simulation for social service design. In: IJCAI/AAMAS Workshop on Massively Multi-agent Systems (2018)
17. Šišlák, D., Volf, P., Jakob, M., Pěchouček, M.: Distributed platform for large-scale agent-based simulations. In: Dignum, F., Bradshaw, J., Silverman, B., van Doesburg, W. (eds.) AGS 2009. LNCS (LNAI), vol. 5920, pp. 16–32. Springer, Heidelberg (2009). https://doi.org/10.1007/978-3-642-11198-3_2
18. Sornette, D., Maillart, T., Ghezzi, G.: How much is the whole really more than the sum of its parts? $1 + 1 = 2.5$: superlinear productivity in collective group actions. PLoS ONE **9**(8), e103023 (2014)
19. Thung, F., Bissyande, T.F., Lo, D., Jiang, L.: Network structure of social coding in GitHub. In: Software Maintenance and Reengineering, CSMR (2013)
20. Tumer, K., Agogino, A.: Distributed agent-based air traffic flow management. In: Autonomous Agents and Multiagent Systems, AAMAS 2007. ACM (2007)
21. Webber, W., Moffat, A., Zobel, J.: A similarity measure for indefinite rankings. ACM Trans. Inf. Syst. **28**(4), 1–38 (2010)
22. Zhu, J., Zhou, M., Mockus, A.: Patterns of folder use and project popularity: a case study of GitHub repositories. In: Proceedings of the 8th ACM/IEEE International Symposium on Empirical Software Engineering and Measurement, ESEM 2014. ACM (2014)

Towards Profile and Domain Modelling in Agent-Based Applications for Behavior Change

Jean-Paul Calbimonte[✉], Davide Calvaresi, Fabien Dubosson, and Michael Schumacher

eHealth Unit, Institute of Information Systems,
University of Applied Sciences and Arts Western Switzerland (HES-SO),
Sierre, Switzerland
`jean-paul.calbimonte@hevs.ch`

Abstract. Health support programs play a vital role in public health and prevention strategies at local and national levels, for issues such as smoking cessation, physical rehabilitation, nutrition, or to regain mobility. A key success factor in these topics is related to the appropriate use of behavior change techniques, as well as tailored recommendations for users/patients, adapted to their goals and the continuous monitoring of their progress. Social networks interactions and the use of multi-agent technologies can further improve the effectiveness of these programs, especially through personalization and profiling of users and patients. In this paper we propose an agent-based model for supporting behavior change in eHealth programs. Moreover, we identify the main challenges in this area, especially regarding profile and domain modeling profiles for healthcare behavioral programs, where the definition of goals, expectations and argumentation play a key role in the success of a intervention.

Keywords: MAS · Behavior change · Profiles · Domain models

1 Introduction

Personalization is a key factor for succeeding in changing the behavior of users, especially in the context of health support programs. In concrete use-cases like smoking cessation, nutrition, or physical rehabilitation, the profile of the user (or patient) can help defining different strategies and approaches to attain the desired goals, which may significantly differ from the ones tailored for other peers. Modeling the different interactions between users and health professionals, and/or support personnel, is a fundamental step towards the digitalization of these processes. The advantages of using IT solutions to support these interactions are manifold: it allows providing streamlined support to participants, it facilitates the implementation of guidelines and best practices, it can increase the effectiveness of the program, and it can potentially reduce interaction costs.

ⓒ Springer Nature Switzerland AG 2019
Y. Demazeau et al. (Eds.): PAAMS 2019, LNAI 11523, pp. 16–28, 2019.
https://doi.org/10.1007/978-3-030-24209-1_2

Agent-based models are a particularly promising technology in this context. Agent models allow representing not only the type of actions and behaviors of participating entities, but also their assumptions, goals, background knowledge, and plans. These elements can relate to both users following a behavior change program (e.g., patients) and those supporting the program (e.g., caregivers), whose interactions can partially be assumed by a software agent. However, existing agent-based models focus on different aspects and it is generally difficult to adapt them to specific characteristics of health-support programs. More specifically, most of these models do not fully address the elements relevant for behavior change, or require extensive adaptation and mapping to profile models.

In this paper, we identify key challenges for health support applications targeting behavior change, and we describe key requirements for implementing systems that can effectively address those challenges. We then propose a novel agent-based model for behavior change, exploiting existing persuasion and comportment models in eHealth [19,25], and incorporating the development of domain models, and user profiles. In particular, we discuss how this model can be adapted to a real use case, in the domain of smoking cessation. This model leverages well studied behavior change research [13], incorporating as added value the usage of multi-agent systems that can encapsulate user-agent interactions, coaching, mediation, and personalized interactions, also including aspects related to argumentation and domain-specific context [11].

The paper is organized as follows. In Sect. 2 we introduce the smoking cessation example use case, in Sect. 3 we describe the challenges of behavior change in eHealth. Section 4 details the requirements derived form the challenges while Sect. 5 presents the propose model. Related work is discussed in Sect. 6 before concluding with a proposed road-map.

2   Use-Case: Smoking Cessation

Smoking is a public health concern, as it produces chemical, routinary and social addiction [14]. Different measures have been adopted through the years to counter this issue, including prevention and media campaigns, increasing tobacco prices, or the introduction of smoke-free policies [3]. Given the proven benefits of stopping to smoke [3], there are many approaches for quitting this habit, although the hardest addictions to fight are related to routine and social behaviors. Smoking cessation interventions, backed up by health professionals and providing continuous support, can help individuals attaining this goal. However, they are often costly in terms of time and resources, with mitigated results if they do not consider the personal context of the participants. Hence, a personalized eHealth support system has the potential to achieve comparable results to those provided by a traditional clinic-based intervention, with the low cost associated with a public health approach. In the literature, there have been a number of approaches to address this issue, such as using expert systems [24], which provides cost-effective means of intervening in smoking cessation. However, there has also been evidence that the impact of smoking cessation support can substantially increase in social scenarios [23].

In this paper we use smoking cessation as a running example of a behavior change issue, given the omnipresence of this issue worldwide, and considering the availability of prevention and public health programs supporting this type of initiatives in Switzerland. Concretely, we take the example of the smoking cessation program named «J'arrête de fumer» (JDF), launched in 2015 in the canton of Valais and soon expanded to all the French-speaking cantons in Switzerland. The program was implemented as a Facebook community consisting of individuals willing to quit smoking on the same day. It allowed participants to share their approaches and techniques, and to support each other throughout the difficult periods of smoking cessation. After six months, out of 7000 participants, 13.5% definitely stopped smoking [9]. From the experience of this program, we can identify some of the advantages and opportunities of a social network eHealth intervention, while also considering the numerous challenges, as we will see next.

3   Challenges

Behavior change is a challenging problem, especially regarding health-related issues and lifestyle. There are different factors that need to be taken into account in order to achieve effective outcomes, including the attitude, emotional issues, social pressure, self-perception, etc. [13]. Given that each person has a particular background and context, even if the behavior change goals are similar, the strategies and techniques need to be personalized. As it can be seen in classic behavior change models such as the Trans-theoretical model (Fig. 1) of stages of change [19], participants may fall under different states, for which intervention may require completely different strategies. The use of digital solutions for supporting behavior change holds the promise of providing higher effectiveness, increasing the level of personalization, allowing massive outreach, and reducing intervention costs. In the following, we identify the main challenges that digital behavior change applications face, in the context of health support programs.

– *Communication.* Interactions with participants require the use of appropriate means of communication, adapted to their needs, in terms of technology

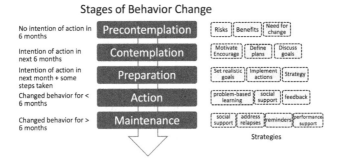

Fig. 1. The Trans-theoretical model of behavior change [19].

(e.g., usage of audio, chatbots, messaging), frequency, length, etc. A poor choice of communication technologies can lead to early abandon, or to misuse of the health support application.

- *Engagement.* Participants may quickly abandon a health program if it looses focus, if it does not provide any tangible or meaningful response, or if it deviates from the expected goals. Even if results in the very short term are not usually possible, the participant at least expects useful interactions, motivations, rewards, or support aligned with the initial objectives.
- *Personalization.* Behavior change actions will increase effectiveness if they are tailored to the user context and situation. Health programs need to model the user, or at least the relevant factors that play a key role in the scope of the targeted behavior. At least, it is important to elaborate a basic profile of the user, and determine at which stage she is, and how to track her changes and progress during the intervention in order to tailor future actions.
- *Continuous learning.* Humans interactions and behaviors are dynamic, and require to be updated constantly. An automated health support system must deal with these changes and learn from them, potentially building patterns and user models that exploit previous interactions in order to match and predict future activities.
- *Argumentation.* Changes in activities and behavior can be motivated in different ways, and arguments supporting or opposing an idea or an action, can be part of a strategy in order to persuade a participant. Argumentation needs to be built around knowledge in the area, and must be directed depending on the state of the participant and her context. Computational argumentation theories [13] need to be adopted in order to automatize the establishment of argument construction and dialogue.
- *Domain specifics.* Persuasion, argumentation and personalization require relevant knowledge of the domain of application. This knowledge needs to be organized and modeled so that it can be used for building arguments, adapting to context, or to elaborate strategies for personalization. These domain models [5] also require the participation and validation of experts, and the usage of existing ontologies and metamodels.

4   Requirements

The challenges described previously lead to the elicitation of requirements for a behavior change support system. To illustrate the process we take as example the smoking cessation use case. The requirements can be summarized as follows:

1. *Structured & instantaneous interactions.* Participants must interact with the system through instantaneous messaging, with constrained interactions. It is important to limit the dialog length in order to avoid tiredness and losing the focus of the intervention. The usage of instantaneous messaging is convenient as it allows for multi-platform interactions, including the use of mobile devices, and integration with existing messaging systems through chatbots.

2. *Symmetric/Asymmetric communication.* In many scenarios, participants may interact with the system primarily through asymmetric dialogues [12], allowing for structured, shorter and targeted input from the user [5]. This mechanism provides more control to the system, as it can pose the arguments that the user may confirm, answer, and/or react to. For example, for asking about cigarette consumption, the system may pose questions about the context (is the cigarette necessary, is the user alone, at work, what is the mood, etc.), allowing predefined response sets. This makes the interaction quicker, less error-prone, and more focused. Conversely, in other scenarios (e.g., emotion and feedback processes), less constrained dialogues can be allowed, possibly relying on natural language processing, polarity and sentiment analysis.

3. *Social interactions.* Participants must be able to interact with their peers, establishing virtual connections. A fundamental added value of an intervention is the network of social connections with other participants that can support, provide advice, reflect on their own goals, etc., through the duration of a health program. For example, successful smoking quitters may provide tips to other participants about dealing with morning anxiety, or how to cope with the temptation of cigarettes during social events. It has been shown in the literature that this type of social support has an important impact on behavioral change success [22].

4. *State-dependent interactions.* Interactions with users must be adapted to the stages of the program in which they currently are, characterised as states during the behavior change process (as in Fig. 1). The system should keep track of the stages that a certain participant has passed, and use the corresponding strategy depending on that. For example, during contemplation the interactions may focus on the definition of plans and goals for quitting smoking, during maintenance the emphasis will be on addressing relapse events and performance support. Moreover, during each stage, the system may establish fine-grained states, e.g., during the preparation stage for smoking cessation the participant may be: assessing her level of dependence, registering smoking patters, tracking cigarettes, defining short term goals, etc.

5. *Profile learning.* The system must build a profile of each participant, based on the states that she passed through, and the data acquired through asymmetric dialog interactions, and feedback loops. The profile will constitute part of a local knowledge base for each participant, subject to privacy protection. For instance, a profile for smoking cessation may include the demographic information entered at the start of the program, a nicotine dependence assessment through the Fagerstrom test, cigarette consumption, mood and desire level according to hour-of-day, and contextual situations, etc.

6. *Behavior analytics.* Every participant may be addressed considering her behavior history, as recorder during the program, and also according to the behavior of other participants. Based on the analysis of the dialogue interactions, the system should identify behavior patterns that will have an impact on the personalization of the intervention for her. For example, based on sentiment analysis of the interactions, or on the tracking of cigarettes (e.g., recent relapse, or anxiety episodes), the system may opt to strengthen

motivation factors, which would have more impact than for another participant with different behavior patterns. Furthermore, the system may cluster
similar participants according to their behavior.

7. *Persuasive argumentation.* The system must use domain-modelled arguments
in order to attempt to persuade the participant using suitable arguments,
matching both her context and profile. Arguments can be structured as concepts surrounding a certain problem/solution: e.g., its causes, benefits, associated risks, opportunities; or linked to goals, factual information, evidence,
preferences, and opinions. For example, a smoker during a cessation phase
may be suffering a motivation crisis after a month of quitting. An appropriate argument to boost motivation to sustain the cessation may be to point
out that evidence shows that after the first month the relapse crisis decrease
substantially. However, for a participant that just started the process this
argument might have little effect. The usage of computational persuasion
techniques [13] needs to be included to power this type of features.

8. *Scalability.* The support system must scale to large numbers of participants,
potentially reaching thousands of users simultaneously, without degrading the
quality of experience.

5 Design Principles

Following the requirements detailed in the previous section, we present a multi-
agent model for a behavior change system. emphasizing its main components:
domain modelling, user profiling, argumentation, stage/state management, and
communication. This model is based on the concept of user-dedicated agents that
interact with each participant individually through conversational messaging,

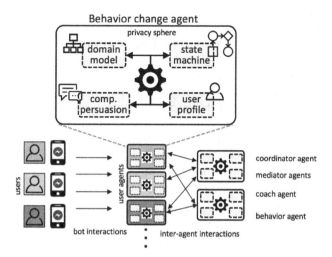

Fig. 2. A model for agent-based behavior change support applications.

while being able to keep a local knowledge base composed of the user profile and behavior. At the same time, each of these agents can interact with each other directly or through mediator agents, in cases where collaboration is required, or if further coaching/information is needed. The minimal components of the model are depicted in Fig. 2. Each behavior change agent is a lightweight software entity in charge of a single participant. Each of these agents manages the state of the participant through a state machine that reflects the different stages (and inner states), as the program progresses. It also progressively constructs a profile of the user, based on the interactions it has/had, and possesses a domain model that contains information relative to the behavior that is targeted (e.g., a model of smoking cessation issues/interactions). In addition, it includes a computational persuasion model that structures argumentation related to the domain model, and that chooses strategies of action according to the participant stages and profile. The data and profile information remains within the private sphere of each agent, which is not permeable to other agents unless passing through privacy preserving filters. The model incorporates the participants as users that interact with their corresponding behavior change agent through messaging. The agent responds embodied as a conversational application, and agents may interact among them depending on their different roles:

- Coordinator agent: it manages the addition/removal of participants and their corresponding agents in the program, it manages general stage changes, and regulates interactions within the system, including changes in the domain model (which can be forwarded to the rest of agents), incorporation of new program rules, enforcement of agreed regulations.
- Mediator agents: these are in charge of managing interactions among behavior change agents. For instance, if certain agent requires to share action plans with another one, a mediator will be activated to manage these interactions. Mediators are necessary, as they can forward agents to the most relevant peers, depending on their needs and profiles.
- Coach agents: these agents provide support, motivation, information and strategy resources to behavior change agents. In many occasions, the argumentation of each individual agent may not cover a specific situation, and the coach may be required to intervene, potentially connecting with a non-virtual coach, e.g., a professional in tobacco addiction.
- Behavior agents: these are in charge of building collective profiles of behavior, feeding from the aggregation of individual agent information. This allows the elaboration of common patterns that can help grouping participants or finding common strategies for increasing the success of the program. For instance, it may identify groups of users that are struggling with relapse episodes, or those who appear to have motivational breakdowns.

As depicted in Fig. 3, our model and its main conceptual components can also be related to aspects found in well-known behavior change models such as the I-Change model [25]. This model also incorporates different stages (as in the model in Fig. 1), although it adds different elements, such as predisposing, information, motivation and ability factors, which have incidence on several aspects

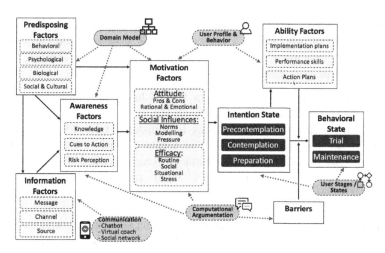

Fig. 3. The I-Change model of behavior change [25], and its relation to the different elements of our proposed agent-based model (rounded boxes).

of the behavior change process. Our agent-based approach has the flexibility to adapt to such behavior change models. For instance, the user profiling can be used to model motivation factors, and to characterize action plans and skills. Similarly, argumentation and persuasion can be used to confront awareness and information factors to barriers or obstacles.

In the following, we present the design principles of our approach, explaining through concrete examples how they relate to our agent-based model.

Conversational Multi-agent Ecosystem. The behavior change multi-agent model requires direct and personalized communication with the participants in the health program. Given that these interactions are crucial in order to set up behavioral goals, define strategies, implement actions, motivate and support the chosen actions, etc., the communication choices need to be chosen carefully. A chatbot-based interface has the advantage of being deployable in social networks, and that it can implement asymmetric dialogues natively. Moreover, it allows immediate responsiveness while reaching thousands of users simultaneously. In our model, each of these behavior change agents manages a single participant, keeping private their personal profile information and states, although with the possibility of sharing certain information through the mediator and behavior agents at a higher level. This multi-agent design enables both the encapsulation of per-user information/profiles, and the potential interaction among them in order to exploit the fact that multiple participants may face similar situations.

State-Driven Interactions. As it has been shown in the Trans-theoretical and the I-Change models, stages and participant states play a fundamental role in order to organize strategies and adapt interventions to the current context. For instance, in a smoking cessation program a key step is to quantify consumption during the preparation stage, by explicitly communicating with the agent each time a cigarette is lit. This can be modeled as a loop-repeating state of cigarette tracking during the preparation stage, which may lead to a self-consciousness state where the participant is aware, not only of how much she smokes, but also under which circumstances it happens.

User Modelling. As it has been seen in the I-Change model [25], motivation and ability factors have a direct impact on the progress of the desired behavior change. In the proposed model, this is translated into a user profile that characterizes the participant, not only in terms of basic information such as demographics, or domain-specific assessments (e.g., nicotine dependence), but also in terms of plans, goals, and skills (which are particular to each individual), as well as attitudes, social factors, and efficacy. For instance, the user profile of a smoking cessation participant may establish strategies for coping with crisis, such as preferred alternatives to cigarettes: running early in the morning instead of smoking, or switching to a patch in case of anxiety. Having this information in the profile may help the behavior change agent to adapt its advice accordingly.

Domain Modelling. Each domain of application for a particular health issue requiring behavior change, has its specific concepts and terminology, as well as inherent logics. The different physiological, psychological, emotional, motivational factors are different for each domain, and this specificity needs to be considered. Our behavior change model incorporate domain models that formally define these elements. A domain model identifies *problems* and *solutions*, and different concepts associated to these, e.g., the causes of a problem, risks, motivations; or the costs and side-effects of a solution, benefits, opportunities of a solution, etc. Other types of concepts can also be defined in the domain model, such as facts and evidence (e.g., verifiable information items), goals (e.g., personal, societal), opinions (subjective) and preferences [5]. This structured information, typically organized as ontologies, can be fed to the behavior change agents in order to manage awareness and motivation factors throughout the intervention.

Computational Persuasion. Argumentation in an asymmetric dialogue for behavior change has the underlying purpose of implementing certain action. This requires the usage of persuasion techniques, potentially using the most suitable argumentation elements for the current situation. For example, during the action/trial stage of the I-Change model, a participant trying to quit smoking may have a moment of lack of motivation, due to a perceived weight gain during the cessation period. The behavior change agent may then use the domain model to choose the most appropriate argument to try to introduce motivation factors to the participant. Probabilistic approaches [13] can be implemented within the agent in order to determine the most suitable course of action.

Privacy. Finally, the model introduces the need for bounding the range of action of each behavior change agent to its corresponding participant. This is important in order to preserve and protect sensitive data, e.g., in the user profile, behavior data, stages/states, and other private information. In any case it is necessary to define mechanisms for sharing part/aggregated data at the macro, level, with the intention of fostering collaboration among individual agents, as well as to generate and analyze behavior patterns among groups of agents.

6 Related Work

Multi-agent systems (MAS) have been used in the past for supporting eHealth interventions in different areas, as they are able to model human-like behaviors and dynamics. Behavior change systems have also been studied extensively in the context of personalized and ubiquitous computing [17], although lacking the integration of interventions into support or coaching systems. As it is explained in a survey summarizing some of the relevant work on this topic [15], assistive technologies still need to explore potential opportunities regarding the incorporation of techniques that specialize and personalize behavior change interventions. Other lines of research include exploring strategical argumentation [21], or the formalization of preferences and arguments within NLP interactions [4].

Concerning the utilization of social networks for supporting health and well-being programs, there have been several initiatives, although with mixed results. In particular, social networks have been used in previous attempts at providing community-based platforms for smoking cessation. Tweet2Quit is one such example [18], showing promising potential for the development of online support systems. However, these results still show no conclusive evidence on the effect of social interactions or the effectiveness of information messages. Other approaches have included WhatsApp and Facebook as social platforms, for instance targeting smoking relapse prevention [6], or smoking cessation in young adults [20]. Digital assistants have become popular in recent years, and have been used under different contexts, exploiting vocal command interfaces. A study focusing on smoking cessation advice [2] was conducted comparing Siri and Google Assistant against simple Web search, and showed that in fact, the use of these assistants is often not better than a manual search. Early attempts to design virtual coaches for smoking cessation [10] have only provided initial ideas and requirements, while concrete implementations remain to be developed. Beyond smoking-related use-cases, chatbot-based solutions and prototypes have been presented in other contexts, such as dietary & food counselling [1], healthy lifestyle programs [8], or primary care patient intake [16].

7 Road-Map

In this paper we presented an abstract model that considers behavior change models as basis for developing multi-agent-based systems that automatize the support of participants in healthcare programs. This model is a starting point towards the implementation of effective and personalized support systems that are able to effectively take into account domain models and user profiles to tailor the type of intervention. Although this constitutes a first step in this direction, a significant number of future contributions are required to achieve this goal:

– *Behavior change ontologies.* The inclusion of vocabularies and ontologies for description, discovery, provenance and exchange within behavior change agents is of particular importance. These ontologies can formalize the knowledge of the domain models, and help structure the argumentation graphs that can be used later for the respective computations.

– *Domain models.* Specific models should be developed for each domain. The existence of public libraries of these models can help enriching agent-based systems in areas such as physical rehabilitation, medication adherence, physical activity, sleep training, etc.

– *Agent coordination and negotiation.* Although the proposed model includes the definition of goals, which can be used within the argumentation component, it remains to specify what mechanisms will be implemented in order to incorporate computational persuasion into the agent execution logic. While existing approaches [13] offer potential solutions, it remains to be studied how to incorporate the learning process (e.g., evolution of the participant, or reuse of other participants' behavior) in order to enrich the model.

– *Cooperation.* The specification of cooperation protocols for participating agents is an important topic of study, in order to enable clustering participants, finding common problems and targeting community-based interventions that focus on similar issues. This reinforces the social-nature of the proposed approach and its inherent benefits in the context MAS.

– *Implementation.* The implementation of the proposed model is challenging, both form the technical (integration of multi-agent and behavior change approaches), and the application point of view (evaluation of the system on a real environment with a concrete participants). For this purpose, we plan to apply the model presented here in the future editions of the JDF smoking cessation program in Switzerland. KPIs to evaluate implementations shall consider both technical indicators as well as persuasion metrics.

– *Privacy.* Given the potentially sensitive nature of profile and behavior information, privacy concerns need to be thoroughly studied and addressed. Ensuring privacy protection, using different approaches spanning from obfuscation to anonymity guarantees, will be expected, adopting ethics-by-design methodologies [7].

References

1. Angara, P., et al.: Foodie fooderson a conversational agent for the smart kitchen. In: CASCON, pp. 247–253 (2017)
2. Boyd, M., Wilson, N.: Just ask Siri? A pilot study comparing smartphone digital assistants and laptop Google searches for smoking cessation advice. PLoS ONE **13**(3), e0194811 (2018)
3. Centers for Disease Control and Prevention: Quitting smoking among adults-United States, 2001–2010. Morb. Mortal. Wkly Rep. **60**(44), 1513 (2011)
4. Cerutti, F., Tintarev, N., Oren, N.: Formal arguments, preferences, and natural language interfaces to humans: an empirical evaluation. In: ECAI, pp. 207–212 (2014)

5. Chalaguine, L., et al.: Domain modelling in computational persuasion for behaviour change in healthcare (2018). arXiv preprint arXiv:1802.10054
6. Cheung, Y.T.D., et al.: Using WhatsApp and Facebook online social groups for smoking relapse prevention for recent quitters: a pilot pragmatic cluster randomized controlled trial. J. Med. Internet Res. **17**(10), e238 (2015)
7. d'Aquin, M., Troullinou, P., O'Connor, N.E., Cullen, A., Faller, G., Holden, L.: Towards an ethics by design methodology for AI research projects. In: Proceedings of the AAAI/ACM Conference on AI, Ethics, and Society, pp. 54–59. ACM (2018)
8. Fadhil, A., Gabrielli, S.: Addressing challenges in promoting healthy lifestyles: the al-chatbot approach. In: Proceedings of the 11th EAI International Conference on Pervasive Computing Technologies for Healthcare, pp. 261–265. ACM (2017)
9. Folly, L., Riedo, G., Felder, M., Falomir-Pichastor, J.M., Desrichard, O.: Rapport de l'évaluation externe du programme «J'arrête de fumer» sur Facebook. Sur mandat du Fonds de Prévention du Tabagisme (2016)
10. Grolleman, J., van Dijk, B., Nijholt, A., van Emst, A.: Break the habit! Designing an e-Therapy intervention using a virtual coach in aid of smoking cessation. In: IJsselsteijn, W.A., de Kort, Y.A.W., Midden, C., Eggen, B., van den Hoven, E. (eds.) PERSUASIVE 2006. LNCS, vol. 3962, pp. 133–141. Springer, Heidelberg (2006). https://doi.org/10.1007/11755494_19
11. Hunter, A.: Opportunities for argument-centric persuasion in behaviour change. In: European Workshop on Logics in Artificial Intelligence, pp. 48–61 (2014)
12. Hunter, A.: Modelling the persuadee in asymmetric argumentation dialogues for persuasion. In: 24th International Joint Conference on Artificial Intelligence (2015)
13. Hunter, A.: Towards a framework for computational persuasion with applications in behaviour change. Argument & Computation (Preprint), 1–26 (2017)
14. Jones, A.M.: Health, addiction, social interaction and the decision to quit smoking. J. Health Econ. **13**(1), 93–110 (1994)
15. Kennedy, C.M., Powell, J., Payne, T.H., Ainsworth, J., Boyd, A., Buchan, I.: Active assistance technology for health-related behavior change: an interdisciplinary review. J. Med. Internet Res. **14**(3), e80 (2012)
16. Ni, L., Lu, C., Liu, N., Liu, J.: MANDY: towards a smart primary care chatbot application. In: Chen, J., Theeramunkong, T., Supnithi, T., Tang, X. (eds.) KSS 2017. CCIS, vol. 780, pp. 38–52. Springer, Singapore (2017). https://doi.org/10.1007/978-981-10-6989-5_4
17. Oinas-Kukkonen, H.: A foundation for the study of behavior change support systems. Pers. Ubiquitous Comput. **17**(6), 1223–1235 (2013)
18. Pechmann, C., Pan, L., Delucchi, K., Lakon, C., Prochaska, J.: Development of a Twitter-based intervention for smoking cessation that encourages high-quality social media interactions via automessages. JMIR **17**(2), e50 (2015)
19. Prochaska, J.O., Velicer, W.F.: The transtheoretical model of health behavior change. Am. J. Health Promot. **12**(1), 38–48 (1997)
20. Ramo, D.E., Thrul, J., Chavez, K., Delucchi, K.L., Prochaska, J.J.: Feasibility and quit rates of the tobacco status project: a Facebook smoking cessation intervention for young adults. J. Med. Internet Res. **17**(12), e291 (2015)
21. Rosenfeld, A., Kraus, S.: Strategical argumentative agent for human persuasion. In: ECAI, vol. 16, pp. 320–329 (2016)
22. Tsoh, J.Y., et al.: A social network family-focused intervention to promote smoking cessation in Chinese and Vietnamese American male smokers: a feasibility study. Nicotine Tob. Res. **17**(8), 1029–1038 (2015)
23. Velicer, W., Prochaska, J., Redding, C.: Tailored communications for smoking cessation: past successes and future directions. Drug Alcohol Rev. **25**, 49–57 (2006)

24. Velicer, W.F., et al.: An expert system intervention for smoking cessation. Addict. Behav. **18**(3), 269–290 (1993)
25. de Vries, H., Mesters, I., Van de Steeg, H., Honing, C.: The general public's information needs and perceptions regarding hereditary cancer: an application of the integrated change model. Patient Educ. Couns. **56**(2), 154–165 (2005)

Towards Agent-Oriented Blockchains: Autonomous Smart Contracts

Giovanni Ciatto[1] , Alfredo Maffi[1] , Stefano Mariani[2] ,
and Andrea Omicini[1(✉)]

[1] Alma Mater Studiorum–Università di Bologna, Bologna, Italy
{giovanni.ciatto,alfredo.maffi,andrea.omicini}@unibo.it
[2] Università di Modena e Reggio Emilia, Modena, Italy
stefano.mariani@unimore.it

Abstract. Features of blockchain technology (BCT) such as decentralisation, trust, fault tolerance, and accountability, are of paramount importance for multi-agent systems (MAS). In this paper we argue that a principled approach to MAS-BCT integration cannot overlook the foundational character of agency—that is, *autonomy*. Accordingly, we present a custom BCT implementation where autonomy is placed in *smart contracts* (SC) interpreted as software *agents*. We show how agency can enhance SC expressiveness with autonomy, situatedness, sociality, and intelligence, and highlight the limitations of state-of-art BCT in supporting MAS design and implementation.

Keywords: Autonomy · Smart contracts · Blockchain ·
Multi-agent systems

1 Introduction

The notion of *smart contract* (SC) as a way of automating the verification of properties of transactions according to application-level criteria is a warhorse for most famous 2nd and 3rd generation blockchain technologies (BCTs)—such as Ethereum [24] and HyperLedger Fabric [1]. There, the blockchain is not only a decentralised, secure, and fault-tolerant ledger tracking assets transactions, but a full-fledged distributed computing platform handling the lifecycle of computational processes called smart contracts. Smart contracts are intended as trustworthy intermediaries amongst mutually-untrusted parties that need to interact. Accordingly, their ultimate goal is to replace and possibly augment real-world contracts [22].

Real-world contracts are essentially *passive* containers of terms regulating the side effects of an interaction amongst two or more mutually-untrusted parties in a specific context, as in the case of a seller and a buyer of a house whose obligations and rights depend on properties beyond the asset being traded—for instance, seller's actual ownership of the house, house legal compliance to security standards, etc. In case of a controversy, a real-world contract would *not*

Y. Demazeau et al. (Eds.): PAAMS 2019, LNAI 11523, pp. 29–41, 2019.
https://doi.org/10.1007/978-3-030-24209-1_3

actually *enforce* those side effects: SC, instead, are meant first of all meant to do that in an *automatic* way. The example in [23] is a vending machine as a smart contract, automating the intercourse between a client and the product provider.

So, SC do not just replace real-world contracts: they *augment* them with automation. Yet, what is smart in a smart contract? In [23], "smartness" apparently stems from developers hard-coding useful behaviours into some software or cyber-physical system—so, they are smart as much as their program is.

However, in the real-world, contracts are "augmented" in many ways, thus suggesting that automating their enforcement could be just the starting point. For instance, given a real-world contract, a trusted third-party such as a magistrate *(i)* could be asked to provide the rightful interpretation of the contract against the law, *(ii)* should decide which parties are right and which are wrong in a controversy, and *(iii)* might take action to ignite the enforcement of the side effects—i.e. invalidating the deal. More generally, many organisms in the real world are in charge of *pro-actively* monitoring trading in certain business domains – such as finance, communications, real estate, public administration contracting, etc. – with the duty of triggering the appropriate sanctioning procedures, if needed. The key here is *pro-activity*—meaning "making something happen", rather than simply reacting to events: so, a pro-active SC has the potential to be really smart—for instance, by actively pushing the parties in a contract to actually abide by their obligations.

From a computational viewpoint, pro-activity requires *(computational)* *autonomy*: which is something that current implementations of SC do not provide. In fact, SC are typically implemented as purely *reactive* computational processes [3,19] which only encapsulate state and behaviour – as in OOP –, not their *control flow*—as in agents and multi-agent systems (MAS) [15]. Instead, we argue that *enhancing SC with autonomy* – or, in other words, *interpreting SC as agents* – is a promising step towards the full development of the BCT potential.

Along these lines, the contribution of the paper is threefold:

- we discuss why SC and BCT are not currently ready for computational autonomy, why that is an issue, and how MAS could work as a source of abstractions and mechanisms to overcome current limitations
- we articulate a long-term research roadmap meant to blend agent-oriented and BCT abstractions and techniques in a coherent way, by drawing the notions of agent and SC closer based on autonomy
- we propose and design a novel notion of *rational* and *autonomous* smart contracts, which we endow with typical agents features such as computational autonomy, situatedness, inferential capabilities, and sociality

As a solid ground to root our discussions, and also to enable further research efforts, we deliver Tenderfone, a proof-of-concept implementation based on Tendermint [10] of a custom blockchain supporting such a novel notion of SC, as the first step along the outlined roadmap, aimed at narrowing both the modelling and implementation gap between SC and agency.

2 Autonomy in Smart Contracts

The concept of smart contract has no formal definition. The term has been introduced in [22] to define a *"computerized transaction protocol that executes the terms of a contract"*. There, the author conceives SC as a digital version of real world contracts capable of *actively: (i)* regulating the interaction between two or more parties while enforcing the terms of the contract, *(ii)* clarifying unambiguously the implications of this interaction, *(iii)* minimising exceptions, both malicious and accidental, and *(iv)* minimising the need for trusted intermediaries. According to this vision, SC can be used as a means for reducing the transaction costs related to the execution of real world contracts (essentially by eliminating or reducing the need for a middleman) as well as an opportunity for creating new kinds of business and social institutions.

At present, many instantiations of the original definition have been proposed by 2nd–3rd generation BCT. Despite some minor differences, they all share some crucial common traits that make it possible to grasp what the mainstream interpretation of a SC actually is: a *reactive* computational process executing a program on top of a blockchain. In fact, even though in most cases SC are not explicitly described as reactive, such a feature is apparent when looking at the technical documentation[1]—for instance, as exemplified by the request/response interaction mode always triggered by off-chain entities (such as end users).

In order to better understand the nature of SC, let us provide a quick overview of how a generic blockchain works. By abstracting away from peculiarities of specific implementations, a blockchain consists of a peer-to-peer (P2P) network of nodes, most of which participate to a consensus algorithm aimed at making them jointly behave as a single, consistent, and fault-tolerant virtual machine executing SC. The blockchain is built in such a way that every information or asset possibly manipulated by the system itself – there including SC – is cryptographically-secured through one-way hash functions, and made hard to tamper with by means of consensus, redundancy, and replication.

More precisely, BCT can be conceived as a three-layered system:

1. The bottom layer is composed by a number of *validators* that enable and support *State Machine Replication* (SMR) [18], aimed at *ordering* the transactions concurrently occurring in the distributed system by storing transactions on a hash-chain data structure – the *ledger* – which is prohibitively difficult to tamper with. This layer – here, the *ledger-based SMR engine* – makes all validators *eventually* agree on *who* makes *what* happen, *when*.
2. The middle layer consists of the SC *interpreter*—that is, the program actually executing SC. Due to replication, the interpreter is actually composed by a number of distributed processes running in parallel, as the validators, which thanks to the ledger engine execute every SC in the same way.
3. The top layer is the *application level*, where SC are executed.

---

[1] https://solidity.readthedocs.io/en/v0.5.3/introduction-to-smart-contracts.html, https://hyperledger-fabric.readthedocs.io/en/release-1.3/chaincode4ade.html.

End users – that is, off-chain entities – interact with the top layer to affect the ledger, either by issuing assets transactions or by deploying/invoking smart contracts. Once invoked, a SC may invoke another one in turn. Technically, all triggering events are *transactions*, as events aimed at altering the state of the ledger, thus: *(i)* they must be registered by the bottom layer, and *(ii)* they may affect the application level—through SC. In particular, end users are allowed to deploy (that is, publish on the blockchain) the source code of a SC by issuing a deployment transaction. Then, technically, several replicas of the same program are instantiated, one for each node of the underlying P2P (sub)network in charge of validating the transaction. Thanks to consensus, when triggered the many replicas of the SC are executed as a single entity, in a coherent and consistent way. Once a SC is published (that is, it has been deployed), end users are allowed to invoke it by issuing an invocation transaction. Then, the computation expressed by the SC program, aimed either at updating the SC internal status or producing some result value according to that status, is started.

In summary, based on a thorough analysis of the most established BCT [1, 24] we can define SC more precisely by their features:

user-centric — they are created and deployed by end users, for end users

transparent — their source code can be inspected by any participant

immutable — their source code cannot be altered after deployment

trustworthy — as transparent and immutable

reactive — they cannot take action unless triggered from off the chain

stateful — each smart contract encapsulates its own internal state and exposes a set of methods regulating how it can be updated—as in OOP

deterministic — their execution is always deterministic—their output depends on their input and state, which are guaranteed to be consistent by the underlying SMR engine

synchronous — they interact with both end users and other SC through a synchronous request-response mechanism ($\approx$ method call)—as in OOP

As already observed by others [20], the more rigorous description emphasises a discrepancy between the full potential of SC and their mainstream interpretation, hence the way they are implemented, and in turn their expressive power: the lack of *control flow encapsulation* implies the lack of the most basic *computational autonomy*—roughly, the capability of deciding *when* to do something.

According to [13], object and agents both encapsulate state and behaviour. They differ instead because agents encapsulate control flow (so, they are *proactive*), while objects do not (they are just *reactive*). Thus, *computational autonomy* is the most foundational feature of software *agents* [15]. On a technical note, this implies *asynchronous* message-passing as the default means of interaction—in contrast with OOP (and SC) synchronous communication.

Besides being autonomous, software agents are expected to be:

situated [14, 21] — Agent practical reasoning and actions are bound to the environment where they occur, there including the space-time fabric

social — Agents may overcome their own individual limitations by interacting with others to achieve a goal—either their own or a common one. This includes both explicit communication mechanisms, such as message passing, and implicit ones, such as stigmergy [17]

goal-driven [6] — Agents gear their course of actions towards a goal either implicitly embedded in their design and programming (goal-driven) or explicitly represented as a cognitive abstraction (goal-governed)

3 A Roadmap to Agency for Smart Contracts

According to the state-of-art of BCT, SC lack all of the agent features mentioned in Sect. 2, which would help them fully realise their potential. For instance, a SC can not perform any task involving periodic, delayed, or scheduled action without the explicit intervention of an end user. In other words, without external invocation a SC is unable to act. By the way, this exemplifies the lack of computational autonomy as well as the lack of situatedness—in time, in particular. Whereas sociality of SC could be debatable, goal-drivenness is limited by the fact that the goal is not explicitly represented, thus the SC can neither observe, reason, manipulate their own goal nor act deliberately to achieve it.

Nevertheless, the aforementioned limitations do not depend on technical limitations of the blockchain itself, or, on conceptual flaws in the modelling of SC; instead they depend on the choice of the design paradigm adopted for SC, that is, OOP. There, the autonomy of objects is not considered by design, as objects are *servants* whose behaviour constrained by their interface—ironically, a sort of contract itself. On the contrary, agents and MAS explicitly grounds their novelty and expressive power on the basic notion of autonomy [13].

Accordingly, we propose for SC the roadmap to agency as depicted in Fig. 1:

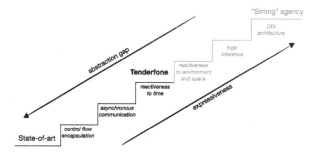

Fig. 1. Smart contracts: the roadmap to agency

1. encapsulation of control flow (for *computational autonomy* [15])
2. asynchronous interaction (for *social autonomy* [4])
3. reactiveness to time, space, environment (for situatedness)
4. logic inference (for goal-drivenness, weak agency)
5. BDI architecture (for goal-drivenness, strong agency)

Encapsulation of Control Flow. Smart contracts should encapsulate their own control flow [15], so they can be technically interpreted as *autonomous* agents, able to deliberate their own course of actions regardless of the external stimuli. Being proactive by no means prevents SC to behave reactively.

Asynchronous Interaction. Since synchronous invocation directly contrasts with social autonomy [4], interaction should be *asynchronous*. Technically, the current practice of (remote) method call could be replaced by *asynchronous message-passing*, for instance tracking each message exchange on the blockchain as a *transaction*. This more naturally lends SC to a *social* interpretation where a set of interacting SC can be seen as a set of communicating agents collaborating towards a common goal. As further desirable implications, asynchronous communication would *(i)* enable SC to carry out long-running computations without making others starve, and *(ii)* prevent some well-known subtleties arising when SC developer do not properly take into account recursive calls [2,11].

Reactiveness to Time, Space, Environment. Autonomy of SC enables *situatedness*—for instance, in the time dimension, since autonomous SC can *pro-actively* decide when to take action according to time-aware criteria. Other dimensions of situatedness are not discussed here for the sake of simplicity.

Logic Inference. The term "inference" may be interpreted as the capability to infer new information from existing one, or, to (dis)prove that some information stem from some other. The latter acceptation is particularly appealing for SC, since the process of checking whether interaction conforms to some rules can be represented as a theorem proving process ("the interactions are compliant") against a set of axioms and hypotheses (rules and interactions, respectively).

This is the perspective we foster by adopting *Logic Programming* (LP), in particular Prolog, as the language of choice for programming SC [5,8]. LP-based SC are close to *rational agents*—that is, agents capable of bringing about *goal-driven* reasoning, planning, deliberation, etc. A rational SC may take the information stored on the blockchain as the logic theory against which to prove the goal they encode—for instance, compliance to a set of invariants.

BDI Architecture. A stronger notion of goal-drivenness – making agents *goal-governed* – can be achieved by resorting to a full-fledged *Belief-Desire-Intention* (BDI) architecture [16] to structure reasoning of rational SC as *cognitive agents*. Along that perspective, each SC acts to satisfy a set of *desires*, by adopting a number of *intentions*, based a corpus of *beliefs*, that it brings about through a library of *plans*. Desires are an explicit representation of the long-term goals to be achieved or maintained by a SC—for instance, some invariant properties for each set of transactions they process. Intentions are the short-term commitments that an agent makes towards the satisfaction of its desires—for instance, the set of procedures that a SC carries out for checking compliance to a specific policy of a specific transaction. Beliefs are a representation of the state of the "world" in which SC are living, stemming from either their perception of the environment (for instance, the state of the blockchain they see) or from the communication with other SC (i.e., the messages or the implicit information they receive from other SC. Finally, plans represent the procedural knowledge that agents need to achieve their goals, which may be either encoded by developers, acquired dynamically by other agents, or generated by agents themselves through deliberation and means-ends reasoning.

4 Towards Autonomous SC with Tenderfone

As a first stop in our investigation, we propose Tenderfone[2], a language and associated interpreter for the execution of autonomous, asynchronous, time-aware, and logic-based SC, implemented on top of the ledger-based SMR engine Tendermint [10]. First, we model the language for programming SC, then we describe the Tenderfone Interpreter, emphasising the assumptions required for the underlying BCT. In fact, as we chose Tendermint as our implementation platform, any other BCT satisfying such assumptions could be used instead.

4.1 A Declarative, Asynchronous, Time-Aware Language for SC

Tenderfone language is a declarative language based on First Order Logic (FOL), hence the associated Tenderfone Interpreter is essentially a logic-based reasoning engine. In particular, Prolog syntax and the tuProlog engine [7,9] are adopted [5,8]. Accordingly, a Tenderfone SC can be interpreted as a reasoner proving goals either pro-actively pursued or coming from end users or other SC. Goals are expressed as FOL terms in Prolog syntax, likewise the information encapsulated as part of the SC state, which, in logic terms, constitutes its Knowledge Base (KB)—the corpus of axioms and rules against which theorem proving happens. The KB is split in two: *(i)* the *static* KB stores the *immutable* knowledge endowed to the SC by its creator (the developer), and represents the "program" to be executed; *(ii)* the *dynamic* KB tracks information which may be altered by the smart contract itself, hence represents its (encapsulated) mutable state.

The language constructs described below[3] directly reflect the aforementioned distinguishing features of Tenderfone SC, as follows.

---

[2] Source code publicly available at [12].

[3] We rely on Prolog standard notation for input/output arguments: + is an input, + is an output, ? can be both, whereas @ is a *ground* input.

Computational Autonomy. Autonomy is enabled by the interplay between a few distinct mechanisms, among which the Tenderfone Interpreter plays a crucial role—Subsect. 4.2. A first enabler is the `init(+Args)` callback, specifying what SC should do as its very first action. There the developer may decide to take advantage of time-awareness and, possibly, asynchronous message passing, to specify a pro-active behaviour in which *(i)* the SC periodically executes tasks, *(ii)* there including reception of messages and *(iii)* deliberation about whether and when to actually process them. This is technically enabled by a clever combination of `receive/2` and time-aware constructs, both described in the following.

The semantics enforced by Tenderfone Interpreter guarantees that deployment of a valid smart contract can only succeed if goal `init/1` can be proven using arguments `Args` provided by the transaction issued by end user U. In case of success, the new SC is actually deployed, and its KB is stored on the blockchain, otherwise no SC is deployed and an error description is returned.

Asynchronous Interaction. Tenderfone smart contracts interact through asynchronous message passing, as follows:

- `send(+Message, @ReceiverID)` is a built-in construct that adds to the outbox of the current SC `Message`, to be dispatched to `ReceiverID`. If execution is successful, a correspondent `receive/2` of the smart contract whose identifier is `ReceiverID` will be triggered by an invocation transaction.
- `receive(+Message, @SenderID)` is a callback that specifies what the SC should do every time it is triggered by an invocation transaction regarding `Message`, as sent by either a end user (through `invoke/2`) or another SC (through `send/2`) identified by `SenderID`.
- `answer(+Message, @SenderID, -Result)` is a callback that specifies how the SC should answer (`Result`) every time it is triggered (through a call to `observe/3`, last paragraph) by an end user whose identifier is `SenderID`.

An invocation transaction issued by entity E towards SC carrying message M is valid only if the KB of SC entails `receive(Message, SenderID)`, where `Message` $= M$ and `SenderID` $= id(E)$. In that case, the current state of SC dynamic KB is committed to the blockchain; otherwise, any change to SC dynamic KB and outgoing message queued by `send/2` are dropped.

Reactiveness to Time. Tenderfone sensibly assumes that the underlying BCT provides a global notion of (logical) time, T_g, maintained through consensus, hence consistently observable every time a new block is created. The following built-in constructs are then available to Tenderfone developers, to let SC observe time (time-awareness) and act based on it (reactiveness to time):

- `now(-Timestamp)` retrieves the last value of T_g shared through consensus, as it is stored in the block whose commit triggered the executing SC
- `when(@Instant, +Goal)` triggers callback `receive(Goal, Me)` – where `Me` denotes the executing SC – as soon as $T_g \geq$ `Instant`

- `delay(@Interval, +Goal)` triggers goal `receive(Goal, Me)` as soon as $T_g \geq T'_g + $ `Interval`, where T'_g is the value of time when `delay/2` was invoked
- `periodically(@Period, +Goal)` triggers callback `receive(Goal, Me)`, then does so again as soon as $T_g \geq t_i = t_0 + (i \cdot$ `Period`$)$, where t_0 is the time when `receive/2` was first invoked, until some `receive(Goal, Me)` fails

Variables `Timestamp` and `Instant` both represent an instant in time – such as `datetime(Y, ..., SS)`, – whereas variables `Interval`, `Delay`, and `Period` represent an interval of time – such as `seconds(SS)`, ..., `years(Y)`.

Miscellaneous. The following built-in constructs are also provided as general-purpose facilities:

- `self(-ID)` retrieves the ID of the current SC
- `owner(-ID)` retrieves the ID of the *owner* of the current SC
- `set_data(@Key, ?Value)` either stores the (`Key`, `Value`) pair in the dynamic KB of the current SC or replaces (`Key`, `Whatever`), if present
- `get_data(?Key, ?Value)` checks if a pair matching (`Key`, `Value`) exists within the current SC dynamic KB

End User API. Users can interact with Tenderfone smart contracts pretty much as they do with state-of-art smart contracts:

- `deploy(@StaticKB, +Args, -ScID)` creates a SC whose source code is `StaticKB`, and triggers its callback `init/1` with arguments `Args`.
- `invoke(+Goal, @ScID)` triggers callback `receive(Goal, UserID)` on the SC `ScID` for calling user `UserID`—with an all-or-nothing semantics
- `observe(+Query, @ScID, -R)` triggers callback `answer(Query, U, R)` – where `U` denotes the invoking user – on the SC `ScID`, failing if and only if the callback fails. In any case, *all* side effects possibly occurred are dropped, as `observe/3` is intended as a pure *inspection* primitive.

4.2   The Tenderfone Interpreter

Invocation transactions published by end users deliver a single message (`Goal`) aimed at triggering the `receive/2` callback of a SC. Conversely, messages sent by SC are implemented as *spontaneous* transactions generated by validators themselves—which now encapsulate their own flow of control. In a similar way, postponed, delayed, and periodic computations are designed as messages sent by a SC to itself, hence are *spontaneous* transactions, too.

The Tenderfone Interpreter takes care of ordering transactions spawned during system operation, provided that the following critical assumptions hold. Let V be the amount of validators in Tenderfone, then, at some time t, each one is executing a copy of all SCs deployed before t. Since execution of all SCs is aligned by consensus, then for each callback executed by a SC, V copies of its triggering transaction have *actually* been published and committed on the blockchain: one for each validator. As a consequence, there is a 1:V correspondence between the amount of messages possibly sent by each SC and the corresponding amount of transactions actually committed on the blockchain. This property is crucial to let an external observer discriminate among legitimate and forged transactions, as further discussed in the following.

Trust problems may arise since validators may technically generate *spurious* transactions out of thin air, aimed at triggering a SC S even if no other entity sent a message to S, nor S scheduled any computation. This is a potential violation of SC computational autonomy, other than an undesirable security hole—for instance, vulnerable to DOS attacks. As a countermeasure, Tenderfone guarantees that unless messages are sent by legitimate users, they are considered valid if and only if V copies of each are actually on the blockchain as part of as many transactions. Messages are thus considered actually "sent" only when the Vth copy of the corresponding transaction has been committed on the blockchain by the consensus algorithm—pluggable, in Tenderfone. Validators may of course still forge messages, but, unless other validators are corrupted too, they will be simply ignored. Computations reactive to time are realised through spontaneous transactions, too: each validator keeps track of the computations scheduled by all SC and generates a transaction as soon as their deadlines are reached.

5 Use Case: Public Tender

In the following we shortly describe a use case for Tenderfone SC which is instead out of reach for state-of-art SC: the handling of a public tender.

Public tenders are a trust-critical application that could easily benefit from the adoption of BCT and SC by easily cutting out the cases where: *(i)* one or more submitters lie about the timing of their submission, *(ii)* one or more corrupted employees tamper with one or more submissions, or *(iii)* one or more submissions are disclosed before the public tender is over. The SC described below can be adopted as a countermeasure to the aforementioned issues.

Figure 2 shows the source code of an "auctioneer" SC handling a public tender. After deployment, and as long as the tender is open, it continuously collects submissions sent by other SC or end users. More precisely, it *(i)* knows when to open the tender and its duration from input, *(ii)* after deployment, waits until the opening date, then moves into the **open** state and schedules closing of the tender when due, *(iii)* accepts submissions as long as the tender is open, and *(iv)* exposes submissions only *after* the tender has been closed.

Finally, it is worth emphasising what makes Tenderfone SC more expressive than the state-of-the-art SC: *(i)* computational autonomy, enabling SCs to set their own goals upon deployment and act as soon as the tender needs to be opened/closed without the need for external stimuli, and *(ii)* temporal situatedness, enabling SC to perceive time and perform time-dependant computations.

```
% assume opening date & duration are provided upon deployment
init([OpeningDate, Duration]) :-
    now(Now), OpeningDate > Now, % ensure opening date in the future
    set_data(tender_opening, OpeningDate), % store opening date
    set_data(tender_duration, Duration), % store duration
    set_data(tender_status, will_open), % tender will eventually open
    when(OpeningDate, open_tender). % schedule tender opening

receive(open_tender, Sender) :-
    self(Sender), % only this smart contract can open the tender
    get_data(tender_status, will_open), % ensure not already opened
    set_data(tender_status, open), % tender is now open
    get_data(tender_duration, Duration), % retrieve tender duration
    delay(Duration, close_tender). % schedule tender closing

receive(close_tender, Sender) :-
    self(Sender), % only this smart contract can close the tender
    get_data(tender_status, open), % ensure tender is open
    set_data(tender_status, closed). % tender is now closed

receive(submission(Offer), Sender) :-
    get_data(tender_status, open), % ensure tender is open
    set_data(submitter(Sender), submission(Offer)). % store submission

answer(submission(Submitter), _, Result) :- % no constraint on asker
    get_data(tender_status, closed), % ensure tender is open
    get_data(submitter(Submitter), Result). % retrieves the submission
```

Fig. 2. A Tenderfone SC autonomously managing a public tender

6   Conclusion

The notion of smart contract is increasingly getting a well-deserved attention, as a potentially-disrupting way of cutting out middle-man agencies (i.e., costs) and humans (i.e., errors and misinterpretations) from asset transactions of any kind. Nevertheless, currently-available SC implementations are more automatic than smart: they can check compliance of contracts automatically, yet their "smartness" is bound by the hard-coded reactive behaviour designed for them.

This is why in this paper we push SC beyond their current status towards the realisation of their intended purpose, that is, *replacing* and *augmenting* real-world contracts. Along that line, we resort to the most appropriate source of abstractions: agents and multi-agent systems. Hence, we endow SC with autonomy, situatedness, and rationality; we draw a roadmap for SC towards agency; finally, we provide an implementation of SC as agents with Tenderfone [12].

References

1. Androulaki, E., et al.: Hyperledger fabric: a distributed operating system for permissioned blockchains. In: 13th EuroSys Conference (EuroSys 2018). ACM, New York (2018). https://doi.org/10.1145/3190508.3190538
2. Atzei, N., Bartoletti, M., Cimoli, T.: A survey of attacks on ethereum smart contracts (SoK). In: Maffei, M., Ryan, M. (eds.) POST 2017. LNCS, vol. 10204, pp. 164–186. Springer, Heidelberg (2017). https://doi.org/10.1007/978-3-662-54455-6_8

3. BangBit Technologies: The power of smart contracts on the blockchain: how can businesses get the advantage? Medium, May 2018. http://medium.com/p/b8abd5086caf

4. Castelfranchi, C.: Guarantees for autonomy in cognitive agent architecture. In: Wooldridge, M.J., Jennings, N.R. (eds.) ATAL 1994. LNCS, vol. 890, pp. 56–70. Springer, Heidelberg (1995). https://doi.org/10.1007/3-540-58855-8_3

5. Ciatto, G., Calegari, R., Mariani, S., Denti, E., Omicini, A.: From the blockchain to logic programming and back: research perspectives. In: Cossentino, M., Sabatucci, L., Seidita, V. (eds.) WOA 2018–19th Workshop "From Objects to Agents". CEUR Workshop Proceedings, vol. 2215, pp. 69–74 (2018)

6. Conte, R., Castelfranchi, C.: Cognitive and Social Action. UCL Press, London (1995). http://books.google.com/books?isbn=1857281861

7. Denti, E., Omicini, A., Ricci, A.: tuProlog: a light-weight prolog for internet applications and infrastructures. In: Ramakrishnan, I.V. (ed.) PADL 2001. LNCS, vol. 1990, pp. 184–198. Springer, Heidelberg (2001). https://doi.org/10.1007/3-540-45241-9_13

8. Idelberger, F., Governatori, G., Riveret, R., Sartor, G.: Evaluation of logic-based smart contracts for blockchain systems. In: Alferes, J.J.J., Bertossi, L., Governatori, G., Fodor, P., Roman, D. (eds.) RuleML 2016. LNCS, vol. 9718, pp. 167–183. Springer, Cham (2016). https://doi.org/10.1007/978-3-319-42019-6_11

9. Kowalski, R.A.: Predicate logic as programming language. In: Information Processing 74 - Proceedings of the 1974 IFIP Congress, pp. 569–574. North-Holland Publishing Company (1974)

10. Kwon, J.: Tendermint: consensus without mining (2014). https://tendermint.com/static/docs/tendermint.pdf

11. Luu, L., Chu, D.H., Olickel, H., Saxena, P., Hobor, A.: Making smart contracts smarter. In: ACM SIGSAC Conference on Computer and Communications Security (CCS 2016), pp. 254–269. ACM Press, New York (2016). https://doi.org/10.1145/2976749.2978309

12. Maffi, A.: Tenderfone GitLab repository. https://gitlab.com/pika-lab/blockchain/tenderfone/tenderfone-sc

13. Odell, J.: Objects and agents compared. J. Object Technol. **1**, 41–53 (2002). https://doi.org/10.5381/jot.2002.1.1.c4

14. Omicini, A., Ricci, A., Viroli, M.: Timed environment for Web agents. Web Intell. Agent Syst. **5**(2), 161–175 (2007). http://content.iospress.com/articles/web-intelligence-and-agent-systems-an-international-journal/wia00111

15. Omicini, A., Ricci, A., Viroli, M.: Artifacts in the A&A meta-model for multi-agent systems. Auton. Agent. Multi-Agent Syst. **17**(3), 432–456 (2008). https://doi.org/10.1007/s10458-008-9053-x

16. Rao, A.S., Georgeff, M.P.: An abstract architecture for rational agents. In: Proceedings of the 3rd International Conference on Principles of Knowledge Representation and Reasoning (KR 1992), pp. 439–449. Morgan Kaufmann (1992)

17. Ricci, A., Omicini, A., Viroli, M., Gardelli, L., Oliva, E.: Cognitive stigmergy: towards a framework based on agents and artifacts. In: Weyns, D., Parunak, H.V.D., Michel, F. (eds.) E4MAS 2006. LNCS (LNAI), vol. 4389, pp. 124–140. Springer, Heidelberg (2007). https://doi.org/10.1007/978-3-540-71103-2_7

18. Schneider, F.B.: Implementing fault-tolerant services using the state machine approach: a tutorial. ACM Comput. Surv. **22**(4), 299–319 (1990). https://doi.org/10.1145/98163.98167

19. Seijas, P.L., Thompson, S.J., McAdams, D.: Scripting smart contracts for distributed ledger technology. Report 1156, IACR Cryptology ePrint Archive (2016). http://eprint.iacr.org/2016/1156
20. Stark, J.: Making sense of blockchain smart contracts. CoinDesk, June 2016. https://www.coindesk.com/making-sense-smart-contracts/
21. Suchman, L.A.: Plans and Situated Actions: The Problem of Human-Machine Communication. Cambridge University Press, New York (1987)
22. Szabo, N.: Smart contracts (1994). http://www.fon.hum.uva.nl/rob/Courses/InformationInSpeech/CDROM/Literature/LOTwinterschool2006/szabo.best.vwh.net/smart.contracts.html
23. Szabo, N.: Formalizing and securing relationships on public networks. First Monday **2**(9) (1997). http://ojphi.org/ojs/index.php/fm/article/view/548/469
24. Wood, G.: Ethereum: a secure decentralised generalised transaction ledger (2014). http://ethereum.github.io/yellowpaper/paper.pdf

Towards Topological Analysis of Networked Holonic Multi-agent Systems

Ahmad Esmaeili[1(✉)], Nasser Mozayani[2], Mohammad Reza Jahed-Motlagh[2], and Eric T. Matson[1]

[1] Purdue University, West Lafayette, IN 47907, USA
{aesmaei,ematson}@purdue.edu
[2] School of Computer Engineering, Iran University of Science and Technology, Tehran, Iran
{mozayani,jahedmr}@iust.ac.ir

Abstract. Interaction networks, either being implicitly or explicitly specified between the agents, play a crucial role in all multi-agent systems. These structures define and limit the ways the agents should interact with their peers, and hence help to manage the coordination problems in large-scale systems. It is widely accepted that the structure of an interaction network plays a significant role in the performance of the systems. In this article, we use the interaction network of the initial agent population to construct a holonic multi-agent system. Being based on agent interaction networks, the performance of the resulting holonic multi-agent system highly depends on the structure of the underlying agent network. Here, we study this dependency in more details. The study is carried out by applying the holonification algorithm on various network topologies and assessing the constructed holonic structure in a task environment.

Keywords: Multi-agent systems · Holonic multi-agent systems · Network topology

1 Introduction

Multi-agent Systems (MASs) are proven to be highly successful in modeling and solving large-scaled real-world problems and the simulation of complex phenomena, thanks to their intrinsic distributed nature [20]. The way the system components should interact with each other to achieve their personal or the system-wide goals is very important in the design of a MAS, and the more complex the problems get, the higher loads of interactions emerge as the result of heterogeneity and multiplicity of the components. Such a high load of interactions is inevitable, mainly because of the limitations in capabilities and rationality of the agents in dealing with large complex problems in which they need to act in concert with their counterparts towards a system level goal. The new

© Springer Nature Switzerland AG 2019
Y. Demazeau et al. (Eds.): PAAMS 2019, LNAI 11523, pp. 42–54, 2019.
https://doi.org/10.1007/978-3-030-24209-1_4

area of networked multi-agent systems (NMAS) concentrates on the interaction patterns among the agents and components of a MAS and the way the interconnections can be utilized to organize and hence improve the performance and the entire system [11,13].

One of widely used and essential methods for tackling the interaction loads in MASs and complementing the agency definition, with the focus on model simplification and uncertainty reduction, is the use of multi-agent organizations [6]. The organizational structures in MAS are usually defined in terms of roles, relationship and authority structures in order to dictate a certain interaction configuration among the agents, in such a way that the overall performance of the system is improved. There are dozens of organizational models proposed and used in the literature such as teams, coalitions, hierarchies, holarchies, congregations, federations, to name a few [6,9]. Considering a MAS as an open system, numerous types of agents, in terms of their capabilities and access to resources, can take part in its design and deployment. It is widely accepted that the overall system performance can be largely affected, positively or negatively, by the way such heterogeneous society of the agents are put together to form groups or teams [8].

This paper concentrates primarily on the holonic structures builted in multi-agent systems (HMASs). Holons, as the building block of HMASs, are self-similar composition of agents that are organized in a multi-level structure that is called "holarchy". Such multi-level assemblies of agents have broad application in complex problems, thanks to their capacity in modeling multi-agent systems at several granularity levels [15]. The way that the holarchy is constructed based on the selection of possible holons for specific tasks or access to the available resources has a substantial role in the success of HMASs. Due to its excessive importance on the performance of a HMAS, this process, under the name of "holonification", has been studied in numerous research endeavors, resulting in several methods for building a holarchy and managing its dynamics during its lifetime - such as the ones presented in [1,7,10] to name a few. The available mechanisms range from negotiation and communication based ones as in [10] to graph theory based greedy approaches in [1,7].

We believe that there is no similar research dedicated to the topological analysis of holonic multi-agent systems. Here we present an experimental study on the effects of multi-agent network topologies on the structure and performance of HMASs. This would help system designers choose an appropriate interaction networks in MASs.

The organization of the presented materials is as follows: Sect. 2 provides a short introductory to holonic structures and HMAS, alongside the concepts and corresponding terminologies that are utilized in this paper; Sect. 3 presents the detailed explanation of the proposed framework; Sect. 4 provides the empirical results of this study; and at the end, Sect. 5 concludes the paper with some directions for the future work.

2   Holonic Multi-agent Systems

In Greek, the phrase "holon" refers to something that is a whole ("holos") and a part ("-on" suffix) at the same time. Coined by "Arthur Koestler", an Hungarian philosopher, the term was uses to describe the observations in hierarchically self-similar structures of nonliving, biological or social organizations [12]. He believed that there is no entity deemed to be a whole or a part in an absolute sense, but rather, all of the (non)living and social systems demonstrate the hybrid characteristics of being sub-wholes or sub-parts. In the holonic terminology, the parts of a larger self-similar structures are called "sub-holons" and the larger self-contained wholes that embraces these subordinates are called "super-holon". Holonic concepts are not circumscribe to be defined and discussed in philosophy only; but they are well-exploited in the definition of hybrid and hierarchical organizations that exhibit the solidity, cooperation, and autonomy characteristics of holonic systems among many others [17]. There is no wonder that multi-agent community has also conducted many research endeavors to benefits such holarchical organizations to manage its tasks and resources.

The general rules of holonic systems as the Open Hierarchical Systems are characterized by Koestler as follows [3].

– A tree-like construction can be utilize to represent a holonic system.
– A holon is a self-contained entity meaning that while being composed of other holons, is itself a part of a larger holon.
– Adaptability to changes in strategies and following principles is a core feature of a holon.
– The hierarchical position of a holon specifies the abstraction level of its actions. That is, the higher level a holon stands in, the more abstract and complex actions it demonstrates.
– A holon is capable of communicating its counterparts at the same holarchical level or the ones at different levels. The latter category of the communications are managed by special managerial holons called "heads".

Adopting the concepts of holonic systems to organize the relationships between the agents of a MAS in a hierarchical sub/super-holon manner has resulted in the creation of Holonic Multi-Agent Systems (HMAS). Following the aforementioned rules of holonic systems, a HMAS is obliged to have an adaptable multi-level structure, meaning that its constituent holons feature a flexible autonomy and the ability to change their compositions and arrangements. According to the flexible autonomy, the holistic goals are set and managed by the heads of super-holons whereas the member sub-holons employ their own strategies or decide about their membership inside a super-holon. On the other hand, the holons can unite to form a holonic whole, or they can be dissolved to form multiple holonic parts. In a HMAS, there are two potential types of interactions: (i) between the holons of the same level; and (ii) between a holon and the head of its immediate sub/super holon. A holarchy with four layers, containing an example set of communication and interaction links is depicted in Fig. 1. In this figure, the head holons are characterized by red color and as we

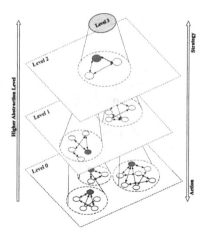

Fig. 1. A holarchy with four granularity levels. (Color figure online)

move from top of the structure to the bottom layers the level of abstraction is decreased causing the most realistic and reactive actions to be performed by the holons of the bottom most level.

Holonic solutions are provably effective to the modeling and solution of problems with intrinsic hierarchical or self-organization formations [16]. Thus, these structures have been successfully applied to numerous complex applications ranging from flexible manufacturing systems [4] to transportation [2] and health organizations [18].

It goes without saying that all the promising advantages of HMASs in solving real-world complex problems depend on the way such systems are constructed and managed during their life time. From our point of view, carrying out a deep-rooted study about the roles of system components and design parameters on the performance is crucial for devising solutions that can be employed in various fields, and a HMAS is not an exception. This paper concentrates on the role that the communicative connection patterns play in the performance of multi-agent holarchies. The outcomes of this study will help HMAS designers develop effective and efficient algorithms for their tasks.

3   Proposed Holonic Model

3.1   Holonic Interaction Network

As stated earlier, there is always a network structure in a MAS, as the result of the interaction and communication patterns that the agents establish with their peers. Such an interaction network can be explicitly applied by the designers or imposed by the problem and its environment. They can also be implicitly present as the result of agents communicative or capability limitations. It is worth noting that such interaction and communication networks can substantially lighten the complexity of the system and its coordination tasks due to the fact that the agents often do not (and cannot) maintain detailed information about all components of the system but only the ones in their vicinity, especially in large scale scenarios. The essence of the interaction networks both in MASs and HMASs can be modeled by a graph. In this graph, the agents (holons) are presented by the vertices, and the interaction/communication links by the edges. Furthermore, the graph can be (non)directional and (un)weighted depending on the problem and system characteristics.

In this paper, an unweighted and non-directional graph is assumed to model the multi-agent network, which is shown by $MAN\langle A, I \rangle$, with $A = \{a_1, \ldots, a_n\}$ as the set of all agents and $I = \{(a_i, a_j) | i \neq j; a_i, a_j \in A\}$ as the set of all possible links between them. This network can be alternatively presented by a symmetric matrix defined as in Eq. 1.

$$\Lambda(a_i, a_j) = \begin{cases} 1 & \text{if } (a_i, a_j) \in I \\ 0 & \text{otherwise} \end{cases} \tag{1}$$

Figure 2 shows a representative example of the above-mentioned network representation.

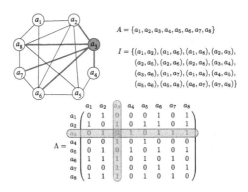

Fig. 2. Matrix representation of an example multi-agent network.

The network modeling that was presented above for a MAS can be extended for HMAS in order to be used in the holonification process. This extension starts with representing the holons at the bottom most level of the holarchy, named "base holons". We denote the set of all n base holons by $H^0 = \{H_1^0, H_2^0, \ldots, H_n^0\}$, where $H_i^0 = a_i \in A$. Additionally, the set of base interactions (the ones among the base holons) is denoted by $I^0 = \{(H_m^0, H_n^0), (H_k^0, H_l^0), \ldots\}$, where:

$$\forall (H_i^0, H_j^0) \in I^0 : \exists a_i, a_j \in A | (a_i, a_j) \in I \tag{2}$$

We can use similar notations to represent the set of all holons together with their corresponding interaction networks at different levels of the holarchy.

Assuming λ levels for the holarchy, the top most universal holon is denoted by H_u^λ and for all intermediate levels we have:

$$H_i^\tau = \{H_1^{\tau-1}, H_2^{\tau-1}, \ldots, H_\eta^{\tau-1}\};$$

$$0 \leq \tau < \lambda, \quad H_t^1 \subseteq H^0,$$

$$\bigcup_t H_t^1 = H^0, \quad \bigcup_t H_t^{\lambda-1} = H_u^\lambda \tag{3}$$

where the i-th holon of layer τ and the number of its sub-holons are denoted by H_i^τ and η respectively. It is worth noting that for the sake of coordination simplicity, we have assumed the holons do not overlap, i.e. the are merged whenever there is a need for them to share a member. Formally speaking, we have:

$$\forall H_i^\tau, H_j^\tau \in H_k^{\tau+1}: \quad H_i^\tau \cap H_j^\tau = \varnothing \tag{4}$$

Furthermore, each holon (agent) owns a set of skills that indicate their capability in solving a problem or accessing a specific resource. Formally, the skill set of holon H_i^l is denoted by $hs_i^l = \{s_1, s_2, \ldots, s_{ns_{i,l}}\}$, where $ns_{i,l}$ is the number of skills the holon has. On the other hand, $HS = \{s_1, s_2, \ldots, s_{ns}\}$ denotes the set of all skills defined in the system. According to this definition, each skill s_i is a separate entity that can be owned by several holons. Moreover, we have differentiated the set of interactions inside each holarchical level. Using the similar notation as in the interactions of the base level, the overall set of holarchical interactions is denoted by HI as follows:

$$HI = \{HI^0, HI^1, HI^2, \ldots, HI^{\lambda-1}\} \tag{5}$$

where λ is the number of levels in holarchy; and HI^i is the set of all interactions in level i, which can be represented by a symmetric matrix similar to the way that we illustrated in Fig. 2. Formally, we have:

$$HI^i = \{(H_j^i, H_k^i) | \Lambda_i(H_j^i, H_k^i) = 1; 1 \leq j \neq k \leq n_i\} \tag{6}$$

In Eq. 6, Λ_i is the adjacency matrix specifying the presence of an interaction between the holons of level i; and HI^i is the set of all holonic pairs between which there is an interaction, i.e. the corresponding matrix item is 1. The sets of HI are determined during the holonification and self-organization stages; and we assume that there is no inter-level interaction in our representation. On top of that, the sets of the interaction links in the base layer and the inter-agent links of the original $MAN\langle A, I\rangle$ are basically the same, that is, $HI^0 = I$. Finally, the entire holarchy defined as above, is denoted by $\langle H, HI\rangle$.

3.2 Network-Based Holonification

Holonification can be considered as a variant of the clustering problem. Assuming the initial holonic network composed of the agents and their interaction, i.e. $HN\langle H^0, I^0\rangle$, any graph clustering algorithm that groups the agent population based on specific criteria is NP-hard, and so is the holonification itself [5]. The holonification algorithm used in this paper is based on the bottom-up approach proposed in [8]. More specifically, we rank the agents according to the number of triangles that they can form using their connections with the peers in their vicinity. Simply put, the rank of an agent determines the number of agents in its vicinity (connected directly) that are also neighbors. This measure is known as the local clustering coefficient in the network theory [14]. According to Watts and Strogats, there is a tendency in real-world social networks to form groups of densely connected entities [19]. Here, we have used this intuition to drive the holonification process of an initial NMAS. That being said, the rank of an agent is defined as Eq. 7.

$$R(a_i, \langle A, I \rangle) = \frac{\triangle_{\langle A,I \rangle}(a_i)}{\wedge_{\langle A,I \rangle}(a_i)} = \frac{2(CN_{\langle A,I \rangle}(a_i))}{N_{\langle A,I \rangle}(a_i)(N_{\langle A,I \rangle}(a_i) - 1)} \tag{7}$$

where $\triangle_{\langle A,I \rangle}(a_i)$ is the number of triangles that agent a_i is a vertex of; $\wedge_{\langle A,I \rangle}(a_i)$ is the number of triples (two edges and three vertices) on agent a_i; $N_{\langle A,I \rangle}(a_i)$ is the number of agents that agent a_i is directly connected to, that is, $N_{\langle A,I \rangle}(a_i) = |a_j : I(a_i, a_j) = 1|$; and finally, $CN_{\langle A,I \rangle}(a_i)$ is number of a_is neighbors connected to each other. Formally speaking, $CN_{\langle A,I \rangle}(a_i) = |\{I(a_j, a_k) : a_j, a_k \in N_{\langle A,I \rangle}(a_i), I(a_j, a_k) = 1\}|$. It should be noted that Eq. 7 can be utilized for any arbitrary holon H_i^τ in level τ by simply calling $R(H_i^\tau, \langle H^\tau, HI^\tau \rangle)$.

The holonification process starts by the highly ranked base holons initiating the formation of super-holons. Next, these initiators look for the peers in their vicinity that are qualified enough to be added to their super-holon. Depending on the problem domain, the qualification measures can vary from capabilities and diversities to social standing and access to the resources. As soon as a holon joins a super-holon or initiates it, it is removed from the list that contains all the holons ordered based on their ranks. It is worth noting that the joining process might be composed of several interactions between the super-holon's head and the potential member before it agrees to join. As the process and the criteria can be completely domain dependant, we do not discuss it further in this paper. In addition to forming the super-holons, the holonic interaction among the newly formed holons are determined. Given $HN\langle H^\tau, HI^\tau \rangle$ as the holonic network of level τ, we have:

$$\exists H_k^{\tau-1} \in H_i^\tau, H_l^{\tau-1} \in H_j^\tau : I^{\tau-1}(H_k^{\tau-1}, H_l^{\tau-1}) = 1 \Rightarrow I^\tau(H_i^\tau, H_j^\tau) = 1 \tag{8}$$

In other words, the existence of a link between the members of two separate holon in a same level induces the creation of a links between their super-holons. When the ordered list of the holons is empty, the single-layer holonification process is finished, and the result is used to form the super-holons of the upper layers until no new holon is formed and the holonic structure is not updated. Strictly speaking, the holonic network of level i, $\langle H^i, HI^i \rangle$, is used to build the upper level (level $i + 1$) holonic network $\langle H^{i+1}, HI^{i+1} \rangle$ The detailed holonification algorithm is presented in Algorithm 1. In the worst case, only one super-holon is built in each layer with complexity of $O(n^2)$. Hence, the overall time complexity of the algorithm is $O(n^3)$.

Algorithm 1: Holonification Function

Input: $HN\langle H^\tau, HI^\tau \rangle$
Output: H_u^λ

1 **forall the** $H_i^\tau \in H^\tau$ **do**
2 $\quad$ $rankList \leftarrow compute(R(H_i^\tau))$;
3 **end**
4 $orderedList \leftarrow sort(rankList)$;
5 **while** $orderedList \neq \varnothing$ **do**
6 $\quad$ $H^{\tau+1} \leftarrow \varnothing$;
7 $\quad$ $currentHolon \leftarrow orderedList.first$;
8 $\quad$ $H_i^{\tau+1} \leftarrow createHolon(currentHolon)$;
9 $\quad$ **forall the** $H_j^\tau \in Neighbors(currentHolon)$ **do**
10 $\quad\quad$ $success \leftarrow addMember(H_i^{\tau+1}, H_j^\tau)$;
   $\quad\quad$ /* Adds H_j^τ to the newly created super-holon $H_i^{\tau+1}$ and returns
   $\quad\quad$ whether the joining process was successful $\qquad\qquad$ */
11 $\quad\quad$ **if** $success = TRUE$ **then**
12 $\quad\quad\quad$ $hs_i^{\tau+1} \leftarrow hs_i^{\tau+1} \cup hs_j^\tau$; $\qquad$ // super-holon skills are updated
13 $\quad\quad\quad$ $removeFrom(orderedList, H_j^\tau)$;
14 $\quad\quad$ **end**
15 $\quad$ **end**
16 $\quad$ $removeFrom(orderedList, currentHolon)$;
17 $\quad$ $H^{\tau+1} \leftarrow H^{\tau+1} \cup H_i^{\tau+1}$;
18 **end**
19 $I^{\tau+1} \leftarrow \varnothing$;
   // The following loop constructs the new layer's network
20 **forall the** $H_i^\tau \in H^\tau$ **do**
21 $\quad$ **forall the** $H_j^\tau \in Neighbors(H_i^\tau)$ **do**
22 $\quad\quad$ **if** $H_i^\tau.SuperHolon \neq H_j^\tau.SuperHolon$ **then**
23 $\quad\quad\quad$ $I^{\tau+1} \leftarrow I^{\tau+1} \cup (H_i^\tau.SuperHolon, H_j^\tau.SuperHolon)$;
24 $\quad\quad$ **end**
25 $\quad$ **end**
26 **end**
27 **if** $changed(H^\tau)$ **then**
28 $\quad$ **return** $Holonification(HN\langle H^{\tau+1}, I^{\tau+1}\rangle)$
29 **else**
30 $\quad$ $\lambda \leftarrow \tau + 1$;
31 $\quad$ $H_u^\lambda \leftarrow createEmptyHolon()$; $\qquad\qquad$ // the final universal holon
32 $\quad$ $delete(H^{\tau+1}); delete(I^{\tau+1})$; $\qquad\qquad$ // undoing the last construction
33 $\quad$ **forall the** $H_i^\tau \in H^\tau$ **do**
34 $\quad\quad$ $addMember(H_u^\lambda, H_i^\tau)$;
35 $\quad$ **end**
36 $\quad$ **return** H_u^λ
37 **end**

3.3   Performance

The assessment of the suggested model is carried out in a task environment; i.e. the performance is measured based on the ability of the system in completing the incoming tasks. In this environment, tasks of different characteristics arrive in the system at specific intervals. Each task is recognized by a unique ID, the list of skills that are required to accomplish it, and age. As a new task arrives in the system, it is received by the upper-most super-holon. Checking the required skills of the task with the available ones from its sub-holons, the super-holon assigns it to an appropriate member holon. This assignment is continued until the task can be partially executed by a base holon. The task assignment action of the super-holon is one of the minimal set of built-in behaviors that we have implemented for the holons. More specifically, it is assumed that all the holons are able to perform tasks or assign them their sub-holons in the case they have any. They are also capable of reporting the result to their own super-holons.

Let T and T_s be the set containing all tasks introduced and the ones completed successfully by the holarchy, before they expire. The performance of the holarchy is measured using Eq. 9. This metric basically measures the ratio of the overall tasks that have been successfully handled before their deadlines. The more tasks the holarchy was able to manage, the higher performance it exhibits.

$$Performance(\langle H, HI \rangle) = \frac{|T_s|}{|T|} \tag{9}$$

4   Empirical Results

This section discusses the experimental settings and scenarios for the assessment of the proposed approach. We have used a task environment to study the effect of agents' interaction network structure on the entire system performance. To this end, we implemented a test-bed that enabled us to design a multi-agent system with desired interaction network topologies, agent skill distributions, and list of tasks to be fulfilled.

The general specifications of the experiments are listed in Table 1. In this table, $|A|$ is the number of agents; $|HS_i^0|$ is the number of skills that each agent (base holon) has; $task\_age$ specifies the number of steps before the expiration of each task; $|TS_i|$ is the number of skills that each task demands; and finally $|T|$ is the total number of tasks that have arrived in the system during the experimentation. It is also assumed that, the tasks are all of a same length (number of required skills), and it takes 3 simulation steps to complete them, when started. Four network topologies, namely, Small World, Preferential Attachment, 2-D Lattice, and Ring, were experimented. For each of these network topologies 10 different MAN were generated. The skill distributions among the agents were identical in all MANs, and they were exposed to 10 different lists of 5000 tasks, differing in the order, age, and the list of required skills. The results presented here, are the average of the results from all runs.

Table 1. General specification of the experiments.

Property	$|A| = |H^0|$	$|HS_i^0|$	$task\_age$	$|TS_i|$	$|T|$
Value	100	1	$1 \leq rand \leq 2$	10	5000

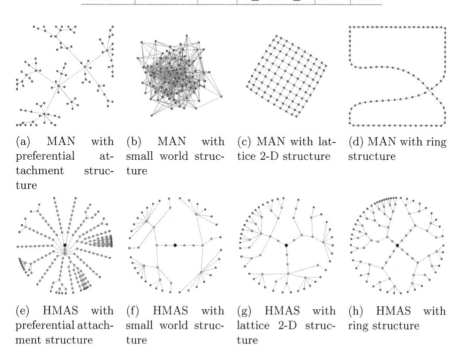

(a) MAN with preferential attachment structure

(b) MAN with small world structure

(c) MAN with lattice 2-D structure

(d) MAN with ring structure

(e) HMAS with preferential attachment structure

(f) HMAS with small world structure

(g) HMAS with lattice 2-D structure

(h) HMAS with ring structure

Fig. 3. Examples of initial multi-agent networks (top) with their holonified structures (bottom) under various network topologies and using the proposed holonification algorithm.

Figure 3 depicts an example for the holonification process on four experimented network topologies. Please note that, for the purpose of clarity in the holonic structures, only the composite holons are visualized. Furthermore, it should be noted that the singleton composite holons have been inserted merely for making the height of sub-structures equal. As it can be seen, the preferential attachment topology has resulted in the formation of composite holons with the smallest sizes; and the small world network structure has lead to relatively larger composite holons. This is due to the abundance of interaction links that most of atomic holons own in the small world model. In other words, having relatively larger set of neighbors has helped them form larger super-holons.

Figure 4 illustrates the performance of the constructed holonic multi-agent systems in assigning the tasks over time. Each point of the plot is the average of all runs under the corresponding network topologies. As it can be seen, HMAS with small world topology has outperformed all other three models. On the other

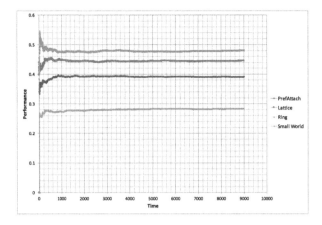

Fig. 4. Performance of experimented holonic models in the task environment.

hand the ring topology exhibited the lowest performance of all topologies. This is due to the fact that small world topology caused the most appropriate holonic formations, in terms of their skill combinations, due to the short average path between the agents.

5   Conclusion

The primary goal of this article was to study the impact of the interaction networks on the performance of holonic multi-agent systems. This was accomplished by purposing a holonic framework based on networked multi-agent systems. The suggested framework utilizes a bottom-up iterative approach to construct the self-contained holonic structure according to the underlying interaction networks. Then we used the model in a highly loaded task environment and monitored the performance of the systems in various experimental settings. According to the results, small world model for multi-agent networks resulted in a better performance and holonic distributions.

In the presented work, we have used a static holonic model for a MAS. It is apparent that in a dynamic environment, the holonic structure needs to be adapted as changes occur. This adaptation would possibly lead to a different interaction network topology from the initial one. We are currently working on dynamic holonic multi-agent systems and suggest this as a future research trend.

References

1. Abdoos, M., Esmaeili, A., Mozayani, N.: Holonification of a network of agents based on graph theory. In: Jezic, G., Kusek, M., Nguyen, N.-T., Howlett, R.J., Jain, L.C. (eds.) KES-AMSTA 2012. LNCS (LNAI), vol. 7327, pp. 379–388. Springer, Heidelberg (2012). https://doi.org/10.1007/978-3-642-30947-2_42

2. Abdoos, M., Mozayani, N., Bazzan, A.L.C.: Holonic multi-agent system for traffic signals control. Eng. Appl. Artif. Intell. **26**(56), 1575–1587 (2013). https://doi.org/10.1016/j.engappai.2013.01.007

3. Adam, E., Mandiau, R.: Bringing multi-agent systems into human organizations: application to a multi-agent information system. In: Jeusfeld, M.A., Pastor, Ó. (eds.) ER 2003. LNCS, vol. 2814, pp. 168–179. Springer, Heidelberg (2003). https://doi.org/10.1007/978-3-540-39597-3_17

4. Barbosa, J., Leitão, P., Adam, E., Trentesaux, D.: Structural self-organized holonic multi-agent manufacturing systems. In: Mařík, V., Lastra, J.L.M., Skobelev, P. (eds.) HoloMAS 2013. LNCS (LNAI), vol. 8062, pp. 59–70. Springer, Heidelberg (2013). https://doi.org/10.1007/978-3-642-40090-2_6

5. Brandes, U., et al.: On finding graph clusterings with maximum modularity. In: Brandstädt, A., Kratsch, D., Müller, H. (eds.) WG 2007. LNCS, vol. 4769, pp. 121–132. Springer, Heidelberg (2007). https://doi.org/10.1007/978-3-540-74839-7_12

6. Deloach, S.A., Matson, E.: An organizational model for designing adaptive multi-agent systems (2004)

7. Esmaeili, A., Mozayani, N., Jahed Motlagh, M.R.: Multi-level holonification of multi-agent networks. In: 12th Iranian Conference on Intelligent Systems (ICIS 2014), pp. 1269–1273. IEEE, Bam (2014)

8. Esmaeili, A., Mozayani, N., Motlagh, M.R.J., Matson, E.T.: The impact of diversity on performance of holonic multi-agent systems. Eng. Appl. Artif. Intell. **55**, 186–201 (2016)

9. Irandoust, H., Benaskeur, A.: Multi-organizational structures. In: Proceedings of Association for the Advancement of Artificial Intelligence, Chicago, pp. 25–33 (2008)

10. Jie, L., Wei-Ming, Z., Bao-Xin, X., Zhong, L.: An organization model in MAS based on Holon. In: IEEE Ninth International Conference on Dependable Autonomic and Secure Computing, pp. 951–957, December 2011. https://doi.org/10.1109/DASC.2011.158

11. Karagiannis, P., Vouros, G., Stergiou, K., Samaras, N.: Overlay networks for task allocation and coordination in large-scale networks of cooperative agents. Autonom. Agents MultiAgent Syst. **24**(1), 26–68 (2010)

12. Koestler, A.: The ghost in the machine (1968)

13. Mesbahi, M., Egerstedt, M.: Graph Theoretic Methods in Multiagent Networks. Princeton University Press, Princeton (2010)

14. Newman, M.: Networks: An Introduction. Oxford University Press, Oxford (2009)

15. Rodriguez, S., Gaud, N., Hilaire, V., Galland, S., Koukam, A.: An analysis and design concept for self-organization in holonic multi-agent systems. In: Brueckner, S.A., Hassas, S., Jelasity, M., Yamins, D. (eds.) ESOA 2006. LNCS (LNAI), vol. 4335, pp. 15–27. Springer, Heidelberg (2007). https://doi.org/10.1007/978-3-540-69868-5_2

16. Rodriguez, S., Hilaire, V., Koukam, A.: Formal specification of holonic multi-agent systems framework. In: Sunderam, V.S., van Albada, G.D., Sloot, P.M.A., Dongarra, J. (eds.) ICCS 2005. LNCS, vol. 3516, pp. 719–726. Springer, Heidelberg (2005). https://doi.org/10.1007/11428862_98

17. Rodriguez, S., Hilaire, V., Koukam, A.: Towards a holonic multiple aspect analysis and modeling approach for complex systems: application to the simulation of industrial plants. Simul. Model. Pract. Theory **15**(5), 521–543 (2007)

18. Ulieru, M., Geras, A.: Emergent holarchies for E-health applications: a case in glaucoma diagnosis. In: IEEE 28th Annual Conference of the Industrial Electronics Society, IECON 2002, vol. 4, pp. 2957–2961. IEEE (2002)
19. Watts, D.J., Strogatz, S.H.: Collective dynamics of small-worldnetworks. Nature **393**(6684), 440–442 (1998)
20. Weiss, G. (ed.): Multiagent Systems, 2nd edn. MIT Press, Cambridge (2013)

Selecting Trustworthy Partners by the Means of Untrustworthy Recommenders in Digitally Empowered Societies

Rino Falcone and Alessandro Sapienza[(⊠)]

Institute of Cognitive Sciences and Technologies, ISTC-CNR,
00185 Rome, Italy
{rino.falcone,alessandro.sapienza}@istc.cnr.it

Abstract. In this work, we want to show that the introduction of categories can strongly improve the performance of recommendation, within the new digitally infrastructured societies. We state that, inside these highly dynamic contexts, in which more and more people are connected to each other but a substantial part of the communication happens between strangers, it is fundamental to restructure the concept of recommendation. We strongly believe that a good solution for many situations would be to combine inferential processes with recommendations, i.e. focusing on recommending categories of agents rather than specific individuals. Specifically, in this work we prove that category's recommendations are more robust to untrustworthy recommenders than individual recommendation. We tested our idea by the mean of a multi-agent social simulation. The results we obtained are in agreement with our hypotheses and can be of important interest for the development of this sector.

Keywords: Social recommendation · Trust · Multi-agent system

1 Introduction

The problem of selecting reliable partners is fundamental in social contexts, and is even more relevant within the web.

We believe that this context deserves to be investigated specifically, both because it has different characteristics that lead to different interaction dynamics [7], and because it is a sector in continuous growth, which everyday involves more and more people and becomes more and more pervasive.

Within these contexts, human and artificial cognitive agents think, elaborate plans and select actions with the aim of realizing specific states of the world. However, it happens very frequently that an agent is not able to carry out his own plan alone (or that it is not convenient for him), and therefore needs to delegate part of his plan to another agent of the network.

Thus, it becomes essential to identify models and methodologies able to evaluate our interlocutors and possibly to select adequate partners for the collaborative goals we want to pursue. When dealing with digital social context, we must however consider that there are different dynamics, with respect to the classical social contexts:

© Springer Nature Switzerland AG 2019
Y. Demazeau et al. (Eds.): PAAMS 2019, LNAI 11523, pp. 55–65, 2019.
https://doi.org/10.1007/978-3-030-24209-1_5

1. Given the very nature of digitally infrastructured social networks, where interaction is not constrained by physical distance, generally each agent tends to interact with many other agents in the network. Thanks to the Internet, more and more people are connected to each other, but a substantial part of the communications occur between people (or artificial agents) who know little or nothing about each other, such as in online social networks.
2. These networks are generally characterized by a high turnover, so that with a certain frequency many agents enter and leave the network.

For all these reasons, some partner selection methodologies may be less effective than before. If in the classical social paradigm we mainly rely on direct experience, or even recommendations, we believe that both these dimensions need to be adapted and integrated in such new contexts. This is because both of these approaches would require the analysis of an excessive amount of interactions, whether direct or reported by someone else.

A good solution for this problem could be to refer to the category tool. That of category is an abstract concept, a useful instrument allowing us to generalize the knowledge we possess [6].

A category is represented by a group of entities/agents, each one possessing homogeneous characteristics. These distinctive traits can be identified or inferred through a set of visible and non-deceptive signs. The categories could also be defined on the basis of very specific traits: in case of human beings, a trait could be somatic traits. For instance, the authors of [9] show that we tend to identify the somatic traits of the most reliable individuals and, in the absence of other information, we will look for partners who have the same traits. Practical examples of social category could be doctors, professors, pharmacists, etc.

The advantages are clear: we are able to evaluate an agent that no one has ever met before only on the basis of his characteristics. We are, in other words, able to obtain information about something/someone we have never met and this through inference, prediction or inheritance. We can generate knowledge about an entity without having any previous experience with it, without anyone ever reporting any information about it, without even having suspected it existed.

Several works have identified the effectiveness of the concept of *category recommendation*, i.e. a combination of the inferential processes of the category with that of the classic recommendation, highlighting its potential within the web. In general, however, this strategy was considered only in the presence of trustworthy recommenders. The purpose of this work is to show the effectiveness of category recommendations even in the presence of potentially unreliable recommenders. Through a simulative approach, we will show how in fact this type of recommendation is more robust than the classic individual one.

The rest of the paper is organized as follows. Section 2 analyzes the state of the art. Section 3 describes the details of the simulation's model, while the actual simulation is discussed, together with the results, in Sect. 4. Section 5 resumes the work.

2   Related Works

The concept of category/stereotype is well known and very frequently used in the literature. It has been widely used for user modeling [12], but more recently it has been applied also to trust modeling.

Tirloe [15] starts modeling group's reputation as an aggregate of individual reputations and proposes a few inferential strategies. Later [13] proposes a group-based reputation system. Here an average performance P_i for the group is computed, which is used as an initial trust value when a new member joins the group. The purpose is to limit the whitewashing in the network, regulating the behavior of the agents in the group, so it is not necessary that this value is precise, as long as it is sufficiently restrictive.

However the groups considered in these works do not require the members to have any element in common.

In [14], the authors propose a Bayesian model to estimate the trustworthiness of the agents by different reputation sources. The realized model computes the trust values on the basis of direct experience, reputation and the "observations of the behavior of groups of agents that share characteristics with the trustee".

The authors of [5] analyze the role of categories for trust evaluations. Their agents are defined by a number of features, determining their behavior. The novelty introduced by the authors is to apply the concept of "kripta" and "manifesta" [1] to the categories. Kripta are the internal features of an agent, representing its internal configuration and determining its behavior. They cannot be directly accessed, but estimated through the manifesta, which are the visible features of an agent. The trustworthiness of an agent cannot be directly accessed, but only be inferred thanks to the manifesta. According to them, categories represents a set of agents possessing similar values for these features, i.e. a category is defined by a set of constraints and the members of a given category have their profile's features bounded in a certain interval. Thus, knowing that an agent belongs to a category means to possess an estimation of its kripta, observing its manifesta. So, in this way it is possible to estimate the agent's trustworthiness.

The contributions described above work with categories, but they still do not provide the possibility to combine recommendations and categories. Recommending categories is a common practice for items and topics recommendations. For instance, [16] talks about collaborative topic modeling for recommending scientific articles. Although this kind of recommendations regards articles, they use the concept of topic for classifying the articles, which is a sort of category. There are very few works in the literature in which category's recommendations are applied to individuals or agents.

The authors of [10, 11] realized StereoTrust, introducing the concept of stereotypes for trust models. Here, the agents own a set of features determining its behavior and the stereotypes contain certain features of the agents and foreseen the outcome of a possible task. Each agent can match one or more stereotypes, which can be aggregated to derive its expected trustworthiness. Thus, this model can be used as a complementary mechanism to provide initial trust values for strangers, especially if nobody knows them. The authors also provide a stereotypes sharing overlay network, which allows the agents to share the information about stereotypes.

In [2, 3] the authors claim that the agents can generalize the experience gained with the partners met through the stereotypes. In other words, they identify classes of agents on the basis of the features they possess. Such stereotypical knowledge is fundamental for reducing the complexity of human decision-making process, and can be successfully applied also in MAS. Although even stereotypes take time to build, a new trustor accessing the network can take advantage of what they call stereotypical reputation, exploiting the generalized knowledge that others have achieved previously. This work also provides a methodology to identify stereotypes starting from features, using machine learning techniques.

At last, the authors of [8] believe that exploiting someone else's stereotypes may be misleading, as "buyers (trustors) may have subjectivity difference in evaluating transactions with sellers (trustees), where different ratings could be given for the same transaction by different buyers". In their work, they built a semantic ontology to represent trustees' attributes and then they apply semantic reasoning over the ontology to generalize the stereotypes. Thus, instead of using the experience of other agents to learn the trust stereotypes, each agent only uses its own experience.

We strongly believe that, in a very heterogeneous and dynamic world, using the experience of the other agents is fundamental, but this information need to be used properly.

The current state of the art clearly showed the utility of category recommendations. With respect to that, our contribute aims to demonstrate that category recommendations are even more robust to a decrease of the recommenders' trustworthiness.

3   Simulative Model

We realized a set of simulations, with the purpose of verifying the utility of individual and category recommendations in different situations. The experiments were realized by the means of NetLogo [17], a multi-agent framework designed specifically for simulations. For the concept of trust and reputations, we will refer to the model proposed by [4].

In the simulations, we chose to model a social network of agents interconnected via the Internet. Unlike what happens in a classical social network, within such a network the physical distance is irrelevant for the purposes of interaction: while interacting with a node, it is not important how close the node is to us[1]. What happens here is that we tend to know many more nodes than in a classical social network, but the degree of knowledge about each individual node decreases.

In the simulation world, we added 200 agents, moving around the world and interact with each other, and 4 generic categories. Each agent belongs to a specific category and its membership is clear and unequivocal.

---

[1] This aspect may become relevant in a very wide network, because of the latency time.

3.1   Setup Phase

At the beginning, these agents start knowing each other. For each shift, each of them interacts with a given percentage of the population, randomly selecting the agents and then asking them to perform the informative task τ. Thus, each requester evaluates the performances of the agents it meets, concerning the task τ, memorizing these performances both for the specific individual and for the category to which it belongs. For the sake of simplicity, we suppose that the subjective perception of the performance coincides with the actual performance, i.e. there is no mistake in the evaluation process of a specific performance. Figure 1 describes all this process.

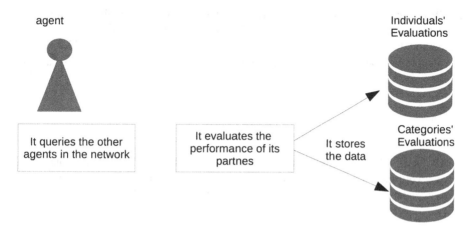

Fig. 1. Setup phase's workflow for an individual agent

At the end of this phase, each agent will have a partial (because it has met just a random subset of the agents) and subjective (it evaluates how the other agents performed with it, but it does not know their objective performances) knowledge of the network. This knowledge depends on the duration of the setup phase (hence the number of interactions that each agent has with others). We have established a fixed duration of 100 ticks.

3.2   Setup Phase

In a next step, a further agent, the trustor, enters the simulative world and needs to select an agent to perform the task τ for it. It therefore addresses a percentage of agents in the world (ranging from 1% to 100%) and asks for two types of recommendation:

1. An individual's recommendation (I): it asks for a recommendation on a specific agent to perform the task. Then it selects the agent who has received the highest number of recommendations.
2. A category's recommendation (C): it asks for a recommendation on a category of agents. Then it randomly selects an exponent of the most recommended category.

Figure 2 describes what happens for individual recommendations. The procedure is similar for category's recommendations.

At last, the trustor compares the objective trustworthiness of the two agents it selects. We decided to compare the *objective trustworthiness* of the agents because we are interested in evaluating the real ability of this approach to identify the most trustworthy agents. The best recommendation type (individual/category) has a higher probability to provide a better trustworthiness. In order to exclude cases in which the differences between the two trustworthiness values are minimal, we have inserted a threshold: there must be a difference of at least 3%. We assign a point to the best approach (I or C).

In this paper, we compare the performance of our algorithmic mechanism with the following approaches:

1. CV (category value): number of times the category C wins, normalized with respect to the number of times the category C wins and the times when the individual method I wins. This value is defined in the interval $[0, +\infty]$. Specifically, the category will perform better than the individual method when it exceeds the value 1.

$$CV = \frac{C}{I}$$

2. EV (error of evaluation): difference between the highest individual's/category's trustworthiness $tw_{highest}$ and the one identified by the individual's/category's recommendation $tw_{selected}$. This value is defined in the interval $[0, 1]$. The more it is

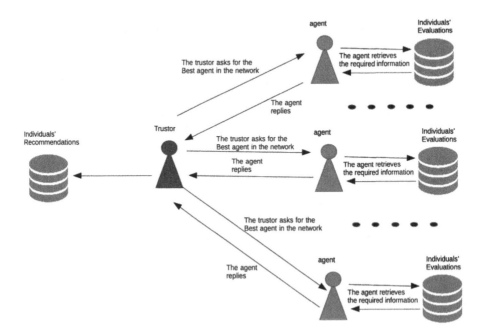

Fig. 2. Testing phase's workflow for a trustor and recommenders

low, the better the method is used. Ideally (for a perfect recommender and a perfect performer) it should be zero.

$$EV = tw_{highest} - tw_{selected}$$

Each measurement is averaged over 500 instances.

4 Simulations and Results

In this experiment, we take into account the possibility that the recommenders may not faithfully report they information they have. In general, each agent possesses a partial and subjective knowledge of the network. He can however report it as it is to the trustor, or he may report a different result. We are not interested in analyzing the motivation beyond this action (which can be due to the aspect of competence or willingness), but we just consider this possibility in our framework. Other works [8] state that it is better to rely on our own information and generalize it to produce new knowledge, rather than using information coming from external sources, such as recommendations. We believe that it is fundamental to exploit external information, but it is necessary to do it carefully.

Each agent is associated with a trustworthiness value as a recommender *twAsRecommender*, a value uniformly distributed between 0 and 1. It is important to underline that this value is different and totally unrelated to the trustworthiness of the same agent for executing the task τ. Starting from *twAsRecommender*, it will be determined how much the agent's recommendation will deviate from the correct one.

Each agent performs a ranking of the agents/categories it knows based on their average performance. In case of equal performances, it also considers the amount of past experience, giving priority to the agents with whom it had more past experience, because the attributed evaluation has been confirmed more times.

In particular, a normal medium-zero distribution and standard deviation equal to

$$\sigma = (1 - twAsRecommender) * NumberOfElements$$

So σ will be inversely proportional to the trustworthiness as a recommender: the more reliable the agent is, the more correct the result will be.

The standard deviation will also depend on the number of items *NumberOf Elements* that can be recommended. This implies that the generic probability of recommending a specific agent (about 0.5% on average) will be much lower than that of recommending a category (about 25% on average). Note that the agents initially do not know any other agent nor have knowledge about the categories. Therefore, the value of *NumberOfElements* will not be fixed, but it will depend on the number of individuals or categories actually encountered.

By the use of a Gaussian distribution with mean 0 and standard deviation σ, a random number will be generated, which will then be truncated considering only the integer part. This last value represents the index of the recommended agent, according to the subjectively realized ranking.

As far as it concerns the trustor, he needs a way to handle the different recommendations coming from the trustees, choosing an *aggregation strategy* to process the information. We chose to give different weight to the recommendations. Specifically, in the experiments, we considered the case where the weight/value of the information is equal to the trustworthiness of the recommender *twAsRecommender* reporting it.

As already said, in this paper we are not interested in calculating the reliability of the recommenders, but we assume that the trustor can freely access this value.

Experimental Setting:

3. World dimension: 33 × 33 patches, wrapping both horizontally and vertically
4. Number of categories: 4, {A, B, C, D}
5. Categories' trustworthiness: A = 80%, B = 60%, C = 40%, D = 20%.
6. σ of categories: 10%
7. Number of agents: 200, 50 per category
8. Setup phase duration: 100 ticks
9. Percentage of interactions in the setup phase: 2%
10. Percentage of agents interviewed by the trustor: {1, 5, 10, 25, 50, 100}%
11. Recommenders' trustworthiness: uniformly distributed between 0 and 1.

In this experiment, we are interested in analyzing how the effectiveness of individual and category recommendations in the contexts considered varies.

The dimensions we are going to evaluate will be:

- The CV, trying to understand when it is better to rely on categories and on individuals.
- The EV, that is the difference between the highest trustworthiness in the network and that of the most recommended individual: the most effective method will tend to minimize this value.

We make an initial premise, before going to consider the results of the experiment. Due to the way in which we have chosen to set up the experiment, the average value of *twAsExecutor* for an agent is equal to 0.5, while its maximum value is equal to 1. This makes 0.5 the maximum value of EV (which is given by the difference between these two previous parameters), at least on average. This is the worst case ever, which would be obtained simply choosing a random agent, without any information on the network.

In Fig. 3, we analyze how the CV changes as the percentage of agents queried by the trustor varies. In particular, we analyze both the case in which the trustor uses weights for the recommendations, and the scenario in which it does not. This second scenario does not analyze the case in which the trustor is able to know the reliability of the recommenders and chooses not to use it - which would be irrational - but rather the case in which this information is not available. For instance, the trustor could have just entered a new network where he does not know anyone.

Figure 3 clearly shows the importance of category evaluations. In the scenario in which the trustor uses weights (orange curve), the category allows getting a better

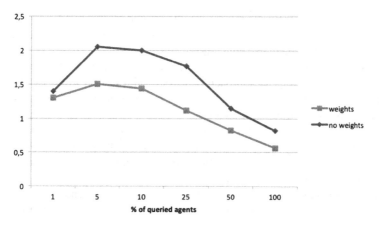

Fig. 3. CV variation using or not using weights for recommendations (Color figure online)

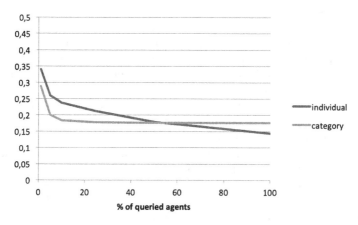

Fig. 4. EV variation using weights for recommendations

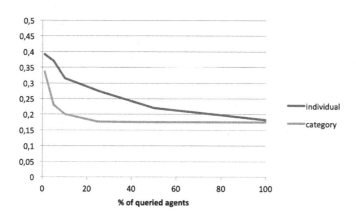

Fig. 5. EV variation not using weights for recommendations

performance, as long as the percentage of agents queried by the trustor does not exceed 25%. This threshold percentage rises up to 50% when the trustor does not know the reliability of the recommenders (blue curve).

To corroborate these results, there is also an analysis of the value of EV. This time we are no more comparing an approach (category) with respect to the other (individual), but we are analyzing how much these two methods allow us to get closer to the optimal performance within the network.

Figure 4 analyzes the scenario in which the trustor is aware of the recommenders' ability. In this case, the category method (gray) allows getting a more precise assessment until the trustor queries 50% of the network; from here on, individual recommendations provide a better performance.

However, when the trustor is not able to evaluate the recommendations (Fig. 5), the role of the category becomes fundamental: it always allows obtaining a better performance.

5   Conclusions

Selecting reliable partners within the digitally infrastructured societies may not be an easy task. In this work we decided to analyze the role of category recommendations, in relation to the classic individual recommendations, in the presence of potentially unreliable recommendations.

We support the idea that the category recommendations play a fundamental role here, which is not necessarily alternative but complementary to that of individual recommendations. We do not believe that the latter must disappear, but that they can coexist. Rather, there are situations in which one method prevails over the other and it is necessary to understand when this happens.

After creating a simulative model taking into account the characteristics of these kind of social networks, we performed a series of simulations, showing that category recommendations can in some cases have performances superior to those of individual recommendations, both in the condition in which the trustor is able to determine the reliability of the recommenders, both if this is not possible.

These results could be of great interest for dealing with this kind of network, since they point out that within the digitally infrastructured societies, in presence of possibly unreliable recommenders, it is more convenient to rely on category recommendations. Even if not satisfactory, this achievement suggests the need to investigate the topic better.

Acknowledgments. This work is partially supported by the project CLARA—CLoud plAtform and smart underground imaging for natural Risk Assessment, funded by the Italian Ministry of Education, University and Research (MIUR-PON).

References

1. Bacharach, M., Gambetta, D.: Trust as type detection. In: Castelfranchi, C., Tan, Y.H. (eds.) Trust and Deception in Virtual Societies, pp. 1–26. Springer, Dordrecht (2001). https://doi.org/10.1007/978-94-017-3614-5_1
2. Burnett, C., Norman, T.J., Sycara, K.: Bootstrapping trust evaluations through stereotypes. In: Proceedings of the 9th International Conference on Autonomous Agents and Multiagent Systems: volume 1-Volume 1, pp. 241–248. International Foundation for Autonomous Agents and Multiagent Systems, May 2010
3. Burnett, C., Norman, T.J., Sycara, K.: Stereotypical trust and bias in dynamic multiagent systems. ACM Trans. Intell. Syst. Technol. (TIST) 4(2), 26 (2013)
4. Castelfranchi, C., Falcone, R.: Trust Theory: A Socio-Cognitive and Computational Model. Wiley, Chichester, April 2010
5. Falcone, R., Piunti, M., Venanzi, M., Castelfranchi, C.: From manifesta to krypta: the relevance of categories for trusting others. ACM Trans. Intell. Syst. Technol. (TIST) 4(2), 27 (2013)
6. Falcone, R., Sapienza, A., Castelfranchi, C.: The relevance of categories for trusting information sources. ACM Trans. Internet Technol. (TOIT) 15(4), 13 (2015)
7. Falcone, R., Sapienza, A., Castelfranchi, C.: Recommendation of categories in an agents world: the role of (not) local communicative environments. In: 2015 13th Annual Conference on Privacy, Security and Trust (PST), pp. 7–13. IEEE, July 2015
8. Fang, H., Zhang, J., Sensoy, M., Thalmann, N.M.: A generalized stereotypical trust model. In: 2012 IEEE 11th International Conference on Trust, Security and Privacy in Computing and Communications (TrustCom), pp. 698–705. IEEE, June 2012
9. FeldmanHall, O., Dunsmoor, J.E., Tompary, A., Hunter, L.E., Todorov, A., Phelps, E.A.: Stimulus generalization as a mechanism for learning to trust. Proc. Nat. Acad. Sci. 115(7), E1690–E1697 (2018)
10. Liu, X., Datta, A., Rzadca, K., Lim, E.P.: Stereotrust: a group based personalized trust model. In: Proceedings of the 18th ACM Conference on Information and Knowledge Management, pp. 7–16. ACM, November 2009
11. Liu, X., Datta, A., Rzadca, K.: Trust beyond reputation: a computational trust model based on stereotypes. Electron. Commer. Res. Appl. 12(1), 24–39 (2013)
12. Middleton, S.E., Shadbolt, N.R., De Roure, D.C.: Ontological user profiling in recommender systems. ACM Trans. Inf. Syst. (TOIS) 22(1), 54–88 (2004)
13. Sun, L., Jiao, L., Wang, Y., Cheng, S., Wang, W.: An adaptive group-based reputation system in peer-to-peer networks. In: Deng, X., Ye, Y. (eds) International Workshop on Internet and Network Economics. WINE 2005. LNCS, vol. 3828, pp. 651–659. Springer, Heidelberg, December 2005. https://doi.org/10.1007/11600930_65
14. Teacy, W.L., Luck, M., Rogers, A., Jennings, N.R.: An efficient and versatile approach to trust and reputation using hierarchical bayesian modelling. Artif. Intell. 193, 149–185 (2012)
15. Tirloe, J.: A theory of collective reputations'. Rev. Econ. Stud. 63, 1–22 (1996)
16. Wang, C., Blei, D.M.: Collaborative topic modeling for recommending scientific articles. In: Proceedings of the 17th ACM SIGKDD International Conference on Knowledge Discovery and Data Mining, pp. 448–456. ACM, August 2011
17. Wilensky, U.: NetLogo: Center for Connected Learning and Computer-Based Modeling, Northwestern University, Evanston, IL (1999). http://ccl.northwestern.edu/netlogo/

Identifying Knowledge
from the Application of Natural Deduction
Rules in Propositional Logic

Fabiane F. P. Galafassi[(⊠)], Cristiano Galafassi, Rosa Maria Vicari,
and João Carlos Gluz

Federal University of Rio Grande do Sul, Porto Alegre, RS, Brazil
`fabiane.penteado@gmail.com`,
`cristianogalafassi@gmail.com`, `rosa@inf.urfgs.br`,
`jcgluz@gmail.com`

Abstract. Intelligent Tutoring Systems (ITS) are technological resources widely used in teaching-learning processes, and their studies are directed, mainly, at distance learning. In this sense, the purpose of this work is the redesign of a Student Model agent, in the context of an ITS applied to the teaching of Natural Deduction in Propositional Logic (NDPL) for computing. It is expected that the agent will be able to identify and represent the students' knowledge states. In the modeling stage, we present the details of the knowledge representation, as well as about the inference mechanism, based on Bayesian networks. Regarding the results, students are satisfied with the Heráclito environment and that the agent achieves its main objective, evidencing the possibility of implementing personalized teaching strategies based on individual characteristics and knowledge from the students.

Keywords: Intelligent Tutoring Systems · Logic for computing ·
Student model

1 Introduction

Among the many technological resources offered to the educational context, Intelligent Tutoring Systems have been widely adopted in teaching-learning processes, most of which are directed to the support of Distance Education, study outside the classroom of traditional class and higher education [11].

An ITS can be designed as a multiagent system, where the agent can be defined as a dynamic system that has the capacity to receive information and act on a certain environment in order to perform a certain task [7]. In this paper we seek to answer the following question: It is possible to identify the level of the student's knowledge about the concepts of Natural Deduction in Propositional Logic using a computational model based on Bayesian Networks, while in the teaching-learning process?

Given that identifying certain characteristics of the student (e.g., knowledge) are fundamental to the development of personalized teaching-learning strategies, the objective of this study was the redesign and development of a model student agent.

© Springer Nature Switzerland AG 2019
Y. Demazeau et al. (Eds.): PAAMS 2019, LNAI 11523, pp. 66–77, 2019.
https://doi.org/10.1007/978-3-030-24209-1_6

Inspired by Vygotsky's theory [12] (in relation to the Zone of Proximal Development - ZPD), this model sought to identify and represent the student's knowledge states, as well as in the learning process, in solving Natural Deduction exercises in a computational teaching environment. In this way, the use of part of this theory is justified, due to the fact that this new Student Model seeks to infer, that is, to estimate the student's knowledge (Real Development Level - RDL) about the concepts of the rules of NDPL. With this information, it is expected to provide the pedagogical support services (mediation and tutoring) to the students with more precision and that is more appropriate to the profile of the student.

The work is organized as follows: Sect. 2 presents the concepts of ITS and personalized teaching, as well as examples of ITS that used knowledge representation in their student models. Section 3 shows the methodology of this work. Section 4 discusses the results obtained and, finally, Sect. 5 concludes about the universe of experiments and projects future work using the new Student Model.

2   ITS and Personalized Learning

ITSs have evolved from the traditional Computer Assisted Instruction Systems of the 1960s to more adaptive learning environments with models with more flexible cognitive theories and teaching-learning strategies. These techniques seek to assist in the teaching and learning process and, for this, seek to understand how students learn [5, 9]. Its main objective is the personalized teaching, which emerged in the 1980s. Conceptually ITS are computer programs designed to incorporate AI techniques, in order to produce a teaching-learning system that: know what they teach, know how to teach and detect how students are learning [6].

In its development, several AI technologies are used, depending on their purpose. However, regardless of the technology used, these systems have as basic components the following models: Student model (initial knowledge about who will learn and, in many cases, also the student's emotional state), Pedagogical model pedagogical tactics - how it will be taught), Expert model (knowledge base on what will be taught), and Interface Model (means for student interaction with the system - represents methods of communication between students and computers, such as graphical interfaces, animated agents, etc.).

These systems reach fine levels of detection of the point of educational content where a student: (a) may have learning problems (cognitive status) and then; (b) it is possible to interfere in a specialized way (for example, making use of a specific learning style, associated with approaches directed to the cognitive and emotional state of that student); (c) how to present the content (what will be taught) in the most appropriate way for each individual.

With these characteristics, an ITS can offer help at any time during the exercise: it allows the student to solve proposed problems step by step (validating the learning), as well as to propose possible solutions of problems from any point of the resolution, through examples or pedagogical tips that point the next step.

Personalized Learning is a teaching-learning strategy used by ITS, Learning Management Systems (LMS) and Massive Online Open Courses (MOOCs) and its implementation is fed by the information of the model: affectivity, cognitive and also of the personality of the student. This information about the affectivity, cognitive and personality model of the student is used so that the challenges, content and even evaluations can be in accordance with the degree of knowledge and the affectivity state of each one. Not always these three models are implemented together, varying their combination or even only one of them being deployed. In order to enable the implementation of a student model, any technologies can be used to represent knowledge, such as neural networks, probabilistic networks, etc., which are typical of AI.

Among the ITS that use personalized teaching concepts, we can cite the AnimalWatch [13] which had its Student Model designed and developed to customize the feedback given to students. This structure occurs in a context that uses a study of threatened species (such as free whales) to solve problems and thus provide the student with the opportunity to select a guidance character as a guide during their activity. Another example is PAT2Math (Personal Affective Tutor to Math) [7] which aims to assist students in solving algebraic problems. It employs several AI algorithms to simulate a teacher who assists and teaches students as they solve first and second-degree equations. The construction of his system is based on the concept of an intelligent learning environment, able to consider the student's emotions, making use of an Animated Pedagogical Agent, which applies pedagogical tactics for motivation and engagement. Another example is the Cardiac Tutor [3] aimed at the medical field and whose objective is to provide intelligent simulation to help medical teams learn procedures on how to manage cardiac arrest. Another example is the Andes [1], a tutorial system for the curricular component of Physics that aims to assist incoming students in the first semesters of the graduation to create equations and graphs while solving classical physics problems. The environment interacts with students using trained problem solving, that is, a method aimed at teaching cognitive skills in which there is a collaboration between the tutor and the student to solve problems. Finally, there is another example that is the AMPLIA (Intelligent Probabilistic Multiagent Learning Environment) [4, 8], an intelligent learning environment designed as an additional resource to support the training and training of medical students. It was developed with the objective of supporting the development of diagnostic rationalization and the modeling of diagnostic hypotheses in the medical field.

3   Proposed Student Model

This new Student Model seeks to infer, that is, to estimate the student's knowledge about the concepts of NDPL rules. In other words, the model seeks to identify the RDL of the student. The ITS scenario of use of this work, part of the presupposition that each exercise of Logic is constituted in a Joint Attention Scene [10], where the dialectical process of mediation between the environment and the student, can allow the latter to evolve its ZPD.

The Student Model agent represents the student model, which in the Heráclito environment is based on the exercise resolution process. According to [2] a student model can be analyzed in three levels of abstraction: operational, behavioral and conceptual. Applying this analysis to the teaching of deduction in Logic models are obtained with the following organization: (a) Operational Level: the model is responsible for verifying whether or not the student can apply the rules of deduction correctly; (b) Behavior Level: the model evaluates if the student can be proficient in their reasoning process to solve a given problem; (c) Conceptual Level: the model indicates the assimilation of the concepts involved in the process of deduction in Logic. It is achieved when the student understands the implications of deduction for other areas of Logic.

The Student Model agent of the Heráclito environment worked only on the first level mentioned above, where it is only verified if the student knows how to properly apply the rules of deduction. With the redesign and implementation of the model of inference to the Student Model, the Heráclito environment will be able to use the behavioral level as well, since in this version it started to have substantial data, inferring statistically how much the student knows or does not about the concepts of natural deduction rules.

To estimate and model the student's knowledge, a Bayesian network composed of 64 observable variables (4 evidences × 16 rules = 64 observable variables) and 16 non-observable variables (10 basic rules and 6 derived rules) was developed. In this network, the unobservable variables represent the probability that the student will know each one of the 16 rules available in the Heráclito environment con-having one variable per rule.

The probability to estimate the student's knowledge was calculated according to 4 evidences (observable variables) that can be extracted from the environment. They are:

- Visualization of the rule concept [True, False]: In this evidence, the student has the possibility to analyze the concept and the standard form of application of the rule before applying it;
- Example view of the rule [True, False]: In this evidence, in addition to the concept, the student can also see an example with the application of the rule (as it was applied) in order to try to elucidate possible doubts;
- Help [True, False]: In this evidence when asked for help, the environment provides the next step (this is calculated by the expert agent) which may be the next rule to be applied or the number of rows (example, line 3 and 5) to which the student must select to apply the next rule and continue with the exercise;
- Correction about the application of the rule [True, False]: Whenever the student applies the rule, it is technically correct or incorrect. In case it is incorrect, the environment will not let the student continue, it is necessary to reapply the same rule correctly or try to apply another rule, but also correct.

Based on these four evidences for each rule (16 rules in all), the inference mechanism begins to estimate the probability of the student to know the given rule. Figures 1 and 2 show an example (using part of the developed network) with the Equivalence and Modus Ponens rules. In Fig. 1, we have the initial values in the evidence and the inference about the knowledge of the rules, while in Fig. 2 we have an example where the student hit the application of the rule Equivalence without using any aid. It is important to mention that Visualization, Example and Help evidence has the same weight, while the correction about the application of the rule plays a major role when calculation its probability.

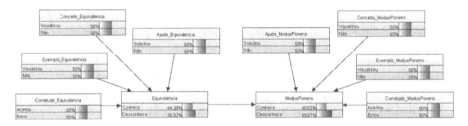

Fig. 1. Variables with the initial values.

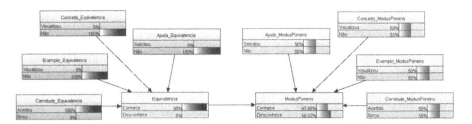

Fig. 2. Inferred values for the variable.

It can be seen in Fig. 2 that the updated evidence is in blue and that the probability of the student to know the rule of Equivalence was updated to 95% since he did not request help and did not view examples or concepts about the rule. The Modus Ponens rule was also updated, from 40% to approximately 44%, since the student demonstrated to know the concepts that preceded this rule. In addition to updating the network in real time, the calculated probabilities are stored for later use.

Considering that the Heráclito environment allows the use of 16 rules, Fig. 3 was adapted to show only the variables that will be estimated by the inference mechanism. The 4 observable variables of each rule were omitted to facilitate visualization of the network structure.

In Fig. 3, two sets of rules can be verified: those that are part of the student's ZPD (represented in yellow) and the others (represented in gray). It should be noted that because it is a network in its initial state, none of the rules was used by the student, that is, there is no evidence about the student's knowledge. In this graphical representation, as previously mentioned, it is believed that the previous knowledge of the student in previous contents, will facilitate the learning of the basic rules of inference, such as the rules of Addition, Conjunction, Equivalence and Double-Negation.

Considering a hypothetical student who performs a few exercises in the environment, the inference mechanism has enough evidence to estimate the student's knowledge about certain rules. In this sense, Fig. 4 presents a hypothetical network where it was inferred that the student knows some rules, as well as, he does not know others. The inference and delimitation of the student's ZPD could be visualized through the evidences observed through the interaction between the student and the teaching environment Heráclito.

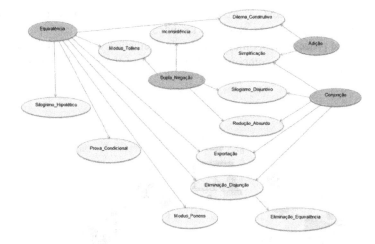

Fig. 3. Initial state of the Bayesian network. (Color figure online)

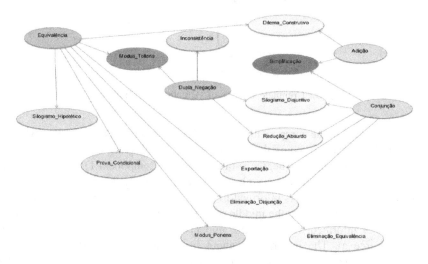

Fig. 4. Example of a ZPD after some interactions. (Color figure online)

In the set of applied rules, which resulted in Fig. 4, it is observed that the student knows the Equivalence and Double-Negation rules (represented in green color). In addition, the network evidences 7 rules that are part of the student's ZPD (represented in the yellow and orange colors): Hypothetical Syllogism, Concurrent Proof, Modus Ponens, Modus Tollens, Inconsistency, Addition, and Conjunction. In addition, it can be verified that the student did not know the Simplification rules (represented in pink) and Modus Tollens (represented in orange color). These rules are represented with different colors since the Modus Tollens rule is part of the student's ZPD, while the Simplification rule is not part of it. The other vertices (represented in gray) represent the rules that the student is expected to learn. It should be noted that the rules represented in the yellow and gray colors were not used by the students, or there is insufficient evidence to infer the student's knowledge about these concepts.

The complete process involving the student's interaction with the environment and the agents together with the components that are part of the Heráclito environment is shown in Fig. 5.

Fig. 5. Complete process of Heráclito environment.

Figure 5 shows all the components that involve the macro process, starting with the user performing an action, going through the 3 agents and returning with the response to the user action. The process begins with the student (Component 1) when interacting with the Heráclito environment through some device (Desktop, Notebook, Smartphone or Tablet). Each user action is informed to the Student Model agent (Component 2).

Assuming the student is in the middle of a test and tries to apply a rule, the Student Model agent is informed, receiving the student's partial test as well as his/her last action (Resource a). The information about its action is stored (Process 2.1) and inserted into the inference mechanism, which updates the student's knowledge (Process 2.2). Once this process is completed, the Student Model agent forwards the information that they have (Resource a) to the Agent Mediator (Component 3), which in turn analyzes their action plans (Process 3.1) and forwards the message to the Agent Expert (Component 4). The Specialist receives the student's partial exam and its last step (Resource a), assesses the status of that action (Process 4.1) and informs the Mediator about what it has discovered (Resource b). With all possible information, the Mediator agent decides which learning strategy should be used and forwards the necessary actions (Resource c) to the Student Model.

If, for example, the attempt to apply a student's rule would result in a scenario where it would be impossible to complete the test, the mediator's action would be to inform the student of this situation and suggest to him that he would go back on his decision, undoing the application of the last rule (even if it is correct), since it would be from the behavioral point of view, prejudicial to the resolution of the exercise. Finally, the Student Model agent applies the action plan (Resource c) defined by the Mediator agent. This process repeats itself at each rule applied and is only terminated when the proof (or argument) closes to the end (successfully completing the exercise) or when the student gives up proving the exercise in question, closing the editor or initiating a new proof (the same or another of your choice).

The student's knowledge network has its duration defined by exercises. That is, it begins in its initial state and changes, being shaped by the student to each action performed in the interaction with the environment. If the same student performs 10 exercises, we will have 10 representations of the student's knowledge that after these sections will make a mean about the concepts that were applied correctly and incorrectly, thus inferring how much this student knows about the rules of deduction applied.

4 Experiments and Results

The experiments had as target audience, students of the undergraduate courses in Computer Science and Software Engineering of a University located in the city of Porto Alegre, RS, Brazil. The experiment was carried out in the second semester of 2018, with the curricular component of Logic for Computing, comprising two mixed classes (students of the two courses), totaling 57 students. The experiment was composed of 1 pre-test and 1 post-test and the application of a form to evaluate questions concerning the teaching environment and its functionalities. The pre-test was applied in the classroom while the post-test was applied in the computer lab. In both cases, the students had 1 h and 15 min to resolve a list containing 10 exercises. It should be noted that the exercises in the two lists were different, but equivalent, in order to allow a direct comparison between the exercises. Only at the end of the exercises did the students complete the environmental assessment form.

The experiments were started by evaluating the students' perception of the Heráclito environment, considering two main groups: Usability/Interface and Tutoring Service. The Usability/Interface data are summarized in the following:

- 84% of the students are satisfied with the efficiency that the tool brings, speeding up and facilitating the test;
- 79% of students are generally satisfied with the interface;
- Over 90% are satisfied with the availability of basic rules and derivatives;
- 89% are satisfied with the demonstration format of the tests.

As we can verify, in general, the students were satisfied with the interface and operation of the environment. As for the Tutoring Service, it is worth mentioning that the strategies in the mediator are generic for all students. The mediator intervenes in the process when the student demonstrates that he or she needs help or trying to take action that will prevent the completion of the test. In addition, some motivational messages, stating how many steps are missing to complete the test (e.g. half the test, missing a few steps) are also forwarded. It can be analyzed that these strategies do not consider the specific knowledge or characteristics of each student. In this sense, more than 75%

were satisfied with the intervention of the tutor when they were in difficulties or trying to take an action that would prevent the conclusion of the test. However, with respect to the other messages, 47% and 44% declare themselves satisfied and indifferent, respectively. Some students pointed out that they were following a different flow of evidence from the tutor and, being informed that only X steps to complete the test were missing, they had to review the test from the beginning to be able to continue.

Next, it is sought to evaluate if there are significant differences between the accomplishment of the exercises in paper and the Heráclito environment. It begins by analyzing the data about the issues solved in Table 1, which shows the number of theorems correctly proved on paper and in the Heráclito environment.

Table 1. Comparison between exercises performed on paper and in the Heráclito environment.

Method	Ex.1	Ex.2	Ex.3	**Ex.4**	**Ex.5**	Ex.6	Ex.7	Ex.8	Ex.9	**Ex.10**	Total
Paper	29	43	40	**8**	**7**	13	16	10	19	**44**	229
Heráclito	43	43	41	**47**	**0**	42	41	41	40	**38**	376
Average	36	43	40,5	**27,5**	**3,5**	27,5	28,5	25,5	29,5	**41**	302,5

It can be seen from Table 1 that the students performed more exercises in the Heráclito environment than on paper. When we observe the absolute quantities, it is possible to verify that only exercises 5 and 10 were more performed on paper. However, although it was more performed on paper, exercise 10 did not present a significant difference compared to the Heráclito environment (MW = 1008; p = 0.078), differently from exercise 5, where there was a significant difference (p = 0.006). In contrast, when analyzing the others, it can be verified that the students performed more often in the Heráclito environment. Only in exercises 2 and 3 there were no significant differences (MW = 1152, p = 0.680 and MW = 1128, p = 0.500, respectively). In the other exercises, p values were 0.001 for exercise 1 and less than 0,000 for the others (exercises 4, 6, 7, 8 and 9), and the Mann-Whitney values were less than 1000.

At the end of the experiments, the students answered 4 questions, respectively, evaluating questions about the natural deduction rules made available by the Heráclito environment. At this stage, the students had the freedom to determine what rules the environment made available to them they believed they had easily used. It is worth mentioning that facilities and difficulties may be associated, mainly, to two factors: interface and theoretical knowledge about the teaching domain. Once the student knows the theory surrounding the rule he is trying to apply, it is important that the steps for applying the rule are intuitive. In this respect, the Heráclito environment detaches itself by working with the application of rules in a manner like that carried out by the teacher in the classroom.

Table 2, divided by basic rules (10) and derivatives (6), shows the students' perception, the percentage of correct answers and errors in the corresponding applications, and the average probability of the students knowing this rule (calculated by the agent).

Analyzing Table 2, regarding the basic rules, it can be observed that 82% of the students pointed to the CJ rule as being what they believed to be the easiest to use, which corroborates the fact that they have agreed to apply the rule in 86% of the time.

Table 2. Comparison between students' perception and performance and the Student Model.

Rules	Facility	Difficulty	Correct	Incorrect	Total	Knowledge
Addition (AD)	67%	9%	90%	10%	380	83%
Conjunction (CJ)	82%	5%	86%	14%	488	80%
Simplification (SP)	65%	5%	90%	10%	448	66%
Modus Ponens (MP)	95%	2%	75%	25%	954	65%
Double-Negation (DN)	30%	4%	41%	59%	17	49%
Elimination of Disjunction (–Dj)	25%	16%	100%	0,0%	7	73%
Introduction of Equivalence (+Eq)	16%	18%	36%	64%	11	45%
Elimination of Equivalence (–Eq)	39%	25%	100%	0%	368	80%
Close Conditional Proof (PC)	51%	84%	84%	16%	159	70%
Close Reduction to Absurdity (RAA)	11%	60%	15%	85%	27	23%
Constructive Dilemma (DC)	35%	67%	12%	87%	8	19%
Export (EXP)	28%	54%	50%	50%	20	42%
Inconsistency (INC)	26%	40%	39%	61%	18	38%
Modus Tollens (MT)	100%	11%	50%	50%	99	41%
Disjunctive Syllogism (SD)	56%	35%	79%	21%	98	59%
Hypothetical Syllogism (SH)	16%	35%	11%	89%	9	18%

In this case, the average calculated probability of the students knowing this rule is 80%. Another important fact is related to the rule –Dj (Elimination of Disjunction), where few students pointed out facilities and some pointed difficulties, but students applied the rule correctly every time (7 times). Although they have always correctly applied the rule, the probability of students knowing this rule is only 73%, since this rule is associated with other rules, which these students did not demonstrate knowledge throughout the test. The same can be explained for the rule –Eq (Elimination of Equivalence).

Still in Table 2, but considering the derived rules, it can be observed that, unlike the basic rules, the students' perception of the difficulties and difficulties found in the application of derived rules, in some cases, does not corroborate attempts to apply the rules. Considering, for example, the MT rule (Modus Tollens), 100% of the students indicated that it is easy to use the rule, but they miss their application 50% of the time.

On the other hand, 56% of the students emphasized ease in using the SD rule (Disjunctive Syllogism), and 79% of the attempts were successfully applied.

In addition, as additional information, it is worth mentioning that the correlation between the facilities and difficulties pointed out by the students and the average probability of knowing the rule is 0.61 and −0.21, considering the basic rules. As for the derived rules, the correlation is 0.56 and −0.12, respectively. It is worth noting that the correlation presented in the basic rules is stronger than the correlations obtained for the derived rules, which can be explained by the teaching domain. All theorems can be proved using only the basic rules of inference, as well as being taught before the derived rules. Nevertheless, when comparing the total applications of the basic rules with respect to the derived rules, we notice a greater number of attempts to apply the basic rules, which allows students to be clearer about the facilities and difficulties they are facing.

5   Conclusions

The present work presented a redesign for Student Model agent applied to the Heráclito environment, which consists of an ITS for teaching Logic for Computing. One of the advantages provided by this new agent is the ability to estimate student knowledge individually, allowing the tool to use personalized learning concepts.

As shown, considering the universe of experiments, the tool presented satisfaction indexes above 75% regarding usability. In the tutorial service, the students showed themselves to be in favor of the interactions of the tutor when they had some type of difficulty. However, some motivational messages were not well received, achieving indifference rates of 44% and only 47% satisfaction. However, when analyzing the students' efficiency using the environment, in comparison with the paper tests, there is a significant increase in the number of exercises solved, from 229 to 376 (Table 1). In addition, it has been observed that in most cases, students did significantly better using Heráclito. It is important to emphasize that the students had the first contact with the environment before the post-test, where they received training of only 15 min.

Nevertheless, by analyzing the results of the inference mechanism, it was found that there was a correlation between the rules that were said to be easy and difficult in relation to their percentages of correctness and errors, respectively. In addition, to evaluate the effectiveness and quality of the inference about knowledge of the rules, a comparison was made between the evolution of knowledge learned for each rule and the history of correctness and errors in the applications (of each student). It was verified that in comparing students' knowledge with the use of rules, in approximately 83% of the time the data were consistent, emphasizing the accuracy of the inference mechanism. In this sense, it can be established that the proposed Student Model presents a high accuracy rate when comparing the students' historical knowledge with the application of the rules.

Considering the positive results about the inference of the student's knowledge, on the theme, and the representation of the student's knowledge, a range of possible future works is opened focusing the Mediator Agent, allowing the environment to walk to personalized teaching considering the individual knowledge of each student.

References

1. Conati, C., Gertner, A.S., VanLehn, K., Druzdzel, M.J.: On-line student modeling for coached problem solving using bayesian networks. In: Jameson, A., Paris, C., Tasso, C. (eds.) User Modeling. ICMS, vol. 383, pp. 231–242. Springer, Vienna (1997). https://doi.org/10.1007/978-3-7091-2670-7_24
2. Dillenbourg, P., Self, J.: People power: a human-computer collaborative learning system. In: Frasson, C., Gauthier, G., McCalla, G.I. (eds.) Intelligent Tutoring Systems ITS 1992. LNCS, pp. 651–660. Springer, Heidelberg (1992). https://doi.org/10.1007/3-540-55606-0_75
3. Eliot, C.R., Woolf, B.P.: A simulation-based tutor that reasons about multiple agents. In: Proceedings of the 13th National Conference on Artificial Intelligence (AAAI-96), pp. 409–415. AAAI/MIT Press, Cambridge (1996)
4. Flores, C.D.: Negociação pedagógica aplicada a um ambiente multiagente de aprendizagem colaborativa. Tese de Doutorado. Instituto de Computação. UFRGS (2005)
5. Gluz, J.C., Galafassi, F.F.P., Mossmann, M., Vicari, R.M.: Heráclito: a dialectical tutor for logic. In: Proceedings 16th Portuguese Conference on Artificial Intelligence EPIA, Açores, Portugal, vol. 8154. pp. 1–2. Springer, New York (2013)
6. Nwana, H.S.: Intelligent tutoring systems: an overview. Artif. Intell. Rev. **4**(4), 251–277 (1990)
7. PAT2Math. Personal Affective Tutor to Math. Disponível em (2018). http://pat2math.unisinos.br/. Acesso em 21 Jan 2019
8. Russel, J.S., Norvig, P.: Artificial Intelligence: A Modern Approach, 3rd Edn. Editora Prentice Hall (Pearson Education), Upper Saddle River (2010)
9. Seixas, L.M.G.: Estratégias Pedagógicas para um Ambiente Multiagente Probabilístico Inteligente de Aprendizagem – AMPLIA. CINTED/UFRGS. Programa de Pós-Graduação em Informática na Educação. Tese de Doutorado (2005)
10. Self, J.A.: Bypassing the intractable problem of student modelling. Intell. Tutoring Syst.: Crossroads Artif. Intell. Educ. **41**, 1–26 (1990)
11. Tomasello, M.: The Cultural Origins of Human Cognition. Harvard University Press, Cambridge (2001)
12. Vicari, R.M.: Tendências em inteligência artificial na educação no período de 2017 a 2030: SUMÁRIO EXECUTIVO/Serviço Nacional de Aprendizagem Industrial, Serviço Social da Indústria. SENAI, Brasília (2018)
13. Vygotsky, L.S.: Thought and Language. M.I.T. Press, Cambridge (1986)
14. Woolf, B.P.: Building intelligent interactive tutors: student-centered strategies for revolutionizing e-learning. Department of Computer Science, University of Massachusetts. Editora Elsevier, Amherst (2009)

Network Effects in an Agent-Based Model of Tax Evasion with Social Influence

Fernando Garcia Alvarado[1,2]($\boxtimes$)

[1] Centre d'Economie de la Sorbonne,
University of Paris 1 Pantheon-Sorbonne, Paris, France
fernando.garcia@unive.it
[2] Department of Economics, Ca' Foscari University of Venice, Venice, Italy

Abstract. An Agent-Based Model (ABM) accounting for tax-morale and loss-aversion was implemented over different network systems with social interactions at the local level to study the phenomenon of tax evasion. This ABM is an innovative model which integrates endogenous characteristics of heterogeneous agents and proposes a more relaxed assumption on the information exchanged between agents as compared to previous social models. The current study gives an insight on the possibility that choosing specific network structures may yield to more realistic outcomes. Moreover, this ABM manages to replicate both individual and aggregate results from previous experimental and computational models of tax evasion. A clearcut novelty might be the non-linear channel through which the network centrality enhances a positive effect on the aggregated level of tax compliance. There is a large area of action for public policy makers to further research the presented results about how audit rates, fines and tax morale non-linearly increase income disclosure, whereas tax rates have a non-linear negative impact on tax compliance.

Keywords: Agent-based models · Tax evasion · Complex networks

1 Introduction

Following the influential paper published by Allingham and Sandmo [1] exploring the rationale behind tax evasion phenomenon, a vast literature has congregated around the modeling of tax compliance. A non-negligible portion of income tax research has explored the mechanisms surrounding social interaction among the agents, particularly in agent-based modeling. Mittone and Patelli [2] delved into the psychological motives of tax compliance inherent to a society composed by three heterogeneous types of agents: full-compliers, imitators, and full-evaders (free-riders). The objective of their endeavor was bound to the analysis of aggregate tax behavior in function of the initial composition of the taxpaying population under two different audit schemes; uniform and tail auditing.

This project has received funding from the ITN ExSIDE European Union's Horizon 2020 research and innovation programme under the Marie Sklodowska-Curie grant agreement No 721846.

© Springer Nature Switzerland AG 2019
Y. Demazeau et al. (Eds.): PAAMS 2019, LNAI 11523, pp. 78–89, 2019.
https://doi.org/10.1007/978-3-030-24209-1_7

A comprehensive compilation of literature may include Davis et al. [3] who find stable equilibria both under low and high enforcement schemes, linked by a non-linear and asymmetric transition; Hokamp and Pickhardt [4] introduced an exponential utility function for agents in order to induce more realistic results; and Korobow, Johnson and Axtell [5] introduced a network structure but also considered individuals who possessed heterogeneous characteristics and intrinsic perceptions about the enforcement regime.

Stepping forward into a more contemporary literature review, Andrei et al. [6] contributed an additional aspect to be taken into account for agent-based models of income tax evasion. The authors found that the network structure underlying the societal arrangement has a significant impact in the decision process dynamics; principally, individuals tended to disclose a larger fraction of their income whenever they embodied networks with higher levels of centrality. Amongst the number of social structures tested, the Erdos-Renyi random network and the Power Law networks may incentive agents to comply the most given their larger capacity of propagating information and influence dissemination. The usage of network structures in models with 'social pressure' are everyday more frequent. A convenient example is the one by Billari et al. [7] in which agents must choose a partner based on the mutual proximity with respect to age and social status in a dynamic framework; this approach will be particularly handy for the model implementation in Sect. 3.

Alm, Bloomquist and McKee [8] conducted a social experiment intended to learn about the burden of peer effects and social pressure in the context of tax compliance. The conclusions reached by the authors discuss how agents have a statistically significant positive effect in the tax disclosures of their 'neighbors' or 'people with whom they frequently share information'; when an agent is surrounded by honest (cheating) individuals, the agent itself starts to behave in a more honest (cheating) manner.

2   A Taxpayer's Decision to Evade

Tax compliance decision-making is ordinarily modeled as a gamble or an investment opportunity involving one risky asset (undisclosed income) and a risk-free asset (disclosed income), the micro-founded expected utility to be optimized with respect to the fraction of income declared d may well be defined as:

$$EU[d] = p \cdot U(X) + (1 - p) \cdot U(Y), \qquad (1)$$

where X is the net income after taxes and penalties in case an audit takes place, and Y is the net income after taxes in case no audit takes place.

Promptly substituting X and Y in terms of the gross earned income I, the penalty rate θ applied to the undisclosed fraction of income in case an audit occurs, and the applicable tax rate τ, reformulates Eq. 1 to:

$$EU = (1 - p) \cdot U[I - \tau(d \cdot I)] + p \cdot U[I - \tau(d \cdot I) - \theta\tau(I - d \cdot I)] \qquad (2)$$

Solving for optimality conditions, the rational taxpayer will declare less than its actual income if the expected tax payment on undeclared income is less than the regular rate, that is, whenever $p \cdot \theta < 1$; moreover, the fine rate must be larger than 1. There is a widely known substantial drawback for this model in the sense that it highly overestimates the tax evasion rate.

Akin to the adjustment outlined by Hokamp and Pickhardt [4], a power utility function is imputed into the model outlined in Eq. 2. Discarding for simplicity the subindex, yet considering for each agent i and each time t, the utility function of every single agent is characterized in Eq. 3.

$$U(d, W) = (1 + d)^{\kappa} W^{(1-\rho)} \tag{3}$$

where the variables are denoted as: period-wealth $W = \{X, Y\}$, the fraction of declared income $d \in [0, 1]$, loss-aversion $\rho \in (0, 1)$, and tax-morale $\kappa \in [0, 1]$. In this sense, a higher the tax morale yields a larger utility of complying; while a higher loss-aversion would yield a lower utility on wealth.

Tax morale has been a recurring matter in the models of tax compliance ever since Myles and Naylor [9] asserted a social conformity framework in which agents attained an additional utility from conforming to the established social norms. Despite the complications to accurately define tax morale, hereafter tax morale will be understood as an umbrella term, in the sense of Luttmer and Singhal [10], enclosing intrinsic motivation, reciprocity, culture, biases and social influences. Next in order, loss aversion will be understood as the well-known wealth effect described by Tversky and Kahneman [11].

A remark for the current tax decision model is the non-matchable income assumption, meaning that an auditor from the Tax Agency does not know beforehand the individuals' incomes. If a society would happen to account for a non-negligible matching system for its labor market, the assumption may be relaxed to take into consideration only the non-matchable portion of the agents' stipends without sacrificing any of the models' intuitions and results.

2.1 Subjective Audit Rate

The individuals' subjective probability of being audited is updated based on their past experience. Moreover, their audit beliefs are likewise updated by the behaviors of their 'neighbors', defined as the agents with whom they frequently exchange information, as in Alm, Bloomquist and McKee [8]. Hereafter, the subjective audit probability perceived by agent i at time t can be defined as a weighted average of the agent's prior experience (temporal updating) and the signals from its neighboring individuals (geographical updating) last period.

The universe of agents coexists in a predefined network structure with (local) social interactions and each period agents exchange information with their neighbors, however they never get to know the entire situation nor the composition of the society in which they inhabit. Afterwards, agents update their own perceived audit probability by means of a weighted average of three possible channels: their subjective audit rate in the previous period (prior), their own recalling of past audits (memory), and the signals they received from their neighbors (social influence).

$$\hat{p}_{i,t+1} = \lambda_1 \hat{p}_{i,t} + \lambda_2 \sum_{s=1}^{S_i} \frac{A_{i,t-s}}{S_i} + (1 - \lambda_1 - \lambda_2) \sum_{j \neq i}^{N_{i,t}} \frac{1}{N_{i,t}} \sum_{s=1}^{S_j} \frac{A_{j,t-s}}{S_j} \qquad (4)$$

where λ_1 and λ_2 are convex averaging weights, $A_{i,t-s}$ is valued one if the agent i was audited in the period $(t-s)$ and zero otherwise, S_j is the memory or number of audit periods that agent j can recall in the past, and $N_{i,t-1}$ is the number of neighbors of agent i at time t.

3   Implementation of the Agent-Based Model

There are key distinctions that difference ABM's from mathematical models. Arguably one the most germane attributes of any Agent-Based Model is its intrinsic capability of embodying plentiful heterogeneous agents, all possessing unique aspects and personalities. Accordingly, each agent is heterogeneous by acquiring specific built-in characteristics. Secondly, individuals base their decision process in their own subjective probabilities of being audited and not in the true audit rates. Lastly, agents coexist in neighborhoods inside a larger societal structure which allows for information exchange at a local level.

Similarly to Korobow et al. [5], this model includes the three listed attributes, however there is a key difference in the assumptions about shared information. Korobow et al., for example, implemented their model under the hypothesis that individuals shared their own, personal 'payoffs' for tax evasion among their neighborhoods, however, they acknowledged the unlikelihood of such delicate information becoming public in real-life scenarios. In order to outplay this limitation, now agents communicate solely their memory about previous audits and update their subjective probability of being audited in conjunction with the frequency of audits perceived by themselves and their immediate neighbors.

Stepping into the realm of the current work, agents are constituted as individuals embroidered by personal traits: tax-morale, loss-aversion, income, age and an initial subjective probability of being caught evading taxes. Moreover, the tax-morale and loss-aversion parameters are dynamic, increasing stochastically with respect to age. On any occasion in which an agent would happen to grow into an age above 65, it would be removed from the network analogous to a retired individual would exit the labor market; to replace the empty node left inside the network, a new individual, aged 18 and with its own particularities, would replace the available position.

Tax morale is initialized from a society-level parameter for the entire network, whereas loss-aversion is entirely endogenous for each individual. For a society level tax-morale of $\kappa_S \leq 0.5$, individual morale is modeled as $\kappa \sim U(0, 2\kappa_S)$. Endorsing the notion of loss-aversion as the preference of avoiding a loss over attaining a win, coupled by the endowment effect in which an individual would rather pay a higher rate to retain something it owns (net income) than to receive another thing it does not own (taxes), it follows that a local and endogenous loss-aversion parameter (ρ) may well be defined as the relative income position held by the individual with respect to its neighbors divided by the neighborhood size $|N_i|$ (including the agent) plus one, where the highest loss-aversion measures pertain the most affluent agents.

$$\rho_i = \frac{\text{rank}(I_i)}{|N_i| + 1} \tag{5}$$

This definition allows the global distribution of individual loss-aversion of ρ to be symmetric around 0.50. The distribution of (ρ) resembles a bell-shape tendency, at least when contrasted against the original Uniform$\sim U(0,1)$.

Enhancing audits to shift from random to endogenous and regarding the income effect on tax compliance, a modification was made on the Tax Agency's audit strategy. It would not be a surprise that a Tax Agency would be more inclined into targeting individuals whose eye-catching income stands out from the sample. Ergo, proceeding for each agent, the endogenous probability of being audited is set in accordance to its income level, where individuals with higher salaries have larger probabilities of being audited. Following, the endogenous audit rate q for agent i is the true audit rate p multiplied by the ratio of the agent's income over the average income of the population, shown in Eq. 6.

$$q_i = \frac{I_i}{\sum_{j=1}^{N} I_j} \cdot Np \tag{6}$$

Notwithstanding the adjustment implemented for the endogenous audit rates, the mean value of q remains equal to the true audit rate p; allowing for consistent testing of parameters. To see this it suffices to sum over all agents i and divide by N in both sides of Eq. 6.

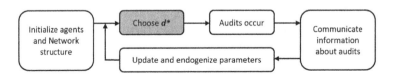

Fig. 1. Simplified process flowchart

Figure 1 depicts the decision process mechanism in a rather simplified manner. An artificial society is structured as a network, where each agent is initialized with exogenous parameters $\{\kappa_0, \rho_0, q_0, \hat{p}_0, I_0, age_0\}$ and chooses an optimal fraction of income to declare d^*. Afterwards, audits take place and agents communicate 'signals' or information regarding the audit process. Next, agents update and endogenize parameters $\{\kappa_t, \rho_t, q_t, \hat{p}_t, I_t, age_t\}$ and repeat the decision process. Every agent repeats the cycle until it is retired from the labor market.

3.1   Network Structure

Immediately upon the parameter booting, whether endogenous or not, lies the second cornerstone of the ongoing Agent-Based model with social pressure:

the network formation process. Embracing the methodology followed by Andrei et al. [6], a selection of nine different underlying network structures where tested ensuing comparisons and contrasts among one another: two types of random graphs, small words, large world, Watts-Strogatz, ring, wheel and two types of scale-free networks.

Figures 2 and 3 display an Erdos-Renyi random graph and a random geometric graph, respectively, in a toroidal world which 'wraps up' both vertically and horizontally. Albeit both graphs having the exact number of agents, links and degree distribution, its interesting how the physical arrangement appears to be strikingly different. The ABM simulations where implemented in the *Netlogo* software, where the default ordering of agents follows the random geometric structure of Fig. 3. All network structures, except for the fitness function model, where implemented using the 'nw' extension of *Netlogo*.

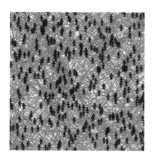   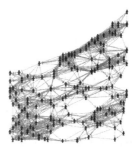

Fig. 2. Erdos-Renyi   **Fig. 3.** Random geom.   **Fig. 4.** Fitness model

Figure 4 presents a fitness function network in a Cartesian environment without 'wrapping'. This is a specific type of scale-free networks, following a mathematical specification to determine or not an association between any two given individuals. Inspired on the social interaction Agent-Based model with spatial components devised by Billari et al. [7], individuals are constrained to link only with 'relevant others' within their reach in terms of age and social position. Attending to this notion, an artificial society was emulated on a Cartesian plane where the x-axis features the agents' age whilst the y-axis represents the individuals' income. First, a newly created set of agents is randomly assigned individual age and salaries and positioned in their corresponding coordinates inside the plane. Then, each time-step, agents advance one unit horizontally, and, stochastically increase their income, shifting north in the plane on the long-run. The procedure continues for each agent until they reach a sufficiently advanced age, in which case they 'retire' from the labor market and are replaced by an offspring endowed with a fraction (two-thirds) of the exiting agent's wealth and being positioned at the left edge, starting their own working life.

Figure 4 depicts a pyramidal society after 60 timestamps where the top-right corner positions are occupied by old, wealthy individuals, the top-left corner is void (juvenile millionaires) and a dense bottom-left edge reveals a large amount of young agents with low or middle incomes. Evidently, it would be plausible to speculate that in the real world a person would discuss his or her fiscal matters rather exclusively with people of their own age and income level (social status).

4   Results

The main objective of the following section is understanding the effects of different regressors on the fraction of income declared at the society level. The Behavior Space tool incorporated in the *Netlogo* software allowed for a simulation of 21,890 simulations ran over 729 different possible parameter combinations: $\tau = \{25\%, 35\%, 45\%\}$, $p = \{2\%, 6\%, 10\%\}$, $\kappa = \{10\%, 25\%, 40\%\}$, $\theta = \{2, 4, 10\}$, and nine different network structures; each simulation accounted for 350 agents and fixing the probability updating weights to $\lambda_1 = \lambda_2 = \lambda_3 = 1/3$.

The analysis of the parameters is specified in Table 1 along with their respective significance codes. Keeping in mind the nature of the outcome variable d to be bounded between zero and one, a specific statistical model must be applied for data analysis. The results produced by the simulation were tested under a Tobit model censored for minimum and maximum values of zero and one, respectively, boundaries included. Moreover, quadratic coefficients where added to study the non-linear interactions of each parameter.

Table 1 delineates the different linear and non-linear effects that each parameter imposes in the fraction of income disclosed. Column (1) and Column (2) both deal with the effects of tax rates, audit rates, fines and tax-morale. The last regressors in Column (1) take into consideration the average closeness-centrality of all individuals in the underlying network where agents coexist; the closeness-centrality is interpreted as 'how easily a node may be reached from all other nodes'. Hereby and after closeness will be understood as the inverse of the average distance of a node to all other nodes; where the distance between two nodes is the shortest path in which one node may reach the other. Consequently, a node who requires few steps to reach other nodes will have a lower average distance, implying a larger closeness within the network. On the other hand, Column (2) controls for each network structure by adding one dummy variable for each type while keeping the Erdos-Renyi random-graph as the baseline case, allowing for comparisons with the results by Andrei et al. [6].

Opening the analysis of the Tobit model, tax rates seem to impose a negative effect on tax compliance, yet such impact seems to marginally increase for very large levels of tax duties. This effect, which can be interpreted from a positive estimated coefficient for τ and a negative estimated coefficient for τ^2, as seen in Table 1, is represented in Fig. 5 where tax compliance decreases non-linearly with respect to the tax rate. A basal development of any taxation model is the understanding of how tax rates behavior reflect an impact on the collected revenues from the Tax Agency's point of view. The Laffer Curve is the representation of tax revenues as a function of the tax rate. Governments cannot over-raise the

Table 1. Dependent variable: Aggregate $[d]$

Tobit model	Closeness	Dummy variables
Regressors	(1)	(2)
Intercept	−2.143***	−2.146***
τ: tax_rate	−3.392***	−3.392***
τ^2: tax_rate^2	2.348***	2.347***
p: audit_rate	4.060***	4.060***
p^2: audit_rate^2	−12.550***	−12.550***
θ: fines	0.055***	0.055***
θ^2: fines^2	−0.003***	−0.003***
κ: tax_morale	1.841***	1.841***
κ^2: tax_morale^2	−1.503***	−1.503***
closeness	0.577***	
closeness^2	−0.971***	
Random_Geom		−0.002
Lattice		−0.045***
Pref_Attach		0.001
Fitness_Model		0.004*
Ring		−0.081***
Small_Worlds		−0.022***
Watts_Strogatz		−0.006**
Wheel		−0.045***

Signif. codes: '***' 0.001 '**' 0.01 '*' 0.05

tax rate as it would incentive agents to evade taxes, reducing the governmental revenue. Figure 6 details the corresponding Laffer Curve for the simulated society.

An outcome from Table 1 that falls in line with common sense is the positive coefficient for audit rates; as the true probability of being audited increases, a larger proportion of agents experience audits, which in turn communicate the event to their neighbors and the information about a harsher enforcement environment becomes public knowledge, ensuing higher tax compliance among individuals. The quadratic term of the audit rate suggests that, despite the notion of larger audit rates implying higher tax compliance, this policy tool will tend to lose effect as the audit probabilities start turning 'too high'. Fines (or penalties), represented by the parameter θ in this model, retain a somewhat secondary role at inhibiting tax evasion. Analogous to findings in the tax policy literature, see for example Alm, Jackson and McKee [12], fine rates have statistically significant effects to deter evasion even though their estimated coefficients are rather low. Fines help deter evasion only up to some degree given that in the model specification they only appear interactively with the true audit rate p forming

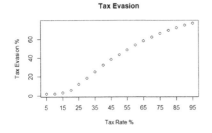

Fig. 5. Tax evasion as a function of τ **Fig. 6.** Laffer curve

the enforcement criterion θp. Ergo, for relatively high values of p, parameter θ loses its strength. The resulting non-linear effects of audit rates on tax evasion have relevance for public policy, shedding light on a possibility that raising audit rates and strengthening enforcement schemes may have marginally decreasing effects. Side by side with these results, Kirchler et al. [13] point out that policy makers should concentrate less in penalties and enforcement, and instead, focus on policies aiming to heighten voluntary compliance.

It may be wise to commence the discernment of tax morale by acknowledging how fundamentally difficult it is to measure a society's morale. However, miscellaneous interpretations could typify a government's control over a society's tax morale through a larger participation and political inclusion of citizens or even by generating a feeling over how well the budget is being spent. Relying on citizen's perception of their trust on institutional authorities may be, as well, a proxy conjecture about societal morale. Adopting the assumption, however, that tax-morale is not only measurable but mutable, it has a positive, non-linear, and statistically significant effect on tax compliance, that is, individuals endowed with a higher tax-morale would be more inclined to disclose their true incomes and thus diminish their fiscal evasion. Consequently, societies whose citizen's tax-morale is low should be more concerned in establishing an agenda which would encourage taxpayers' involvement within the society and policies targeting the promotion of how resources are being 'well spent'.

The concluding parameter in Column (1), the closeness centrality of the network, previously defined, yielded a statistically significant positive effect in the aggregate tax compliance and a negative coefficient on its squared transformation. There exists, therefore, a non-linear channel through which closeness in a network may stimulate tax compliance at the aggregate level. Perhaps these peer-effects gain their impetus from the spread of information and the availability of knowledge regarding the audit frequency.

Column (2) provides a deeper look into the dynamics of closeness centrality by recurring to dummy variables in the Tobit model. Even more, the closeness centrality for each structure may be seen in Table 2 to serve as reference.

Reminiscent of the Erdos-Renyi graph as the baseline case, the random geometric and the preferential attachment networks do not have a statistically significant different repercussion regarding tax behavior. Lattice, ring, small

Table 2. Closeness centrality measures

Network	Closeness	Network	Closeness	Network	Closeness
Erdos_Renyi	0.3734	Pref_Attach	0.3806	Ring	0.0113
Random_Geom	0.1714	Small_worlds	0.2362	Lattice	0.0808
Fitness_model	0.3631	Watts_Strogats	0.2418	Wheel	0.5035

worlds and wheel structures impose a curtailed effect on tax evasion, statistically significant lower than the benchmark; these effects may be seen in the statistically significant negative coefficients that these dummies attained in Table 1. Watts-Strogatz worlds seem to retain a statistically significant reduced effect with respect to the benchmark, nonetheless the estimated coefficient is relatively modest in comparison to the alternative networks. Ultimately, the fitness function model conveys a small increase in the aggregate tax levels, nevertheless limited to a minor statistical significance. As a final word, the closeness of wheel networks, as seen in Table 2 is markedly high, however it is not efficient in the sense of enhancing tax compliance; consequently, a large centrality is no guarantee for discouraging tax evasion. A possible explanation may be that, for each network, the loss-aversion distribution changes. The fitness model, based on income proximity, accounts for the fastest speed of bell-shape convergence of ρ, making it close to reality, whereas other structures have large fractions of agents with very low, or very high, loss-aversion levels.

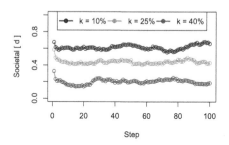

Fig. 7. Aggregate tax compliance   **Fig. 8.** Mean subjective probability

A robustness check took into account the aggregate convergence results provided by previous ABM's of tax compliance. Figures 7 and 8 illustrate the emergence of a bottom-up compliance behavior, both in the fraction of aggregate declared income and for the average perceived audit probability. In Fig. 7, even if the agents act independently and do not know the exact declared income of others, they converge to an aggregate level of tax compliance; the oscillating convergence at three different steady states is presented with respect to their respective levels of societal tax morale, for $\kappa = \{10\%, 25\%, 40\%\}$ and $p = 5\%$,

$\theta = 2$, and $\tau = 30\%$. In Fig. 8, in spite of the seemingly accurate mean perceived probability, a t-test proved that agents overestimated the true audit rate for $p = 2\%$ and $p = 6\%$ yet they underestimated it at the $p = 10\%$ level; where $\kappa = 25\%$, $\theta = 2$, and $\tau = 30\%$. Accordingly, agents consistently fail to discover the true audit rate both individually and collectively.

Alm et al. [14] studied individual tax evasion by means of economics and discovered that over two thirds of individuals either fully-evade or fully-comply, generating a dichotomous distribution of the share of income disclosed; a behavior which is not supported by the standard expected utility theory. Figure 9 depicts the last idea that the power utility model has to offer by reproducing the dichotomous behavior of individual taxpayers found in economic experiments for different levels of tax morale. Intriguingly, a power utility model with social interactions may be able to replicate not only the aggregate, but also the individual level results found in the literature of experimental economics.

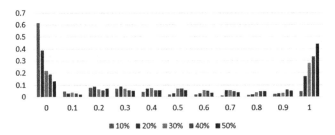

Fig. 9. Histogram of individually declared income for varying *tax-morale*

5   Conclusions

An expected utility theory tax evasion model was presented under a power-utility function specification and implemented through an Agent-Based model with heterogeneous agents and local social interactions, simulated over different underlying network structures. Agents have limited knowledge about their surroundings yet may acquire endogenous parameters of loss-aversion and audit rates, depending not only on their income levels but also in the corresponding ones from their neighbors. An exploratory setup shed light in the possibility of choosing specific network structures which may yield a more realistic result, particularly for the calibration of endogenous parameters as loss-aversion. Following, a fitness-function model that accounts for age and social status (income) was questioned and deemed to be appropriate for modeling taxpayers' behavior. In top of that, the assumption on the information exchanged is relaxed from communicating evasion rates and payoffs to simply sharing their past memories about the occurrence or not of former audits.

There is a large area of action for public policy makers in the further study of how audit rates and fines non-linearly increase tax compliance, yet both tools tend to lose effect whenever over-enforced. Whilst tax rates have a non-linear negative impact on income disclosure, tax morale offers an opportunity for governments with an unreceptive image among their citizens to call for a larger voluntary tax contribution by attending for a better public image of government spending or by strengthening their political inclusion. Moreover, an interesting property of the model specification is its capability of reproducing both individual behavioral patters and aggregate convergence levels of tax compliance as the encountered in experimental economics literature. Lastly, a novel parameter for the closeness centrality of the networks was tested and found to be a non-linear channel through which societies may converge to higher tax compliance rates for more closely connected social structures.

References

1. Allingham, M.G., Sandmo, A.: Income tax evasion: a theoretical analysis. J. Public Econ. **1**(3–4), 323–338 (1972)
2. Mittone, L., Patelli, P.: Imitative behaviour in tax evasion. In: Luna, F., Stefansson, B. (eds) Economic Simulations in Swarm: Agent-Based Modelling and Object Oriented Programming, vol. 14. Springer, Boston (2000). https://doi.org/10.1007/978-1-4615-4641-2_5
3. Davis, J., Hecht, G., Perkins, J.: Social behaviors, enforcement, and tax compliance dynamics. Acc. Rev. **78**, 39–69 (2003)
4. Hokamp, S., Pickhardt, M.: Income tax evasion in a society of heterogeneous agents: evidence from an agent-based model. Int. Econ. J. **24**(4), 541–553 (2010)
5. Korobow, A., Johnson, C., Axtell, R.: An agent-based model of tax compliance with social networks. Nat. Tax J. **30**(3), 589–610 (2007)
6. Andrei, A.L., Comer, K., Koehler, M.: An agent-based model of network effects on tax compliance and evasion. J. Econ. Psychol. **40**(C), 119–133 (2014)
7. Billari, F., Diaz, B.A., Fent, T., Prskawetz, A.: The wedding-ring. Demographic Res. **17**(3), 59–82 (2007)
8. Alm, J., Bloomquist, K.M., McKee, M.: When you know your neighbour pays taxes: information, peer effects, and tax compliance. In: Working Paper Series No. 6775. Victoria University of Wellington (2017)
9. Myles, G., Naylor, R.: A model of tax evasion with group conformity and social customs. Eur. J. Polit. Econ. **12**(1), 49–66 (1996)
10. Luttmer, E.F.P., Singhal, M.: Tax morale. J. Econ. Perspect. **28**(4), 149–168 (2014)
11. Tversky, A., Kahneman, D.: Availability: a heuristic for judging frequency and probability. Cogn. Psychol. **5**, 207–232 (1973)
12. Alm, J., Jackson, B., McKee, M.: Estimating the determinants of taxpayer compliance with experimental data. Nat. Tax J. **45**(1), 107–114 (1992)
13. Kirchler, E., Hoelzl, E., Wahl, I.: Enforced versus voluntary tax compliance: the "slippery slope" framework. J. Econ. Psychol. **29**(2), 210–225 (2008)
14. Alm, J., McClelland, G.H., Schulze, W.D.: Why do people pay taxes? J. Public Econ. **48**(1), 21–38 (1992)

A New Deep Hierarchical Neural Network Applied in Human Activity Recognition (HAR) Using Wearable Sensors

Zahra Ghorrati$^{(\boxtimes)}$ and Eric T. Matson

Purdue University, West Lafayette, IN 47907, USA
{zghorrat,ematson}@purdue.edu

Abstract. Human Activity Recognition (HAR) using wearable sensors is becoming more practical in the field of security and health care monitoring. Deep and Machine learning techniques have been widely used in this area. Since smartphones and their applications are the parts of daily life, they can be very helpful in data gathering and online learning in HAR problems. In this paper, a new hierarchical neural network structure with the hierarchical learning method is presented and applied to the HAR. The proposed model is a deep learner neural network without using heavy computations that CNN-based deep learners usually suffer from. This makes the suggested model suitable for being embedded in agent and multi-agent based solutions and online learning, especially when they are implemented in small devices such as smartphones. In addition the hidden layer of the first section of the proposed model benefits automatic nonlinear feature extraction. The extracted features are proper for classifications. Handling the dimension of data is one of the challenges in HAR problem. In our model, data dimension reduction is automatically performed in the hidden layers of the different network sections. According to the empirical results, our proposed model yields better performance on the Opportunity data sets, compared to the similar ML algorithms.

Keywords: Human Activity Recognition · Deep learning ·
Wearable sensors · Agent · Multi-agent

1 Introduction

Recently, human activity recognition problem has become a popular research field due to the large number of applications it can be used in. It plays a main role in several research areas such as health care, military, behavior analysis, agent, multi agent modeling and human interaction systems [1–3]. The pioneering work on HARP was in the late 90s [4]. They focused on proving the high reliability of the accelerometer for posture and motions detection. HAR problem is considered a classical pattern recognition (PR) problem [5], so techniques are applied in PR problems are considered as solutions in this area. In HAR the input data come

© Springer Nature Switzerland AG 2019
Y. Demazeau et al. (Eds.): PAAMS 2019, LNAI 11523, pp. 90–102, 2019.
https://doi.org/10.1007/978-3-030-24209-1_8

from different types of sensors such as external, wearable and hybrid. Depending on the types of the sensors used in HAR, different machine learning approaches are applied to recognize human activities. Among them, external sensors are useful in security and monitoring, however, due to the limitation of using these sensors, wearable sensors are more preferable. Cameras are among the widely used external sensors, but as mentioned in [6], there are some problems about using them, such as *privacy* (people do not like to be monitored by camera in their daily life), *tracking specific target* (attaching the video to the specific target for activity monitoring is difficult), and *computation problem* (video processing is computationally expensive and needs more resources). Due to the problems that external sensors have, recently wearable based HAR has become more popular and has been widely used. Examples of wearable sensors are accelerometers, gyroscopes, and sound sensors. Some of them are listed in [6,7]. more over, wearable sensors are useful for the necessary treatment of the patients at their home after they face some problems such as heart attack, diabetes, or Parkinson disease [8].

HAR can usually be defined as a time series problem. Such a definition can be as follows:

Given a window W of time interval from t_i to t_j, that includes the set of time series $S = \{S_0, ..., S_{k-1}\}$ from each of the k measured features, determining the activity, performed during the time W from the predefined set of the activities, is the goal. Examples of the activities are walking, eating, sitting, etc. Due to the different sensors used in HAR problem, dimension reduction and feature extraction are challenges in this area. PR methods have been widely used to reduce the dimension and extract the features from the data. There are many approaches for feature extraction in time series data. One of them is using the statistical features in Time-domain such as mean, variance, correlation between axes, mean absolute deviation, root mean square, standard deviation [9]. Another approach is based on frequency-domain features such as Fourier transform, and the Wavelet transform [9]. The next approach is mapping and transforming the feature from the current space to the new space. The mapping approach can be linear or nonlinear. Principal Component Analysis (PCA) [10] and Linear Discriminant Analysis (LDA) are a standard linear technique used in dimension reduction and feature extraction for HAR and PR problems. In [11,12] PCA finds an orthonormal subspace. PCA's basis vectors are in the directions of maximum variance of input variables. Overall PCA transforms a number of correlated variables into a number (that could be smaller number) of uncorrelated variables called principal components. Another version of the PCA called kernel PCA (KPCA) that is the nonlinear PCA used for the dimension reduction in HAR problem [13,14]. PCA is a proper method for data representation so is not essentially has the optimum features proper for class separability [15]. While for classification problems, is more useful to reach maximum discrimination [16]. Hence, LDA can be the alternative choice for the dimension reduction in classification problem, but still the problem suffers from the linearity of the method. In our proposed method we used a nonlinear automatic dimension reduction in the output of the hidden layer of each section of the model. Machine learning techniques try to extract the high-level information from the low-level data. Some PR approaches for HAR problem were surveyed in [5] such as decision tree, support vector machine, naive Bayes (NB), and hidden Markov models. However, the aforementioned methods have some problem for example High Correlation features of the signals come from some sensors such as acceleration or heart rate affect the necessary assumption in order to use the Naive Basie (NB) approach [5]. Other different classifiers were compared in [17] including C4.5 (J48) decision tree, multi-layer perception, logistic, k-nearest neighbor (kNN), and meta-algorithms such as boosting and bagging. They also introduced K-nearest neighbors (KNN) as the best classifier, but KNN has problem to classify the activities, effectively, that are similar. The most popular machine learning techniques for PR and HAR problem are deep learning neural network. Different deep learning approaches are proposed for HAR problem. Among the deep learning techniques Convolutional Neural Network (CNN) is the famous one, however training deep CNN requires the heavy calculation and sources which makes it challenging for real-time classification. So due to the computational limits of the smart phones, deep CNN techniques are not a proper choice for using in real-time classification in this device. A user-independent deep learning is proposed in [18], the model is a CNN, combines local and global features come from CNN and characteristics of the time series data respectively. [18] proposed using the CNN for extracting the local feature and statistical features together. However the results just based on the data come from accelerometer. Recently [19] researched the different proposed data fusions and classifiers such as kalman filtering and deep-learning algorithms. The paper focuses on wearable sensors and mobile devices. They categorised different methods and compared their strength and weaknesses in HAR problems also introduced some open research direction in the area. [20] surveys some existing deep learner approaches for HAR problem. In this paper the proposed model is compared with several deep-learning model that tested on Opportunity data set and mentioned in the survey paper. The rest of the paper arranged as follows: section two proposes a new deep learner model, architecture and training algorithm. Section 3 provides experiment and results over the Opportunity data set as a benchmark and finally section four summarizes our conclusion.

2   Proposed Model

In this section a new hierarchical deep neural network is proposed. Figure 1 shows the architecture of the proposed network.

2.1   Architecture

As it is shown in the Fig. 1 The proposed model has several sections. Each section made up of the three layers. First layer is an input, second is a hidden and third one is an output layer that classifies the patterns of the input data. Except the first section that takes its input from the time window of the output of the sensors, Input of each section can be constructed from the output of the previous section's hidden layer, using two different methods:

– Passing through the filters having the different time coefficients.
– Applying the different time delays.

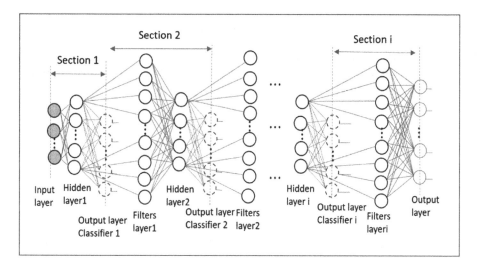

Fig. 1. The architecture of the proposed model

The output layer of the last section is the output of the network. The following formulas show the related equation for the input and output of the different sections:

$$I(t) = [X(t)^T, X(t-1)^T, \ldots, X(t-T)^T]^T \tag{1}$$

I is the input of the first layer where $X(t)$ is the prepossessed data from the outputs of the sensors at t. Here T is the time window of inputs.

$$O^{(i,j)}(t) = [o_1^{(i,j)}(t), \ldots, o_n^{(i,j)}(t)]^T \tag{2}$$

$o_n^{(i,j)}$ shows that the output of the layer j of the section i of the network. n shows the neuron's number in the same layer. The output for the first layer of Sect. 1 is:

$$O^{(1,1)}(t) = I(t) \tag{3}$$

The output of the first layer of the section i for i=2, 3,.. are as follows:

$$O^{(i,1)}(t) = [S_1^{(i)}(t)^T, S_2^{(i)}(t)^T, \ldots, S_k^{(i)}(t)^T]^T \tag{4}$$

As it mentioned above two different methods are suggested for constructing the input of each layer from The output of the previous layer hence, $S_k^{(i)}$, constructed input for the next layer, could be calculated from any of them:

- *Method1:* input created by Passing the previous layer's output from filters, having the different time coefficients.

$$S_k^{(i)}(t) = (1 - \alpha_k)S_k^{(i)}(t - \Delta) + \alpha_k O^{(i-1,2)}(t) \tag{5}$$

where α_k is a time coefficient for k–th filter.
- *Method2:* input created by applying the different time delays on the outputs of the previous layer.

$$S_k^{(i)}(t) = O^{(i-1,2)}(t - (k - 1)\Delta) \tag{6}$$

Here Δ called delay, $T - \Delta$ is the overlapping time between the windows.

In each layer the activation function will be applied to the multiplication of the weight and output

$$O^{(i,j)}(t) = F(W^{(i,j)}O^{(i,j-1)}(t)) \tag{7}$$

where F is the activation function and $W^{(i,j)}$ is the weight between the layer of *j-1* to *j* for section i of the network, for *j=2,3,...*

2.2   Learning Algorithm

Training the network is hierarchical. Network is trained as a series of the sections and each section is trained separately. Training is started from the first section in series and will be continued to the last one. In the network the Primary sections will represent the low-level actions and middle sections represent middle-level actions and the last section represent high-level actions. The cross entropy is used as an error function in each section. The updating rules of the weights by minimizing the error function is explained below. Training of the whole network is different from the training of the NN in side of the each section and is hierarchical. During the training phase, the whole network is supposed as a series of the sections. Training starts from the first section and will be continued to the last one separately in a sequence. After completing the training of the NN of the same section, each step, the last layer of the NN in same section will be omitted and the output of its hidden layer will be send as an input to the next section that is positioned after this section in the series. Following same procedure, the next NN will be trained as a usual NN, and again the last layer of the same NN will be omitted and the output of the hidden layer will be send to the next one and it will be continued to reach the last NN in the series. The last layer of the last NN is the out put of the network and will not be omitted. Figure 1 shows the network structure and different sections in the network.

$$E = -\sum_t \sum_l c_l(X(t)) \log O_l^{(i,3)}(t) \tag{8}$$

where $O_l^{(i,3)}(t)$ is the lth output of the *third* layer of the section i of the network, and $c_l(X(t))$ shows the class of the input data $(X(t))$ as follows:

$$c_l(X(t)) = \begin{cases} 1, & \text{if } X(t) \in \text{ class } l \\ 0, & \text{if } X(t) \notin \text{ class } l \end{cases} \quad (9)$$

$$O_l^{(i,3)}(t) = F(W_l^{(i,3)}O^{(i,2)}(t)) \quad (10)$$

where $W_l^{(i,3)}$ is the lth row of the weight matrix from the layer two to layer three of the section i of the network.

$$O^{(i,2)}(t) = F(W^{(i,2)}O^{(i,1)}(t)) \quad (11)$$

Using the gradient method, updating the weights in layer 2 and 3 of each section of the network is as follows:

$$\Delta W_l^{(i,3)} = -\eta \frac{\partial E}{\partial W_l^{(i,3)}} \quad (12)$$

Due to the hierarchical nature, HAR problem has, deep Learning (DL) approaches are suitable for it [13, 18, 21, 22] in [20]

$$\Delta W^{(i,2)} = -\eta \frac{\partial E}{\partial W^{(i,2)}} \quad (13)$$

$$\frac{\partial E}{\partial W_l^{(i,3)}} = -\sum_t \frac{c_l(X(t))}{O_l^{(i,3)}(t)} F'(W_l^{(i,3)}O^{(i,2)}(t))(O^{(i,2)}(t))^T \quad (14)$$

$$\frac{\partial E}{\partial W^{(i,2)}} = -\sum_t \sum_l \frac{c_l(X(t))}{O_l^{(i,3)}(t)} F'(W_l^{(i,3)}O^{(i,2)}(t))$$
$$[(W_l^{(i,3)})^T . F'(W_l^{(i,2)}O^{(i,1)}(t))](O^{(i,1)}(t))^T \quad (15)$$

3   Experiment and Results

To evaluate the performance of the proposed model we used Opportunity (Op) data set [23, 24]. The data set is available in UCI repository. The original data set included different sensors: body worn, Object, and Ambient, which are used for gathering data while users' daily activities are applied". In our experiments, the data come from wearable sensors which included 7inertial measurement units, 12 3D acceleration sensors are considered for HAR problem. They used 30 per second sampling rate for sensor signals. In this paper three of the 4 existing subjects in the data set and 6 runs per subject are used. Activity of Daily Living (ADL) characterized by a natural execution of daily activities are included 5 of the runs. To generate many activity instances and for enriching the data set, the 6th run that is called "drill" run that is a predefined activities is executed, and Each subject execute a scripted sequence. For example, the ADL1, ADL2, ADL3, ADL4, ADL5 and Drill, of Subject S1 contain 51116, 32224, 33273, 32955, 30127 and 54966, records, respectively. Each record is further comprised of 113 real valued sensory readings and the time information is not included. There are 2 different focuses in this data set our first focus is classifying modes of locomotion that is 5 classes which are standing, sitting, lying, walking and no action and next, we focus on classifying mid-level actions called gesture used for recognizing the arm movements which has 18 classes for example, open door, close door, open dishwasher, close dishwasher, etc and no action. The structure used for the experiments is the proposed method1, already explained in Sect. 2. Different structures of the proposed model are tested for both experiment. The different structures started from one section to 4 sections were tested in each experiment. Activation function used in each node of the middle layer of the each section is tangent hyperbolic and for the last layer sigmoid function has been used. The results are reported in Tables 1 and 2. The method1 that explained in Sect. 2 is used for both experiments. The accuracy of each subject reported individually for the different structure. For testing the proposed model independent from the subjects, the accuracy for all the subject with different structure is also reported in the last column of Tables 1 and 2.

3.1   Experiment 1

For the first experiment we used the proposed model for classifying the 5 classes (i.e. modes of locomotion). the parameters set was: 50 neurons for the hidden layer and four filters with different coefficient in each section and the values selected for the coefficient of the filters are as follows alpha1 = .99, alpha2 = .66, alpha3 = .33, alpha4 = .01. They are same for all the sections of the model. For each subject the first 3 ADLs and drill of each subject used as a training data also ADL4 and ADL5 used as a testing data for the same subject. Total (Train+test) performance for each subject individually and for whole data for the different structure of proposed model reported on Table 1. According to the result the proposed model with four sections has the better performance. This is because in each section of the proposed model the past histories of the activity are memorized and the model can memorized more histories by adding more sections. Since the activity recognition is hierarchically, the performance of the model on recognizing those activities that are needed more past histories, is better. Second reason related to the nature of the Neural network. By adding more layers in neural network the classifier become more complex that means the classifier will have better performance until doesn't overfit the data. Since early stopping method has been used in each section, there is no overfitting on the data then by adding more sections the performance of the model is higher. This is shown on Fig. 2. It is shown in the figure the training error and testing error is decreasing in each epoch. Early stopping is a form of regularization used to avoid overfitting during the training of machine learner. By using this method training stops when the testing error increases while the training error decreases. To be able to compare the performance of the proposed model with other models, several methods from [22] and [25] are used in Table 4. As it is shown in the Table 2, our proposed model has better performance for subject 2 and 3. Comparing to the other methods For subject 1, the proposed model has the better performance than method no 1 and 2. The Receiver Operator Characteristic (ROC) curve for total (Train+test) and test data for the proposed model are shown in Figs. 4 and 5 respectively. According to the Fig. 4 the Curves are closer to the top-left corner. Since, for the classifiers, curves closer to the top-left corner shows a better performance, proves that the proposed method shows the high performance for classifying the locomotion with 5 classes in the experiment. A confusion matrix (CF) is a table that is used to describe the performance of a classification model is shown in Fig. 3. The CF is based on the 4 sections used in the proposed model and for classifying the 5 locomotion classes The predicted class (Output Class) are shown on the rows and the columns correspond to the true class (Target Class). The number of the instances recognized correctly by the model are shown in diagonal cell of the matrix. The incorrectly classified observations have been shown in off-diagonal cells. The number and the percentage of the total number of observations are presented in each cell in inner matrix. In the outer right side of the main matrix the percentages of all the instances predicted which is belong to each class, and classified correctly and incorrectly, are shown.

3.2   Experiment 2

In this experiment 18 classes ie mid-level actions are used from OP data set for classification. The number of the neurons used in the hidden layer of section1, section2, section3 and section4 are 150, 50, 100 and 50 respectively. The number of the filters and their coefficients in the each section are the same as used in the previous experiment. Also, In this experiment, followed by [22] and [25] we used Drill and first two sets of ADLs (ADL1 and ADL2) of each subject as the training data and ADL3 as the testing data. The accuracy for each subject is individually reported in Table 3. Table 3 shows that Our proposed model with 4 sections outperforms all other structures for the same model. It shows that the proposed model have higher performance when we have a deeper structure. Due to the several tested has done in this paper. Results shows that in overall the performance on the S2 and S3 is better than the other subject. [25] also reported that their proposed method perform better on S2 and S3. In [26] they reported the better performance for their proposed method on the test set. Since they used S2 as a test set in their experiments and reported the performance on the test set, this might be one of the reason why they reach high performance on their test set include *Null class* for both method DeepConvLSTM and Baseline CNN. In their paper they report the result for the locomotion classes Baseline CNN = 0.912 DeepConvLSTM = 0.930 and for the gesture class Baseline CNN = 0.883 and DeepConvLSTM = 0.915 which is a exceptional performance compare to the other method, but they didn't provide the performance for each subject separately. Compared to other existing models the result in Table 4 show that our proposed model has a higher performance in recognizing the mid level activities for all the subjects.

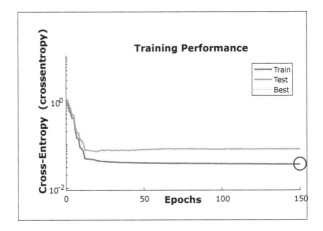

Fig. 2. Locomotion error with 5 classes

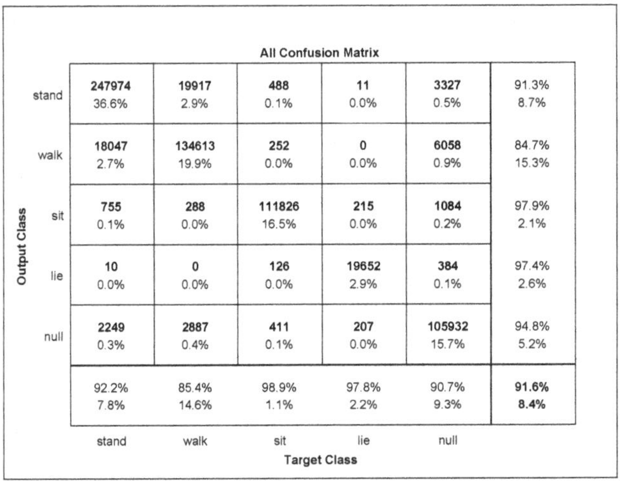

Fig. 3. Confusion matrix of the all data for the locomotion with the 5 classes

Table 1. Total and test performance of different section of the proposed model for each subject with 5 classes

Sec no.	Subject1 (s1)		Subject2 (s2)		Subject3 (s3)		*All* subjects	
	Tot	Test	Tot	Test	Tot	Test	Tot	Test
1	82.90	73.80	91.50	87.98	89.85	80.85	87.39	84.35
2	86.61	80.06	93.37	88.60	91.87	82.67	90.45	86.84
3	87.81	81.21	93.61	88.66	92.86	83.39	91.20	87.29
4	89.83	81.67	94.15	89.00	93.39	83.80	91.62	87.31

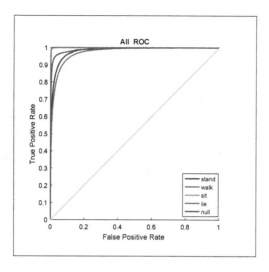

Fig. 4. ROC of the all data for Locomotion with 5 classes

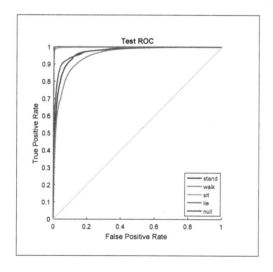

Fig. 5. ROC of the test data for Locomotion with 5 classes

Table 2. Comparing the accuracy of the different classifier for the locomotion with 5 classes

No.	Method	S1	S2	S3
1	1NN [25]	89.8	89.8	88.4
2	SPO+1NN [25]	89.7	89.9	88.4
3	SPO+1NN+Smooth [25]	92.7	92.7	90.8
4	SVM [25]	92.8	88.8	87.3
5	SPO+SVM [25]	93.1	89.2	87.4
6	SPO+SVM+smooth [25]	94.5	90.0	89.1
7	Integrated frame work [25]	94.5	91.7	90.8
8	Proposed method	89.83	94.15	93.39

Table 3. Total and test performance of different section of the proposed model for each subject with 18 classes

Sec no.	Subject1 (s1)		Subject2 (s2)		Subject3 (s3)		*All* subjects	
	Tot	Test	Tot	Test	Tot	Test	Tot	Test
1	85.10	70.83	94.47	88.86	91.14	85.80	89.26	87.21
2	88.25	84.35	95.64	90.15	93.46	87.73	91.92	89.19
3	91.01	84.42	96.95	90.21	95.51	88.07	93.17	89.19
4	91.83	85.25	97.19	90.22	96.0	88.10	95.11	89.23

Table 4. Comparing accuracy of different classifier for gesture with 18 classes

No.	Method	S1	S2	S3
1	1NN [25]	79.3	73.9	63.8
2	SPO+1NN [25]	80.9	75.7	80.2
3	SPO+1NN+Smooth [25]	84.5	80.4	84.2
4	SVM [25]	83.4	79.4	78.1
5	SPO+SVM [25]	86.9	81.5	82.6
6	SPO+SVM+smooth [25]	88.2	82.6	84.1
7	integrated frame work [25]	86.8	82.7	86.8
8	MV [22]	83.7	74.3	80.7
9	DBN [22]	80.0	74.1	79.3
10	CNN [22]	87.0	82.5	85.8
11	Proposed method	91.83	97.19	96.0

4 Conclusion

In this paper a new hierarchical deep Neural network is proposed for human activity recognition. Two different learning methods are presented for the training of the proposed model. The model has an automatic nonlinear feature extraction that are proper for the classification. Network has the different section that apply data dimension reduction automatically in the hidden layers of each one. Opportunity data set is used for testing the performance of the proposed model as a benchmark. Compare to the several existing methods including CNN the proposed model has the good performance in recognizing the locomotion with 5 classes and outperforms other seven existing models and has the best performance to recognize 18 classes of the mid-level actions. Adding more sections to the network had the positive impact on the performance of it and deeper network could be able to recognize the activities with the higher performance. Also it shows that the deeper model has potential to recognize the higher level activities.

References

1. Fatima, I., Fahim, M., Lee, Y.-K., Lee, S.: A unified framework for activity recognition-based behavior analysis and action prediction in smart homes. Sensors **13**(2), 2682–2699 (2013)
2. Gomez, M.A., Chibani, A., Amirat, Y., Matson, E.T.: Iort cloud survivability framework for robotic aals using harms. Robot. Auton. Syst. **106**, 192–206 (2018)
3. Kim, M., et al.: A harmsbased heterogenous human-robot team for gattering and collecting. Adv. Robot. Res. **2**, 201–217 (2018)
4. Foerster, F., Smeja, M., Fahrenberg, J.: Detection of posture and motion by accelerometry: a validation study in ambulatory monitoring. Comput. Hum. Behav. **15**(5), 571–583 (1999)
5. Avci, A., Bosch, S., Marin-Perianu, M., Marin-Perianu, R., Havinga, P.: Activity recognition using inertial sensing for healthcare, wellbeing and sports applications: a survey. In: 2010 23rd International Conference on Architecture of Computing Systems (ARCS), pp. 1–10. VDE (2010)
6. Lara, O.D., Labrador, M.A., et al.: A survey on human activity recognition using wearable sensors. IEEE Commun. Surv. Tutor. **15**(3), 1192–1209 (2013)
7. Mukhopadhyay, S.C.: Wearable sensors for human activity monitoring: a review. IEEE Sens. J. **15**(3), 1321–1330 (2015)
8. Mariani, B., Jiménez, M.C., Vingerhoets, F.J., Aminian, K.: On-shoe wearable sensors for gait and turning assessment of patients with parkinson's disease. IEEE Trans. Biomed. Eng. **60**(1), 155–158 (2013)
9. Olszewski, R.T.: Generalized feature extraction for structural pattern recognition in time-series data. Technical report, School of Computer Science, Carnegie-Mellon University, Pittsburgh, PA (2001)
10. Pearson, K.: LIII. On lines and planes of closest fit to systems of points in space. London Edinburgh Dublin Philos. Mag. J. Sci. **2**(11), 559–572 (1901)
11. Fergani, B., et al.: Evaluating a new classification method using PCA to human activity recognition. In: 2013 International Conference on Computer Medical Applications (ICCMA), pp. 1–4. IEEE (2013)

12. M'Hamed Bilal Abidine, B.F.: Evaluating a new classification method using PCA to human activity recognition
13. Hassan, M.M., Uddin, M.Z., Mohamed, A., Almogren, A.: A robust human activity recognition system using smartphone sensors and deep learning. Future Gener. Comput. Systems **81**, 307–313 (2018)
14. Kuspa, K., Pratkanis, T.: Classification of mobile device accelerometer data for unique activity identification (2013)
15. Lerner, B., Guterman, H., Aladjem, M., Dinstein, I., Romem, Y.: Feature extraction by neural network nonlinear mapping for pattern classification. In: Proceedings of the 13th International Conference on Pattern Recognition 1996, vol. 4, pp. 320–324. IEEE (1996)
16. Bengio, Y., et al.: Learning deep architectures for AI. Found. Trends® Mach. Learn **2**(1), 1–127 (2009)
17. Wu, W., Dasgupta, S., Ramirez, E.E., Peterson, C., Norman, G.J.: Classification accuracies of physical activities using smartphone motion sensors. J. Med. Internet Res. **14**(5), e130 (2012)
18. Ignatov, A.: Real-time human activity recognition from accelerometer data using convolutional neural networks. Appl. Soft Comput. **62**, 915–922 (2018)
19. Nweke, H.F., Teh, Y.W., Mujtaba, G., Al-Garadi, M.A.: Data fusion and multiple classifier systems for human activity detection and health monitoring: review and open research directions. Inform. Fusion **46**, 147–170 (2019)
20. Wang, J., Chen, Y., Hao, S., Peng, X., Hu, L.: Deep learning for sensor-based activity recognition: a survey. Pattern Recogn. Lett. (2018)
21. Ronao, C.A., Cho, S.-B.: Human activity recognition with smartphone sensors using deep learning neural networks. Expert Syst. Appl. **59**, 235–244 (2016)
22. Yang, J., Nguyen, M.N., San, P.P., Li, X., Krishnaswamy, S.: Deep convolutional neural networks on multichannel time series for human activity recognition. In: IJCAI, vol. 15, pp. 3995–4001 (2015)
23. Roggen, D., et al.: Collecting complex activity datasets in highly rich networked sensor environments. In: 2010 Seventh International Conference on Networked Sensing Systems (INSS), pp. 233–240. IEEE (2010)
24. Chavarriaga, R., et al.: The opportunity challenge: a benchmark database for on-body sensor-based activity recognition. Pattern Recogn. Lett. **34**(15), 2033–2042 (2013)
25. Cao, H., Nguyen, M.N., Phua, C., Krishnaswamy, S., Li, X.: An integrated framework for human activity classification. In: UbiComp, pp. 331–340 (2012)
26. Ordóñez, F.J., Roggen, D.: Deep convolutional and lstm recurrent neural networks for multimodal wearable activity recognition. Sensors **16**(1), 115 (2016)

Approximating Multi-attribute Resource Allocations Using GAI Utility Functions

Charles Harold[1]([⊠]), Mohan Baruwal Chhetri[1], and Ryszard Kowalczyk[1,2]

[1] Swinburne University of Technology, Melbourne, Australia
{charold,mchhetri,rkowalczyk}@swin.edu.au
[2] Systems Research Institute, Polish Academy of Sciences, Warsaw, Poland

Abstract. The design of Multi-Attribute Double-Sided Auctions (MADSA) is an important problem being examined in a variety of domains. Despite significant efforts, an ideal compromise between expressiveness of preference representation and the tractability of MADSA mechanisms is still subject to much debate. In this paper, we propose a MADSA mechanism whereby bids are placed in the form of Generalised Additive Independent-Decomposable (GAI-D) utility functions. We show that by applying a set of constraints on the composition of these functions a relaxation of the Kalai bargaining solution becomes tractable for large double-sided markets. Experimental results show that the proposed mechanism provides efficient results when compared to the well known k-priced greedy market mechanism.

Keywords: Generalised additive utility functions ·
Multi-attribute double-sided auctions · Bargaining solutions

1 Introduction

The design of market mechanisms that can efficiently allocate multi-attribute items amongst groups of agents is an open problem being examined in a variety of problem domains including the allocation of: virtual machines [2,6,16,21], network bandwidth [12,14], plug-in electric vehicle charge points [3] and many others. Much of the literature in these fields examines the use of *multi-attribute double-sided auctions* (MADSA) to find efficient allocations of goods. However, design of these mechanisms is complicated by several (often in-compatible) objectives that need to be considered; such as: tractability, budget balance, individual rationality, incentive compatibility and allocative efficiency [16,23].

Primarily, this research examines allocative efficiency and its inherent trade-off with the tractability of markets. It is well known that increasing the information presented to a market often increases its allocative efficiency [4,22]. However, this extra information adds computational complexity when arbitrating (or pricing) market pairings [4,22,30]; leading to a trade-off between tractability of the market and the preference representation of participants. Subsequently, an

© Springer Nature Switzerland AG 2019
Y. Demazeau et al. (Eds.): PAAMS 2019, LNAI 11523, pp. 103–114, 2019.
https://doi.org/10.1007/978-3-030-24209-1_9

abundance of research [6,16,21,30] has examined different preference representation models that can be used in tractable market mechanisms. Despite this, an appropriate model for preference representation in MADSA is still missing.

In this paper we define a special case of Generalized Additive Independence-Decomposable (GAI-D) utilities [10]. We show that adherence to constraints on the composition of these utilities leads to a natural relaxation of the Kalai bargaining solution that keeps pricing tractable. To validate the performance and versatility of this approach we use the motivating example of allocating parking spaces and power charging facilities amongst a set of autonomous vehicles. Specifically, we conduct a series of experiments where multi-attribute bids from car-parks and electric vehicles are placed into a double-sided market mechanism. Each possible pairing is then priced using our proposed approach and the common k-pricing mechanism [23]; a greedy algorithm is then employed to select the final bid pairings. Comparison of results shows that our approach is highly effective in markets where a "win-win" scenario exists.

The remainder of this paper is organised as follows. After first defining its motivating scenario (Sect. 2) this paper presents a brief overview of the literature relating to mechanism design and bargaining solutions (Sect. 3). Section 4 defines our proposed mechanism. Sections 5 and 6 then detail our methods of analysis, present a summary of results and discuss their implications. Section 7 concludes the paper by summarising our research and outlining potential extensions to the proposed mechanism.

2   Motivating Scenario

Currently, in many major cities around the world up to 30% of traffic in metropolitan areas can be attributed to cars looking for parking spaces [19]. The economic, environmental and social costs of this have sparked research into parking guidance systems that direct vehicles to available parking [1,11,26]. However, the parking guidance systems reviewed do not consider the integration of *autonomous electric vehicles* (AEVs) into these systems. We consider this to be an important consideration for several reasons, including:

(1) AEVs will be able to balance power usage and parking costs so that inherently there will exist price points at which parking becomes more expensive than driving around meaninglessly. Rational vehicles will then avoid utilising parking resources, potentially adding to road congestion.
(2) As electric vehicle usage has expanded so has the literature examing the allocation of Plug-in Electric Vehicle (PEV) points [3,25]. We consider PEV allocation as a specific case of parking/charging time allocation where both items need to be purchased in equal quantity.

This research proposes that the aforementioned issues can be addressed through the application of an efficient economic market mechanism. More specifically, we consider this problem a resource allocation problem amongst a set of autonomous self-interested agents; therefore subject to tradeoffs between allocative efficiency and tractability.

3   Related Work

The benefits of resolving resource allocation issues through *auctions* have been studied extensively in the field of *Multi-Agent Systems* (MAS) [28]. However, complications arise when the goods to be allocated by these auctions have multiple attributes, such as the case when parking-time, distance and power-charge rate attributes are included in the allocation of AEV parking facilities. Given that AEV parking requires allocating such complex goods, the application of *Multi-Attribute Auctions* (MAAs) to allocate parking and charging resources for AEVs seems intuitive.

Allowing for unique configurations of multi-attribute goods for each bidder has, in-general, yielded better results than creating predetermined lots for bidders to bid over [4,22]. One method by which bidders can define their own configuration of goods is via a package bid (defining the amount of each attribute a bidder requires and the bid price). Much of the literature related to arbitration (or pricing) of multi-attribute package bids has focused on adaptation of the single item Vickrey auction, the most prevalent of which being the extensions proposed by Clarke and Groves, yielding the VCG mechanism [20]. However, as discussed at length by Rothkopf [20] this generalisation of the Vickrey auction has several issues, including: "problems related to capital limited bidders", "problems associated with various kinds of cheating", "the fact that strategies in sequences of strategy-proof auctions may not be strategy-proof". Furthermore, the VCG pricing mechanism is not budget balanced [20,24,28]. Thus, similarly to Schnizler et al. [24], we conclude that the k-pricing mechanism[1] is more practical than VCG pricing. Subsequently, we use k-pricing as a representative example of package bidding pricing in our experimentation.

A known limitation of single package bid market mechanisms is that bids cannot be changed by the auction house (as it may make participation non-individually rational). While many package based mechanisms try and address this issue (such as: XOR bidding, iterative markets etc.) this research considers the use of *utility bidding* most applicable in this context. However, the use of utility functions within an auction context faces two key challenges: (1) Tractability: The solution of arbitrary multi-dimensional bargaining problems is intractable [7]. (2) Elicitation: Defining utility functions in many practical scenarios has been shown to be non-trivial [5,10].

Definition 1. *A multi-attribute utility bid defined over a set of attributes has two components: (1) - the domain of values for each attribute that yields non-negative utility, and (2) - a (utility) function with codomain $\mathbb{R}_0^1$ for each combination of attribute assignments made within their respective domains.*

---

[1] When arbitrating bids k-pricing allocates the bid package defined by the bidder (assuming the vendor has sufficient volume of goods) at a price (P) between the two bids. Specifically, the excess value (difference between buyer offer B_o and vendor reserve V_r) is allocated between bidder and vendor according to some ratio k, that is $P = k \cdot (B_o - V_r) + V_r$ [24].

Arbitration (or pricing) of utility based bidding in auctions is often based on established results in game theory, known as bargaining solutions. Two of the most common bargaining solutions discussed in the literature are the Nash [18] and Kalai [15] solutions. The Nash solution seeks to maximize the product of excess utility gained through trade; while the Kalai (or egalitarian) solution minimizes the differences between utilities. The primary tradeoff between these solutions is that the Nash solution does not respect *resource monotonicity* (no party should lose utility when more goods are available to allocate), while the Kalai solution lacks *scale invariance* (i.e., the solution does not depend on the range or scale of the utility functions, only their shape). Computing bargaining solutions for multi-attribute utility functions is $\mathcal{NP}$-$\mathcal{H}$ [7] and thus intractable in many real world markets. Subsequently, the literature has explored a plethora of ways to restrict the forms of utility functions and create tractable bargaining solutions. Here we define one restricted form of utility functions, Generalised Additive Independent Utility (GAI). A GAI utility function is additively separable (or modular), with some subset of attribute members being non-disjoint [8]. Such functions exhibit some of the desirable tractable properties of *additive utility* while still supporting attribute interdependence [10].

Example 1. Given some budget, an AEV wants to purchase charging facilities at a car-park. With its value of money (m) dependent on the power offered (p), and its value of time (t) related to the power offered, the vehicle may then represent its utility using a decomposed GAI function, formally: $u_1(m)+u_2(t,p)+u_3(p,m)$.

Irrespective of bidding and pricing mechanism the clearing of an auction whereby multiple buyer and seller pairs are considered at the same time is known as a *double-sided auction* (DSAs)[2] [16]. In general, finding the ideal pairings of a DSA is an $\mathcal{NP}$-$\mathcal{H}$ combinatorial optimisation problem [29]. Accordingly, several means of approximating solutions to the DSA have been proposed in the literature, such as: Greedy approximations [2,6,21], Integer Programming approximations [12,14,29,30], Iterative auctions [3,13] and others. As our research focuses on pricing and bidding mechanisms we consider the simplest of these approaches (from an implementation perspective), greedy approximations. Greedy allocation mechanisms use a heuristic to identify and subsequently remove the best pairing from the market, this is done iteratively until the market is cleared.

A *multi-attribute double-sided auction* (MADSA) is a combination of the two aforementioned auctions that can resolve bids of multiple attributes from multiple buyers and sellers. Five common criterion used in the analysis of MADSA are [23]:

- *Economic efficiency (EE)*: specifically Pareto efficiency, refers an allocation of goods that cannot be changed to offer more utility to other participant/s without inducing a loss for other participant/s [27].
- *Individual rationality (IR)*: is satisfied when an agent does not risk a loss of utility by participating in the market [16].

---

[2] We only discuss non-continuous or call-market mechanisms in this paper.

- *Budget balance (BB)*: if an auction house makes a profit then it is weakly budget balanced, if the auction house neither loses or gains money through trading then the auction is strictly budget balanced [16].
- *Incentive compatibility (IC)*: Specifically *Bayesian-Nash incentive compatibility* (BNIC) is where a participant will bid truthfully when they can assume competitors also are bidding truthfully [17].
- *Tractability (T)*: A common assumption is that market mechanism must run in polynomial time [16].

Of all the impossibility results achieved in micro-economics, arguably the most relevant in the field of mechanism design is the Myerson-Satterthwaite result. Myerson and Satterthwaite [17] showed that it is *impossible* for any mechanism to simultaneously satisfy IR, BNIC and BB while being *ex*-post efficient[3]. This has created much discussion in the literature as to which of these properties is least significant in a practical context.

In summary, the literature would suggest that use of a MADSA where agents are able to express their preferences effectively would be highly applicable in the allocation of parking and charging facilities in the future. However, there are a variety of limitations when applying existing mechanisms directly to this problem. Our research shows that utility based bidding within the auction context is under represented in the literature despite its promising merits. Therefore, we propose to examine other means of defining utility functions that are both tractable and expressive within a MADSA context.

4 Overview of Conditional Utility Bidding

In an attempt to address issues regarding expressiveness and computational complexity of resolving pricing/arbitration in MADSA bidding this research proposes a bidding mechanism called *conditional utility bidding* (CUB). CUB is a special case of decomposed GAI utility functions whereby constraints are placed on the composition of utility functions. We show that given a set of utility bids conforming to this composition the arbitration (or pricing) of all bid pairs in a MADSA becomes tractable by taking a relaxation of the Kalai solution.

Formally, given a set of attributes to allocate, $\{x, y, z\}$, many utility functions can be composed as follows: $U(x, y, z) = U(x) + U(y|x) + U(z|x, y)$. That is, if each bidder can define how they value x, $[U(x)]$, then how they value y given some amount of x, $[U(y|x)]$ and finally how they value y given certain values of x and y, $[U(z|x, y)]$, then the Kalai solution (noted by $\cap$) of the original functions $U_b(x, y, z)$ and $U_s(x, y, z)$ (utility of buyer and seller respectively) can be approximated by resolving each attribute in a strict ordering. For example, compute a value of x using $U_s(x) \cap U_b(x)$, yielding some allocation for x, noted as X. Then compute y by solving $U_s(y, X) \cap U_b(y, X)$, yielding Y. Finally compute

---

[3] Myerson and Satterthwaite [17] define an *ex*-post efficient market as one that awards the good to the bidder with a higher valuation (be that seller or buyer).

z by solving $U_s(z, X, Y) \cap U_b(z, X, Y)$ This process can be continued for any arbitrary number of attributes.

Consideration of the mechanism described yields several questions, namely:

(a) Does this mechanism yield Pareto efficient results?
(b) Variables arbitrated first clearly have an advantage over those arbitrated later, can this be avoided?
(c) How can the domain over which a function is valid be determined for a previous attribute assignment?
(d) Can such functions be generated at runtime by autonomous-agents?

The remainder of this section addresses issues (b) and (c). Section 6 will address issues (a) and (d).

To deal with issue (b) *variable bias*, we take advantage of the lack of scale invariance of the Kalai solution by allowing bidders to assign weights to different attributes. In doing so, bidders can force the arbitration to bias more important attribute mediations in their favor. To keep the utility functions normalized over $\mathbb{R}_0^1$, the sum of all weights must equal 1. Formally, a two dimensional description of utilities can be specified as follows:

$$U(x, y) = \alpha \cdot U(x) + \beta \cdot U(y|x) \Big| \alpha + \beta = 1 \;\&\; U(\bullet) \mapsto \mathbb{R}_0^1 \; \forall \bullet \in \mathbb{R}_\zeta^\phi$$
$$Where \; \phi \; nd \; \zeta \; are \; the \; edges \; of \; the \; specified \; bid \; domain.$$

Example 2. If agent s prefers x over y, i.e., $s : x \succ y$, and agent b prefers y over x, i.e., $b : x \prec y \Rightarrow \alpha_s \succ \alpha_b$. This means that the value of x will be mediated with a focus on maximizing the utility of the seller $U_s(x)$. It follows that in future attribute mediations the utility of the bidder $(U_b(y))$ will have preference, as $\alpha_b \prec \alpha_s \Rightarrow \beta_b \succ \beta_s$. Intuitively, this means that the agent who offers the most leniency in determining the first attribute is offered a better outcome for subsequent attributes.

Whilst defining preferences does offer more flexibility to each bidder, clearly this only partially mitigates the weighting given to attributes being mediated first.

In our examination of issue (c) *determining domain intersects of decomposed functions*, we propose that each function is decomposed further into a triple of functions. Consider $U(y|x)$, rather than defining a two dimensional function $U : x, y \mapsto \mathbb{R}_0^1$ the bidder decomposes this function into a pair of transform functions $T : x, y \mapsto p$ and $T^{-1} : x, p \mapsto y$ and a utility function $U_p : p \mapsto \mathbb{R}_0^1$. This definition allows each bidder to specify how combinations of attributes define internal "*goal variables*" (e.g. maximize time over cost). The advantage of this approach to utility composition is two-fold. Firstly, it respects separation of concerns; that is, one function defines the utility of a goal variable and the others define how other attributes relate to that goal variable. Secondly, this composition allows each bidding party to define their own goal variables, while still allowing for direct mediation of any bid pairs in the market. This is achieved by ensuring T is bijective (U_p can be any arbitrary utility function). By making this restriction it is apparent that T^{-1} can be applied to compute the range of y given some fixed value of x (assuming the original range of p is known).

Example 3. If a bidder defines a cost function $U : c \mapsto \mathbb{R}_0^1 \mid \forall c \in \mathbb{R}_1^5$ (c in \$) and a decomposed function set of $U : p \mapsto \mathbb{R}_0^1 \mid \forall p \in \mathbb{R}_2^3$ (p in \$ per hour), $T : t, c \mapsto p$ and $T^{-1} : p, c \mapsto t$, then for any cost c we can compute the values of t that the bidder would accept (using T^{-1}). We can then use T to map U_p to $U_t : t, c \mapsto \mathbb{R}_0^1$. This means that any arbitrary combination of assigned attribute values and a single new attribute can be formed to make a new goal variable. Thus, any goal variables defined can then be compared against each other (any bid pair in the market can have its bargaining solution computed).

In summary, it is apparent that any bids defined as a collection of transform functions (adhering to the aforementioned decomposition) can have the domain of each attribute computed given the domain of each goal variable and dependent previous attribute assignments.

5   Experimental Evaluation

To examine the performance of CUB we define two types of agents, cars and car-parks, both of which have the capacity to map an input state to an ideal allocation of goods from the market. Both agents also have methods for composing utility functions such that an ideal allocation has utility 1 and other attribute assignment utilities fall off according to some demand profile (see Table 1)[4].

Table 1. Higher order function factories for agent utility functions

	Name	Function
Utility functions	Boulware	$(start, end, \zeta) \mapsto \begin{array}{ll} s > e & U_x(x) = 1 - e^{\zeta \cdot x - e}/e^{s \cdot \zeta - e} \\ s \le e & U_x(x) = e^{\zeta \cdot x - e}/e^{s \cdot \zeta - e} \end{array}$
	Ramp	$(min, max) \mapsto U_x(x) = (x - min)/(max - min)$
Transform functions	Division	$(scale) \mapsto (f, b) \mapsto (g) = f.apply(g \cdot scale)/b)$
	Id	$() \mapsto (f, \bullet) \mapsto (g) = f.apply(g)$

For the purposes of testing we establish three configurations of demand profiles for both agent types (see Table 2). For each of these demand profiles we use a set of 16 fixed combinations of bidder tuning values (all combinations of the preference models in Table 3) and a set of 16 randomly determined tuning values. This gives us a total of 96 types of experiments falling into six *categories* (three with fixed tuning values and three randomised). Each experiment consists of randomly generating 100 car and 50 car-park states, these are subsequently mapped to bids by each agent. These bids are submitted to a market where the results are calculated for both CUB and k-priced package bids.

---

[4] In our testing framework a bid also entails a start time for the parking allocation, these are used to filter possible pairings, this puts limitations on the efficiency of scheduling, a complex issue discussed in detail by Fujiwara et al. [9] and others.

Table 2. Agent utility functions and transforms

Agent	Attribute	Function	Parameters	Transform	Parameters
Car	Cost	Ramp	(maxPrice, 0)	Id	-
	Time	Boulware	(1, idealUse, 1)	Division	(2)
	Power	Ramp	(0, idealPower)	Id	-
Car-park	Cost	Ramp	(minPrice, minPrice · 2)	Id	-
	Time	Boulware	(maxPower, 0, 0.4)	Division[†]	(4)
	Power	Boulware	(maxUse, 0, 0.1)	Division[‡]	(1)

[†] *This is Id in experiments 1, 3, 4 and 6*
[‡] *This is Id in experiments 1, 2, 4 and 5*

Table 3. Preference models

Bias	Car type				Car-park type			
	A	B	C	D	i	ii	iii	iv
Power	33%	50%	25%	25%	33%	50%	25%	25%
Time	33%	25%	50%	25%	33%	33%	50%	25%
Cost	33%	25%	25%	50%	33%	33%	25%	50%

We compute 200 experiments for each of the 96 experiment types and aggregate their results by category, forming data-sets. The results of these experiments are summarized in the box-plots shown in Fig. 1. The *total utility* (*TU*) and efficiency (μ) results are computed using the set of allocation results A.

$$TU = \sum_{i=1}^{|A|} U_{si}(A(i)) \cdot U_{bi}(A(i)) \quad \& \quad \mu_t = \sum_{i=1}^{|A|} \frac{U_{si}(A(i)) \cdot U_{bi}(A(i))}{A_t(i)}$$

6   Discussion

Our analysis of CUB is structured as follows; firstly we highlight key characteristics in our data sets (Fig. 1) and postulate explanations for their presence. We then discuss the theoretical merits of CUB with consideration to the aforementioned five common criterion of MADSAs. Subsequent discussion synthesises this analysis into a set of early observations of CUB.

Two significant points of note when examining total utility (Figs. 1.1.1–1.1.6) are:

1. The range of CUB data in sets 1.1.1–1.1.3 is much larger than 1.1.4–1.1.6. As CUB uses a greedy approach to pairing it follows that bid pairs offering higher utility are paired. Evidently, many good pairings exist in random markets where a variety of bidder preferences are present. Subsequently, the randomised markets see more consistent results; thus reducing the *range* of the box-plots 1.1.4–1.1.6.

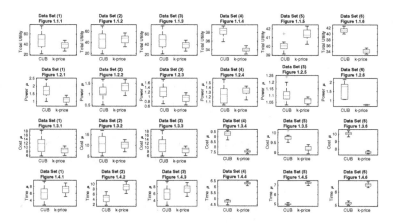

Fig. 1. Data set summary, sets (1–3) fixed tuning values and sets (4–6) are randomized

2. The drop in utility offered by CUB in Fig. 1.1.5. As this data-set is generated when both agents strongly value time; it follows that there is limited opportunity for compromises. That is to say that when both sides of the market strongly value a particular asset, there is no way for the CUB market to find an effective solution.

When considering power efficiency (Figs. 1.2.1–1.2.6) it can be seen that the non-random market composition scenarios (1.2.1–1.2.3) follow the utility results (1.1.1–1.1.3). That is, the total utility result dominates any small changes in the volume of power allocated. However, randomised profiles appear to yield different results (1.2.4–1.2.6). As one side of the market (the car-parks) will always prefer to provide less power (in this model), then as functions provided become less concessionary the volume of goods traded is decreased. This is best illustrated by the change in data sets 3 and 6, both of which see increases in the power efficiency. This seems to imply that the efficiency of the allocation of goods is strongly related to the competition for those goods. That is, when a good is under strong demand it is allocated in small volumes (proportional to the utility gained from its allocation), and when a good is under weak demand it is allocated more freely, this is a desirable quality of markets [6].

Results regarding cost efficiency (Figs. 1.3.1–1.3.6) illustrate the strong linear relation between cost and utility, that is all results trend with those of the total utility. This holds for all data-sets except set 5. Given the digression in set 5 is of %3, we conjecture that this result simply implies that the cost mediated by CUB was smaller than that of k-pricing. This linear relation is expected as both car and car-parks utilize linear cost functions. In consideration of time efficiency (1.4.1–1.4.6) what is apparent is that the CUB mechanism achieves lower quality results than the k-pricing mechanism. As aforementioned time is under the strictest opposition according to the utility functions defined. Given this, and the points made above, it can be stated that no good outcome for this attribute exists for both parties. Thus, our results show that as bidding over specific attributes becomes stronger the quality of CUBs results decrease. Conversely, when given sets of differing utilities CUB appears to exploit trade-offs between participants.

In addition to preliminary empiric analysis of CUB we also consider its theoretical merits within the context of MADSA. To conduct this analysis we consider the five key features of markets, as mentioned in [23]:

- *Individual Rational:* (IR) Within our implementation of CUB the utility offered by *each* attribute is non-negative. CUB is therefore IR.
- *Budget Balance:* (BB) As the payment from each bidder goes directly to the vendor it is understood that CUB is strictly budget balanced.
- *Tractability:* (T) The described CUB bidding mechanisms requires computation of each bid pairing; each pairing (using brute force) requires examination of each attribute within the overlapping variable domains. Yielding a polynomial time complexity of: $O(n \cdot m \cdot p \cdot d)$, given: (n) = number of buyers, (m) = number of sellers, (p) = number of variables, (d) = maximum number of discrete states considered for each variable.
- *Economic Efficiency:* (EE) At this point CUB is not *ex*-post *Pareto* efficient. This is because conditional utility bids decomposed according to CUB exhibit supermodularity in comparison to their ideal Kalai solution.
- *Incentive Compatibility:* (IC) As CUB is budget balanced, individually rational and *ex*-post efficient we can state that CUB is definitely *not* incentive compatible (as per the Myerson-Satterthwaite result [17]).

As aforementioned, defining utility functions for complex resources is an entirely non-trivial problem [10]. However, we have shown that when defining utilities within the CUB mechanism an intuitive decomposition of utility functions exists. Furthermore, within the simplistic scenario of AEV parking allocation we have defined a set of higher-order functions that can produce utilities at run-time based on agents' state. Accordingly, we suggest that when allocating resources of limited attributes with clearly definable inter-dependencies the generation of utilities at run-time is not unrealistic.

In summary, empiric evidence suggests that the effectiveness of CUB is highly dependent on the market context within which it operates. That is, when no efficient market pairings exist CUB preforms poorly, yet as better pairings exist CUB is able to find and exploit these pairings, producing superior results to existing mechanisms. Additionally, theoretical analysis has highlighted several other important features of CUB with respect to tractability, individual rationality, budget balance and economic efficiency.

7   Conclusion

This research has examined one of many open problems in the field of auction mechanism design, that of preference representation. Consideration of the literature and functional requirements of markets in the context of allocating vehicle parking has led to a new market mechanism CUB. Subsequent experimental examination has yielded insights into the strengths and weaknesses of CUB and highlighted areas of the literature not yet fully explored. While empiric evidence suggests CUB is highly efficient, further research is required to produce a more generally applicable market mechanism.

There are numerous ways this research may be extended, including:

- The theoretical analysis of CUB presented does not address issues of: coalition proof-ness, false name bidding, counterspeculation, participation without capital, and other important considerations in mechanism design [20].
- While evidence suggest CUB efficiently explores high-dimensional problem spaces it is not yet *ex*-post Pareto efficient. Consequently, an adaptation that further exploits the solution space local to CUBs results seems like a promising line of research.

References

1. Alajali, W., Wen, S., Zhou, W.: On-street car parking prediction in smart city: a multi-source data analysis in sensor-cloud environment. In: Wang, G., Atiquzzaman, M., Yan, Z., Choo, K.-K.R. (eds.) SpaCCS 2017. LNCS, vol. 10658, pp. 641–652. Springer, Cham (2017). https://doi.org/10.1007/978-3-319-72395-2_58
2. Baranwal, G., Vidyarthi, D.P.: A fair multi-attribute combinatorial double auction model for resource allocation in cloud computing. J. Syst. Softw. **108**, 60–76 (2015)
3. Bhattacharya, S., Kar, K., Chow, J.H., Gupta, A.: Extended second price auctions for plug-in electric vehicle (PEV) charging in smart distribution grids. In: American Control Conference (ACC), pp. 908–913. IEEE (2014)
4. Bichler, M., Kalagnanam, J.: Configurable offers and winner determination in multi-attribute auctions. Eur. J. Oper. Res. **160**(2), 380–394 (2005)
5. Boutilier, C., Bacchus, F., Brafman, R.I.: UCP-networks: a directed graphical representation of conditional utilities. In: Proceedings of the Seventeenth Conference on Uncertainty in Artificial Intelligence, pp. 56–64. Morgan Kaufmann Publishers Inc. (2001)
6. Chichin, S.: An open market for trading cloud services. Ph.D. thesis, Swinburne University of Technology (2016)
7. Conitzer, V., Sandholm, T.: Complexity results about nash equilibria. arXiv preprint cs/0205074 (2002)
8. Engel, Y., Wellman, M.P.: Multiattribute auctions based on generalized additive independence. J. Artif. Intell. Res. **37**, 479–525 (2010)
9. Fujiwara, I., Aida, K., Ono, I.: Applying double-sided combinational auctions to resource allocation in cloud computing. In: 2010 10th IEEE/IPSJ International Symposium on Applications and the Internet (SAINT), pp. 7–14. IEEE (2010)
10. Gonzales, C., Perny, P.: GAI networks for utility elicitation. KR **4**, 224–234 (2004)
11. Houissa, A., Barth, D., Faul, N., Mautor, T.: A learning algorithm to minimize the expectation time of finding a parking place in urban area. In: 2017 IEEE Symposium on Computers and Communications (ISCC), pp. 29–34. IEEE (2017)
12. Iosifidis, G., Koutsopoulos, I.: Double auction mechanisms for resource allocation in autonomous networks. IEEE J. Sel. Areas Commun. **28**(1), 95–102 (2010)

13. Izakian, H., Ladani, B.T.e.e.: A continuous double auction method for resource allocation in computational grids. In: IEEE Symposium on Computational Intelligence in Scheduling, CI-Sched 2009, pp. 29–35. IEEE (2009)

14. Jain, R., Walrand, J.: An efficient mechanism for network bandwidth auction. In: NOMS Workshops 2008 IEEE Network Operations and Management Symposium Workshops, pp. 227–234. IEEE (2008)

15. Kalai, E.: Proportional solutions to bargaining situations: interpersonal utility comparisons. Econ.: J. Econ. Soc. 1623–1630 (1977)

16. Kumar, D., Baranwal, G., Raza, Z., Vidyarthi, D.P.: A systematic study of double auction mechanisms in cloud computing. J. Syst. Softw. **125**, 234–255 (2017)

17. Myerson, R.B., Satterthwaite, M.A.: Efficient mechanisms for bilateral trading. J. Econ. Theory **29**(2), 265–281 (1983)

18. Nash Jr, J.F.: The bargaining problem. Econ.: J. Econ. Soc. 155–162 (1950)

19. Rhodes, C., Blewitt, W., Sharp, C., Ushaw, G., Morgan, G.: Smart routing: a novel application of collaborative path-finding to smart parking systems. In: 2014 IEEE 16th Conference on Business Informatics (CBI), vol. 1, pp. 119–126. IEEE (2014)

20. Rothkopf, M.H.: Thirteen reasons why the vickrey-clarke-groves process is not practical. Oper. Res. **55**(2), 191–197 (2007)

21. Samimi, P., Teimouri, Y., Mukhtar, M.: A combinatorial double auction resource allocation model in cloud computing. Inform. Sci. **357**, 201–216 (2016)

22. Sandholm, T.: Expressive commerce and its application to sourcing: how we conducted $35 billion of generalized combinatorial auctions. AI Mag. **28**(3), 45 (2007)

23. Schnizler, B., Neumann, D., Veit, D., Weinhardt, C.: A multiattribute combinatorial exchange for trading grid resources. In: Proceedings of the Research Symposium on Emerging Electronic (2005)

24. Schnizler, B., Neumann, D., Veit, D., Weinhardt, C.: Trading grid services-a multiattribute combinatorial approach. Eur. J. Oper. Res. **187**(3), 943–961 (2008)

25. Shafie-khah, M., et al.: Optimal behavior of electric vehicle parking lots as demand response aggregation agents. IEEE Trans. Smart Grid **7**(6), 2654–2665 (2016)

26. Tasseron, G., Martens, K., van der Heijden, R.: The potential impact of vehicle-to-vehicle communication on on-street parking under heterogeneous conditions. IEEE Intell. Transp. Syst. Mag. **8**(2), 33–42 (2016)

27. Varian, H.R.: Intermediate microeconomics; a modern approach (2009)

28. Wooldridge, M.: An Introduction to Multiagent Systems. Wiley, Hoboken (2009)

29. Xia, M., Stallaert, J., Whinston, A.B.: Solving the combinatorial double auction problem. Eur. J. Oper. Res. **164**(1), 239–251 (2005)

30. Zhang, Y., Xu, K., Shi, X., Wang, H., Liu, J., Wang, Y.: Design, modeling, and analysis of online combinatorial double auction for mobile cloud computing markets. Int. J. Commun. Syst. **31**(7), e3460 (2018)

Multiagent Reinforcement Learning Applied to Traffic Light Signal Control

Carolina Higuera[1(✉)] [iD], Fernando Lozano[2] [iD], Edgar Camilo Camacho[1] [iD],
and Carlos Hernando Higuera[3] [iD]

[1] Universidad Santo Tomás, Bogotá, Colombia
{carolinahiguera,edgarcamacho}@usantotomas.edu.co
[2] Universidad de los Andes, Bogotá, Colombia
flozano@uniandes.edu.co
[3] Universidad Pedagógica y Tecnológica de Colombia, Tunja, Colombia
carlos.higuera@uptc.edu.co

Abstract. We present the application of multiagent reinforcement learning to the problem of traffic light signal control to decrease travel time. We model roads as a collection of agents for each signalized junction. Agents learn to set phases that jointly maximize a reward function that encourages short vehicle queuing delays and queue lengths at all junctions. The first approach that we tested exploits the fact that the reward function can be splitted into contributions per agent. Junctions are modeled as vertices in a coordination graph and the joint action is found with the variable elimination algorithm. The second method exploits the principle of locality to compute the best action for an agent as its best response for a two player game with each member of its neighborhood. We apply the learning methods to a simulated network of 6 intersections, using data from the Transit Department of Bogotá, Colombia. These methods obtained significant reductions in queuing delay with respect to the fixed time control, and in general achieve shorter travel times across the network than some other reinforcement learning based methods found in the literature.

Keywords: Adaptive traffic light signal control · Best response ·
Coordination graphs · Game theory · Machine learning ·
Multiagent reinforcement learning · Variable elimination

1 Introduction

As the number of vehicles in circulation increases, the problem of vehicular traffic congestion in urban areas becomes unbearable. In Bogotá, one of the most congested cities in Colombia, the average commute time is 72 min each way [2]. In Bogotá, traffic light control is done through fixed-time signaling that adheres to the recommendations of the German methodology RILSA (Richtlinien für Lichtsignalanlagen) [16]. However, this open loop strategy does not respond dynamically to variations in traffic demand.

© Springer Nature Switzerland AG 2019
Y. Demazeau et al. (Eds.): PAAMS 2019, LNAI 11523, pp. 115–126, 2019.
https://doi.org/10.1007/978-3-030-24209-1_10

In this paper, we test solutions to decrease travel times based on multiagent reinforcement learning, modeling the problem as a multiagent Markov Decision Process (MDP). A collection of agents learns to minimize vehicle queuing delays and queue lengths at all junctions. Our primary contribution is the coupling of algorithms to conventional RL, to ensure coordination in multiagent environments. In our first approach (Q-VE) agents are modeled as vertices in a coordination graph and the joint action is found with the variable elimination algorithm. The second method (Q-BR) follows the work done by [3], which computes the action for an agent as the best response of a two player game with each member of its neighborhood.

We tested our methods in a Bogotá's network with 6 junctions using the SUMO simulator [10], with traffic flow data supplied by the Transit Department. We compared the performance against the fixed time control currently used, and with other reinforcement learning methods. In our experiments Q-VE and Q-BR achieve average reductions of $54, 99\%$ and $63, 49\%$ in queueing delay over fixed time control, respectively.

This paper is organized as follows: in Sect. 2 we present a brief literature review of the application of reinforcement learning to traffic signal control. In Sect. 3 we present the problem definition as a multiagent MDP, states, actions, and reward function. In Sect. 4 we describe the learning algorithms. In Sect. 5 we present experimental results and a discussion. Finally, in Sect. 6 we present some conclusions.

2   Previous Work

Reinforcement Learning (RL) is a Machine Learning technique in which an agent learns a task through its interaction with the environment. The process can be described as a Markov Decision Process, where for every discrete time k, the agent receives a state s_k and performs an action a_k to reach its goal. As feedback, the agent receives a reward r and moves to a new state s_{k+1}. In RL, the agent must map in the factors $Q(s_k, a_k)$ the expected utility that he would receive if he took action a_k in state s_k and he would behave optimally from then on. With those factors. the agent can build a policy $\pi(s, a)$ which has the information about how to complete the task, indicating the probability of applying action a to maximize its expected utility [17].

RL has been applied previously to the problem of adaptive traffic control. Usually, a learning agent is assigned to one or more junctions and must learn a policy to reduce congestion. In a simplified problem, each agent learns independently. For example Camponogara and Krauss Jr [1] formulate the problem as a distributed stochastic game, where each agent learns independently assuming that the environment is stationary. Oliveira et al. [14] modified and applied Q-Learning so that each agent manages stochastic traffic patterns.

However, for the traffic signal problem the environment is non-stationary. Thus, a key feature of a multiagent RL algorithm is the mechanism for policy coordination between agents. This can be incorporated at various points in the formulation of the RL problem, or directly in the learning algorithm. Examples of the former include the work of Wiering [18], where each agent attempts to estimate the likelihood of state transitions by the other agents. Richter et al. [15] incorporates to the state vector the traffic flow of the neighboring intersections. Li et al. [12] include the waiting time of stopped vehicles of neighboring junctions in the reward function for each agent. Examples of coordination in the learning algorithm are given by Xu et al. [19], who modify the action selection mechanism in Q-learning by the incorporation of a Bayes based estimation of the likelihood of action selection for other agents. El-Tantawy et al. [3] present a more efficient approach in which the estimates made by each agent are limited to its neighborhood, and each agent always selects the action that maximizes the reward function in its neighborhood.

3 Problem Definition and Notation

The problem can be formally described as a collaborative multiagent MDP model. In particular we employ the setting of Guestrin [6], in which each agent only has dependencies with a small neighborhood. The model is as follows:

- A discrete time $k = 0, 1, 2, 3, \ldots$.
- A set of n agents $\mathcal{N} = \{N_1, N_2, \cdots, N_n\}$.
- A finite set of actions $\mathcal{A}_i$ for each agent i. The joint action $\mathbf{a} \in \mathcal{A}$, where $\mathcal{A} = \mathcal{A}_1 \times \cdots \times \mathcal{A}_n$.
- A set of states $\mathcal{S}$. The state $\mathbf{s}^k \in \mathcal{S}$ describes the environment at time k.
- A finite set of observations Ω_i for each agent i. The observation $o_i^k \in \Omega_i$ provides the agent i with state information s^k.
- A state transition function $T = \mathcal{S} \times \mathcal{A} \times \mathcal{S} \rightarrow [0, 1]$.
- An observation function $\mathcal{O} : \mathcal{S} \times \mathcal{A} \times \Omega_1 \times \cdots \times \Omega_n \rightarrow [0, 1]$, that defines the probability $p(o_1^k \cdots o_n^k | \mathbf{s}^k, \mathbf{a}^{k-1})$.
- A reward function $R_i : \mathcal{S} \times \mathcal{A} \rightarrow \mathbb{R}$, that returns to agent i a reward r_i^k. The global reward is defined as $R(\mathbf{s}^k, \mathbf{a}^k) = \sum_{i=1}^{n} r_i^k$.

3.1 Actions

In a signalized junction there are phases that give right of way to one or more nonconflicting movements. An agent takes an action by selecting a new phase, or deciding to prolong the current one.

3.2 State Space

The state contains information about all the agents. Because of our locality assumption, each agent i observes only the variables that are relevant for its decision making, o_i^k. For an agent with i edges, the observation vector has the following items:

- Hour (h) to include that traffic has a cyclical temporal dynamic
- Maximum queue length (in vehicles) in edge i (q_i)
- Queuing delay (in minutes) of stopped vehicles in edge i (w_i)

In order to maintain a notation consistent with the RL literature, the agent's observation about its environment, o_j^k $\forall j \in \mathcal{N}$, will be represented as the state s_j^k hereafter.

3.3 Reward Function

Our reward function encourages short queue lengths and waiting time experienced by the vehicles throughout the road.

$$r_i = -\sum_{k=1}^{edges} \beta_q(q_k)^{\theta_q} + \beta_w(w_k)^{\theta_w} \quad \forall i \in \mathcal{N} \tag{1}$$

Where, $edges$ is the number of approaches of agent i. q_k and w_k are the maximum queue length and queuing delay in edge k. β_q and β_w are coefficients to set priority. θ_q and θ_w balance queue lengths and waiting times across approaches. In addition, $\beta_q, \beta_w, \theta_q, \theta_w \in [0,1]$ and $\beta_q + \beta_w = 1$. However, finding the specific values for these parameters is problem-dependent.

4 Learning Algorithms

It is important that decisions made at the individual level result in decisions close to the optimal for the group. In the case of traffic control, each agent should coordinate its actions only with its adjacent agents or neighbors. Guestrin *et al.* in [5] describe a method for coordinated RL in which the global function Q is splitted into a linear combination of the Q functions for each agent:

$$Q(\mathbf{s}, \mathbf{a}) = \sum_{i=1}^{|\mathcal{N}|} Q_i(s_i, a_i) \tag{2}$$

The update rule for the local Q_i factors is similar to the one used in Q-Learning for a single agent. In the multiagent case, the update uses temporary differences of the global error:

$$Q_i(s_i^k, a_i^k) := Q_i(s_i^k, a_i^k) + \alpha \left[R(\mathbf{s}^k, \mathbf{a}^k) + \gamma \max_{a' \in \mathcal{A}} Q(\mathbf{s}^{k+1}, \mathbf{a}') - Q_i(s_i^k, a_i^k) \right] \tag{3}$$

The problem of coordination is to find at each step the joint action:

$$\mathbf{a}^* = \underset{a' \in \mathcal{A}}{\operatorname{argmax}} \, Q(\mathbf{s}^{k+1}, \mathbf{a}') \tag{4}$$

We consider two ways for solving this problem, coordination graphs and best response by neighborhoods.

4.1   Coordination Graphs

A coordination graph, $G = (\mathcal{V}, \mathcal{E})$, represents problems where agent $i \in \mathcal{V}$ needs to coordinate its actions with its neighbors $\Gamma(i) = \{j : (i,j) \in \mathcal{E})\}$. The global Q function can be discomposed into terms corresponding to the edges in $\mathcal{E}$ [7]:

$$Q(\mathbf{s}, \mathbf{a}) = \sum_{(i,j) \in \mathcal{E}} Q_{ij}(s_{ij}, a_i, a_j) \tag{5}$$

Where s_{ij} is the discrete joint observed state for agents i and j, $\mathbf{s}_i \cup \mathbf{s}_j$.

To find the optimal joint action $\mathbf{a}^*$ in (4), we use the variable elimination algorithm (VE) proposed by Gaustrin et $al.$ [4]. Agents are eliminated in a predefined order. To remove agent i, it calculates the $conditional$ $payoff$ $function$, defined as the maximum value that the agent is able to contribute to the Q function of the system, given by the sum of the factors Q_{ij} that the agent has in common with its neighbors $\Gamma(i)$. Moreover, the agent finds its $conditional$ $strategy$, that is, the action $a_i \in \mathcal{A}_i$ that it must apply to maximize its contribution. Once the agent i communicates the conditional payoff function to one of its neighbors, it is eliminated and new dependencies (edges) are generated between the agents involved in the payoff function. This process is repeated until only one node remains in the graph, who finds the action a_i^* that maximizes its conditional payoff function. Based on this, the conditional strategy for the other agents is found, a_j^*, doing this procedure in the reverse order of elimination. At the end, the individual actions make up the joint action $\mathbf{a}^*$ for the whole graph. The complete VE algorithm is shown in Algorithm 1.

To find nearly optimal policies for each agent, we use a multiagent version of Q-Learning proposed by Kok in [8]. Given the action $\mathbf{a}^*$ and joint state s_{ij}^k, we update the factors Q_{ij} for each edge $(i,j) \in \mathcal{E}$ with the following formula. The learning algorithm is summarized in Algorithm 2.

$$Q_{ij}(s_{ij}^{k-1}, a_i^{k-1}, a_j^{k-1}) := (1-\alpha)Q_{ij}(s_{ij}^{k-1}, a_i^{k-1}, a_j^{k-1}) +$$
$$\alpha \left[\frac{r_i^k}{|\Gamma(i)|} + \frac{r_j^k}{|\Gamma(j)|} + \gamma Q_{ij}(s_{ij}^k, a_i^*, a_j^*) \right] \tag{6}$$

4.2   Best Response

We follow the work done by El-Tantawy et $al.$ in [3], in which each agent participates in a two player game with its neighborhood $\Gamma(i)$. Agent i creates and updates a model θ that estimates the likelihood of action selection for each neighbor $j \in \Gamma(i)$. The probabilities are calculated according to the number of visits to the state-action pair $v(s_{ij}^k, a_j^k)$, as:

$$\theta_{ij}\left(s_{ij}^{k-1}, a_j^{k-1}\right) = \frac{v(s_{ij}^{k-1}, a_j^{k-1})}{\sum\limits_{a_j \in \mathcal{A}_j} v(s_{ij}^{k-1}, a_j)} \tag{7}$$

Algorithm 1. Variable Elimination Algorithm

Require: coordination graph of the system $G = (\mathcal{V}, \mathcal{E})$; order of elimination of agents
$\quad\quad \mathcal{O} \subseteq \mathcal{V}$; set of neighbors for each agent $\Gamma(i)$

1: **function** VARIABLEELIMINATION(s_{ij}^k)
2:     **for** each agent $i \in \mathcal{O}$ **do**
3:         **if** agent i is the first to eliminate **then**
4:             $k \equiv$ next agent to eliminate, $k \in \Gamma(i)$
5:
$$\phi_{kj} = \max_{a_i} \left[\sum_{j \in \Gamma(i)} Q_{ij}(s_{ij}^k, a_i, a_j) \right]$$
6:         **else if** agent i is the last to eliminate **then**
7:             $\phi_{ii} = \max_{a_i}[\phi_{ii}(a_i)]$
8:         **else**
9:             $k \equiv$ next agent to eliminate, $k \in \Gamma(i)$
10:
$$\phi_{kj} = \max_{a_i} \left[\sum_{j \in \Gamma(i)} Q_{ij}(s_{ij}^k, a_i, a_j) + \phi_{ik}(a_i, a_k) \right]$$
11:         **end if**
12:         Send ϕ_{kj} to next agent to eliminate
13:     **end for**
14:     **for** each agent i in the reverse order of $\mathcal{O}$ **do**
15:         **if** agent i was the last one eliminated **then**
16:             Get $a_i^* = \text{argmax}_{a_i}[\phi_{ii}(a_i)]$
17:             Send to the previous agent a_i^*
18:             Send $\max_{\mathbf{a}} Q(\mathbf{s}, \mathbf{a}) = \max_{a_i} \phi_{ii}(a_i)$
19:         **else**
20:             Expect from neighboring agents a_k^*, a_j^* and $\max_{\mathbf{a}} Q(\mathbf{s}, \mathbf{a})$
21:             Get $a_i^* = \text{argmax}_{a_i}[\phi_{kj}(a_k^*, a_j^*)]$
22:         **end if**
23:     **end for**
24:     **return** $a_i^* \quad \forall \quad i \in \mathcal{V}$
25: **end function**

Then, agent i learns the joint policy with each $j \in \Gamma(i)$, and updates the Q factors for each state-action pair, according to:

$$Q_{ij}^k \left(s_{ij}^{k-1}, a_{ij}^{k-1} \right) = (1 - \alpha) Q_{ij}^{k-1} \left(s_{ij}^{k-1}, a_{ij}^{k-1} \right) + \alpha \left[r_i^k + \gamma \max_{\mathbf{a}' \in \mathcal{A}} Q(\mathbf{s}^k, \mathbf{a}') \right] \quad (8)$$

Where $\max_{\mathbf{a}' \in \mathcal{A}} Q(\mathbf{s}^k, \mathbf{a}')$ corresponds to the maximum expected value of the Q factor for the whole system, starting from the current global state $\mathbf{s}^k$. Because of the locality assumption this factor simplifies to the best response of agent i with respect to its neighbor j, as shown by El-Tantawy *et al.* [3]:

$$br_i^k = \max_{a_i \in \mathcal{A}_i} \left[\sum_{a_j \in \mathcal{A}_j} Q_{ij} \left(s_{ij}^k, a_{ij} \right) \times \theta_{ij} \left(s_{ij}^k, a_j \right) \right] \quad (9)$$

Algorithm 2. Multiagent Q-Learning with coordination graphs (Q-VE)

Require: coordination graph of the system $G = (\mathcal{V}, \mathcal{E})$; order of elimination of agents
$\mathcal{O} \subseteq \mathcal{V}$; set of neighbors for each agent $\Gamma(i)$

1: **for** each edge $(i, j) \in \mathcal{E}$ **do**
2:     Initialize $Q_{ij}(s_{ij}, a_i, a_j)$ optimistically
3: **end for**
4: **for** each episode **do**
5:     Initialize the observed state s_i for all agents $i \in \mathcal{V}$
6:     **for** each decision time k **do**
7:         Get joint action $\mathbf{a}^k$ with $\epsilon-$greedy as action selection method
8:         For each agent $i \in \mathcal{V}$ apply $a_i \in \mathbf{a}^k$, observe r_i^k y $\mathbf{s}_i^k$
9:         Get $s_{ij}^k = \text{DISCRETIZATION}(\mathbf{s}_i^k \cup \mathbf{s}_j^k) \ \forall \, (i, j) \in \mathcal{E}$
10:         Find $\mathbf{a}^* = \max_{\mathbf{a}} Q(\mathbf{s^k}, \mathbf{a}) \to \text{VARIABLEELIMINATION}(s_{ij}^k \ \forall (i,j) \in \mathcal{E})$
11:         **for** each edge $(i, j) \in \mathcal{E}$ **do**
12:             Update Q_{ij} factors with Eq. 6
13:         **end for**
14:         For each agent $i \in \mathcal{V}$ update $s_i^{k-1} \leftarrow s_i^k$
15:     **end for**
16: **end for**

Finally, all agents choose the best response, the action that maximizes the Q factor at their neighborhood level, regardless of the policies of other members:

$$a_i^* = \text{argmax}_{a_i \in \mathcal{A}_i} \left[\sum_{j \in \Gamma(i)} \sum_{a_j \in \mathcal{A}_j} Q_{ij}\left(s_{ij}^k, a_{ij}\right) \times \theta_{ij}\left(s_{ij}^k, a_j\right) \right] \tag{10}$$

The learning procedure is summarized in Algorithm 3.

As a final remark, note that in both Algorithms 2 and 3, the Q values are initialized optimistically. That means, with the highest reward, in order to encourage exploration to non visited state-action pairs [17].

5   Experimental Results

Both methods were simulated in a network with 6 intersections of Bogotá, as shown in Fig. 1. The information regarding the vehicular flow and the fixed-time control was provided by the District Mobility Office [13]. Simulations were done through the SUMO simulator [10] and the TraCI environment [11].

Each agent has two actions or phases. They have a minimum green time (20 seconds for Q-VE and 14 seconds for Q-BR) to ensure safe crossing. Furthermore, the parameters in the reward function (1) were set experimentally as $\beta_q = 0.3$, $\beta_w = 0.7$, $\theta_q = 1.75$ and $\theta_w = 1.75$, since these values work well in our case.

To compare Q-VE and Q-BR methods with some previously used in the literature, we implement independent Q-learning to follow the approach proposed by Camponogara *et al.* in [1]. Also, the coordination method proposed by Xu *et al.* in [19] in which it is induced by the estimation of the mixed strategy of other

---

Algorithm 3. Multiagent Q-learning with best response (Q-BR)

Require: set of agents $\mathcal{N}$, set of neighbors for each agent $\Gamma(i)$
1: **for** each agent $i \in \mathcal{N}$ **do**
2:    **for** each neighbor agent $j \in \Gamma(i)$ **do**
3:       Initialize $Q_{ij}(s_{ij}, a_i, a_j)$ optimistically
4:       Initialize model for policy estimation $\theta_{ij}(s_{ij}, a_j) = 1/|\mathcal{A}_j|$
5:    **end for**
6: **end for**
7: **for** each episode **do**
8:    Initialize the observed state $\mathbf{s}_i$ for all agents $i \in \mathcal{N}$
9:    **for** each decision time k **do**
10:       Get joint action $\mathbf{a}^k$ with ϵ–greedy as action selection method
11:       Apply $a_i \in \mathbf{a}^k$ for each agent $i \in \mathcal{N}$
12:       **for** each agent $i \in \mathcal{N}$ **do**
13:          **for** each neighbor agent $j \in \Gamma(i)$ **do**
14:             Observe $\mathbf{s}_i^k$, r_i^k, $\mathbf{s}_j^k$ and a_j^{k-1}
15:             Form $s_{ij}^k = \text{DISCRETIZATION}(\mathbf{s}_i^k \cup \mathbf{s}_j^k)$ and $a_{ij}^{k-1} = a_i^{k-1} \cup a_j^{k-1}$
16:             Update policy model with Eq. 7
17:             Find the maximum expected value of the Q factor using Eq. 9
18:             Update Q_{ij} factors with Eq. 8
19:             Update $s_{ij}^{k-1} \leftarrow s_{ij}^k$
20:          **end for**
21:          Compute action a_i^* that corresponds to best response with all
             neighbors using Eq. 10
22:       **end for**
23:    **end for**
24: **end for**

---

agents by Bayes likelihoods. However, our implementation differs in two main points. First, we keep our reward function. Second, we learn a Q function for each agent only taking into account adjacent agents. Our purpose is to measure the performance of several learning strategies in our network with our reward function.

Figure 2 presents learning curves obtained by Q-VE, Q-BR, independent learning and RL with coordination induced by Bayes likelihoods. For each agent, we give the average reward during the last 10 days and the corresponding value for the fixed time control strategy (denoted by FT). After 100 episodes, we observe significant improvement with Q-VE and Q-BR over the FT strategy. Also, we found that the method based on Bayes likelihoods performs poorly on this framework, in comparison with the other strategies. We believe that this could be the result of not frequent visits to all state-actions pairs, which affects the beliefs and therefore, the updating of posterior probabilities for the estimation of the mixed strategy of adjacent agents. On the other hand, we found surprisingly that the reward evolution with independent learning is very similar to the one obtained by the coordinated method Q-BR. With both methods, all agents achieve better rewards than with other approaches. Nonetheless, we

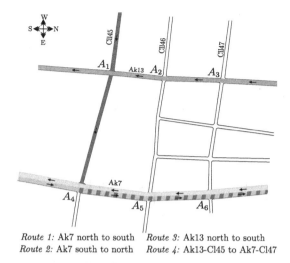

Route 1: Ak7 north to south   *Route 3:* Ak13 north to south
Route 2: Ak7 south to north   *Route 4:* Ak13-Cl45 to Ak7-Cl47

Fig. 1. Test framework for multiagent traffic control

believe that the policy learned by Q-BR can positively influence other variables that are not included in the reward function, due to coordination between neighboring agents.

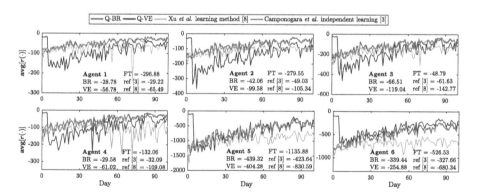

Fig. 2. Agents learning curves. With Q-VE and Q-BR it was achieved a better reward in comparison with FT control. However, with Q-BR we get better average rewards after 100 training episodes in almost all agents.

In order to compare the performance of Q-VE and Q-BR, we present in Table 1 indicators as: maximum average queue length per intersection (veh), average queuing delay per vehicle (s/veh), and average speed (m/s). We found large reductions in the delay experienced by the vehicles at the six junctions. For most agents, Q-BR achieves a larger improvement than Q-VE. We believe this is

Table 1. Average queue length, queuing delay and speed measurements to evaluate performance of policies learned

Method	Average queue (veh)						Average waiting time (s/veh)						Average speed (m/s)					
	A1	A2	A3	A4	A5	A6	A1	A2	A3	A4	A5	A6	A1	A2	A3	A4	A5	A6
FT	8.8	7.3	4.0	7.6	10.9	8.0	32.1	45.6	23.8	25.1	50.7	59.1	3.1	3.1	4.0	6.8	4.6	3.7
Q-VE	3.8	2.9	4.7	3.0	7.6	7.8	15.0	21.6	13.6	11.5	19.9	20.1	5.1	4.4	2.4	7.2	3.9	3.5
Q-BR	3.7	4.0	4.6	1.8	9.7	8.3	8.3	10.9	9.7	8.8	23.4	27.9	5.0	5.4	3.9	8.2	4.1	3.9
Q-ind [1]	3.6	4.1	4.6	2.4	9.9	8.5	8.2	11.3	10.0	8.4	23.6	28.6	4.9	5.1	3.9	8.0	4.1	3.8
Q-Xu [19]	3.8	4.8	5.0	4.2	11.0	9.1	20.9	30.0	29.0	26.7	44.1	57.1	5.3	4.6	3.4	7.0	3.5	3.0

due to the action selection method of Q-BR, which is based on neighborhoods, and chooses the phases according to the state of each section of the network. This result supports the assumption that the actions of the agents influence only their neighborhood and agents outside can be considered independent. Hence, to get the joint action that maximizes the objective, it is not necessary to consider the whole system, but neighborhoods determined by direct influences on traffic flow. This decreases the computation required to obtain the joint action, but increases the amount of information that must be observable.

In Table 2 we present travel time across the main routes of the network, as showed in Fig. 1. Q-VE and Q-BR achieve reductions of at least 14% and at most 48% with respect to FT. The largest reductions are obtained with Q-BR, which agrees with the larger average speed and smaller waiting times shown in Table 1. It is interesting to note that Q-BR policy generate green waves along arterials, as show in Fig. 3, seeking for the progression of big groups of vehicles along successive junctions. The sensitivity to traffic allow the policies to assign the appropriate phases to balance the waiting time of the vehicles, without compromising the average speed.

Table 2. Average travel time (in minutes) for selected routes using fixed time control and the policies learned

Method	Route 1	Route 2	Route 3	Route 4
FT	2.41	4.17	1.65	5.58
Q-VE	1.74	**2.17**	1.41	2.90
Q-BR	**1.52**	2.33	1.04	**2.75**
Q-ind [1]	2.44	3.26	**0.93**	3.72
Q-Xu [19]	4.20	5.33	1.02	5.67

We conclude pointing out some advantages and deficiencies that we infer from our results. First, distributing the reward function into contribution per agent, together with the principle of locality, simplifies the problem, since the Q factors can be splitted into dependencies between agents. This is represented by the coordination graphs, which are favorable for the application of the VE algorithm.

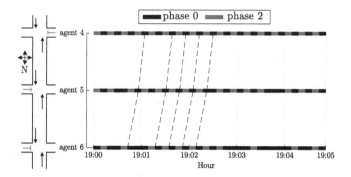

Fig. 3. Space-time diagram for route 1, Ak7 north to south, with Q-BR policy. At some intervals, agents 4, 5 and 6 coordinate their actions to generate a platoon.

This method allows an exact solution to the joint action selection problem [9]. However, as the algorithm eliminates agents, neighborhoods change and may include ones that are not adjacent, thus, may not have direct communication. The method would require an estimation of the Q factors for nonadjacent agents.

A difficulty with the VE algorithm is that it delivers the joint action at the end of the second transmission. A faster alternative is the Max-Plus algorithm, developed by Kok in [8]. On the other hand, the coordination strategy based on BR presents good scalability, due to communication between agents is known a priori. However, policies in the neighborhood are not shared knowledge, so a greater transmission of information is required to estimate and model the behavior of neighbors.

6 Conclusions

We have presented two multiagent RL methods for the problem of traffic light signal control. We implement two different methods to achieve coordination between agents, Coordination Graphs with the Variable Elimination (Q-VE) and Best Response (Q-BR). We tested them in simulation in a road of Bogotá.

Our results show that Q-VE and Q-BR reduces average waiting time per vehicle for more than 55%, and average queue length by intersection by more than 30%. It is interesting to note that the policies obtained by our algorithms prioritize green waves along routes where the major demand is.

References

1. Camponogara, E., Kraus, W.: Distributed learning agents in urban traffic control. In: Pires, F.M., Abreu, S. (eds.) EPIA 2003. LNCS (LNAI), vol. 2902, pp. 324–335. Springer, Heidelberg (2003). https://doi.org/10.1007/978-3-540-24580-3_38
2. Department, N.P.: Dnp advierte que se avecina colapso de movilidad en las principales capitales (2016). https://www.dnp.gov.co/Paginas/DNPadvierte queseavecinacolapsodemovilidadenlasprincipalescapitales.aspx

3. El-Tantawy, S., Abdulhai, B., Abdelgawad, H.: Multiagent reinforcement learning for integrated network of adaptive traffic signal controllers (MARLIN-ATSC): methodology and large-scale application on downtown toronto. IEEE Trans. Intell. Transp. Syst. **14**(3), 1140–1150 (2013). https://doi.org/10.1109/TITS.2013.2255286

4. Guestrin, C., Koller, D., Parr, R.: Multiagent planning with factored MDPS. In: NIPS-14, pp. 1523–1530. The MIT Press (2001)

5. Guestrin, C., Lagoudakis, M.G., Parr, R.: Coordinated reinforcement learning. In: Proceedings of the Nineteenth International Conference on Machine Learning, ICML 2002, pp. 227–234. Morgan Kaufmann Publishers Inc., San Francisco (2002)

6. Guestrin, C.E.: Planning under uncertainty in complex structured environments. Ph.D. thesis, Stanford University, Stanford, CA, USA (2003). https://pdfs.semanticscholar.org/ac33/ea3606d5a50f3893b1d5dd964904a5291545.pdf

7. Kok, J.R.: Cooperation and learning in cooperative multiagent systems (2006)

8. Kok, J.R.: Cooperation and learning in cooperative multiagent systems. Ph.D. thesis, University of Amsterdam (2006)

9. Kok, J.R., Vlassis, N.: Collaborative multiagent reinforcement learning by payoff propagation. J. Mach. Learn. Res. **7**(Sep), 1789–1828 (2006)

10. Krajzewicz, D., Erdmann, J., Behrisch, M., Bieker, L.: Recent development and applications of SUMO - Simulation of Urban MObility. Int. J. Adv. Syst. Measure. **5**(3&4), 128–138 (2012)

11. Krajzewicz, D., Erdmann, J., Behrisch, M., Bieker, L.: Traci - SUMO (2017). http://sumo.dlr.de/wiki/TraCI

12. Li, T., Zhao, D., Yi, J.: Adaptive dynamic programming for multi-intersections traffic signal intelligent control. In: 2008 11th International IEEE Conference on Intelligent Transportation Systems, pp. 286–291 (2008). https://doi.org/10.1109/ITSC.2008.4732718

13. Bogota District Mobility Office: Vehicular Flow and Phase Diagrams (2015)

14. de Oliveira, D., Bazzan, A.L.C., da Silva, B.C., Basso, E.W., Nunes, L.: Reinforcement learning based control of traffic lights in non-stationary environments: a case study in a microscopic simulator. In: ResearchGate, vol. 223 (2006)

15. Richter, S., Aberdeen, D., Yu, J.: Natural actor-critic for road traffic optimisation. In: Proceedings of the 19th International Conference on Neural Information Processing Systems, NIPS 2006, pp. 1169–1176. MIT Press, Canada (2006)

16. Robles, D., Ñanez, P., Quijano, N.: Control y simulación de tráfico urbano en colombia: Estado del arte. Revista de Ingeniería **0**, 59–69 (2009), https://ojsrevistaing.uniandes.edu.co/ojs/index.php/revista/article/view/245

17. Sutton, R.S., Barto, A.G.: Reinforcement Learning : An Introduction. MIT Press, Cambridge (1998). https://mitpress.mit.edu/books/reinforcement-learning

18. Wiering, M.: Multi-agent reinforcement learning for traffic light control (2000)

19. Xu, L.H., Xia, X.H., Luo, Q.: The study of reinforcement learning for traffic self-adaptive control under multiagent markov game environment. Math. Probl. Eng. **2013**, e962869 (2013). https://doi.org/10.1155/2013/962869

QoS-Aware Agent Capabilities Composition in HARMS Multi-agent Systems

Mohamed Essaid Khanouche[1,2(✉)], Nawel Atmani[1], Asma Cherifi[1],
Abdelghani Chibani[2], Eric T. Matson[3], and Yacine Amirat[2]

[1] Medical Computing Laboratory, Faculty of Exact Sciences,
University of Bejaia, 06000 Béjaïa, Algeria
`essaid.khanouche@univ-bejaia.dz`
[2] LISSI Laboratory, UPEC University, 94400 Vitry-Sur-Seine, France
`{abdelghani.chibani,amirat}@u-pec.fr`
[3] M2M Lab/RICE Research Center, Purdue University, West Lafayette, IN, USA
`ematson@purdue.edu`

Abstract. With the increasing adoption of Internet of Things (IoT) technologies, the number of agents offering equivalent capabilities is increasing more and more. The services of these capability equivalent agents may have different Quality of Service (QoS) levels. Therefore, the selection of the most appropriate services that best match some given requirements becomes a challenging issue in the HARMS (Human, Agent, Robot, Machine, Sensor) multi-agent systems. In this paper, a Social Group optimization-based QoS-aware agents services Composition Algorithm (SG-QCA) is proposed to enable HARMS interaction layer with the capability of composing agents services in large-scale IoT services environments. The simulation results show that for both randomly generated and real datasets, the proposed approach is scalable and achieves a near-to-optimal composition in a reduced composition time compared to other services composition approaches.

Keywords: Internet of Things (IoT) · HARMS systems ·
Services composition · Quality of Service (QoS) ·
Social Group Optimization (SGO)

1 Introduction

The Internet of Things (IoT) is a new computing paradigm where billions of smart objects (i.g., Smartphones, services robots, public displays) are interconnected through a variety of communication technologies such as Bluetooth, WiFi, ZigBee and GSM [1]. These smart object are instantiated in the cloud as communicating agents having different capabilities that represent the functions performed by their linked sensors/actuators and that are abstracted in IoT environments as *agent services*. The composition of agents services is an organization

© Springer Nature Switzerland AG 2019
Y. Demazeau et al. (Eds.): PAAMS 2019, LNAI 11523, pp. 127–138, 2019.
https://doi.org/10.1007/978-3-030-24209-1_11

process allowing the delivery of an added-value service (composite service) by combining the capabilities of individual agent service (atomic service) in order to satisfy given requirements. In the context of the HARMS multi-agent system model defined by five layers, the main challenge is how the HARMS interaction layer will be able to select, in a transparent way, the most appropriate agents services to be part of the composition, defined in the organization layer as an abstract plan, in order to satisfy as much as possible user's functional and non-functional requirements (see Fig. 1). The latter correspond to global QoS constraints that can be expressed as upper or lower bounds imposed on the QoS attributes values of the composite service requested by users [2].

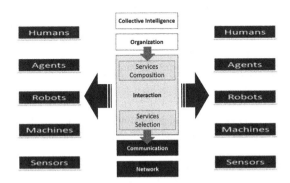

Fig. 1. Agents services composition in a HARMS multi-agent system.

Several researches have been conducted to deal with the composition problems under user's global QoS constraints (e.g., [2–7]). The population-based services composition approaches [7–10] are used to find a trade-off between the optimality of the compositions and the composition time. However, many parameters need to be initially adjusted in these approaches. To deal with this limitation, a population-based optimization method that requires few initialization parameters is used in this paper to solve the agents services composition for HARMS in the context of large-scale IoT environments. Indeed, a Social Group optimization-based QoS-aware agents services Composition Algorithm (SG-QCA) is proposed to find the near-to-optimal compositions (i.e., those that satisfy the QoS constraints and offer the best utility value in terms of QoS) while reducing the composition time. The SG-QCA algorithm is based on the Social Group Optimization (SGO) method [11] and performs in three phases: initializing phase, improving phase and acquiring phase. Note that the second phase of the SGO method is improved when applied to the services composition.

The remainder of this paper is organized as follows. Section 2 summarizes the related work on QoS-aware services composition approaches and discuses the novelty of the approach proposed in this paper. In Sect. 3, the services composition model and an overview of the SGO optimization method are presented. Section 4 details the proposed QoS-aware agents services composition algorithm, whereas Sect. 5 provides its performances evaluation. Finally, Sect. 6 concludes this work and outlines some future work.

2 Related Work

According to the used solving method, the QoS-aware services composition approaches proposed in the literature can be classified into five categories: (i) Integer Linear Programming-based (ILP) approaches, (ii) Pareto optimality-based approaches, (iii) graph-based approaches, (iv) QoS constraints decomposition-based approaches and (v) machine learning-based approaches [12]. Furthermore, another category of services composition approaches that is not pointed by this classification concerns the population-based approaches.

The authors in [3] consider the probability of each execution path in a composition and solves the services composition problem using Integer Programming method. In [13], a theoretical complexity analysis of the plan-based QoS-aware services composition problem is proposed and the mixed ILP method is applied to solve this problem. Pareto-based approaches are based on the principle of Pareto dominance in terms of QoS [4,14]. For instance, the authors in [14] consider the QoS fluctuation using the coefficient of variation concept, prunes the dominated candidate services in terms of QoS and uses Mixed Integer Programming technique to find the near-to-optimal composition. The graph-based approaches model the QoS-aware services composition as a path search problem in a graph [5]. For example, in [5], a services composition approach combining a graph optimization method and a local/global search strategy is proposed to find the composition with a good trade-off between the composition time and the composition optimality in terms of QoS. The QoS constraints decomposition-based approaches decompose the global QoS constraints imposed on the overall composition into local constraints associated to each abstract service of the composition [6,15]. Some services composition approaches use machine learning techniques such as the clustering [2] or the reinforcement learning [16]. In population-based approaches, a population of compositions is evaluated and improved during several iterations until finding the near-to-optimal composition in terms of QoS. The approach proposed in [7] is based on genetic algorithms, whereas that proposed in [8] is based on the Teaching Learning-Based Optimization (TLBO) method [17]. Three algorithms based on Artificial Bee Colony optimization method are proposed to solve the QoS-aware service selection problem in the context of composition process [9]. In [10], a dynamic services composition approach using an hybrid adaptive genetic algorithm and an Ant Colony Optimization method is proposed.

Although the ILP-based QoS-aware services composition approaches [3,13] are able to find the optimal composite service, their time complexity increases exponentially with the problem size. Furthermore, in Pareto optimality-based approaches [4,14], the space search of the composition is reduced by filtering out the compositions that are dominated by other compositions. However, the number of compositions increases exponentially with the number of services leading thus to an excessive composition time [4]. Consequently, these two categories of approaches are not suitable for large-scale services environments such as Internet of Things. In addition, the population-based QoS-aware services composition approaches [7–10] require generally a carefully initialization of a high number of parameters in order to achieve satisfactory performances in terms of composition time and optimality. Unlike the aforementioned approaches, in this paper, the QoS-aware agents services composition is addressed using the *Social Group Optimization* (SGO) algorithm [11] that is characterized by a few initialization parameters and a high exploration capability of the compositions search space.

3   Background

3.1   HARMS and Services Composition Modelling

The HARMS (Human, Agent, Robot, Machine, Sensor) is a layered model for building multi-agent systems with self-organizing, adaptable, autonomous, indistinguishable and mobile actors. This model can be divided into five layers: network, communication, interaction, organization and collective intelligence (Fig. 1) [18]. The *network* layer represents the basic communication between the system actors such as humans, software agents, robots, machines, and sensors. The *communication* layer allows the basic information exchange capability between all of system actors. The *interaction* layer represents the means to let the system actors being able to react according to the received messages. The *organization* layer enables the different actors to be assigned activities based on the indistinguishability concept. Indeed, when there are a number of system actors with the same capability (i.e., indistinguishable actors), the capability to solve a goal must be the only selection criterion between the indistinguishable system actors. The *collective Intelligence* behavior in a collection of agents, robots and humans can lean in a number of different directions.

In the context of IoT-based applications, HARMS allows any actor to take the lead part of a multi-agent system when receiving a request from a human asking for an assisted service. The latter represents the user's functional requirements and can be modeled as a composition plan $CP = \langle AS_1, ...AS_i, ..., AS_m \rangle$ with m abstract services. Each abstract service $AS_i = \{cs_1^i, ..., cs_j^i, ..., cs_n^i\}$ is executed by n functionally equivalent candidate services. A candidate service cs_j^i is an invokable concrete service and is represented by a vector $QoS(cs_j^i) = (qos_{1,j}^i, ..., qos_{q,j}^i, ..., qos_{k,j}^i)$, where $qos_{q,j}^i$ $(1 \leq q \leq k)$ is the value of the qth QoS attribute. The commonly used QoS attributes in the literature include *cost, reliability, availability, throughput,* and *response time* [15]. A composite service $CC_l = \langle cs_{l,j_1}^1, .., cs_{l,j_i}^i, ..., cs_{l,j_m}^m \rangle$ $(1 \leq j_i \leq n)$ is obtained by selecting one candidate service from each abstract service of the composition plan CP. The QoS of a composite service CC_l is represented by a vector $QoS(CC_l) = (Q_{1,l}, ..., Q_{q,l}, ..., Q_{k,l})$, where $Q_{q,l}$ is the aggregated value of the qth QoS attribute, which is calculated from the values of the qth attributes of candidate services selected for the composition by considering the composite service structure [15].

3.2   Social Group Optimization Algorithm

The Social Group Optimization (SGO) method is a population-based algorithm highlighting that a group of persons have much more ability to solve a given problem compared to the ability of a single person [11]. Each person has a knowledge level in a given topic and the person who has the highest knowledge level is considered as the best person in the group. The SGO method performs in the three following phases:

Initialization Phase: During this phase, the parameters of the algorithm are initialized, such as the initial population, the maximum number of iterations $Maxiter$, the population size $Popsize$ that represents the number of persons in a group and the number of topics D. The initial population of persons is generated randomly. Each person l is represented by a vector $X_l = (x_{l,j}^1, ..., x_{l,j}^i, ..., x_{l,j}^D)$ where $x_{l,j}^i$ is the jth knowledge level of the lth person in the ith topic.

Improving Phase: In this phase, each person l in a given group improves his/her knowledge according to the best person $best$ in the group. Formally:

$$X_{lNew} = c \times X_{lOld} + r_1 \times (X_{best} - X_{lOld}) \tag{1}$$

where r_1 and c are random numbers generated in the interval $[0, 1]$. A fitness function f is used to evaluate the knowledge of each person in the group. When the new knowledge of the person l is better than his/her old knowledge in terms of the fitness function, the new knowledge is replaced by the old one.

Acquiring Phase: During this phase, each person l in the group improves his/her knowledge by interacting simultaneously with a randomly selected person e and the best person $best$ in the group as follows:

$$X_{lNew} = \begin{cases} X_{lOld} + r_1 \times (X_l - X_e) + r_2 \times (X_{best} - X_e) \text{ if } f(X_l) \text{ is better than } f(X_e) \\ X_{lOld} + r_3 \times (X_e - X_l) + r_4 \times (X_{best} - X_e) \text{ otherwise} \end{cases} \tag{2}$$

where r_1, r_2, r_3 and r_4 are random numbers generated in the interval $[0, 1]$. If the new knowledge of the person l is better than his/her old knowledge then the new knowledge of the person l replaces his/her old knowledge.

4   The Proposed Algorithm: SG-QCA

In this paper, a Social Group optimization-based QoS-aware agents services Composition Algorithm (SG-QCA) is proposed. The services composition problem accounting for QoS constraints is modelled and solved using the SGO method. The group of persons in SGO algorithm represents the population of compositions in the context of services composition. A person $X_l = (x_{l,j}^1, ..., x_{l,j}^i, ..., x_{l,j}^D)$ represents the lth concrete composition $CC_l = (x_{l,j}^1, ..., x_{l,j}^i, ..., x_{l,j}^m)$, where $x_{l,j}^i$ is the index of the jth candidate service in the ith abstract service of the lth composition. Table 1 shows the terms matching between the SGO algorithm and the QoS-aware services composition.

Table 1. The SGO algorithm versus the QoS-aware services composition.

SGO algorithm	QoS-aware services composition
Social group	The population of services compositions
Knowledge level	The index of a candidate service in a composition
Topic	An abstract service
Person	A service composition in the population
Fitness function	The utility value in terms of QoS
Best person	The best services composition in terms of the utility value

4.1 The SG-QCA Algorithm Phases

Initialization Phase: In this phase, the parameters of the SG-QCA algorithm are initialized: the randomly created initial population of compositions, the maximum number of iterations $Maxiter$ and the number of compositions in the population $Popsize$.

Improving Phase: During this phase, each composition CC_l is evaluated using a utility value in terms of QoS $F(CC_l)$ that is calculated as the weighted sum of its QoS attributes by accounting for the user's preferences with respect to each QoS attribute. Improving a composition based on the best composition in terms of utility value and the composition itself, may not lead to a satisfactory performance since some compositions may have a low utility values. Therefore, the mean of the compositions is used in this paper to improve the compositions in an interval that contains high utility values. Accordingly, a composition CC_l is improved using the best composition in terms of utility value CC_{best} and the mean compositions CC_{Mean} in the population. Formally:

$$CC_{lNew} = CC_{lOld} \oplus r_1 \times (CC_{best} \ominus r_m \times CC_{Mean}) \tag{3}$$

where r_1 is a random number generated in the interval $[0,1]$ and r_m is a random number equal to 1 or 2. Note that, $\oplus$ and $\ominus$ are specific operators that will be defined in Sect. 4.2. The mean composition CC_{Mean} is calculated as follows:

$$CC_{Mean} = 1/Popsize \sum_{l=1}^{Popsize} CC_l \tag{4}$$

In the case where the new utility value of the composition CC_l is better than its old one, the composition CC_l is replaced in the population. Algorithm 1 summarizes the improving phase steps of the SG-QCA algorithm.

Acquiring Phase: In this phase, each composition CC_l is improved according to a randomly selected composition CC_r and the best composition CC_{best} in terms of utility value in the population. Formally:

$$CC_{lNew} = \begin{cases} CC_{lOld} \oplus r_1 \times (CC_l \ominus CC_r) \oplus r_2 \times (CC_{best} \ominus CC_r) & \text{If } F(CC_l) \text{ is better than } F(CC_r) \\ CC_{lOld} \oplus r_3 \times (CC_r \ominus CC_l) \oplus r_4 \times (CC_{best} \ominus CC_r) & \text{otherwise} \end{cases} \tag{5}$$

Algorithm 1. The improving phase of the SG-QCA algorithm

Input : $Popsize, CC_{best}, CC_{Mean}$, a population, $BestSol$.

1: **for** $l = 1$ **to** $Popsize$ **do**
2:     Calculate CC_{lNew} using Eq. (3);
3:     **if** $F(CC_{lNew}) > F(CC_{lOld})$ **then**
4:         CC_{lNew} replace CC_{lOld};
5:         **if** $F(CC_{lNew}) > F(BestSol)$ and CC_{lNew} satisfies the QoS constraints **then**
6:             $BestSol = CC_{lNew}$;
7:         **end if**
8:     **end if**
9: **end for**

Output : A new population and $BestSol$.

In the case where the new utility value of the composition CC_l is better than its old one, the composition CC_l is replaced in the population. Algorithm 2 summarizes the acquiring phase steps of the SG-QCA algorithm.

Algorithm 2. The acquiring phase of the SG-QCA algorithm

Input: $Popsize$, a population, $BestSol$.

1: **for** $l = 1$ **to** $Popsize$ **do**
2:     Calculate CC_{lNew} using Eq. (5);
3:     **if** $F(CC_{lNew}) > F(CC_{lOld})$ **then**
4:         CC_{lNew} replace CC_{lOld} ;
5:         **if** $F(CC_{lNew}) > F(BestSol)$ and CC_{lNew} satisfies the QoS constraints **then**
6:             $BestSol = CC_{lNew}$;
7:         **end if**
8:     **end if**
9: **end for**

Output: A new population and $BestSol$.

The phases of the SG-QCA algorithm are described in Algorithm 3.

4.2   The Operators Used in SG-QCA Algorithm

In the SG-QCA algorithm, the operators $\oplus$ and $\ominus$ are used in the improvement process. The *subtraction operator* $\ominus$ is defined based on the candidate services indexes. Given two compositions CC_u and CC_v from the population, if the index of a candidate service of the new composition $CC_u \ominus CC_v$ is lower than the lower bound of the candidate services indexes, the index of this candidate service will be replaced by the lower bound value. The *addition operator* $\oplus$ is also defined based on the candidate services indexes. Given two compositions CC_u and CC_v from the population, if the index of a candidate service of the new composition $CC_u \oplus CC_v$ is higher than the upper bound of the candidate services indexes, the index of this candidate service will be replaced by the upper bound value.

Algorithm 3. The SG-QCA algorithm phases

Input: *Popsize*, *Maxiter* and the initial population.

1: **while** $it \leq Maxiter$ **do**
2:     $BestSol = 0$;
3:     Find CC_{Mean} and CC_{best}.
4:     The improving phase is carried out using Algorithm 1.
5:     The acquiring phase is performed using Algorithm 2.
6: **end while**

Output: The near-to-optimal composition.

---

5   Evaluation and Simulation Results

The SG-QCA algorithm was evaluated in simulation using Matlab R2014b running on a machine equipped with a 64-bit Windows OS, an Intel Core i3-6006HQ CPU with a frequency of 2 GHz and 8 GB RAM. The services compositions considered in the simulation scenarios have a sequential structure. The performances evaluation of the SG-QCA algorithm is carried out using two kinds of datasets: a random dataset and a real dataset. In the randomly generated dataset, the QoS values of the candidate services were synthesized following the values reported in [19] that can represent the services in any service-oriented domain. The real data corresponds to the QWS dataset that includes 9 QoS attributes values of 2507 web services [20]. In the considered services composition scenarios, for both randomly generated and real datasets, each candidate service is described by five QoS attributes. The population size *Popsize* is set to 15 and the maximum number of iterations *Maxiter* is set to 100.

5.1   Performance Metrics

The performances of the SG-QCA algorithm are compared to those of the mobility-enabled Teaching Learning-based QoS-aware services Composition Algorithm (TL-QCA) [8]. The metrics considered for the evaluation are: (*i*) the *composition time* that represents the composition time required by each services composition algorithm (SG-QCA and TL-QCA) to obtain the near-to-optimal composition, (*ii*) the *utility value* of the best composition in terms of QoS obtained with each algorithm, and (*iii*) the *optimality* that defines the ratio between the utility value of the best composition obtained in the case of each algorithm and the utility value of the optimal composition obtained with an exhaustive search algorithm.

5.2   Simulation Results

The performances evaluation of the two composition algorithms are carried out according to two services composition scenarios that are described in Table 2:

Table 2. The simulation parameters of the two services composition scenarios

Simulation parameters	Services composition scenarios	
	Scenario 1	Scenario 2
The number of abstract services	3	10
The number of concrete services	30 to 120	60 to 510
The number of simulations	10	50
Dataset type	Random	Real and random

Scenario 1. The first services composition scenario aims at measuring and comparing the composition time and the optimality of the composition provided by the SG-QCA and the TL-QCA algorithms.

Composition Time: In this simulation, the SG-QCA and TL-QCA algorithms are compared in terms of the composition time. Figure 2 shows that the composition time of the two algorithms increases with the number of concrete services. This result is due to the fact that the time required to find the concrete service that could be part of a composition increases with the number of available concrete services in the IoT environment. However, the SG-QCA has a low convergence time then the TL-QCA because during the execution of the acquiring phase, the compositions are improved considering the best composition instead of considering only the randomly selected one. This allows a better exploration of the search space and therefore improves the convergence of the algorithm.

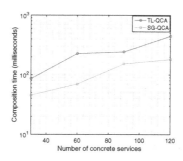

Fig. 2. Composition time vs. the number of concrete services (scenario 1).

Optimality of the Composition: This simulation aims at comparing the optimality of the compositions obtained in the case of the SG-QCA and TL-QCA algorithms. Figure 3 shows that the optimality obtained in the case of the SG-QCA and TL-QCA algorithms decreases slightly when the number of concrete services increases but the SG-QCA algorithm remains more efficient than the TL-QCA algorithm. This is due to the fact that 100 iterations are not enough for these algorithms to fully explore the search space of the compositions in order to find the near-to-optimal composition.

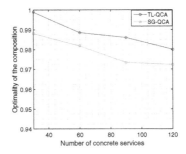

Fig. 3. Optimality vs. the number of concrete services (scenario 1).

Scenario 2. The aim of this scenario is to test the scalability of the SG-QCA algorithm regarding the number of concrete services. To do this, the composition time and the utility values of the composition provided by the SG-QCA and TL-QCA algorithms are measured and compared.

Composition Time: In this simulation, we measure the variation of the composition time taken by the SG-QCA and TL-QCA algorithms against the number of candidate services. Figure 4 shows that the composition time of the two algorithms increases slightly with the number of concrete services. Similarly to the first scenario, the time required to find the concrete service that could be part of a composition increases with the number of candidate services. In addition, the SG-QCA algorithm has a lower composition time compared to TL-QCA because it converges quickly to the best composition thanks to the acquiring phase.

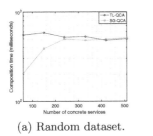
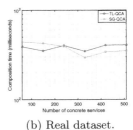

(a) Random dataset.　　　　　　(b) Real dataset.

Fig. 4. Composition time vs. the number of concrete services (scenario 2).

The Utility Value: In this simulation, we compare the utility values of the compositions provided by the SG-QCA and TL-QCA algorithms. As shown in Fig. 5, the utility value of the SG-QCA algorithm decreases slightly when the number of concrete services increases but remains better than that obtained by the TL-QCA algorithm which decreases significantly and in continuous manner. This result is due to the better strategy used by the SG-QCA algorithm to explore the search space, which selects the most appropriate services in terms of QoS for the composition process.

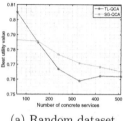

(a) Random dataset.

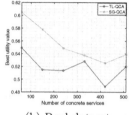

(b) Real dataset.

Fig. 5. Utility value vs. the number of concrete services (scenario 2).

6   Conclusion and Future Work

In this paper, a Social Group-based QoS-aware agents services Composition Algorithm (SG-QCA) is proposed in large-scale IoT environments to enable HARMS with the capability to make QoS-aware services composition. The SG-QCA algorithm guaranties a low composition and convergence time due to it's acquiring phase that allows a better exploration of the search space. The simulation scenarios carried out on both randomly generated and real datasets show that the SG-QCA algorithm is very promising in terms of composition time and achieves a composition with a satisfactory optimality. As future work, we plan to deal with the energy consumption during the services composition since the IoT objects offering the candidate services are resource-limited devices.

References

1. Yaqoob, I., et al.: Internet of things architecture: recent advances, taxonomy, requirements, and open challenges. IEEE Wirel. Commun. **24**(3), 10–16 (2017)
2. Khanouche, M.E., Attal, F., Amirat, Y., Chibani, A., Kerkar, M.: Clustering-based and QoS-aware services composition algorithm for ambient intelligence. Inf. Sci. **482**, 419–439 (2019)
3. Zheng, H., Zhao, W., Yang, J., Bouguettaya, A.: Qos analysis for web service compositions with complex structures. IEEE Trans. Serv. Comput. **6**(3), 373–386 (2013)
4. Chen, Y., Huang, J., Lin, C., Hu, J.: A partial selection methodology for efficient QoS-aware service composition. IEEE Trans. Serv. Comput. **8**(3), 384–397 (2015)
5. Rodriguez-Mier, P., Mucientes, M., Lama, M.: Hybrid optimization algorithm for large-scale QoS-aware service composition. IEEE Trans. Serv. Comput. **10**(4), 547–559 (2017)
6. Alrifai, M., Risse, T., Nejdl, W.: A hybrid approach for efficient web service composition with end-to-end QoS constraints. ACM Trans. Web (TWEB) **6**(2), 7:1–7:31 (2012)
7. Deng, S., Wu, H., Tan, W., Xiang, Z., Wu, Z.: Mobile service selection for composition: an energy consumption perspective. IEEE Trans. Autom. Sci. Eng. **14**(3), 1478–1490 (2017)
8. Deng, S., Huang, L., Hu, D., Zhao, J.L., Wu, Z.: Mobility-enabled service selection for composite services. IEEE Trans. Serv. Comput. **9**(3), 394–407 (2016)

9. Wang, X., Xu, X., Sheng, Q.Z., Wang, Z., Yao, L.: Novel artificial bee colony algorithms for QoS-aware service selection. IEEE Trans. Serv. Comput. **12**, 247–261 (2016)
10. Mistry, S., Bouguettaya, A., Dong, H., Qi, A.K.: Metaheuristic optimization for long-term IaaS service composition. IEEE Trans. Serv. Comput. **11**(1), 131–143 (2018)
11. Satapathy, S., Naik, A.: Social group optimization (SGO): a new population evolutionary optimization technique. Complex Intell. Syst. **2**(3), 173–203 (2016)
12. Khanouche, M.E., Amirat, Y., Chibani, A., Kerkar, M., Yachir, A.: Energy-centered and QoS-aware services selection for internet of things. IEEE Trans. Autom. Sci. Eng. **13**(3), 1256–1269 (2016)
13. Gabrel, V., Manouvrier, M., Murat, C.: Web services composition: complexity and models. Discrete Appl. Math. **196**, 100–114 (2015)
14. Wang, S., Zhou, A., Yang, M., Sun, L., Hsu, C.H. et al.: Service composition in cyber-physical-social systems. IEEE Trans. Emerg. Top. Comput. (2017)
15. Sun, S.X., Zhao, J.: A decomposition-based approach for service composition with global QoS guarantees. Inf. Sci. **199**, 138–153 (2012)
16. Ren, L., Wang, W., Xu, H.: A reinforcement learning method for constraint-satisfied services composition. IEEE Trans. Serv. Comput. (2017)
17. Rao, R.V., Savsani, V.J., Vakharia, D.P.: Teaching-learning-based optimization: an optimization method for continuous non-linear large scale problems. Inf. Sci. **183**(1), 1–15 (2012)
18. Lewis, J., Matson, E.T., Wei, S., Min, B.: Implementing harms-based indistinguishability in ubiquitous robot organizations. Robot. Auton. Syst. **61**(11), 1186–1192 (2013)
19. Al-Masri, E., Mahmoud, Q.H.: QoS-based discovery and ranking of web services. In: 2007 16th International Conference on Computer Communications and Networks, pp. 529–534. IEEE, August 2007
20. Al-Masrib, E., Mahmoud, Q.H.: Investigating web services on the world wide web. In: Proceedings of the 17th International Conference on World Wide Web, pp. 795–804. ACM (2008)

MASS CUDA: A General GPU Parallelization Framework for Agent-Based Models

Lisa Kosiachenko, Nathaniel Hart, and Munehiro Fukuda$^{(\boxtimes)}$ (iD)

Computing and Software Systems, University of Washington,
Bothell, WA 98011, USA
ekosyachenko@gmail.com, nathanielbhart@gmail.com, mfukuda@uw.edu
http://depts.washington.edu/dslab

Abstract. GPU-based parallelization of agent-based modeling (ABM) has been highlighted for the last decade to address its computational needs for scalable and long-run simulations in practical use. From the software productivity viewpoint, model designers would prefer general ABM frameworks for GPU parallelization. However, having transited from single-node or cluster-computing platforms to GPUs, most general ABM frameworks maintain their APIs at the script level, delegate only a limited number of agent functions to GPUs, and copy agent data between host and device memory for each function call, which cannot ease agent description nor maximize GPU parallelism. To respond to these problems, we have developed the MASS (Multi-Agent Spatial Simulation) CUDA library that allows users to describe all simulation models in CUDA C++, to automate entire model parallelization at GPU, and to minimize host-to-device memory transfer. However, our straightforward implementation did not improve the parallel performance. Focusing on the data-parallel computation with GPU, we examined MASS overheads in GPU memory usage and developed optimization techniques that reduce kernel context switches, optimize kernel configuration, use constant memory, and reduce overheads incurred by agent population, migration, and termination. These techniques improved Heat2D and SugarScape's execution performance, respectively 3.9 times and 5.8 times faster than the corresponding C++ sequential programs. This paper gives details of our GPU parallelization techniques for multi-agent simulation and demonstrates the MASS CUDAs performance improvements.

Keywords: Agent-based simulation · GPU parallelization ·
Simulation platforms

1 Introduction

Agent-based models (ABMs) have gained in popularity as a method of observing emergent collective group behavior of many agents, each with its own itinerary,

© Springer Nature Switzerland AG 2019
Y. Demazeau et al. (Eds.): PAAMS 2019, LNAI 11523, pp. 139–152, 2019.
https://doi.org/10.1007/978-3-030-24209-1_12

agenda, and behavior. For practical applications, ABMs need to be able to scale up their problem sizes, e.g., an immune system simulation of 64 thousand cells [8], a metropolitan traffic of 180 thousand vehicles [3], and an influenza epidemic among 200 million citizens [7]. Parallelization has provided a solution to ABMs scalability issue from its inception. To better fit fine-grained computation of each agent behavior as well as tightly-coupled inter-agent communication, ABM parallelization expanded its platforms from cluster systems to GPGPUs (General-Purpose GPUs). It has improved GPU-based parallelization techniques through the following three stages: (1) application-specific ABM parallelization, (2) development of more generalized parallelization techniques, and (3) automated parallelization with general ABM frameworks.

Ideally, general ABM frameworks should inherit GPU-based parallelization techniques developed so far from the first two stages. However, this assumption is not always true. Most ABM frameworks have transited from their previous single-node or cluster-computing platforms to GPUs, which resulted in problems inherent to reuse of their software assets. They reuse the original high-level APIs in Java or Logo; keep describing separate agent schemas in XML; maintain most agents and their environmental states in host memory; delegate only a limited number of agent functions to GPUs; and thus copy agent data to GPU for each function invocation. Despite the intention to facilitate smooth transition to GPUs for better parallelization, these implementations limit model descriptivity and performance improvement.

To address these limitations in the current ABM frameworks, we took a different approach that allows model developers to maintain all agent and environmental data at the GPU level and to describe/execute their behaviors in CUDA C++, while the main program running at CPU serves as a simulation scenario to schedule their invocations. We implemented this approach in the CUDA version of our multi-agent spatial simulation (MASS CUDA) library. The major contributions of our work are two-fold: (1) applying the model-view-presenter (MVP) software architecture to the deployment of all agents and their simulation environments to GPU and (2) presenting optimization techniques to fit this deployment strategy.

The rest of this paper is organized as follows: Sect. 2 looks at related work in GPU-parallelized ABM; Sect. 3 presents MASS CUDA's software architecture; Sect. 4 discusses our performance optimizations; Sect. 5 demonstrates its execution performance; and Sect. 6 concludes with a brief discussion of planned future work.

2 Related Work

This section describes how MASS CUDA differs from other GPU-based ABM parallelization in terms of (1) application-specific parallelization, (2) generalized parallelization techniques, and (3) general ABM frameworks.

2.1 Application-Specific Parallelization

Within a few years of the CUDA architecture being announced in 2007, (mostly in 2009–2013), many ABM applications were parallelized, directly using GPG-PUs. Their application domains vary across biology (e.g., agent-based model simulations of tuberculosis (TB) [8]), physics (such as molecular dynamics simulation on hybrid CPU-GPU computing platforms [6]), computational science (e.g., ant colony optimization [5]), and social, behavioral, and environmental studies (e.g., agent-based traffic simulation with CUDA [15]).

TB epidemic [8] implemented a collision map on the GPU shared memory to avoid agent collision. It also sorted an array of agents to garbage-collect the space for future agents. Molecular dynamics [6] used array sorting, too, while its intention was to rebalance the number of agents residing on each array element. Ant colony optimization [5] focused on OpenMP/GPU hybrid computation where OpenMP took care of each ant agents tour construction process, while a GPU maintained the spatial data, (i.e., a list of nearest neighboring cities) to perform parallel selection of the next cities. Traffic simulation [15] has treated each road segment as a circular queue to move vehicle agents to the next road segment in a FIFO order, which not only eliminates garbage-collecting overheads but also coalesces memory accesses with an array of the queues.

As these techniques have been tuned to each different application, of importance is to consider how they can be adapted to general ABM frameworks. For instance, although agent sorting would work to garbage collection in many ABM applications, agent environmental data could not be always modeled, using a collision map or an array of queues. In other words, we need more generalized data structures to represent simulation environments.

2.2 Generalized Parallelization Techniques

GPU-based parallelization techniques began to be generalized around 2016, initially focusing on GPU memory hierarchy and limited capacity of GPUs. Attention was paid to where in device memory and how to map agent and environmental data.

Latency hiding was proposed by Aaby et al. [1] to partition a grid of agents into small blocks to fit fast shared memory. This mechanism updates agent states quickly and thereafter exchanges them with neighboring blocks. GPU delegation [9] maintains agent states on host memory and delegates their popular behavioral functions (such as collision avoidance, flock centering, and velocity matching) to GPU as passing environmental data to these functions. This delegation strategy fitted well with a limited amount of device memory and clearly separated agents states and functions. Agent pooling [11] allocates a fixed capacity of space to hold the maximum number of agents to be created during computation. It quickly recruits available space by swapping a pair of pointers, one for a terminating and the other for a spawning agent.

Despite their goals for broader uses, they still suffer from their drawbacks as general techniques. Latency hiding is challenging whenever changing the size or a dimension of agent grid; GPU delegation cannot maximize GPU parallelism beyond a limited number of agent functions; and agent pooling is bound to the fixed scalability of an agent population.

2.3   General ABM Frameworks

FLAME GPU [13] jumped at the chance of GPU-based parallelization in 2009. As in its former implementation with MPI, FLAME generates agent templates from XML-based agent schemas, so that users can implement architecture-agnostic agent code using templates. Turtle Kit [12] is a Logo-based spatial ABM platform, implemented in Java. Its strategy in GPU parallelization is to develop a GPU library of various agent behaviors, plugged in from Logo users. Clearly, Turtle Kit is an example of adapting GPU delegation to its framework. MCMAS [10] is another ABM framework that delegates agent functions from Java to GPU. To parallelize entire agent models, called model parallelization, MCMAS enabled users to call any user-defined GPU functions from Java.

However, these frameworks expose drawbacks in model descriptivity and performance improvement, both inherent to reuse of their software assets. FLAMEs XML-based agent schemas and MCMAS model parallelization increase complexity of agent definition and description in two programming languages, (i.e., XML/Java versus CUDA). FLAMEs lack of shared-space concept increases the number of messages exchanged among agents, each maintaining spatial data independently. Finally, GPU delegation cannot maximize GPU parallelism due to frequent host-to-device memory copies of agent and spatial data.

Comparing with the related work, MASS CUDA realizes a general **Agents** class, facilitates multi-dimensional **Places** environments, and allows users to describe all models in CUDA C++. It promotes the concept of model parallelization by maintaining and computing all agents and their environments at GPU.

3   MASS: Multi-agent Spatial Simulation Library

The MASS library is a general ABM framework, available in Java and C++[1] to parallelize ABM over a cluster system. MASS CUDA is the GPU version to run ABMs in the same programing concept as MASS Java and C++. **Places** and **Agents** are the two main base classes in MASS. **Places** is an architectural-independent multi-dimensional array that is used as a simulation environment and is distributed over a cluster system or directly allocated in GPU device memory, depending on a platform to run an ABM program. **Agents** is populated over a user-defined **Places** where each agent resides in a given place, interacts with others on the same place, and migrates from one place to another, all resulting in forming an emergent corrective group behavior.

---

[1] http://depts.washington.edu/dslab/MASS/.

3.1   Programming Model

The **main( )** program simply behaves as a simulation scenario to schedule **Places** creation, **Agents** population, and their computation, all that are however executed in parallel over computing nodes of a cluster system or with many cores in a GPU. To facilitate this model parallelization, MASS provides **main( )** with the MASS interface summarized in Table 1. Note that we now focus on only MASS CUDA specification in the following discussions.

Table 1. MASS CUDA specification

Methods	Descriptions
Places *createPlaces( )	Instantiates a user-derived Places in GPU memory
Places.callAll(funcId)	Invokes a given function of all places with GPU
Places.exchangeAll(nbrs)	Read neighboring places' internal data into nbrs[]
Places.getElements( )	Retrieves all place objects
Agents *createAgents( )	Populates a user-derived Agents in GPU
Agents.callAll(funcId)	Invokes a given function of all agents with GPU. It may call the system built-in functions including kill( ), spawn( ), and migrate( )
Agents.manageAll( )	Performs agent termination, replication, and migration, each scheduled in the last callAll( )
Agents.getElements( )	Retrieves all agent objects

Each model is described in CUDA C++ variadic templates and is derived from either the **Place** or **Agent** class. It defines each object state in either **PlaceState** or **AgentState** and implements all behaviors in respective functions.

To outline how to describe ABM in MASS CUDA, let us consider two simulation examples: Heat2D and SugarScape. The former is a spatial simulation that observes heat dissemination over a 2D metal plate. The latter is an agent simulation that observes a survival process of agents, each searching for sugar.

Heat2D can be coded with two components: (1) **main( )** as its simulation scenario and (2) the **Metal** class as the spatial model. The **main( )** function instantiates 2D **Metal** places, calling **metal=Places::createPlaces<Metal, MetalState>(size, size)**; sets up the initial metal temperature through **metal→callAll(Metal::init)**; and thereafter falls into a cyclic simulation that repeats calling **metal→exchangeAll(Metal::disseminate)** and **callAll(Metal::update-Heat)**. The **Metal** class defines temperature in **MetalState** and implements its functions including **init**, **disseminate**, and **updateHeat**, each initializing temperature in every single place, disseminating it to the neighbors, and calculating the new temperature.

SugarScape can be implemented with three components: (1) **main( )** as the simulation scenario, (2) the **Sugar** class as the spatial model, and (3) the **Ant** class as the agent model. As shown in Listing 1.1, **main( )** function instantiates 2D **Sugar** places (lines 3–4); populates **Ant** agents over **Sugar** (lines 5–6); and thereafter goes to a cyclic simulation (lines 8–17) where each place increments sugar and pollution amount (line 9), exchanges pollution with its neighbors (lines 10–11), and updates its pollution with the average (line 12). On the other hand, each agent migrates from one place to another in search for sugar (lines 13–14) and metabolizes itself that may deposit pollution or starve to death (lines 15–16).

Each model is also described in CUDA C++, using its templates. Listing 1.2 gives a snapshot of the **Sugar** and **Ant** classes used in SugarScape, each respectively derived from the **Place** and **Agent** classes. Each model needs to include **callMethod** (line 7 in Sugar and line 20 in Ant) that is invoked from **main( )** through **callAll** or **exchangeAll**. The **callMethod( )** method is used to receive functionId as an argument and to dispatch the call to the corresponding model behavioral function (lines 11–13 in **Sugar** and lines 24–25 in **Ant**). The model designer can describe any place and agent behavior in these functions. In the SugarScape example shown in Listing 1.2, the actual **Sugar** and **Ant** behaviors are implemented in **incSugarAndPollution( )**, **avePollutions( )**, **updatePollution( )**, **metabolize( )** and **migrate( )**.

Listing 1.1. SugarScape's main( ) function as the simulation scenario

```
1 int main( ) {
2 Mass::init( );
3 Places *places=Mass::createPlaces<Sugar,
4                    SugarState>(0, 2, {500, 500});
5 Agents *agents=Mass::createAgents<Ant,AntState>
6             ( 1, nAgents, NULL ); // NULL arguments
7 vector<int*> nbr; // create neighborhood
8 for ( int t = 0; t < max_time; t++ ) {
9    places->callAll(Sugar::INC_SUGAR_POLLUTE);
10   places->exchangeAll(&nbr,
11                       Sugar::AVE_POLLUTIONS);
12   places->callAll( Sugar::UPDATE_POLLUTION);
13   agents->callAll( Ant::MIGRATE);
14   agents->manageAll( );
15   agents->callAll( Ant::METABOLIZE);
16   agents->manageAll( );
17   }
18 Mass::finish( );
19 }
```

Listing 1.2. SugarScape's simulation models: Sugar and Ant

```
1 class Sugar: public mass::Place {
2 public:
3    const static int INC_SUGAR_POLLUTE = 0;
4    const static int AVE_POLLUTIONS = 1;
5    const static int UPDATE_POLLUTION = 2;
6    MASS_FUNCTION Sugar(Mass::PlaceState *stat);
7    MASS_FUNCTION virtual void callMethod
8                            (int funcId, void *arg);
9 private:
10   SugarState* myState;
11   MASS_FUNCTION void incSugarAndPollution( );
12   MASS_FUNCTION void avePollutions( );
13   MASS_FUNCTION void updatePollution( );
14 };
15 class Ant: public mass::Agent {
16 public:
17   const static int METABOLIZE = 0;
18   const static int MIGRATE = 1;
19   MASS_FUNCTION Ant(mass::AgentState *state);
20   MASS_FUNCTION virtual void callMethod
21                            (int funcId, void *arg);
22 private:
23   AntState* myState;
24   MASS_FUNCTION void metabolize( );
25   MASS_FUNCTION void migrate( );
26 };
```

Note that data inputs to or outputs from models on GPU take a form of passing arguments to **Places/Agents** functions or calling their **getElements( )** functions to retrieve their states. For best performance, **main( )** should give initial data to GPU through **createPlaces/Agents( )** at the beginning of simulation, avoid passing arguments to places or agents during computation, and finally call **Places/Agents.getElements( )** at the end of simulation.

3.2   MASS CUDA Architecture

The MASS library architecture is based on the Model-View-Presenter (MVP) pattern. As illustrated in Fig. 1, View represents the API of the MASS library;

Model represents the data model on both GPU and CPU; and Presenter represents the dispatcher in charge of coordinating the interaction between Model and View, taking care of memory transfers between CPU and GPU (if necessary), and launching GPU kernels.

Since a user-derived class that is instantiated either on the host or the device cannot be mutually executed or accessed programmatically, MASS CUDA separates model behavior and state into Place/Agent and PlaceState/AgentState respectively. An array of concrete behavior classes are instantiated both on the host and device, as well as an array of state classes of equal size. As described in Fig. 2, each behavior instance is assigned a unique state instance. Memory transfer is achieved by copying only the state array between host and device. This in turn means that two minimal memory transfers may occur: one from host to device to initialize model states in GPU and the other from device to host to retrieve their final results.

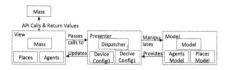

Fig. 1. High-level architecture of the MASS CUDA library

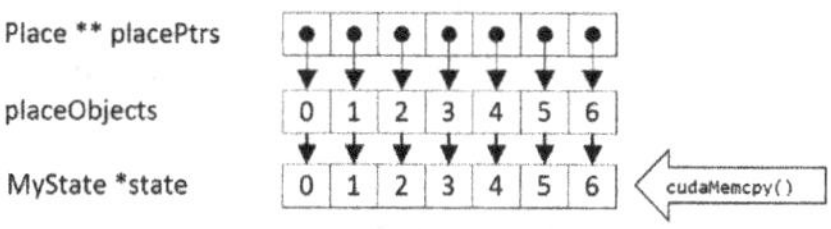

Fig. 2. Separation of behavior and state

Figure 3 is an interaction chart that illustrates a control transition from a user application all the way to GPU. Called from the views static template function, either **createPlaces<T,S>( )** or **createAgents<T,S>( )**, the presenter instantiates PlacesModel or AgentsModel as well as allocates the corresponding PlacesState or AgentsState in the device memory. Once simulation elements are created, the user application begins issuing instructions to the API such as

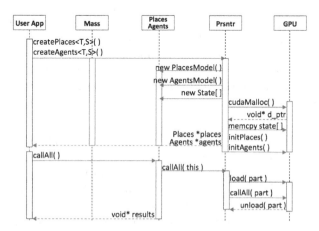

Fig. 3. View, presenter, and model interaction

callAll, exchangeAll, and manageAll. The presenter relays these calls to the corresponding kernel functions. A kernel function has all the GPU threads calculate their own index of simulation entities, (i.e., places or agents), and invoke a given behavioral function simultaneously.

4   Optimization Techniques to Run ABM on GPU

This section discusses optimization techniques for model parallelization using GPU. Although MASS CUDA was designed to describe all models in CUDA C++, to entirely parallelize them at the GPU level, and to minimize memory transfers, our straightforward implementation did not maximize GPU parallelism. As GPU computing is based on data parallelism, the efficient use of GPU cache memory is the key to performance improvement. Since MASS library supports not only agents but also spatial simulation, we particularly examined the overheads that slow down GPU computation from the viewpoints of (1) spatial simulation and (2) agent simulation.

4.1   Space Parallelization

We have looked at the following three performance factors that influence GPU kernel execution: (a) kernel context switches, (b) kernel configuration, and (c) device memory hierarchy.

Avoiding Kernel Context Switches. Spatial simulation in many cases computes wave propagation, heat diffusion, and airflow, all that involve data exchange among neighboring cells, followed by state update in each cell. In MASS CUDA, this corresponds to an exchangeAll( ) invocation followed by a callAll( ) call. The former function is used to collect data from the provided array of neighbors and save it into the message array in each place. These messages are then used by the subsequent callAll( ) that executes another user-defined function on all the place objects in a collection. However, every method call from the host results in switching a kernel context and flushing cached data. To avoid an additional context switch, we combined the exchangeAll( ) and callAll(funcId) functionalities in exchangeAll(funcId) as one GPU kernel call, which allows data to be exchanged and cached in the same context for the continuous uses.

Optimizing Kernel Configuration. The number of blocks in the kernel and the number of threads per block must be specified when the kernel is configured. If a single block requests too many resources, the number of blocks concurrently supported by GPU decreases. We measured the execution performance of 1000×1000 Head2D simulation while changing the number of threads per block. Figure 4 shows 24 threads per block as the best configuration. Spatial simulation in general divides a space into cells and has each cell maintain its regional attributes such as its coordinates, wave height, temperature, air pressure, etc., which eventually occupy a large memory space. Therefore, a smaller number of threads per block can fit simulation subspaces in the limited cache memory and have higher cache hit ratio. As a matter of fact, Table 2 demonstrates higher L2 cache hits with 24 threads per block.

Using Constant Memory. Frequently accessed data needs to be maintained in memory spaces closer to threads. In particular, local memory gives the shorter memory access latency for read-only data. We decided to store in constant memory MASS read-only parameters that define each place's neighborhood, i.e., communication channels. This memory allocation leads to a noticeable performance improvement.

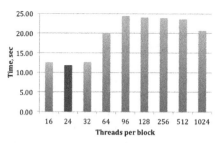

Fig. 4. Heat2D's variable performance with 16-1024 threads per block

Table 2. Profiling results for MASS CUDA's exchangeAll( )

GPU kernel	24 threads per block	512 threads per block
Compute time (%)	69%	87%
Ave. duration (msec)	4.26	9.12
Achieved occupancy	25%	69%
L2 cache hit rate	77%	17%
Device DRAM reads	6.3M	20,980.0M
Device DRAM writes	3.0M	5.1M

4.2 Agent Parallelization

Contrary to spatial simulation, agents show their dynamic action at run time. We look at the following four agent behaviors that influence GPU kernel execution: (1) initial population, (2) migration, (3) cloning, and (4) termination.

Agent Population. MASS CUDA prepares the **map( )** function in the **Agent** class, which allows a user to decide how to populate agents over places, specifically or randomly. In many cases, a user-specific agent population may be difficult to parallelize, because a creation of agent i depends on that of agent $i - 1$. In addition, random agent distribution at the GPU level, (i.e., using cuRAND) cannot perform faster unless the range of random numbers is quite large, i.e., 10 million[2], which may not be realistic in the current device memory size to limit the number of agents. Since agent initialization is just one-time computation before an application starts a cyclic simulation, MASS CUDA initializes an array of agent states on the host memory with either a user-specific **map( )** or the **srand( )** function, and thereafter copies it to the device memory.

---

[2] https://nidclip.wordpress.com/2014/04/02/cuda-random-number-generation/.

Agent Migration. Agent conflict resolution has been studied at the user level such as the use of collision map [8] and the single-threaded execution of collision-prone simulation subspaces, (e.g., intersections in traffic simulation) [4]. Needless to say, model designers hope to use system-level, automatic conflict resolutions. MASS CUDA provides the following three options:

1. **Non-deterministic last-get-space migration**
   As the fastest baseline conflict resolution, each GPU thread that computes a different agents move, simply overwrites the previous agents footstep on the same place. Therefore, the last thread to mark its agents footstep there gets that place. Although this scheme works fastest without any synchronization overheads, each simulation run obtains non-deterministic results.
2. **Smallest-ID-get-space with atomicCAS( )**
   When several agent threads try to migrate to the same place, the atomic-CAS( ) function from the CUDA standard library is used to select an agent with the smallest index. Using this algorithm makes the simulation reproducible. However, it does not allow users to modify the conflict resolution algorithm between migrating agents.
3. **User-provided conflict resolution**
   Each place has an array of agents that want to migrate to this place. Agents register their intent by saving their pointer into that array. For example, if agents migrate to an immediate neighbor such as north, west, south or east, as shown in Fig. 5(a), they register their pointers into the corresponding slot of the destination place's agent array, as illustrated in Fig. 5(b). Thereafter, each place picks up only one agent from its array. A user can describe how to prioritize this array elements.

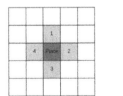

Agent* potentialNextAgents[4]:

(a) Next locations to migrate (b) An array of migrating agents

Fig. 5. User-provided conflict resolution

Agent Replication and Termination. MASS CUDA uses agent pooling. The justification is based on our ABM survey and benchmark test design [14], which identified only a few biological or ecological applications (e.g., TB simulation [8]) as the representatives that repeat spawning and terminating agents during their simulation. Most ABMs in social, behavioral, and economic sciences tend to keep all agents alive, (e.g., social network [2]) or to only lose some of them but not to spawn new entities at all (e.g., influenza epidemics [7]). To implement agent pooling, MASS CUDA allows a user to allocate extra space in **createAgents( )** and to replicate agents at run time by having GPU threads advance a shared pointer to a next available space with **atomicAdd( )**.

5 Performance Analysis

We chose Head2D as a spatial simulation and SugarScape as an agent simulation, parallelized them with MASS CUDA, and measured their execution performance. For this analysis, we used an Ubuntu Linux 14.04 machine with Intel Xeon CPU E5-2630 v3 at 2.4 GHz and 32 GB host memory. The GPU card adapted to this machine is GeForce GTX Titan with 2688 CUDA cores at 876 MHz and 6 GB device memory. The CUDA compiler is version 8.0.

5.1 Performance Improvements with Implementation Techniques

Figure 6 dissects the MASS CUDA's execution performance in spatial parallelization. For this analysis, Heat2D of $1,000 \times 1,000$ places was simulated over 3,000 iterations. The biggest contribution was provided through optimizing the number of threads per block for kernel launches. The second best was avoiding a context switch between GPU kernels through combining exchangeAll( ) and callAll( ) functions to execute in one GPU kernel call. The smallest but still significant contribution was made by the use of constant memory for storing kernel parameters.

For agent parallelization, we focused on agent conflict resolutions. Figure 7 compares the performance of the three resolutions we discussed in Sect. 4.2 when running SugarScape over 100 iterations. Our evaluation was conducted as increasing its simulation space from 100×100 to $1,000 \times 1,000$ places where 2,000 to 200,000 agents were populated. (Note that the size was limited by the 6 GB device memory.) The fastest is non-deterministic conflict resolution, the second fastest is the default resolution using atomicCAS, and the slowest is the user-specified algorithm that is 40% slower than non-deterministic resolution.

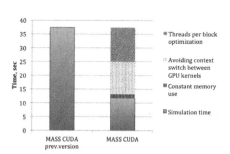

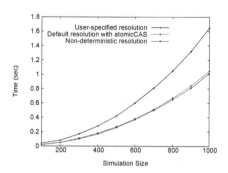

Fig. 6. Performance improvement with space parallelization

Fig. 7. Execution performance of agent migration

5.2 Comparison of MASS CUDA, Bare GPU Parallel, and CPU Sequential Executions

Using Heat2D and SugarScape, we evaluated MASS CUDAs execution performance in spatial and agent parallelization, by comparing it with bare GPU parallel and CPU sequential executions. For this purpose, we coded these two applications in CUDA C++ and C++ in an ad-hoc manner without using MASS.

Figures 8 and 9 summarize their executions of Heat2D and SugarScape respectively when increasing the space size up to 1,000 × 1,000 places. Although MASS CUDA is obviously slower than bare GPU executions due to its general ABM coordination overheads, it performed 3.9 times and 5.8 times faster than the sequential C++ version of Heat2D and SugarScape respectively. These improvements are better than our MASS C++ performance evaluation [14] that used four CPUs. Although it is hard to make any compatible comparisons with other general ABM frameworks on GPU, due to their different test cases and platforms, we feel that MASS CUDAs 5.8-time speed-up of agent execution (in SugarScape) is quite comparable to MCMASs Prey-Predator execution on GPU that performed approximately three times better than its corresponding sequential version [10].

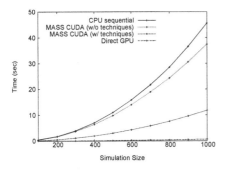
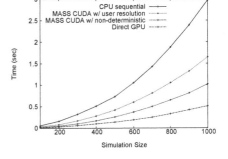

Fig. 8. Execution of different implementations of Heat2D

Fig. 9. Execution of different implementations of SugarScape

6 Conclusions

MASS CUDA was designed to generalize data structures of agents and their environment, to describe all models in CUDA C++, and to parallelize entire models at GPU, each addressing the drawbacks of application-specific GPU parallelization, generalized GPU parallelization techniques, and other general ABM frameworks. Our space and agent parallelization techniques improved the execution performance of Heat2D and SugarScape 3.9 times and 5.8 times better than the corresponding C++ sequential versions respectively.

At present, our evaluation is limited to only two applications. To practicalize MASS CUDA, we should adopt some techniques from application-specific and general parallelization techniques to the library. For this purpose, we are planning on three main areas of future work: (1) benchmarking MASS CUDAs programmability and execution performance with more ABM applications, (2) implementing agent garbage collection as part of MASS CUDA, and (3) combining MASS CUDA and C++ to use a multi-GPU cluster for scaling up the simulation space and the number of agents.

References

1. Aaby, B.G., Perumalla, K.S., Seal, S.K.: Efficient simulation of agent-based models on multi-GPU and multi-core clusters. In: Proceedings of the 3rd International ICST Conference on Simulation Tools and Techniques, SIMUTools 2010, pp. 29:1–29:10. ICST, Torremolinos, Spain, March 2010
2. Ang, C.S., Zaphiris, P.: Simulating social networks of online communities: simulation as a method for sociability design. In: Gross, T., et al. (eds.) INTERACT 2009. LNCS, vol. 5727, pp. 443–456. Springer, Heidelberg (2009). https://doi.org/10.1007/978-3-642-03658-3_48
3. Balmer, M., Meister, K., Nagel, K., Axhausen, K.W.: Agent-based simulation of travel demand: structure and computational performance of MATSim-T. Work report no. 504, ETH Zurich, Switzerland, July 2008
4. Barceló, J., Ferrer, J., Garcéa, D., Grau, R.: Microscopic traffic simulation for ATT systems analysis. a parallel computing version. In: 25th CRT, August 1998
5. Blum, C.: Ant colony optimization: introduction and recent trends. Phys. Life Rev. **2**(4), 353–373 (2005)
6. Brown, W.M., Wang, P., Plimpton, S.J., Tharrington, A.N.: A efficient algorithm for molecular dynamics simulation on hybrid CPU-GPU computing platforms. In: Proceedings of the 12th Int'l Conference on Natural Computation, Fuzzy Systems and Knowledge Discovery, pp. 1357–1363, Changsha, China, August 2016
7. Chao, D.L., Halloran, M.E., Obenchain, V.J., Longini Jr., I.M.: FluTE, a publicly available stochastic influenza epidemic simulation model. PLoS Comput. Biol. **6**(1), 517–527 (2010)
8. D'Souza, R.M., Marino, S., Kirschner, D.: Data-parallel algorithms for agent-based model simulations of tuberculosis on graphics processing units. In: Proceedings of Agent-Directed Symposium - ADS09, pp. 21:1–21:12, San Diego, CA. SCS, March 2009
9. Hermellin, E., Michel, F.: GPU delegation: toward a generic approach for developing MABS using GPU programming. In: Proceedings of the 2016 International Conference on Autonomous Agents & Multiagent Systems, pp. 1249–1258. International Foundation for AAMAS, Singapore, May 2016
10. Laville, G., Mazouzi, K., Lang, C., Marilleau, N., Herrmann, B., Philippe, L.: MCMAS: a toolkit to benefit from many-core architecure in agent-based simulation. In: an Mey, D., et al. (eds.) Euro-Par 2013. LNCS, vol. 8374, pp. 544–554. Springer, Heidelberg (2014). https://doi.org/10.1007/978-3-642-54420-0_53
11. Li, X., Cai, W., Turner, S.J.: Supporting efficient execution of continuous space agent-based simulation on GPU. Concurrency Comput. Pract. Experience **28**(12), 3313–3332 (2016)
12. Michel, F.: Translating agent perception computations into environmental processes in multi-agent-based simulations: a means for integrating graphics processing unit programming within usual agent-based simulation platforms. Syst. Res. Behav. Sci. **33**(6), 703–715 (2013)

13. Richmond, P., Walker, D., Coakley, S., Romano, D.: High performance cellular level agent-based simulation with flame for the GPU. Briefings Bioinf. **11**(3), 334–347 (2010)
14. Shih, C., Yang, C., Fukuda, M.: Benchmarking the agent descriptivity of parallel multi-agent simulators. In: Bajo, J., et al. (eds.) PAAMS 2018. CCIS, vol. 887, pp. 480–492. Springer, Cham (2018). https://doi.org/10.1007/978-3-319-94779-2_41
15. Strippgen, D., Nagel, K.: Using common graphics hardware for multi-agent traffic simulation with CUDA. In: Proceedings of the 2nd International Conference on Simulation Tools and Techniques, pp. 62:1–62:8. ICST, Rome, Italy, March 2009

Multi-agent Coordination for On-Demand Data Gathering with Periodic Information Upload

Yaroslav Marchukov[(✉)] and Luis Montano[(✉)]

Instituto de Investigación en Ingeniería de Aragon (I3A),
University of Zaragoza, C/Mariano Esquillor, s/n, 50018 Zaragoza, Spain
{yamar,montano}@unizar.es

Abstract. In this paper we develop a method for planning and coordinating a multi-agent team deployment to periodically gather information on demand. A static operation center (OC) periodically requests information from changing goal locations. The objective is to gather data in the goals and to deliver it to the OC, balancing the refreshing time and the total number of information packages. The system automatically splits the team in two roles: workers to gather data, or collectors to retransmit the data to the OC. The proposed three step method: (1) finds out the best area partition for the workers; (2) obtains the best balance between workers and collectors, and with whom the workers must to communicate, a collector or the OC; (3) computes the best tour for the workers to visit the goals and deliver them to the OC or to a collector in movement. The method is tested in simulations in different scenarios, providing the best area partition algorithm and the best balance between collectors and workers.

Keywords: Multi-agent system · Data gathering ·
Connectivity constraints

1 Introduction

In the present work we develop a method for planning and execute a multi-agent team deployment to gather data in some scenario. In every cycle of the mission the robots have to reach different locations of interest, periodically requested by a static Operation Center (OC), taking measurements and uploading the information to the OC. It will select new goals for the next cycle of request. The OC and the robots have a limited communication range, thus the robots would have to approach to the OC in order to upload the information. A first basic solution is the classical robot deployment towards the objectives, returning all of them to the OC with the new information captured. But for large scenarios it could be very inefficient due to the long time devoted for travelling. An alternative solution is to use some of the robots as information *collectors*, improving this

ⓒ Springer Nature Switzerland AG 2019
Y. Demazeau et al. (Eds.): PAAMS 2019, LNAI 11523, pp. 153–167, 2019.
https://doi.org/10.1007/978-3-030-24209-1_13

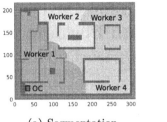
(a) Segmentation

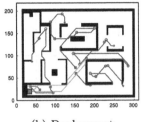
(b) Deployment

Fig. 1. Data gathering of 20 objectives with 5 agents: 4 workers and 1 collector, 5 objectives/worker. In (a), the scenario is divided into 4 segments, 1 per worker. (b) depicts the trajectories of 4 workers (blue lines) visiting 5 objectives each (red circles) and going to transmit data. The collector trajectory is the green line. (Color figure online)

way the time of mission because long journeys are avoided to the rest of robots, which we name *workers*. Depending on times for transmission, for working, and for travelling, a balance between the number of workers and collectors has to be found to minimize the information refreshing time while maximize the number of information packages delivered to the OC. To find a solution to this problem is the objective of the work developed here.

An assumption is that the goals will be every cycle uniformly distributed within the whole scenario, but changing from one cycle to another. We propose to divide the scenario into working zones for the agents, associating one per worker. This way each worker will receive a number of goals approximately proportional to the size of the area. So the workload of the workers will be also proportional to that size. Although a first idea could be to segment the scenario in zones of similar area to balance the workload of the workers, it does not lead always to the best solution, as we will see later. The segments do not change during the mission, and the workers gather data from the goals of their associated segments, delivering the information either directly to the OC or to the closest moving collector, Fig. 1. This way, the team avoids meeting in static rendezvous points to redistribute the working areas of the agents. This would cause a deterioration of the refreshing time of the information. The collectors would need to wait for the workers at each cycle in order to communicate them the distribution of the new segments as well as the next meeting point.

An example of these kind of missions is a fire monitoring, where the locations to monitor and also the frequency of their appearance can change over time. The proposed method can also fit with light changes in other applications such as: human-robot cooperation, where the workers are human operators performing some kind of task in some area and interact during a specified time with a moving robot; warehouse commissioning and logistics, in which the worker robots pickup items and bring them to some collector agents that deliver all the items to the depot point.

The contribution of this work is a technique for planning and executing data gathering missions in connectivity constrained scenarios, working in three steps: (i) the scenario partition in several working areas (so called as segments), each assigned to one worker agent; (ii) the computation of the number of collectors needed for the mission for that partition, their trajectories, and the assignment of workers to meet the collectors or directly to move towards the OC; (iii) the routing for each worker to visit the goals of its assigned area, and synchronize with its assigned collector in movement for the data exchange. The planner is centralized at the OC, but its execution is distributed among the workers for covering its working area and synchronize with the collectors.

For reaching the plan that estimates the best balance between the information refreshing time and the total number of information packages delivered at the OC, the planner evaluates different scenario configurations: three area partition criteria, and different ratios of $\#collectors/\#workers$ in the team. The scenario configuration that provides the best balance is the one selected to be executed.

2   Related Work

We can distinguish between two types of communications in multi-agent coordination: permanent or intermittent. The permanent one is usually used in critical missions, such as monitoring in emergency scenarios [12] or formation control for person guidance [10]. Intermittent communication is more usual in exploration missions [1,8], patrolling [3,9], and data gathering [5]. In this work we use intermittent communication due to the size of the scenario, the communication range and the number of agents.

In patrolling missions [3,9], the agents travel invariant paths through a precomputed graph, re-transmitting the data when they meet each other. Obviously, it will be inefficient to employ this approach for our problem, since the goals appear in different locations, needing to compute the graph with every request cycle. Furthermore, the refreshing time in the OC exponentially increases with each data re-transmission between agents. In our approach, we compute the optimal destinations for the collectors, so they will persistently travel to and from these points and the workers will come to these positions to upload their data, only in the case of having some data to share. So that, only one retransmission is made. This approach is similar in spirit to [6], where an agent performs a persistent task, moving towards other agents to meet them for recharging at the best computed point of their trajectories. In our kind of missions, it is more effective that the collector agents travel invariant paths, being the workers who move to share the data with them, in order to preserve the time of collectors cycles since it delimits the refreshing time.

In [5], the authors develop a method where some workers, with buffer limitations, gather data and transmit it to dynamic collectors. Their collectors are permanently connected to a central server in the entire scenario. They are the only ones capable to upload the data to the server without the need of travel to a unique static depot point, situation considered in our work. Obviously, the travels to a static depot point increase the refreshing time, especially in large scenarios. In our approach the workers remain in their working areas and only travel short paths to the collectors, not needing to go up the OC.

Our method is more flexible because the workers are not enforced to concur with its collector to some fixed rendezvous points, as in classic agent meeting problem [7], since it may become inefficient for big fleets of agents. Instead, the workers decide when and where to share the data with the collector, so that not stopping the motion if it is not needed. In [2], the robots are enabled to transfer deliveries between each other to efficiently reach different delivery locations. However, their system to establish the meeting points is fully centralized, that cannot be directly applied here because our team acts in a distributed way during the execution of the mission.

3   Problem Statement

3.1   Problem Formulation

The problem to solve is planning the deployment of a team of robots in a scenario with connectivity constraints due to obstacles or distances to the OC. This requests for data from different goals to be periodically uploaded them in the OC. We use a grid representation for the scenarios because, as justified bellow, we apply the Fast Marching Method (FMM) [11] as a common tool for several algorithms of our method. We denote a position in the grid as x and a set of positions as $\mathbf{x}$. The positions of the obstacles are denoted as $\mathbf{x}_o$, the position of the OC is expressed as x_{oc}, and the positions of the agents and goals are $\mathbf{x}_a$ and $\mathbf{x}_g$, respectively. The OC periodically requests information from M goal locations, and the team, composed by N robots, is coordinated to move towards the goals, then delivering the information to the OC. The robots can act either as workers (N_w) or as the collectors (N_c), being $N_c + N_w = N$. During the time of the mission, denoted as $T_{mission}$, M remains constant. That is, when OC receives the information from m goals ($m \leq M$), it generates m new goals. Our approach must compute the plan of the mission, previously to deploy the agents. To this end, it must: (i) obtain the working areas for the worker agents, denoted as S_w; (ii) find out the best balance between collector and workers; (iii) pair the workers with the collectors or with the OC to transmit the data, expressed as P_{cw}; iv) compute the trajectories of each collector π_c, according to P_{cw} and S_w. Once the mission starts, each worker computes its path π_w, in order to visit the corresponding goals, $\mathbf{x}_{g_i} \in S_{w_i}$ and go to deliver the information to a collector or OC, according to the association P_{cw}.

Π_w and Π_c are the sets of worker's and collector's paths, respectively, being $\pi_w \in \Pi_w$ and $\pi_c \in \Pi_c$. The times for travelling a path π and paths Π are expressed as $t(\pi)$ and $t(\Pi)$, respectively. The refreshing period from the time in which OC requests information and receives it is $T_{refresh}$. This period is the mean time of the collectors T_c and of the workers that transmit directly to the OC. Naturally, it must be minimal, whilst the number m of goal information

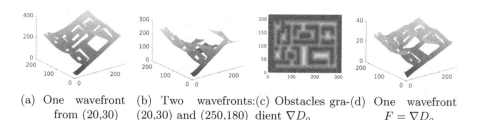

(a) One wavefront from (20,30)   (b) Two wavefronts: (20,30) and (250,180)   (c) Obstacles gradient ∇D_o (d) One wavefront $F = \nabla D_o$

Fig. 2. FMM gradients.

received has to be as large as possible. The problem of computation of trajectories of workers and the collectors can be formally expressed as:

$$\pi^*_{w_{ij}} = \underset{\pi_{w_i} \in \Pi_{w_i}, \; \mathbf{x}_{g_i} \in \pi_{w_i}}{\text{argmax}} \left(|\mathbf{x}_{g_i}| \right) \tag{1}$$

$$\pi^*_{c_j} = \underset{\pi_{c_j} \in \Pi_{c_j}}{\text{argmin}} \left(t(\pi_{c_j}) - \overline{t(\Pi_{w_{ij}})} \right) \tag{2}$$

$$subject\ to\ t(\pi^*_{c_j}) - t(\pi^*_{w_{ij}}) \geq 0 \tag{3}$$

where c_j refers to collector j and w_i to worker i. Equation (1) obtains the optimal route for workers to visit the maximum number of goals $\mathbf{x}_{g_i}$ assigned to the agent w_i from all the possibles Π_{w_i}. Equation (2), computes the trajectory of the collector c_j that minimizes the time the workers must wait for the collector arrival, once that they have visited the goals within its area. $\Pi_{w_{ij}}$ represents the paths of the workers w_i assigned to collector c_j, obtained with Eq. (1), and $\overline{t(\Pi_{w_{ij}})}$ denotes the mean time of these paths. Equation (3) constraint enforces the workers to fulfill the maximum number of their assigned goals, Eq. (1), to meet the collector when it arrives in the current cycle. When a worker and a collector meet each other, the distance between them must be lower than d_{com} and the line-of-sight must not be occluded to establish communication. The three steps achieved by the planner are described in the following sections: (i) scenario segmentation in Sect. 4, (ii) collector's trajectories and segment allocation to workers in Sect. 5, and (iii) workers routing in Sect. 6.

3.2   Fast Marching Method (FMM)

The FMM is applied for several planner steps: the area partition, the path planning for the collectors, and the computation of the best route to the workers visit the goals and synchronize for data delivery. The basic idea of FMM is the propagation of a wavefront from some position x over a static grid, computing a distance gradient ∇D:

$$|\nabla D(x)|F = 1 \tag{4}$$

The wavefront is propagated over every point of the grid with a velocity F, solving Eq. (4). In a simple grid, F takes values of: 0 in positions with an

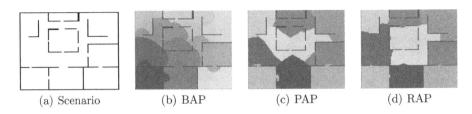

| (a) Scenario | (b) BAP | (c) PAP | (d) RAP |

Fig. 3. Segmentation algorithms for 10 segments.

obstacle, and 1 in free space. Hence the wavefront is propagated uniformly in all the directions, surrounding the obstacles, obtaining the distance gradient ∇D, Fig. 2(a). Descending this gradient from some goal position x_{goal}, we obtain a path from the origin to x_{goal}.

Initializing several wavefronts, the resulting ∇D will represent the distance to the closest origin, see Fig. 2(b). This is used for the segmentation methods of Sects. 4.2–4.3. The positions where the wavefronts collide, are the frontiers of the segments. Varying the values of F, the propagation velocity is non-uniform. The gradient propagates faster for higher values and slower for lower values of F. An example is depicted in Fig. 2(c)–(d). The obstacles gradient ∇D_o is obtained with FMM, Fig. 2(c). Propagating the wavefront, with $F = \nabla D_o$, the resultant gradient obtains lower values in points that are more distant from the obstacles, Fig. 2(d). This property is also used for the segmentation and for associations between collectors and workers in Sect. 5.3.

4   Scenario Segmentation

In this work we develop and evaluate three segmentation algorithms: BAP, PAP and RAP. All of them use the base method FMM. We encourage to visit the link[1], with the proposed segmentation processes in different scenarios.

4.1   Balanced Area Partition (BAP)

The main feature of this segmentation algorithm is that it obtains segments with balanced areas. A uniform FMM wavefront propagation obtains these areas. Firstly, the algorithm computes the gradient from the OC position ∇D_{OC}, which denotes the distance to the OC. Since the team employs N_w workers, the space is divided into N_w segments, with areas $A_{w_i}, i = 1, ..., N_w$, accomplishing $A = \sum A_{w_i}$. The optimal segment area is denoted by $A_{opt} = A/N_w$, measured as number of cells in the grid.

Initially FMM propagates a wavefront from OC, expanding A_{opt} cells. If the total area of expanded cells is higher or equal to $A_{opt}/2$, a heuristic threshold, and the number of already obtained segments is lower than N_w, these cells become a new segment. If not, the expanded cells are added to an adjacent segment of minimum area.

---

[1] http://robots.unizar.es/data/videos/paams19yamar/segmentations/.

The algorithm iterates until classify all the free space A, choosing as wavefront origin, the closest non-classified point to x_{OC} from ∇D_{OC}. The number of extended cells depends on the obstacle distribution in the scenario, since the algorithm requires more iterations to cover the entire area if there are any remaining non-classified small areas. This may also produce bigger segments than A_{opt}, obtaining a lower number of segments than N_w. In this case, the algorithm iteratively halves the biggest segments until obtain N_w. Figure 3(b) illustrates the segmentation for 10 segments. Although the shape of the segments is quite irregular, the areas are equitable, which a priori favours a balanced time for workers in all the segments.

4.2 Polygonal Area Partition (PAP)

Algorithm 1. Procedure for PAP and RAP

Require: Grid, $\mathbf{x}_o$, N_w, Partition type (PAP or RAP)
1: $\nabla D_o \leftarrow compute\_gradient(\mathbf{x}_o)$ ▷ Eq. (4)
2: $\mathbf{x}_c \leftarrow initialize\_centroids(N_w, \nabla D_o)$
3: **If** (PAP) $[S, \mathbf{x}_c] \leftarrow it\_part(\mathbf{x}_c, Grid)$ ▷ Alg. 2
4: **If** (RAP) $[S, \mathbf{x}_c] \leftarrow it\_part(\mathbf{x}_c, \nabla D_o)$ ▷ Alg. 2
5: **return** $S, \mathbf{x}_c$

This algorithm attempts to keep equitable distances between the centroids of the segments and their boundaries with other segments or obstacles. PAP algorithm is summarized in Algorithm 1. The algorithm consists in two main phases: centroid initialization and iteration phase. Firstly, the algorithm obtains the obstacles gradient, corresponding to the distance to them, l.1, as explained in Sect. 3.2, see Fig. 2(c). After that, it iteratively finds the maximum values of this gradient, l.2, which correspond to the largest free spaces, for example rooms. The position of the maximum is the initial location of the centroid of each segment. Since the value of the maximum represents the greatest distance to the closest obstacle, the algorithm removes all the points of the grid within the radius equal to the maximum. This way, we avoid to initialize new centroids of the segments in the same rooms. This procedure is repeated N_w times, one per segment/worker.

After the initialization, the method iteratively moves the centroids until achieving the equilibrium between the distances of the centroids. This procedure is described in Algorithm 2. At first, the method computes the distance gradient from the centroids (l.2), using again FMM. The variable *costmap* takes the values of the basic grid to propagate the wavefronts, so F is 0 or 1 in Eq. (4). Therefore, N_w wavefronts are uniformly propagated in all the directions, one per segment. The positions where the wavefronts collide among them are the boundaries of the segments. The highest value of the gradient of each partition is the farthest position from the centroid $\mathbf{x}_{p_f}$ in l.3. So we move every centroid in the direction of its farthest position in the segment: computing the paths, l.4, and moving the centroids along them, l.5. We encourage the reader to watch the video for better understanding of this procedure. The resulting segments are depicted in Fig. 3(c).

4.3 Room-Like Area Partition (RAP)

Algorithm 2. Iterative Partition (*it_part*)

Require: *Centroids* ($\mathbf{x}_c$), *costmap*
1: **while** !*repeated_positions*($\mathbf{x}_c$) **do**
2:     [$\nabla D_c, S$] ← *gradient_and_partitions*($\mathbf{x}_c$, *costmap*)
3:     $\mathbf{x}_{pf}$ ← *compute_farthest_in_partition*($\nabla D_c, S$)
4:     Π_f ← *gradient_descent*($\nabla D_c, \mathbf{x}_{pf}$)
5:     $\mathbf{x}_c$ ← *move*(Π_f)
6: **end while**
7: **return** $S, \mathbf{x}_c$

This area partition method employs the same procedure that iteratively moves the centroids as PAP. But instead of using the basic grid of the map, in l.4 of Algorithm 1, it uses the obstacles gradient ∇D_o computed in l.1. Then, *costmap* variable takes values of ∇D_o in Algorithm 2. This changes the propagation of the wavefronts, becoming non-uniform. So that the wavefronts cover faster the wide areas, such as rooms, and slow down when reach tight spaces, commonly corresponding to doors, where the wavefronts collide. Using this property, the resulting segments tend to cover the rooms, as can be seen in Fig. 3(d). Because of that, their areas differ from PAP's algorithm.

5 Collectors Trajectories and Segment Allocation

In this section we explain how the planner selects the best number of the collectors used for the mission (based on the workers segments), the computation of their trajectories, and the association of the workers to the collectors to share data.

5.1 Working Time Estimation

The method computes the collectors trajectories based on an estimated working time of their associated workers. During the mission the collectors permanently travel these paths without stopping, being the workers who move to share the gathered data with them.

Since the distribution of the goals will change every cycle, the planner has to estimate an averaged working time in each segment. Assuming the goals are uniformly distributed, we consider the number of goals within each worker segment i will be approximately proportional to its area, obtained as $M_{s_i} = M * A_{s_i}/A$. In order to estimate a fair approximation of the distribution of the goals within a segment, the algorithm automatically places M_{s_i} goals (centroids) within segment S_i using the PAP procedure. This way, the estimated goals are equidistant between them, considering the obstacles. The $NN + 2O$ procedure, explained in Sect. 6.1, computes the shortest tour from each segment centroid to visit the M_{s_i} goals, estimating the working time each worker will spend in its segment.

5.2 Planning Procedure

Algorithm 3. General planning procedure

Require: $Grid, M, N, x_{oc}$
1: $\Pi_c^* \leftarrow \emptyset,\ P_{cw}^* \leftarrow \emptyset,\ S_w^* \leftarrow \emptyset,\ \mathbb{T}_c \leftarrow \emptyset,\ \mathbb{M}_d \leftarrow \emptyset$
2: $\nabla D_{oc} \leftarrow compute\_gradient(x_{oc}, Grid)$
3: **for each** *segmentation* **do**   ▷ BAP, PAP, RAP
4:      **for** $N_c = 0 : N/2$ **do**
5:          $N_w = N - N_c$
6:          $[S_w, \mathbf{x}_{c_w}] \leftarrow segment(grid, N_w)$
7:          $T_{work} \leftarrow estim\_work\_time(S_w)$ ▷ Sect. 5.1
8:          $[\Pi_c, P_{cw}, T_c, M_d] \quad\leftarrow\quad coll\_paths(Grid, N_c,$
             $...x_{oc}, \nabla D_{oc}, \mathbf{x}_{c_w}, S_w, T_{work})$
9:          $\mathbb{T}_c \leftarrow \mathbb{T}_c \cup \{T_c\}, \mathbb{M}_d \leftarrow \mathbb{M}_d \cup \{M_d\}$
10:      **end for**
11: **end for**
12: $[\Pi_c^*, S_w^*, P_{cw}^*] \leftarrow best\_plan$ ▷ Eq. (5)
13: **return** Π_c^*, S_w^*, P_{cw}^*

Based on the average working time estimated for the segments, the plan procedure in Algorithm 3 obtains the needed collectors, their time periods T_c, and their trajectories. The paths of collectors are computed from the gradient to the OC, l.2. It computes the three scenario partitions, l.3. The number of collectors to be evaluated is $N_c = 0..N/2$, l.4, because it makes no sense to devote more than one collector to a single segment. When the system adds a new collector, it renounces to a worker, l.5. This changes the working areas, so the algorithm segments the scenario every iteration, l.6, estimating the working times for the resulting segments, l.7 (Sect. 5.1). Then it computes the paths of the collectors (Π_c) and collector times (T_c), l.8, and associates the workers with the collectors (P_{cw}), obtaining the goals that will be delivered to the OC (M_d), explained in Sect. 5.3. A direct movement of workers to the OC, without using a collector, is also evaluated ($N_c = 0$). The times and the delivered goals are stored, l.9, in order to choose the best plan in l.12 from the different partitions and collectors, using the utility function:

$$U = max\big[\alpha * (1 - \mathbb{T}_c/max(\mathbb{T}_c)) + \beta * \mathbb{M}_d/max(\mathbb{M}_d)\big],\ \alpha + \beta = 1 \qquad (5)$$

In this work, we set the values $\alpha = \beta = 0.5$, giving the same priority to the refreshing time and the number of deliveries. However, these values can be adjusted depending on the kind of mission, i.e. higher values for α in critical missions, such as fire monitoring, and higher values for β in simpler missions, such as surveillance.

5.3 Collector Trajectories and Workers-Collectors Association

An illustrative example of collector computation is depicted in Fig. 4. This method also employs a FMM-based *RAP* procedure to associate the collectors to the workers. It receives the segmented scenario for the workers, Fig. 4(a), and obtains the graph of the worker segments, Fig. 4(b). The vertices of the graph are the centroids of the segments, the edges joining the adjacent vertices. The workers at the segment of the OC and the adjacent ones will upload data directly to the OC, thus their edges are removed from the graph.

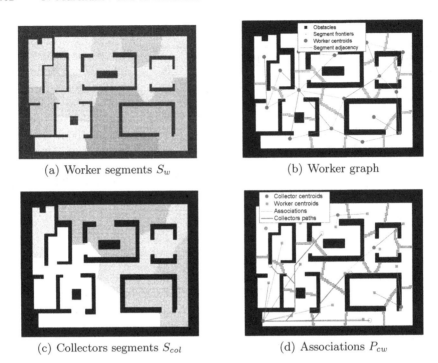

(a) Worker segments S_w (b) Worker graph

(c) Collectors segments S_{col} (d) Associations P_{cw}

Fig. 4. Collectors' path computation and association, for 16 segments (workers) and 4 collectors. In (c), white space are segments of workers that upload directly to the OC

The method iteratively computes the paths of the collectors, associates them with the workers, and estimates the mean refreshing time at the OC. First, it computes the connectivity of the graph, that is the number of edges that has every vertex. Second, it selects N_C vertices of the maximum connectivity, and initializes the centroid of the segments as the initial farthest position to be reached by the collector, $\mathbf{x}_{col}$, before come back to the OC. Then it iteratively moves these centroids, by propagating the gradient ∇D_{front} from the frontiers of the worker segments, depicted with blue points in Fig. 4(b), using Algorithm 2 executing $[S_{col}, \mathbf{x}_{col}] \leftarrow it\_part(\mathbf{x}_{col}, \nabla D_{front})$. This way, the shape of the segments is taken into account, filling faster the smaller and uniform worker segments and slower the largest and irregular ones. The final segments associated to the collectors (S_{col}), which groups the worker segments associated to it, are depicted in Fig. 4(c). The workers of the segments grouped in a collector segment S_{col} share data with the collector that comes to $\mathbf{x}_{col}$, Fig. 4(c). Then, the paths from x_{OC} to each $\mathbf{x}_{col}$ are obtained descending ∇D_{OC}. According to Eqs. (1)–(3), in order to find out a balance between the time of the collector T_c and time of workers to reach $\mathbf{x}_{col}$, each collector path is iteratively contracted until achieving the balance. As can be observed in Fig. 4(c), the method associates not only adjacent workers to upload to OC, but also others corresponding to the next level in the graph until $T_{refresh}$ stops decreasing.

6   Workers Trajectories

Here we develop the trajectory planner that execute the workers to visit the goals and to synchronize with the collector in movement.

6.1   Goals Visit Methods

Each worker has to visit the maximum number of goals in its segment, in such a way that it is able to reach the collector to share the data in some point of its trajectory. The costs to reach the goals are evaluated from the FMM gradient; the distances are the values of the gradient at the goals positions. We use three main routines to obtain the worker's route:

- *Brute Force (BF)*: obtains the optimal solution testing all the possible routes.
- *Nearest Neighbor with 2-opt Improvement (NN+2O)*: a first route is initialized with the *Nearest Neighbor (NN)* procedure. Then, the route is improved by means of a local optimization using 2-opt method [4], that swaps every two edges of the route, goals in our case, checking if the new route outperforms the previous one. This method is able to obtain the routes in real-time (milliseconds), against classic orienteering problem methods, which require minutes to find a solution [13].
- *NN+2O with Time Window (NN+2O-TW)*, and *BF-TW*: with the same structure as the basic *NN+2O* and *BF*, but taking into account a time condition to reach the collector at time, formally expressed as:

$$T_c - t_{tx} >= t_{accum} + t_{g_j} + t_{g_j - c}, j = 1, ..., K \tag{6}$$

where T_c is cycle time for the collector, t_{tx} is the time to transmit the data of already collected information, t_{accum} is the accumulated time of the trajectory, t_{g_j} is the time to reach the next non-visited goal j, $t_{g_j - c}$ is the time from this goal to the collector and K is the number of goals for the worker. When the condition of Eq. (6) is not accomplished, the algorithm stops iterating.

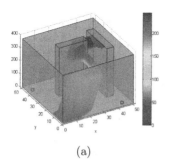   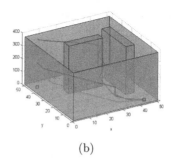

(a)   (b)

Fig. 5. Workers synchronization. In (a), a collector, in movement, creates a dynamic communication area. In (b), a worker goes from blue to red circle, obtaining *Intercepting*, *Waiting*, and *Following* trajectories for $t_{tx} = \{10, 30, 100\}$ sec, are green, blue and red lines, respectively. (Color figure online)

The workers that upload data directly to OC use *BF* to obtain a solution in real-time for instances up to 12 goals (about 50ms), whilst *NN+2O* is used to obtain a suboptimal solution for more than 12 goals. The workers that transmit to a collector employ *BF-TW* for less than 12 goals, otherwise use *NN+2O-TW*. This way the workers upload to the collector every cycle some or all the tasks allocated for them.

6.2 Trajectories for Synchronization

To transmit the data, the workers must remain within the collector communication area during t_{tx} while the collectors are moving Fig. 5(a). This way the agents do not use static meeting points, but synchronize with the collectors in dynamic rendezvous areas, chosen by the workers at each gathering cycle, based on the amount of gathered data to transmit and on the time to meet the collector in a point along its path. The FMM is used to obtain the optimal trajectories to synchronize with a collector in movement to transmit the data. The workers act in three different ways depending on t_{tx}: (i) *Intercepting*: if t_{tx} is much lower than the vertical section of the collectors communication area, so, the worker can simply traverse it (green line in Fig. 5(b)); (ii) *Waiting*: if t_{tx} is equal to the vertical section, the worker can await within the area until it transmits the data (blue line); (iii) *Following*: if t_{tx} is higher than the vertical section, and the worker must follow the collector until fulfill the data transmission (red line).

Note, that if there is an uncertainty in the collector's trajectory or even if it fails during its motion, the worker follows the theoretical collector path until finding it, or up to arriving to OC. This way the mission will be achieved, although the refreshing time will increase and the number of delivered goals during the mission will be reduced.

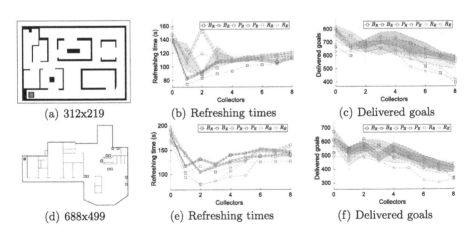

Fig. 6. Results. The red square in (a) and (d) is the OC. The letters B, P, R in the legends refer to BAP, PAP, RAP methods respectively. Sub-index R and E, denote real and estimated values, respectively. The squares represent estimations and the circles the real values. The coloured bands are delimited by the maximum and minimum of the real values. (Color figure online)

7   Results

The method was implemented in C++ and performed in a computer with i7 CPU clocked at 3.4 GHz with 8GB of RAM. We evaluate it by means of simulations in the scenarios of Fig. 6(a) and Fig. 6(d) (extracted from [3]). The results for the planner of Algorithm 3 are evaluated for $N = 20$ agents and $M = 100$ requested goals, $d_{com} = 10$ cells and a constant velocity for the workers and collectors of 2 cell/sec. The time to gather data at one goal is 5 s and to transmit this data is 1 s. The plan execution is also evaluated, based on 20 trials of randomly generated goals, in a 1000 s mission. The mission starts with the agents at OC, the plan is obtained with Algorithm 3 and shared between the agents. Then, in a initialization phase, the workers go to their respective segments and start gathering the first batch of requested goals. The results analysis shows that the mean refreshing times and number of packages delivered at OC for different workers-collectors ratios and the three partition methods, are close to the ones estimated by the planner. Examples of deployments are available in the link[2].

The results are depicted in Fig. 6. Both scenarios present different layouts and difficulties for the team deployment. The mean time to obtain the plan with Algorithm 3, is less than one minute in both scenarios. The complexity of Algorithm 3 is $O(N/2(b_w + b_c + 1)nlogn)$, where: n is the number of free cells in the map, being $nlogn$ the complexity of FMM; b_w is the number of iterations to achieve the balance in the segmentation process for the workers ($b_w = 1$ for BAP); b_c are the iterations to balance the collector segments; the remaining $+1$ is the FMM to obtain the paths of the collectors. The algorithm tests different number of collectors from 0 (baseline for comparison) to 8 ($N/2$). The complexity to obtain the trajectories for a worker i at each cycle is: $O((N_{g_i} + 3)nlogn)$. Requiring $N_{g_i} + 3$ FMM executions, being N_{g_i} the number of goals of the agent i, and the remaining 3 are the FMM's computations: from the agent position, within the communication area, and to the next goal location.

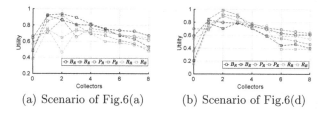

(a) Scenario of Fig.6(a)   (b) Scenario of Fig.6(d)

Fig. 7. Utilities, using Eq. (5)

According to the utilities of Fig. 7 (Eq. (5)), a first clear result is that using collectors is better than not using them. The planner estimates that the best plan for the scenario of Fig. 6(a) is BAP using 2 collectors, although 1 or 3 collectors

---

[2] http://robots.unizar.es/data/videos/paams19yamar/simulations/.

provide similar utilities. For Fig. 6(d) the best is PAP with 2 collectors. The computed utilities for the plan execution are close to the planned ones: the best result in Fig. 6(a) is BAP with 1 collector, and for Fig. 6(d) the execution values match with the estimated ones. Regarding Fig. 6, in mean the plan execution get worse $T_{refresh}$, the time elapsed to deliver the requested the information, only in 9 s, delivering 10 less goals. The little differences found between planned and execution mean values are due to the estimation considers that the number of goals within each segment is proportional to its area, that does not always occur with real goals distribution. It can be concluded that the use of 1–3 collectors provide the best results in the tested scenarios.

Regarding the kind of segmentation, the BAP method that splits the scenario in segments of approximately similar area, works better in the first scenario in which a more homogeneous obstacle distribution is found. The PAP method, which splits the scenario in polygonal segments, works better in the second scenario, where the obstacles are not homogeneously distributed, having large diaphanous areas and narrow corridors. The polygonal segmentation fits better the cleared areas than the other segmentation methods. Anyway, seeing the refreshing time, the number of goals delivered, and the utilities, it can be said that the PAP segmentation provides a good solution for both scenarios.

8   Conclusions

In this paper we have presented a method to plan the deployment of a team of agents to periodically gather information on demand from some a priori unknown goal locations, delivering them to a static operation center. The use of collectors for uploading the information at OC is more useful that directly moving all the robots to the OC, from the point of view of the balance between the refreshing time and the number of delivered goals. We have tested three area partition algorithms, concluding that the PAP segmentation, which splits the scenarios in polygonal areas that fit well the free workspaces, provides good results for one to three collectors in the tested scenarios. As future works, we will include the uncertainty of the trajectories of the collectors for the synchronization with the workers, and will use a training phase to estimate from examples the goals distribution in the scenario.

Acknowledgments. This research has been funded by project DPI2016-76676-R-AEI/FEDER-UE and by research grant BES-2013-067405 of MINECO-FEDER, and by project Grupo DGA-T45-17R/FSE.

References

1. Banfi, J., Li, A.Q., Basilico, N., Rekleitis, I., Amigoni, F.: Asynchronous multirobot exploration under recurrent connectivity constraints. In: 2016 IEEE International Conference on Robotics and Automation (ICRA), pp. 5491–5498, May 2016

2. Coltin, B., Veloso, M.: Online pickup and delivery planning with transfers for mobile robots. In: 2014 IEEE International Conference on Robotics and Automation (ICRA), pp. 5786–5791, May 2014
3. Farinelli, A., Iocchi, L., Nardi, D.: Distributed on-line dynamic task assignment for multi-robot patrolling. Auton. Rob. **41**(6), 1321–1345 (2017)
4. Croes, G.A.: A method for solving traveling-salesman problems. Oper. Res. **6**(6) (1958)
5. Guo, M., Zavlanos, M.M.: Distributed data gathering with buffer constraints and intermittent communication. In: IEEE International Conference on Robotics and Automation (ICRA), pp. 279–284, May 2017
6. Mathew, N., Smith, S.L., Waslander, S.L.: A graph-based approach to multi-robot rendezvous for recharging in persistent tasks. In: 2013 IEEE International Conference on Robotics and Automation, pp. 3497–3502, May 2013
7. Meghjani, M., Manjanna, S., Dudek, G.: Fast and efficient rendezvous in street networks. In: IEEE/RSJ International Conference on Intelligent Robots and Systems (IROS), pp. 1887–1893, October 2016
8. Pei, Y., Mutka, M.W.: Steiner traveler: relay deployment for remote sensing in heterogeneous multi-robot exploration. In: 2012 IEEE International Conference on Robotics and Automation, pp. 1551–1556, May 2012
9. Portugal, D., Rocha, R.: MSP algorithm: multi-robot patrolling based on territory allocation using balanced graph partitioning. In: Proceedings of the 2010 ACM Symposium on Applied Computing, SAC 2010, pp. 1271–1276. ACM (2010)
10. Urcola, P., Montano, L.: Adapting robot team behavior from interaction with a group of people. In: IEEE/RSJ International Conference on Intelligent Robots and Systems (2011)
11. Sethian, J.A.: A fast marching level set method for monotonically advancing fronts. Proc. Nat. Acad. Sci. USA **93**(4), 1591–1595 (1996)
12. Tardioli, D., Sicignano, D., Riazuelo, L., Romeo, A., Villarroel, J.L., Montano, L.: Robot teams for intervention in confined and structured environments. J. Field Rob. **33**(6), 765–801 (2016)
13. Vansteenwegen, P., Souffriau, W., Oudheusden, D.V.: The orienteering problem: a survey. Eur. J. Oper. Res. **209**(1), 1–10 (2011)

Practical Applications of Multiagent Shepherding for Human-Machine Interaction

Patrick Nalepka[1,2(✉)], Rachel W. Kallen[1,2], Anthony Chemero[3], Elliot Saltzman[4,5], and Michael J. Richardson[1,2]

[1] Centre for Elite Performance, Expertise and Training, Macquarie University, Sydney, NSW 2019, Australia
{patrick.nalepka, rachel.kallen, michael.j.richardson}@mq.edu.au
[2] Department of Psychology, Macquarie University, Sydney, NSW 2109, Australia
[3] Center for Cognition, Action and Perception, Department of Psychology, University of Cincinnati, Cincinnati, OH 45220, USA
chemeray@ucmail.uc.edu
[4] Department of Physical Therapy and Athletic Training, Sargent College of Health and Rehabilitation Sciences, Boston University, Boston, MA 02215, USA
esaltz@bu.edu
[5] Haskins Laboratories, New Haven, CT 06511, USA

Abstract. The shepherding problem is interesting for multiagent systems research as it requires multiple actors (e.g., dogs, humans) to exert indirect control over autonomous agents (e.g., sheep, cattle) for containment or transportation. Accordingly, plenty of research has focused on designing algorithms for robotic agents to solve such tasks. Almost no research, however, has utilized this task to investigate human-human or human-machine interactions, even though the shepherding problem encapsulates desirable qualities for an experimental paradigm to investigate the dynamics of human group and mixed-group coordination in complex tasks. This paper summarizes our recent research that has employed the shepherding problem to study complex multiagent human-human and human-machine interaction. The paper concludes with a discussion of practical applications for using the shepherding problem for the design of assistive agents that can be incorporated into human groups or enhance training and human learning.

Keywords: Multiagent coordination · Shepherding · Human-machine interaction

1 Introduction

The shepherding problem involves the indirect control of autonomous agents by one or more actors. The problem poses interesting challenges for multiagent systems research because, in the case of two or more actors, each must coordinate their actions in relationship with other co-actors, and to do so within a task-context that is dynamically responsive to their actions. The problem has many flavors, including the collection of

© Springer Nature Switzerland AG 2019
Y. Demazeau et al. (Eds.): PAAMS 2019, LNAI 11523, pp. 168–179, 2019.
https://doi.org/10.1007/978-3-030-24209-1_14

one or more agents, containment to a specified location, or the transportation of agents to two or more locations. Practical applications to investigating the shepherding problem include, but are not limited to, the design of systems that can herd cattle or other wildlife, assist in human crowd control, rerouting and evacuation, the containment of environmental hazards such as oil-spills, and possibly even find use in areas such as internal medicine to control "herds" of cells to aid in tissue repair [1].

A range of algorithms to solve the shepherding problem have been proposed [2–5], including biomimetic approaches [6], systems designed to herd live animals [7, 8] and policies employed by minimally cognitive agents [9]. The focus of all these approaches is in the design of robotic systems that can solve the task. Little work, if any, has utilized the shepherding problem as a preferred paradigm to investigate human group or mixed-group interactions as its central focus (although see [10] who used a shepherding task to investigate verbal communication in human-robot interaction [HRI]). In addition to being interesting for Engineers, the shepherding problem encapsulates desirable features of a paradigm for Psychologists investigating human group coordination and problem-solving, including task division, behavior-mode switching (e.g., from collection to containment), and adaptation to task perturbations (e.g., addition of new agents), within a task-context that is not under direct control of the shepherding actors.

2 The Shepherding Problem for Human-Human and Mixed-Group Interactions

Our work the past few years involved adapting the shepherding problem to be a useful experimental paradigm to investigate human group coordination [11] and human-machine interaction [12]. An overarching aim of the work is to investigate multiagent goal-directed behavior and develop bio-inspired dynamical models that define the emergence of stable coordinated behavior [12, 13]. The modeling approach features two components. First, the utilization of *dynamical motor primitives* (DMPs) as intrapersonal controllers [14, 15] and second, the utilization of appropriate interpersonal and environmental coupling terms that link motor control to perceptual, task-specific information (e.g., optic, acoustic, haptic) [16]. This approach, which we refer to as *task-dynamic modeling*, seeks to understand the lawful emergence of low-dimensional behavior from movement or action systems that are composed of many degrees of freedom (DoF) [17]. This modeling approach has been used to model individual behavior such as reaching [18], walking and object avoidance [19], as well as human multiagent activities such as coordinating limb movements [20, 21], passing objects [22] and crowd motion [23]. Our research on the shepherding problem sought to expand upon this previous work to include multiagent control and coordination in dynamical task-contexts.

In what follows, we present a summary of our recent work utilizing the shepherding problem for human-human coordination and HMI. We will then conclude with future directions and practical applications of our work. We hope to show that the shepherding problem is not only interesting for Engineers, and Psychologists, but that the insights learned from human behavior can also inform researchers in designing algorithms for other indirect control problems or complex multiagent task scenarios.

2.1 Tabletop Shepherding

Our original task was a video-based task where participants used hand-movements to control their actors (see Fig. 1a) [11]. Participants were free to move their actors (modeled as colored squares, see Fig. 1b) within a fenced region projected onto a translucent tabletop. The task required participants, without talking, to find a strategy to corral and contain either 3, 5, or 7 agents (modeled as spheres, see Fig. 1b for an initial arrangement of 7 agents) within a red target region. The agents exhibited Brownian dynamics and were also repelled away from the participants' controller at a rate inversely proportional to the distance of the nearest actor. The task goal was for participant pairs to corral and contain the agents within the red target region for at least 70% of the last 45 s of 1-min trials. A trial would end prematurely if an agent collided with the surrounding fence, or if all the agents left an area larger than the white annulus (depicted in Fig. 1b). The task was considered solved if participants were able to achieve 8 successful containment attempts within a 45-min experimental period (i.e., completed 8 successful trials).

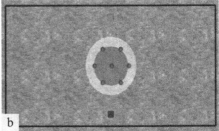

Fig. 1. Experimental setup of [11]. The video task was projected on a translucent tabletop (**a**). Using handheld motion sensors, participants controlled either a blue or orange object which repelled agents, modeled as spheres (shown in **b**). (Color figure online)

During the experiment, two behavioral modes were observed (depicted in Fig. 2). At the start of the experiment, all participants exhibited what we refer to as *search & recover* (S&R) behavior (see Fig. 2a). This behavior involved participants subdividing the task-space in half and individually pursuing and containing the agent that was farthest from the task goal. This behavior was predominant when the agent number to contain was low (i.e., 3 or 5 agents) but led to sub-optimal performance and failure when task difficulty increased (i.e., 7 agents). For those that did not fail when task difficulty increased, participants spontaneously discovered and transitioned to a coordinated mode of behavior we termed *coupled oscillatory containment* (COC) (see Fig. 2b). This behavior involved rhythmic, coordinated hand movements around the entire herd. Interestingly, the stable coordinative patterns that emerged during COC were consistent with the coordinative patterns observed in other human intrapersonal [24] and interpersonal rhythmic coordination tasks [20]. Specifically, participants would engage in either in-phase or anti-phase behavior, with a preference towards in-phase, (visually) symmetric behavior. Participants who discovered this behavior were able to achieve near-ceiling performance and soon after were able to achieve the required 8 points for task success. Although a subset of participants discovered this behavioral mode in the 3 and 5 agent conditions, its likelihood was especially prevalent in the 7-agent condition.

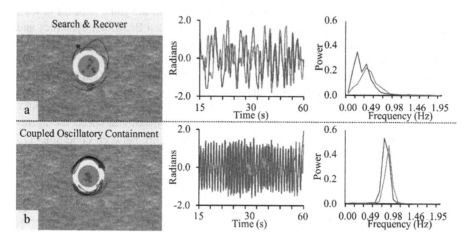

Fig. 2. Behavioral modes observed in the tabletop shepherding task. The black trajectory (**left**) indicates the last 5 s of behavior for both (**a**) and (**b**). Timeseries of last 45 s of behavior (**center**) and spectral analysis of hand movements during trial (**right**) also presented. (**a**) Search & recover involved participants selecting and containing individual agents. (**b**) Coupled oscillatory containment involved coordinated rhythmic movements by both participants around the herd.

The emergence of COC behavior may be the result of specific human-environment interactions that unfold during the experiment. In real sheepdog herding, for example, oscillatory behavior emerges naturally during sheepdog "driving" behavior when sheep at the group fringes escape [25]. Similarly, we have shown that when participants are tasked to complete the tabletop shepherding task with a simplified shepherding artificial actor that reacts to the agent farthest from the task goal (i.e., can only implement S&R), a subset of participants behaved in such a way as to induce COC-like behavior between the participant and the artificial actor which could not perform COC explicitly [26].

2.2   Shepherding While Locomoting

The behaviors observed by participants in the tabletop shepherding task were not unlike what is seen in other animal systems including not only sheepdog herding [25], but also wolf-pack hunting [27] and bubble-net feeding by humpback whales [28]. In these systems, successful containment involves minimizing the lateral movements of the to-be-herded (or hunted) agents. These behaviors have been explicitly encoded in robotic systems (e.g., [2]) but also emerge naturally in minimally cognitive agents [9]. We tested for this dynamic similitude in behavior between robotic and animal systems with human performance by adapting the shepherding problem to a task that required the locomotion of participants across a room-sized space (measuring 6 × 3.48 m).

We tested 39 dyads who completed the shepherding locomotion task while wearing a virtual reality headset attached to backpack-worn computers (see Fig. 3a, top). In virtual reality, participants took the role of a "crash test" dummy and were able to walk along a virtual green field (Fig. 3a, bottom). Like the tabletop version of the task, participants worked together to contain 7 agents. Over the course of 2-min trials, participants had to keep all 7 agents contained anywhere on the game field for at least 70% of the last 45 s of the trial. Again, the agents exhibited Brownian dynamics and were repelled by the colored cubes at the base of each participant's avatar, which was controlled by the participant's head movements. In addition to testing for dynamic similitude of shepherding behaviors across disparate task contexts, the experiment also explored how changing task difficulty affected the coordinated solutions that emerged (as was the case in the tabletop shepherding task by changing the number of agents). Here, task difficulty was manipulated by controlling the maximum speed the agents could move (0.12, 0.20 or 0.28 $\frac{m}{s}$). Dyads were split evenly between conditions (13 dyads each).

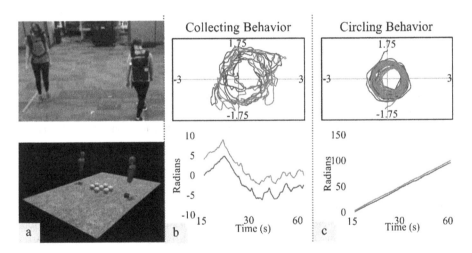

Fig. 3. Locomotory shepherding task and behaviors. (**a**) Participants completed the shepherding task while wear virtual reality headsets connected to portable backpack computers (**top**). Participants embodied "crash-test" dummies and were tasked to contain 7 agents (white spheres depicted in **bottom**) together. Two behavioral modes emerged – collecting behavior (**b**) and circling behavior (**c**). (**top**) Depicts position timeseries in *x, y* coordinates. (**bottom**) Depicts the unwrapped angular position of the participants in reference to the agent's mean position during the last 45 s of the 2nd minute of the trial.

In total, 26 dyads (66.67%) succeeded in the shepherding locomotion task (3 dyads in the 0.20 $\frac{m}{s}$ condition and 10 dyads in the most difficulty 0.28 $\frac{m}{s}$ agent speed condition did not reach the necessary 8 successful containment attempts). For analyses, all dyads who had at least 1 successful attempt were included (which resulted in 5 dyads from the 0.28 $\frac{m}{s}$ agent speed condition remaining excluded). From observing the data, all participants subdivided the task space in half and stayed (more or less) to the opposite side of their partner during the task. Like the shepherding tabletop task, two behavioral modes emerged. The first, termed *collecting,* involved continual changes in direction as participants corralled the agent farthest from the group, and was similar to S&R behavior (see Fig. 3b, top for a timeseries of the behavior). Although participants pursued individual agents, their movements remained coupled to each other, as seen in the coupling in the direction changes in Fig. 3b, bottom, which shows the unwrapped angular timeseries of participant movement in reference to the agent's average position.

The second behavioral mode, depicted in Fig. 3c, involved the persistent, coordinated circling around the entire herd in a fixed direction. This *circling* behavior was more likely to occur as task difficulty increased (from 39.42%, 52.24% to 64.58% of all successful trials for the 0.12, 0.20 and 0.28 $\frac{m}{s}$ agent speed conditions, respectively). Additionally, these dyads who discovered and transitioned to this strategy were sensitive to task difficulty, $F(2,15) = 9.91, p = .002, \eta_p^2 = .57$, such that average walking speed was 0.44 $\frac{m}{s}$, 0.54 $\frac{m}{s}$, and 0.64 $\frac{m}{s}$, respectively. Finally, like COC behavior for the tabletop shepherding task, participants who maintained circling behavior had greater containment time performance ($M = 44.19$ s, $SD = 1.06$) compared to "non-circlers" ($M = 41.73$ s, $SD = 3.17$), $F(1, 28) = 25.11, p < .001, \eta_p^2 = .47$. Consistent with findings from other animal systems [25, 27, 28], as well as minimal agents [9], the human data presented here show that the coordinated solutions humans adopt are the result of an interaction of constraints imposed by the actor and task. Despite differences in constraints acting upon the actors (e.g., being hand-driven in the tabletop shepherding task, and full body driven here), the solutions participants adopt reflect the task demands of maintaining a form of "circling" around the herd to solve the task.

2.3   Shepherding with an Artificial Actor

Returning to the tabletop shepherding task, we have taken insights gleamed from the human data to design a bio-inspired artificial actor that can exhibit both S&R and COC behavioral modes and work effectively with human novices to assist them in reaching success [12]. Interestingly, S&R and COC behavior reflect the two fundamental movement types, or *motor primitives,* hypothesized to underlie goal-directed human movement patterns [14, 15]. Further, these movement primitives can be described by two basic processes in dynamical systems theory. The first are discrete movements, which can be modeled by point-attractor dynamics, and the second are rhythmic movements, defined by limit-cycle dynamics. These relate to the behaviors observed in the tabletop shepherding task as S&R behavior requires discrete selection and movement to a given agent, while COC involved rhythmic oscillations around the entire herd.

These *dynamical motor primitives* (DMPs) have been employed to generate human-like reaching, obstacle avoidance, drumming and racket swinging in both simulation and via end-effector control for a multi-jointed robotic arm [14, 29]. In a HMI task [30], an artificial actor capable of mirroring discrete finger flexion-extensions, as well as rhythmic, oscillatory behavior, reproduced the same stable behaviors seen in the interpersonal behavioral synchrony literature [20, 21]. This same model was also capable of assisting novices to acquire the ability to produce difficult behaviors, providing support that models composed of DMPs have practical use for assisted skill acquisition [31]. Finally, DMPs are hypothesized to describe human-like characteristics of human movement. In the same HMI coordinative task, some participants who worked alongside the artificial actor attributed agency to the agents, providing some evidence for the effectiveness of DMPs [30, 32].

Previous research developing models for DMPs have either focused on non-social, individual behavior [14, 29], or minimally social interactive tasks where the explicit goal is to coordinate one's actions with the agent [30, 32]. Our recent research [12] has sought to expand the hypothesis that DMPs can be suitable control architectures for HMI by designing an agent that can work effectively with novices during the tabletop shepherding task.

A version of the model tested in [12] is presented below (also see Fig. 4a). For more specific experimental implementation, we ask the reader to refer to the paper. The artificial actor, i, for the tabletop shepherding task has an end-point effector control which dictates the r, θ components of its movement in relationship to the center of the target region. The radial component exhibited point-attractor dynamics and is presented in (1),

$$\ddot{r}_i + b_r \dot{r}_i + \varepsilon_r \left(r_i - \left(r_{sf(t),i} + r_{min} \right) \right) = 0 \tag{1}$$

where the radial component of the actor's end-point effector was gravitated towards $r_{sf(t),i}$, which is the radial distance of the targeted agent, defined as the agent farthest from the task goal at time t. Parameter r_{min} is the preferred distance of the agent from the targeted agent to ensure repulsion towards the goal, while parameters b_r and ε_r controlled the degree of dampness and stiffness of the actor's movement. The angular component of the actor's movement is displayed in (2),

$$\ddot{\theta}_l + b_\theta \dot{\theta}_l + \beta \dot{\theta}_i^3 + \gamma \theta_i^2 \dot{\theta}_l + \varepsilon_\theta (\theta_i - \theta_{sf(t),i}) = \left(\dot{\theta}_i - \dot{\theta}_j \right) \left(A + B \left(\theta_i - \theta_j \right)^2 \right) \tag{2}$$

which can exhibit both discrete-like movement seen in S&R behavior, as well as robust oscillatory movement seen in COC behavior. Parameters b_θ and ε_θ are the linear damping and stiffness terms. The Rayleigh ($\beta \dot{\theta}_i^3$) and van der Pol ($\gamma \theta_i^2 \dot{\theta}_l$) escapement terms allow for oscillatory behavior to emerge [33] by manipulating the angular dampness term, b_θ, with the following parameter dynamics function,

$$\dot{b}_\theta + \delta \left(b_\theta - \alpha \left(r_{sf(t),i} - r_\Delta \right) \right) = 0 \tag{3}$$

such that for positive values of b_θ, the actor's endpoint effector will move discretely to the angular component of the targeted agent's location. However, as the distance of the farthest agent from the task goal is within r_Δ, which can be set for example to the bounds of the red target region (see Fig. 4a), b_θ will become negative and a Hopf bifurcation will occur. Here, the fixed-point attractor will lose stability and give rise to limit-cycle dynamics centered on the angular component of the farthest agent's position.

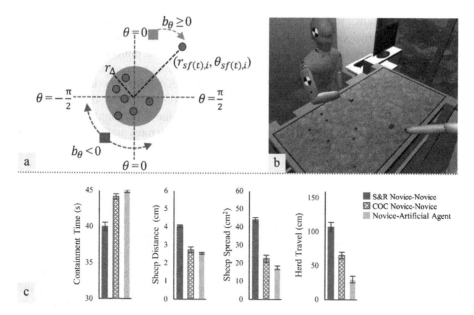

Fig. 4. Virtual tabletop shepherding agent, task depiction and results from [12]. (**a**) Depiction of the tabletop shepherding task space. The artificial actor performed COC (e.g., the blue actor in the figure) when the furthest agent, $sf(t),i$, was within r_Δ distance from the task center. Otherwise, the actor performed S&R behavior (depicted in the orange actor). (**b**) Depiction of virtual reality environment also used in testing. Participants took the perspective of a "crash test" dummy. Here, participants had to keep the agents herded together anywhere on the game field. (**c**) Results from [12] depicting performance differences between novice dyads who exhibited only S&R behavior, those who discovered COC behavior, and novices who performed COC behavior with an artificial actor. (Color figure online)

The coupling function to the right side of (2) couples the angular component of actor i's position and velocity to those of their partner j. The format of the coupling function allows for the model's angular movements of both actors to achieve the stable in-phase and anti-phase modes of behavior observed in [11] and during interpersonal rhythmic coordination more generally [20, 24]. Parameters A and B index coupling strength, such that $|4B| > |A|$ allows for both stable in-phase and anti-phase solutions to emerge. Again, see [12] for more details regarding the model. The artificial actor can also be played with from code downloadable at https://github.com/Multiagent-Dynamics/Human-Machine-Shepherding.

We have run two separate HMI experiments utilizing the table shepherding actor [12] (see Fig. 4b for the virtual reality environment), first where we misled participants to believe they were completing the tabletop shepherding task with another human in a different room (a "Turing-like" manipulation), and a second experiment where deception was not used. In both experiments, the artificial actor was able to work with participants in a virtual reality environment to complete the tabletop shepherding task (see example results in Fig. 4c). In the deception experiment, most participants (63.64% of 11 participants) remained in belief that their virtual partner was human-controlled. In the second, no deception experiment, a sizeable minority (38.89% of 18 participants) believed that, even though it was made explicit to them that their partner was computer-controlled, that the actions of the artificial actor was in fact human-controlled. Taken together, these results suggest that not only is a task-dynamic model of the shepherding task comprised of actor and environmentally-coupled DMPs suitable to reach task success in HMI, but that the interaction by most participants was such that the dynamics were perceived as human-like.

3   Conclusion

Across two very different task contexts utilizing different end-effector control (hand controller in the case of the tabletop shepherding task, and full-body control in the case of the locomotory shepherding task), the coordinative solutions that high-performing participants adopt reflect the most symmetrical arrangement given the constraints imposed on the actor (e.g., upper limit on movement speed, inability to occupy the same physical space) and the constraints of the task itself [34]. Future work seeks to expand on this work to investigate more complex, multistep shepherding problems including transitions from containment to transportation of agents, as well as responses to perturbations on group performance. In these more complex situations, role differentiation and role switching may be necessary to achieve task success, as opposed to the use of identical behaviors observed in our tasks.

The transition from discrete, pursuit behaviors such as S&R to continuous control like COC behavior reflect either behavior destabilization due to increasing task demands (e.g., increasing the number of agents, or increasing their speed) [35], or the transition to behaviors that are either physically or computationally more efficient (e.g., the detection of the "herd" as opposed to scanning between individual agents) [36–38]. Although these coordinated rhythmic behaviors lead to near-ceiling performance, only a subset of participants discovered this strategy, leaving open an opportunity for assistive systems to promote coordination and performance in individual and group tasks.

Indeed, multiagent coordination is ubiquitous to everyday human life which not only fosters new and more efficient modes of behavioral activity, such as when people organize themselves into a bucket brigade, but also plays a fundamental role in human perceptual-motor development and learning, as well as human social functioning more generally [39]. Due to advancements in interactive artificial systems and virtual reality technologies, assistive virtual and robotic agents can play a role in behavioral expertise training and perceptual-motor rehabilitation, enhancing pro-social functioning in children with social deficit disorders, and assisting the elderly and individuals with disabilities with daily life activities.

Taking inspiration from the social aspects of learning, teachers, coaches or tutors can be replaced by artificial actors to provide targeted enhancement in human group performance [40], as was done when participants interacted with our artificial shepherding actor. By embedding assistive systems in group contexts to scaffold learning, artificial actors serve a promising role within human groups. For example, artificial actors embodying human-like dynamics can take the role of humans in situations where recruitment is difficult, such as large-scale training exercises, or to provide more varied team composition or role assignment for more robust team coordination in light of perturbations [41]. In other domains, embodying robotic systems with human-like dynamics may facilitate action prediction and safety in domains such as advanced manufacturing (e.g., handing objects from robot to human), where the movement capabilities of such systems are not readily apparent [42]. Although such human-like dynamics are not necessary for task completion per se, embedding agents with such human-like constraints is expected to enhance HMI [43–45]. Finally, artificial actors play a promising role in "dynamic clamp" methodologies to allow researchers to deduce unidirectional effects of the (artificial) member on the rest of the group to better understand the processes underlying social interactions and diagnosis of social disorders [30, 31, 46].

In summary, our group has taken a human-centered approach to understand multiagent coordination in indirect control problems like the shepherding task. By modeling task dynamics of successful human dyads, we seek to develop bio-inspired artificial actors that can enhance HMI in dynamic task contexts. Not only can the results from our experiments expand understanding to the emergence of stable coordinative patterns in human groups, but the hope is that these insights can also inform the multiagent research community on "human-inspired" solutions to multiagent control problems.

Acknowledgments. NIH Grant R01GM105045, ARC Future Fellowship (Richardson, FT180 100447) and the University of Cincinnati Research Council supported this research.

References

1. Cohen, D.J., James Nelson, W., Maharbiz, M.M.: Galvanotactic control of collective cell migration in epithelial monolayers. Nat. Mater. **13**, 409–417 (2014)
2. Lien, J.M., Rodríguez, S., Malric, J.P., Amato, N.M.: Shepherding behaviors with multiple shepherds. In: Proceedings 2005 IEEE International Conference on Robotics and Automation, pp. 3402–3407. IEEE, Piscataway (2005)
3. Lee, W., Kim, D.: Autonomous shepherding behaviors of multiple target steering robots. Sensors (Switzerland) **17** (2017)
4. Pierson, A., Schwager, M.: Controlling noncooperative herds with robotic herders. IEEE Trans. Robot. **34**, 517–525 (2018)
5. Licitra, R.A., Bell, Z.I., Doucette, E.A., Dixon, W.E.: Single agent indirect herding of multiple targets: a switched adaptive control approach. IEEE Control Syst. Lett. **2**, 127–132 (2018)
6. Strömbom, D., King, A.J.: Robot collection and transport of objects: a biomimetic process. Front. Robot. AI. **5**, 48 (2018)
7. Vaughan, R., Sumpter, N., Henderson, J., Frost, A., Cameron, S.: Experiments in automatic flock control. Rob. Auton. Syst. **31**, 109–117 (2000)
8. Paranjape, A.A., Chung, S.J., Kim, K., Shim, D.H.: Robotic herding of a flock of birds using an unmanned aerial vehicle. IEEE Trans. Robot. **34**, 901–915 (2018)

9. Özdemir, A., Gauci, M., Gross, R.: Shepherding with robots that do not compute. In: Proceedings of the 14th European Conference on Artificial Life, ECAL 2017, pp. 332–339. MIT Press, Cambridge (2017)

10. St. Clair, A., Mataric, M.: How robot verbal feedback can improve team performance in human-robot task collaborations. In: Proceedings of the Tenth Annual ACM/IEEE International Conference on Human-Robot Interaction - HRI 2015, pp. 213–220. ACM Press, New York (2015)

11. Nalepka, P., Kallen, R.W., Chemero, A., Saltzman, E., Richardson, M.J.: Herd those sheep: emergent multiagent coordination and behavioral-mode switching. Psychol. Sci. **28**, 630–650 (2017)

12. Nalepka, P., et al.: Human social motor solutions for human–machine interaction in dynamical task contexts. Proc. Natl. Acad. Sci. **116**, 1437–1446 (2019)

13. Richardson, M.J., et al.: Modeling embedded interpersonal and multiagent coordination. In: Muñoz, V.M., Gusikhin, O., Chang, V. (eds.) Proceedings of the 1st International Conference on Complex Information Systems, pp. 155–164. SciTePress, Setúbal (2016)

14. Ijspeert, A.J., Nakanishi, J., Hoffmann, H., Pastor, P., Schaal, S.: Dynamical movement primitives: learning attractor models for motor behaviors. Neural Comput. **25**, 328–373 (2013)

15. Schaal, S., Kotosaka, S., Sternad, D.: Nonlinear dynamical systems as movement primitives. In: Proceedings of the 1st IEEE-RAS International Conference on Humanoid Robotics. IEEE, Piscataway (2000)

16. Warren, W.H.: The dynamics of perception and action. Psychol. Rev. **113**, 358–389 (2006)

17. Bernstein, N.A.: The Co-ordination and Regulation of Movements. Pergamon Press, Oxford (1967)

18. Saltzman, E., Kelso, J.A.S.: Skilled actions: a task-dynamic approach. Psychol. Rev. **94**, 84–106 (1987)

19. Warren, W., Fajen, B., Fuchs, A., Jirsa, V.: Behavioral dynamics of visually guided locomotion. Coord. Neural Behav. Soc. Dyn. **17**, 45–75 (2008)

20. Schmidt, R.C., Richardson, M.J.: Dynamics of interpersonal coordination. In: Fuchs, A., Jirsa, V.K. (eds.) Understanding Complex Systems, pp. 281–308. Springer, Heidelberg (2008). https://doi.org/10.1007/978-3-540-74479-5_14

21. Oullier, O., de Guzman, G., Jantzen, K.J., Lagarde, J., Scott Kelso, J.A.: Social coordination dynamics: measuring human bonding. Soc. Neurosci. **3**, 178–192 (2008)

22. Lamb, M., Kallen, R.W., Harrison, S.J., Di Bernardo, M., Minai, A., Richardson, M.J.: To pass or not to pass: modeling the movement and affordance dynamics of a pick and place task. Front. Psychol. **8**, 1061 (2017)

23. Warren, W.H.: Collective motion in human crowds. Curr. Dir. Psychol. Sci. **27**, 232–240 (2018)

24. Haken, H., Kelso, J.A.S., Bunz, H.: A theoretical model of phase transitions in human hand movements. Biol. Cybern. **51**, 347–356 (1985)

25. Strömbom, D., et al.: Solving the shepherding problem: heuristics for herding autonomous, interacting agents. J. R. Soc. Interface **11**, 20140719 (2014)

26. Nalepka, P., et al.: Emergence of efficient, coordinated solutions despite differences in agent ability during human-machine interaction. In: Proceedings of the 18th International Conference on Intelligent Virtual Agents - IVA 2018, pp. 337–338. ACM Press, New York (2019)

27. Muro, C., Escobedo, R., Spector, L., Coppinger, R.P.: Wolf-pack (Canis lupus) hunting strategies emerge from simple rules in computational simulations. Behav. Processes. **88**, 192–197 (2011)

28. D'Vincent, C.G., Nilson, R.M., Hanna, R.E.: Vocalization and coordinated feeding behavior of the humpback whale in Southeastern Alaska. Sci. Reports Whales Res. Inst. **36**, 41–47 (1985)
29. Ijspeert, A.J., Nakanishi, J., Schaal, S.: Movement imitation with nonlinear dynamical systems in humanoid robots. In: Proceedings 2002 IEEE International Conference on Robotics and Automation, pp. 1398–1403. IEEE, Piscataway (2002)
30. Dumas, G., de Guzman, G.C., Tognoli, E., Kelso, J.A.S.: The human dynamic clamp as a paradigm for social interaction. Proc. Natl. Acad. Sci. **111**, E3726–E3734 (2014)
31. Kostrubiec, V., Dumas, G., Zanone, P.G., Scott Kelso, J.A.: The virtual teacher (VT) paradigm: learning new patterns of interpersonal coordination using the human dynamic clamp. PLoS ONE **10**, 1–24 (2015)
32. Kelso, J.A.S., de Guzman, G.C., Reveley, C., Tognoli, E.: Virtual partner interaction (VPI): exploring novel behaviors via coordination dynamics. PLoS One **4** (2009)
33. Kay, B.A., Kelso, J.A.S., Saltzman, E.L., Schöner, G.: Space-time behavior of single and bimanual rhythmical movements: data and limit cycle model. J. Exp. Psychol. Hum. Percept. Perform. **13**, 178–192 (1987)
34. Richardson, M.J., Kallen, R.W.: Symmetry-breaking and the contextual emergence of human multiagent coordination and social activity. In: Dzhafarov, E., Jordan, S., Zhang, R., Cervantes, V. (eds.) World Scientific Review, pp. 1–57. World Scientific Publishing Co. (2015)
35. Sternad, D., Marino, H., Charles, S.K., Duarte, M., Dipietro, L., Hogan, N.: Transitions between discrete and rhythmic primitives in a unimanual task. Front. Comput. Neurosci. **7**, 1–13 (2013)
36. Zhang, Z., Sternad, D.: The primacy of rhythm: how discrete actions merge into a stable rhythmic pattern. J. Neurophysiol. (2018). https://doi.org/10.1152/jn.00587.2018
37. Selinger, J.C., O'Connor, S.M., Wong, J.D., Donelan, J.M.: Humans can continuously optimize energetic cost during walking. Curr. Biol. **25**, 2452–2456 (2015)
38. Maurice, P., Hogan, N., Sternad, D.: Predictability, force, and (anti)resonance in complex object control. J. Neurophysiol. **120**, 765–780 (2018)
39. Vygotsky, L.S.: Mind and Society: The Development of Higher Psychological Processes. Harvard University Press, Cambridge (1978)
40. Johnston, J., Sottilare, R., Sinatra, A.M., Shawn Burke, C. (eds.): Building Intelligent Tutoring Systems for Teams. Emerald Publishing Limited (2018)
41. Gorman, J.C., Cooke, N.J., Amazeen, P.G.: Training adaptive teams. Hum. Factors **52**, 295–307 (2010)
42. Mörtl, A., Lorenz, T., Hirche, S.: Rhythm patterns interaction - synchronization behavior for human-robot joint action. PLoS ONE **9**, e95195 (2014)
43. Lorenz, T., Weiss, A., Hirche, S.: Synchrony and reciprocity: key mechanisms for social companion robots in therapy and care. Int. J. Soc. Robot. **8**, 125–143 (2016)
44. Słowiński, P., et al.: Dynamic similarity promotes interpersonal coordination in joint action. J. R. Soc. Interface **13**, 20151093 (2016)
45. Iqbal, T., Riek, L.D.: Human-robot teaming: approaches from joint action and dynamical systems. In: Goswami, A., Vadakkepat, P. (eds.) Humanoid Robotics: A Reference, pp. 2293–2312. Springer, Dordrecht (2019)
46. Słowiński, P., et al.: Unravelling socio-motor biomarkers in schizophrenia. NPJ Schizophr **3**, 8 (2017)

Generating Real Context Data to Test User Dependent Systems - Application to Multi-agent Systems

Pedro Oliveira[1,2(✉)], Paulo Novais[1], and Paulo Matos[2]

[1] Department of Informatics, Algoritmi Centre/University of Minho, Braga, Portugal
pjon@di.uminho.pt
[2] Department of Informatics and Communications,
Institute Polytechnic of Bragança, Bragança, Portugal
{poliveira,pmatos}@ipb.pt

Abstract. This paper, deals with the usually need of data to simulate behavior and efficiency of proposed solutions in several fields, and also knowing that personal data always bring privacy and security issues. This work wants to promote a balanced solution between the need of personal information and the user's privacy expectations. We propose a solution to overcome these issues, and don't compromise the balance between security and personal comfort based on generating real context data of users, that allow to test user dependent systems.

Keywords: Adaptive-system · AmI · Security · Privacy · Simulation · Multi-agent system

1 Introduction

Systems that deal with personal data always bring privacy and security issues, also the balance of these issues, with the need that persons have in interact with spaces in a transparent way and that those spaces smartly adapt to their preferences.

That said, in this project, is proposed a solution to overcome these issues, and don't compromise the balance between security and personal comfort.

In this field some work was done [2,4,9,10], we evaluate and continue to improve that work and develop a more focused solution to solve the presented problem.

Pursuing this effort, we need several information of hundreds of users to test a multi-agent system that simulates the comfort of these users, like in most of the research projects carried out, data are usually needed to simulate behaviour and efficiency of the proposed solutions, since it is necessary to use them to validate and test the research carried out at the most diverse levels.

The development of this project also arises from the need to gather information on the comfort preferences (temperature, humidity, musical playlist, musical

© Springer Nature Switzerland AG 2019
Y. Demazeau et al. (Eds.): PAAMS 2019, LNAI 11523, pp. 180–187, 2019.
https://doi.org/10.1007/978-3-030-24209-1_15

genre, etc.) of multiple users. And besides that, also have the information of how each user adapts their preferences to the place where it is [7]. This information, in addition to being necessary on a large scale (hundreds of users), would also be necessary in a very broad time-frame, always longer than one year. As it is known that comfort preferences normally vary according to a seasonal character, namely at the seasons level.

Getting data with this dimension and involving so many users is a difficult task and, in addition to the users collaboration, would require a high cost, regarding the equipment needed to collect this information [8].

Thus an algorithm was created, which simulates not only the variation of preferences of the different users, but also their daily life, taking into account the different places that it frequents (home, work, leisure places). In addition, the relationship between users is also established, introducing the concept of family and co-workers.

2 Materials and Methods

2.1 Security and Privacy

The technological revolution that is felt, particularly in behavioural analysis fields, IoT or big data, brings significant new challenges, including those related to the type of user information that can be collected, and the knowledge that can be obtained derived from the compilation of this information. Although not necessarily existing the user's authority to collect such information.

This IoT revolution has yet clearly identified problems. In particular, the privacy and security of user data. Foreseeing the dissemination of intelligent spaces, of which the user can, and want to take advantage of the interaction between systems, and the consequent sharing of personal data, this is a theme that needs resolution in a short-term [5].

Obviously at this point there will be the requirements for concessions and commitments on the part of the user.

IoT increases the risk of personal privacy, and the confidentiality and integrity of data in organizations. Some IoT applications for consumers, particularly those related to health and wellness, which store sensitive personal information, and that consumers may not want to share.

Using this solution, all the problems of security and privacy are overcome, without the need of data collection from real users [1].

2.2 The Simulation Algorithm

The developed simulation algorithm has several predefined assumptions that allow the simulation to be as close to reality as possible. These assumptions are defined in the code as input variables and customized according to the simulation needs.

Table 1. Parameters and different delays

Parameter (Delay)	Minimum (minutes)	Maximum (minutes)
Enter Work	−10	10
Enter Home	−30	30
Exit Home	−40	40
Lazer Hours	−90	90

The types of schedule are defined, taking into account the different possibilities, in this case four, then depending on the type of schedule selected, the value for minimum and maximum delay is also defined.

Table 1 defines the four delays to the different schedules, in this table we have the minimum and maximum delay time, that the algorithm uses to generate the random between these limits, and to introduce the generated value in each situation.

The diagram presented at Fig. 1 illustrates more clearly the different processes that the algorithm develops.

The process is started by choosing the number of local systems associated with the user, between 1 and 5, depending on this choice the user is associated with the local systems defined. Consequently when selected the local system associated to the home, users are generated between (0–3) that define the concept of family. With regard to the local system associated with the workplace, co-workers are generated between (0–3) associated with the same workplace. Then, for each generated user, the corresponding time type is defined, so when the introduction of user history for each day is started, it is coherently associated with a type of schedule. Then, it is started the process of entering history information for each user, this introduction is carried out consecutively for each day. Thus during the daily input process, the corresponding time of introduction and delay is generated, taking into account the limits previously defined for this delay. For each daily period the introduction is performed, and new delay random intervals are defined relative to the time set as standard, in order to get as close as possible to the daily reality of the users. In addition to the time, and for each period, are also entered the preferences for the correspondent user. In this case, the following premises were defined:

In 5% of the situations the preference value is changed, introducing in this case the factor of randomness with the limits (−5; 5).

For 15% of the situations, the preference value is changed by introducing the factor of randomness with the limits (−3; 3). In all other situations, the preference value is entered without any change (Table 2).

In this way, the information for this project required to the simulation is obtained, with as many users as necessary, as well for the necessary time period, in this case a 720 day time window was defined, with 1000 users in the system, which originates more than three millions historical records in the database.

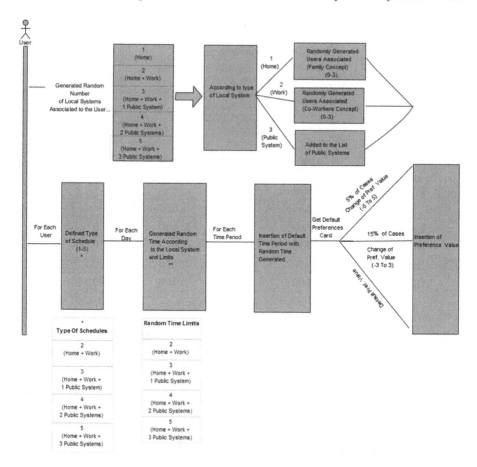

Fig. 1. Diagram - users simulation algorithm

Next, at Table 3, are showed the parameters defined for the four schedules, we try to put these schedules as real as possible, and with that we have the most regular shifts of work, like starting work at 08 h or 09 h of the morning, start at 16 h in the afternoon, or the work by night that starts at 00 h. We set the most normal period of work (eight hours), and with that we can define the correspondent hours of exit home to go work, the enter home hour after work, and also the exit home to do some leisure hours, that is related to the period that the user is not working.

In this way, the information for this project required to the simulation is obtained, with as many users as necessary, as well for the necessary time period, in this case a 720 day time window was defined, with 1000 users in the system, which originates more than three millions history records in the database.

Table 2. Randomness factor

% of Cases	Randomness factor	
	Minimum	Maximum
75%		
15%	−3	3
5%	−5	5

Table 3. Parameters/Schedules

Parameter (Hour)	Schedule			
	Schedule A	Schedule B	Schedule C	Schedule D
Enter work	08h00	09h00	16h00	00h00
Enter home	17h10	18h10	00h10	08h10
Exit home	07h50	08h50	15h50	23h50
Enter lazer	20h00	21h00	10h00	15h00

This process takes few hours, namely for the values defined before, for instance in an average computer it takes three to four hours the process to generate the full dataset of information and the insertion at the database.

The following listing at Listing 1.1 demonstrates a little part of the algorithm, in the case where we select the type of system selected.

Listing 1.1. Part of algorithm implementation

```
switch (randomNumberOfLocalSystemsByUser) {
case 1:
TypeOfSystem = 1;
System.out.println("Home");
idLocalSystem++;
addMoreUsersToSystem(idMasterUser, TypeOfSystem);
DescLocalSystem = ("Home:␣" + idMasterUser + "␣+" +
    idsUsersAtSystem);
genenerateUserSimul.AddLocalSystemWS(idLocalSystem,
    DescLocalSystem);
genenerateUserSimul.insertHistoryRecord(idMasterUser,
    idsUsersAtSystem, idLocalSystem, TypeOfSystem);
break;
case 2:
```

3 Results

3.1 Statistical Analysis

For the simulation results validation, we used the distribution of frequency analysis, using histograms, that is the graphical representation in columns/bars of the dataset previously tabulated and divided into classes [6].

In this case for the different classes, the density of each is shown, as well each percentage, which it represents within each distribution.

As can be verified by the histogram analysis in Figs. 2 and 3, it can be concluded that the different classes are evenly distributed.

As can be seen by analysing the histograms, we can conclude that the different classes are distributed equally.

Describing Fig. 2, we can see in (a) the type of user (0–3), at (b) the number of local systems for each user (0–4), in (c) the number of users at the same home (0–2) (family concept) and at (d) the number of users at the same work (0–3) (co-workers concept).

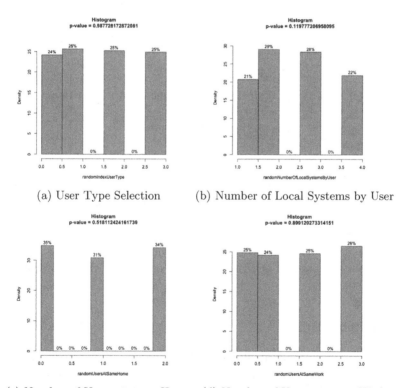

(a) User Type Selection   (b) Number of Local Systems by User

(c) Number of Users at same Home   (d) Number of Users at same Work

Fig. 2. Histogram - user parameters

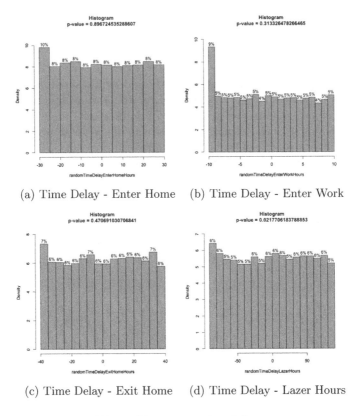

(a) Time Delay - Enter Home   (b) Time Delay - Enter Work

(c) Time Delay - Exit Home   (d) Time Delay - Lazer Hours

Fig. 3. Histogram - time delays

In all histograms for each distribution, we calculate the hypothetical frequency called the P-value, also known as the observed significance level [3], and also validate that all the percentages density are very close, what confirm a evenly distribution.

Describing Fig. 3, we can see in (a) the type of user (0–3), at (b) the number of local systems for each user (0–4), in (c) the number of users at the same home (0–2) (family concept) and at (d) the number of users at the same work (0–3) (co-workers concept).

4   Conclusions

Concluding, we can say that all the work proposed is developed, and all the objectives are achieved. We can use a fully operational solution to simulate how many users we need, in any time period and with the comfort preferences needed for the problem. This work is very important to all type of investigation, that need massive information, and where is needed the simulation of this kind of data, with defined parameters and limits to be as close to reality as possible.

In this case the information generated is used, to test and improve a multi-agent system, that depends from user information, namely behaviour and comfort preferences but also we can adapt it to simulate other type of information.

For future work, the simulation algorithm can be generalized, as much to accommodate as many cases as possible, and with that, the user only need to define and configure the initial parameters for each case, and after that retrieves how many data as he needs for the specific case defined.

Acknowledgments. This work has been supported by FCT Fundação para a Ciência e Tecnologia within the Project Scope: UID/CEC/00319/2019.

References

1. Babar, S., Mahalle, P., Stango, A., Prasad, N., Prasad, R.: Proposed security model and threat taxonomy for the internet of things (IoT). In: Meghanathan, N., Boumerdassi, S., Chaki, N., Nagamalai, D. (eds.) CNSA 2010. CCIS, vol. 89, pp. 420–429. Springer, Heidelberg (2010). https://doi.org/10.1007/978-3-642-14478-3_42
2. Cárdenas, M., Sanz, J.G., Pavón, J.: Testing ambient assisted living solutions with simulations. In: Medina-Bulo, I., Merayo, M.G., Hierons, R. (eds.) ICTSS 2018. LNCS, vol. 11146, pp. 56–61. Springer, Cham (2018). https://doi.org/10.1007/978-3-319-99927-2_5
3. Chaubey, Y.P.: Resampling-Based Multiple Testing: Examples and Methods for P-Value Adjustment (1993)
4. Hoes, P., Hensen, J., Loomans, M., De Vries, B., Bourgeois, D.: User behavior in whole building simulation. Energy Buildings **41**(3), 295–302 (2009)
5. Khan, R., Khan, S.U., Zaheer, R., Khan, S.: Future internet: the internet of things architecture, possible applications and key challenges. In: 2012 10th International Conference on Frontiers of Information Technology (FIT), pp. 257–260. IEEE (2012)
6. Konishi, S., Kitagawa, G.: Information Criteria and Statistical Modeling. Springer, New York (2008). https://doi.org/10.1007/978-0-387-71887-3
7. Schilit, B., Adams, N., Want, R.: Context-aware computing applications. In: First Workshop on Mobile Computing Systems and Applications, WMCSA 1994, pp. 85–90. IEEE (1994)
8. Wang, K.I.K., Abdulla, W.H., Salcic, Z.: Ambient intelligence platform using multi-agent system and mobile ubiquitous hardware. Pervasive Mob. Comput. **5**(5), 558–573 (2009)
9. Yan, D., et al.: Occupant behavior modeling for building performance simulation: current state and future challenges. Energy Buildings **107**, 264–278 (2015)
10. Zimmerman, G.: Modeling and simulation of individual user behavior for building performance predictions. In: Proceedings of the 2007 Summer Computer Simulation Conference, pp. 913–920. Society for Computer Simulation International (2007)

Multimap Routing for Road Traffic Management

Alvaro Paricio Garcia$^{(\boxtimes)}$ (iD) and Miguel A. Lopez-Carmona (iD)

Departamento de Automática, Escuela Politécnica Superior, Universidad de Alcalá,
Campus Universitario, Alcalá de Henares, 28801 Madrid, Spain
{alvaro.paricio,miguelangel.lopez}@uah.es

Abstract. TWM -*Traffic Weighted Multi-maps*- is presented as a novel
traffic route guidance model to reduce urban traffic congestion, focusing
on individual trip and collective objectives considering citizens, individual multi-modal mobility, and heterogeneous traffic groups. They have
different interests, goals and regulation, so new multi-objective cost functions and control systems are required. *TWM* is structured around a
novel control paradigm, based on the generation and distribution of complementary cost maps for traffic collectives (fleets), oriented towards the
application of differentiated traffic planning and control policies. Agents
receive a customized view TWM of the network that is used to calculate
individual route using standard means and tools. The research describes
the TWM theoretical model and microscopic simulations over standard
reference traffic network grids, different traffic congestion scenarios, and
several driver's adherences to the mechanism. Travel-time results show
that TWM can have a high impact on the network performance, leading
to enhancements from 20% to 50%. TWM is conceived to be compatible
with existing traffic routing systems. The research has promising future
evolution applying new algorithms, policies and network profiles.

Keywords: Dynamic traffic assignment · Traffic control ·
Traffic simulation · Vehicle routing · Traffic big data ·
Decision making · Multi-agent systems

1 Introduction

One of the main challenges in the modeling and design of traffic management systems and services is the difficulty of controlling driver's decision making regarding the choice of their routes, in order to match resources and demand in an
optimal and automated way. Currently, Traffic Control System (TCS) coordinate
demand through direct intervention in the network, online information systems,
panels, regulatory policies or restrictions [21]. Drivers, for their part, are increasingly using advanced agent-based navigation systems that adapt and react in real
time to the state of traffic [20]. Thus, the majority of vehicles receive very similar
recommendations and stimuli, which make it difficult to optimize demand and
transfer situations of congestion [16].

© Springer Nature Switzerland AG 2019
Y. Demazeau et al. (Eds.): PAAMS 2019, LNAI 11523, pp. 188–199, 2019.
https://doi.org/10.1007/978-3-030-24209-1_16

There are many proposals and commercial systems that generate individual route recommendations from data sent by users to a TCS [16]. However, these solutions raise multiple deployment questions due to computational resource demands, complexity, and privacy implications. The active participation of vehicles in the generation of data, and the use of Big Data as an element of mobility management, allow the design of alternative demand control models [13].

Smart-Cities require global perspectives that focus not only on traffic individuals (agents) and their contribution to traffic, but also on collective objectives considering citizens, individual multi-modal mobility, and conflicting group interests, leading to the concept of Urban Computing as described in [28]. This fact involve designing new multi-objective cost functions and the corresponding control models that optimize them.

Our goal is to reduce average travel time of all the vehicles in the traffic network, fulfilling individual, collective and regulatory goals and constraints, reducing congestion times in the network. It describes a novel route guidance model called *TWM -Traffic Weighted Multi-maps-*, that is shown to be scalable, technically and economically viable, easy to deploy, compatible with existing platforms, and has a low impact on privacy. TWM is structured around a new control paradigm, based on the generation and distribution of complementary cost maps. Every individual agent receives a customized view of the traffic network. Vehicles are grouped in classes (fleets) that share the same network view. The aggregation of individual decision making tends to satisfy the predefined control policy.

TWM proposal takes into account the individual traffic agent ability to take its own decisions (a) for using any of the known algorithms for K-shortest path (Dijkstra, A, A*, or any variant [7,8,15]) in case of individual route calculation, or (b) having received a TWM-based route calculation, follow it (that will diverge in many occasions from the standard ones). Compatibility with existing routing frameworks based on route-queries for origin/destination (O/D) is direct, as TWM is then applied at the TCS back-end. TWM model is also of application with hyperpaths calculations.

Research main contributions include: (1) a novel traffic route guidance model based on multimap distribution that enable differentiated route selection for individuals and collectives; (2) a microscopic simulation framework for TWM evaluation and algorithm comparisons, and (3) macroscopic and microscopic performance analysis based on the simulations performed for the most basic algorithm and network model. The research has promising future evolution applying new algorithms, policies and network profiles.

1.1 Literature Review

MuTraff deals with the development of an intelligent traffic control system, made up of the design of congestion management mechanisms, from which many parameters susceptible to optimization and control are derived, such as pollution level, noise footprint, prioritization of vehicle type, contingency plans, etc. [2], combined with a hybrid approach of individual vehicle agents that take into account the routing recommendations based on intention-aware policies [5,25]. There are numerous proposals aimed at control and optimization of distributed and centralized type that are data driven [14,24]. [1,20] show a review of this type of multi-agent systems that address the problem using different approaches: automatic negotiation, distributed optimization, predictive routing, predictive control models, and others.

Among the centralized approaches, the proposals for signaling control stand out, proposing the application of predictive control models (MPC) combined with multi-agent models in the urban management of traffic lights at intersections or dynamic control in the incorporation of traffic flows [17,18]. More specific proposals deal for example with the differential criteria applied to electric vehicles and charging stations [24,26].

[4,12] and others have proposed and evolved the hyperpaths formulation and evaluation where not a single route is received by the vehicle agents, but a tree of alternative routes for each origin and destination. Hyperpaths route calculus focuses on the uncertainty and variability of traffic dynamics, and is evaluated based on historical data and applying different analysis techniques [9,19]. Our proposal is complementary to this approach as it focus on the network view that every individual receives and used at hyperpaths calculus. Hyper-path is conceived for individual risk-averse policies design (minimizing travel-time variance), in contrast with TWM that is multi-purpose and combines individual, group and global policies.

MuTraff is a centralized architecture that implements a distributed control for TWM in closed loop of routes of the vehicles [16], with capacities of re-planning. MuTraff feedback is not given explicitly at the microscopic level (of individual routes), and both performance and signaling are given at the mesoscopic level.

Standard navigation system offer shortest routes, derived from real-time density information and historical traffic. Agents (vehicles) make decisions individually, taking as a reference the same source of information, which transfers situations of congestion. This is the so-called *"common resource distribution problem"*, from which the so-called *"Minority Game"* or *"Farol Bar Problem"* derives [23]. It is therefore clear that there is a need for more precise control of vehicle routes, that requires precise individuals feedback and/or highly distributed sensor networks [22,27]. This control could be exercised through individualised management at the microscopic level of each route. However, microscopic control entails problems of scalability, deployment and privacy, so MuTraff proposes an alternative, scalable, non-disruptive control and management methodology with fewer implications for users' privacy. Agent routing decisions may change during the travel, mainly based on the dynamic information received [6] not affecting the aggregated information available at the TCS.

Similar strategies are used in other routing problems such as IP traffic routing strategies (MSTP, SDN) [11] by using distribution of maps with differentiated link weights (link-costs) and shortest-path routing strategies.

2   TWM - Traffic Weighted Multi-maps

Current vehicle traffic agents share the same traffic network maps (roads, paths) whose main path attributes are their physical conditions (number of lanes, length) and also their logical constraints (max speed, traffic allowance, directional senses and others). When we consider the path cost function we cannot modify physical attributes, but we can definitively modify logical ones. If we replace the max speed concept with a cost function that is different for each traffic group of agents, we could generate differentiated network maps for them. Even more, we could have time-dependent maps for them.

The main feature of our proposal, is to generate a traffic management framework (named MuTraff) that can provide differentiated traffic maps (called Traffic Weighted Maps, TWM) for the same area that can fulfill the specific needs of every traffic class. These maps are delivered to the vehicles, depending on multiple factors that are evaluated in a central-station back-end based on multiple criteria. These maps are to be composed in dynamic way combining several sources: historical data, real-time traffic data, real-time events affecting mobility (non-traffic data, but affecting the demand. For instance, a sport event, or a critical incident), and of course, synthetic data extracted from big-data sources. Figure 1 illustrates the basics for TWM generation.

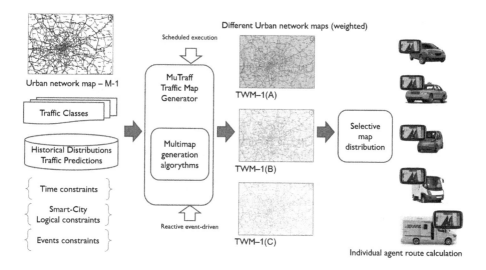

Fig. 1. TWM generation model.

Traffic classes recognize the fact that every type of traffic has specific (a) traffic goals, (b) network constraints, (c) regulations, (d) traffic indicators and (e) individual behaviors, so having a single traffic network map that considers only road descriptions, real-time conditions and traffic density is not enough to cover these specific features. Moreover, though some traffic classes have specific paths (such as bikes), most of the traffic classes share the same paths; management of these specific paths is accomplished by regulation and signaling. But, it can also be covered by specific maps. Multi-map routing strategy shows that this approach is a valid tool to get a better, easy and dynamic traffic management model. Instead of having a heavy set of regulation, signaling, time and geo-fenced constraints that every individual should process, evaluate, and execute, it is easier to have them collected into traffic map collections that are used by the individuals for route selection.

Route selection is the ultimate decision to be taken by traffic individuals and all the preceding issues mentioned can be seen as just factors that influence on it. Traffic individuals behave as agents that take routing decisions based on the available information, their own experience, habits, beliefs, desires and intentions. Available information is formed by the routes proposed by the routing engines, the map information, traffic and road status both real-time and historical data. Multi-maps skew this available information for every fleet, considering the best resource allocation (paths) to conform pseudo-optimal routers that are offered to every fleet. These multi-maps provide a different traffic routing weight for each fleet at each path. For instance, a city center will have different network maps for the fleets taxi, electric vehicles, logistic distributions, and conventional cars. The path weights will be different for each fleet, promoting or penalizing traffic for each path. Of course, these maps can be static or time-dynamic, depending on multiple strategies.

Traffic routes can be generated by the individuals using the network maps and the computing application [16], but also can be generated by a TCS that receives the origin-destination requests for route and delivers a set of possible routes. TWM approach is valid for them as it considers optimal route evaluation against a weighted map. This weighted map can be processed both at the individual and the central station. It is always the individual who decides which route/path to use, but usage of MuTraff will always use a weighted network map.

Individual privacy and data protection is also a main concern in routing systems [10]. No individual route tracking is made as MuTraff is just publishing weighted maps for vehicles groups at certain areas, and then routes and multi-path graphs recommendations contains no individual data. Privacy is preserved. Real-time data is obtained from city sensors and is used to calculated traffic density and congestion.

2.1   Model Formulation

A TWM multimap Π^n is a collection of network maps $[\mu_i^n]$ referring to the same urban area Θ^n and traffic vehicle groups $[\Omega_k^n]$ (called *fleets*) as denoted in 1. Each urban area should have its own set of multimaps. This area could cover a whole city or just sectors.

$$\Pi^n = \{[\mu_i^n]\} \, (\Theta^n, [\Omega_k^n]) \tag{1}$$

Each map instance μ_i^n that belongs to a multimap Π^n is a version Θ_i^n of the traffic network Θ^n, affected by a time constraint set Γ_i^n and applicable for some traffic vehicle groups $[\Omega_k^n]_i$ that are a subset of $[\Omega_k^n]$.

Each urban area Θ^n has a standard traffic network representation formed by a graph of geographical nodes η_k^n connected by edges, being each edge $\epsilon_{k,j}^n$ the traffic link with $l_{k,j}^n$ lanes that connects nodes η_k^n and η_j^n with a weight $\beta_{k,j}^n$. MuTraff multimaps use multiple weight distribution functions $\mathcal{F}^n$ for assigning geographical values to the $\beta_{k,j}^n$ factor for each edge. With this formulation, standard traffic maps use the function $\mathcal{F}_{std}^n$ that just consider lane-speed $S_{k,j}$ for providing the edge weight $\beta_{k,j}^n$.

$$\beta_{k,j}^n = F_{std}^n(\epsilon_{k,j}^n) = \alpha * S_{k,j} \qquad (2)$$

In our initial experiments, we have tried statistical distributions such as normal-N 3 to create weight distributions in the maps that allow traffic dispersion in the network, enabling vehicles to use route alternatives recommendations for each fleet $[\Omega_k^n]$. We scale weights with factor δ ($\delta_{normal.a.b} = normal(a,b)$).

$$F_{normal.a.b}^n(\epsilon_{k,j}^n) = \alpha * S_{k,j} * (1 + \delta_{normal.a.b}) \qquad (3)$$

There will be a population of $[v_i^k]$ vehicles grouped by $[\Omega_k^n]$ fleets. Those vehicles that do not belong explicitly to a fleet, will be assigned to the standard Ω_0^n fleet. The percent of vehicles that use MuTraff at any time is called the adherence factor ψ^n and is calculated as the percent of vehicles not using Ω_0^n.

Vehicles will generate $[T_j^k]$ trips during observations times. Each trip in general is composed by the vehicle identification, the starting timestamp, the starting point (origin node) O_j, the final destination point (node) D_j and tuple with possible intermediate stops P_j.

For the map-distribution approach, depending on each concrete time epoch, each fleet has a specific map μ_i^n that belongs to a multimap Π^n. This map is distributed to its individuals (on-demand or by publication to subscriptions). Vehicles not classified or in general belonging to standard Ω_0^n fleet will use the standard map Θ^n. The vehicle's agent calculate for each trip the shortest-path $r(T_j^k)$ route or hyper-path using the corresponding map (standard or ad-hoc received multimap) valid for this time-interval. This calculation will use some of the available routing algorithms f (Dijkstra, A*, etc).

The agent confidence factor φ_j is a utility function that evolves in time based on previous experiences or available road and traffic information. Agent's route recommendation usage will vary for every individual based on the confidence factor φ_j that should overpass certain subjective threshold K^i.

3   Experiments and Results

Though Traffic Weighted Maps (TWM Π^n) effects on traffic are suitable to be integrated with current macro, meso and microscopic traffic simulators [21], they all use Θ^n maps as urban network representation. We have developed MuTraff simulator MTS over SUMO [3] that implements a car-following microscopic simulation environment.

3.1 Experiments Design

GRID16 network is composed of a matrix of horizontal and vertical roads of 16 horizontal × 16 vertical paths, with uniform edges of 50 m and single or double lanes. The maximum speed is limited to 50 km/h (13,9 m/s). It uses 5 traffic assignment zones (TAZ [3]): TAZ 1 to 4 are located in the external sides of the grid, TAZ 5 covers the whole grid Fig. 2.

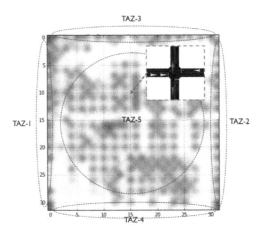

Fig. 2. GRID16 network and TAZ configuration for experiments.

The traffic demand we will use in the experiments is composed by 4 different fleets: cars (44%), taxis (33%), buses (11%) and motorbikes (11%). Zones 1–4 generate directional crossing traffic from side to side, originating from one edge TAZ to an opposite edge TAZ (directional), zone 5 generates random internal traffic. As a reference value we will use the XS and M-size for standard traffic demand. TWM parameters used are: 8 maps per TWM, static weights with $F_{std}^n(\epsilon_{k,j}^n)$ and $F_{normal.0.5,0.5}^n(\epsilon_{k,j}^n)$ (random distribution centered on 0.5 and amplitude of 0.5, named as random05). *Route selection* algorithm $f = $ Dijkstra.

Current experiments consider global traffic network enhancement. They are checked for the whole network at the end of the simulation and also for each edge in the network at every time-step of the simulation: *Routed traffic demand*, as number of vehicles successfully routed against the total traffic demand (global and per fleet). *Mean and median travel time*, as a measure of global travel durations. *Mean and median route distance*, as a measure of global travel distances. *Travel time dispersion*, as an histogram of travel durations, to check how many vehicles have been affected during the experiments. *Variance* would provide us a single measure but a dispersion measure will give us a better insight into how this variance is occurring inside the population.

3.2   Non-TWM Routing in Congested GRID16 Network

This simulation provides the reference for network traffic performance using a full traffic scenario combining internal random and directional traffics without applying the multimap algorithm. Agents use shortest-path algorithm to select the route without predictive routing. Those agents traveling the same trip will use the same route. Figure 3 shows how *traffic congestion starts at the edges* as traffic is trying to enter the network and progressively the network gets congested. and due to the fact that traffic is fully internal, *congestion gets stationary*. Getting deeper inside the initial congestion scenario, we can appreciate how preferred edges selected for the trip routes are being blocked (number of halted vehicles).

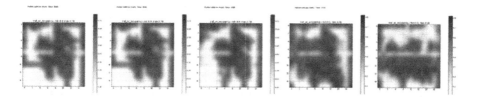

Fig. 3. Grid16. Full traffic not using multimaps, evolution and details.

3.3   TWM Routing Applied to Non-congested GRID16 Network

In order to analyze the effects of TWM on the congested network, we will use several drivers confidence factors to reflect TWM adoption (ψ^n 5%, 10%, 20%, 50% and 100%). Simulation uses XS-size full traffic formed by 1300 vehicles (internal and directional trips). Multi-maps use random05 distribution (normal distributed random) with 8 TWM maps.

Figure 4 shows the histograms corresponding to the different ψ^n mentioned. Each histogram compares no-TWM and 8 maps TWM application scenarios. We can see that even in a low adoption schema as $\psi^n_{0.05}$, travel time starts to enhance. When ψ^n increases over 50% enhancements in mean travel-time are really relevant (23% travel time) growing to 48% for a 100% adoption of TWM. Last histogram shows perfectly how congested trips (green graph) have been reduced or even disappeared (blue graph). Mean route lengths have not changed significantly.

3.4   TWM Routing Applied to Congested GRID16 Network

Now we check the impact of TWM distribution on traffic performance using a congested full traffic scenario (M size, 2800 vehicles). In order to approach a more realistic scenario we use 2 lane paths for the whole network. We use the same random05 maps (uniformly distributed random) with 8 maps distribution. We study just adherence factor $\psi^n_{0.5} = 50\%$ and $\psi^n_1 = 100\%$ values, as they show how much multi-maps can enhance congestion.

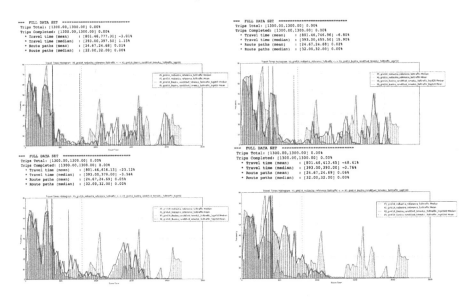

Fig. 4. GRID16 routing XS traffic with $\psi_{0.05}^n$, $\psi_{0.2}^n$, $\psi_{0.5}^n$, ψ_1^n (Color figure online)

As we can see from Fig. 5 histogram, applying multimaps to the near-congested network with $\psi_{0.5}^n$ enhances mean travel-time 19,65% and median over 13%. ψ_1^n raises up to 42% and 28% respectively. As shown, when ψ^n increases, the whole network gets enhanced. Drivers that were having good traffic performance are not affected by the multi-maps, but congested drivers acquire better routers to get to their destination. Specific congestions are cleared and overall travel-time increases. And, moreover, no mean router length is affected. Global metrics for gas emissions and noise are dramatically reduced.

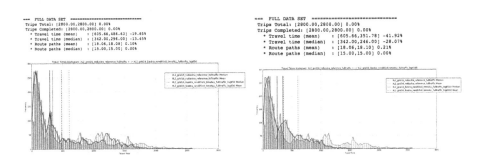

Fig. 5. Grid16-2lanes. Congested network with $\psi_{0.5}^n$ and ψ_1^n.

4   Conclusions and Future Works

Studies in reduced scenarios and with a random map generation, oriented to traffic balancing, have obtained satisfactory results leading to traffic indicators enhancements between 20% and 50%. Experiments conducted with ideal canonical traffic network show that multimap approach improves highly global traffic travel-time, starting at low adoption scenarios, and providing best performance in high-adoption and highly congested situations.

The benefits of the multimap approach include the following: (1) the possibility of automating early and real-time decision making; (2) generation of an integral model for the application of management and control policies; (3) can be offered as a service (SaaS model); (4) it is conceived as a evolutionary planning model, based in traffic feed back and learning cycles; (5) is non-intrusive and compatible with existing traffic management frameworks and traffic agents; (6) reuses existing data (Smart-Cities, OpenData) adding value over them; (7) is compatible with other existing algorithms and techniques; (8) drivers' agents autonomy and privacy is preserved as the multimap model takes into account individual freedom of route choice; (9) it allows for the articulation of contingency plans and the integration of traffic prognosis models.

MuTraff stands out from an innovative perspective in the following: (a) it offers an integrated planning and re-planning model, extensible and open; (b) it enables traffic categorization for application to very different groups and situations; (c) it is replenished and self-learning.

Future work will cover: (a) adding user-perspective for evaluation of TWM impact that will condition the adherence factor; (b) simulation on real cities scenarios; (c) generation of hyper-paths based on TWM; (d) design of a platform architecture for MuTraff real deployment and (e) adding new simulation engines: microscopic and mesoscopic for fast TWM generation responding to real-time incidents.

Acknowledgement. This work was supported in part by the Spanish Ministry of Economy and Competitiveness under Grant TIN2016-80622-P and Grant TEC2013-45183-R.

References

1. Bazzan, A., Klügl, F.: A review on agent-based technology for traffic and transportation. Knowl. Eng. Rev. **29**, 375–403 (2013). https://doi.org/10.1017/S026988 8913000118
2. Bazzan, A.L., Klügl, F.: Introduction to intelligent systems in traffic and transportation. Synth. Lect. Artif. Intell. Mach. Learn. **7**(3), 1–137 (2013). https://doi.org/10.2200/s00553ed1v01y201312aim025. http://www.morganclaypool.com/doi/abs/10.2200/S00553ED1V01Y201312AIM025

3. Behrisch, M., Bieker, L., Erdmann, J., Krajewicz, D.: SUMO - Simulation of Urban MObility: an overview. In: Omerovic, S.U.o.O.A., Simoni, R.I.R.T.P.D.A., Bobashev, R.I.R.T.P.G. (eds.) SIMUL 2011, The Third International Conference on Advances in System Simulation, pp. 63–68. ThinkMind, Barcelona, October 2011. http://elib.dlr.de/71460/

4. Chen, Y., Bell, M.G., Bogenberger, K.: Reliable pretrip multipath planning and dynamic adaptation for a centralized road navigation system. IEEE Trans. Intell. Transp. Syst. **8**(1), 14–20 (2007)

5. Claes, R., Holvoet, T.: Traffic coordination using aggregation-based traffic predictions. Intell. Syst. IEEE **29**, 96–100 (2014). https://doi.org/10.1109/MIS. 2014.73

6. Dell'Orco, M., Marinelli, M.: Modeling the dynamic effect of information on drivers' choice behavior in the context of an Advanced Traveler Information System. Transp. Res. Part C Emerg. Technol. **85**, 168–183 (2017). https://doi.org/10.1016/ j.trc.2017.09.019

7. Dere, E., Durdu, A.: Usage of the A* Algorithm to Find the Shortest Path in Transportation Systems (2018)

8. Dijkstra, E.: A note on two problems in connexion with graphs. Numb. Math. **1**, 269 (1959)

9. Fukuda, D., Ma, J., Yamada, K., Shinkai, N.: Tokyo: Simulating Hyperpath-Based Vehicle Navigations and its Impact on Travel Time Reliability. In: The Multi-Agent Transport Simulation MATSim, pp. 517–522. Ubiquity Press Ltd. (2016). https://doi.org/10.5334/baw.92, https://www.oapen.org/download? type=document&docid=613715

10. Gkoulalas-Divanis, A., Bettini, C. (eds.): Handbook of Mobile Data Privacy. Springer, Cham (2018). https://doi.org/10.1007/978-3-319-98161-1

11. Guleria, A.: Traffic engineering in software defined networks: a survey. J. Telecommun. Inf. Technol. **4**, 3–14 (2016)

12. Michael, G.H.B.: Hyperstar: a multi-path astar algorithm for risk averse vehicle navigation. Transp. Res. Part B Methodol. **43**, 97 (2009)

13. Hu, W., Jin, P.J.: Dynamic origin-destination estimation based on time delay correlation analysis on Location-based Social Network (LBSN) data. In: Transportation Research Board 97th Annual Meeting (2018). http://amonline.trb.org/

14. Ibrahim, H., Far, B.H.: Data-oriented intelligent transportation systems. In: Proceedings of the 2014 IEEE 15th International Conference on Information Reuse and Integration (IEEE IRI 2014), pp. 322–329, August 2014. https://doi.org/10. 1109/IRI.2014.7051907

15. Iqbal, M., Zhang, K., Iqbal, S., Tariq, I.: A fast and reliable Dijkstra algorithm for online shortest path. Int. J. Comput. Sci. Eng. **5**, 24–27 (2018). https://doi.org/ 10.14445/23488387/IJCSE-V5I12P106

16. Liang, Z., Wakahara, Y.: A route guidance system with personalized rerouting for reducing traveling time of vehicles in urban areas. In: 17th International IEEE Conference on Intelligent Transportation Systems (ITSC), pp. 1541–1548 (2014). https://doi.org/10.1109/ITSC.2014.6957652

17. Lin, S., Schutter, B.D., Zhou, Z., Xi, Y.: Multi-agent model-based predictive control for large-scale urban traffic networks using a serial scheme. IET Control Theory Appl. **9**(3), 475–484 (2015). https://doi.org/10.1049/iet-cta.2014.0490. https://digital-library.theiet.org/content/journals/10.1049/iet-cta.2014.0490

18. Luo, R., Bourdais, R., van den Boom, T.J., De Schutter, B.: Multi-agent model predictive control based on resource allocation coordination for a class of hybrid systems with limited information sharing. Eng. Appl. Artif. Intell. **58**, 123–133 (2017). https://doi.org/10.1016/j.engappai.2016.12.005. https://linkinghub.elsevier.com/retrieve/pii/S0952197616302330

19. Ma, J., Fukuda, D.: A hyperpath-based network generalized extreme-value model for route choice under uncertainties. Transp. Res. Part C Emerg. Technol. **59**, 19–31 (2015)

20. Namazi-Rad, M.-R., Padgham, L., Perez, P., Nagel, K., Bazzan, A. (eds.): ABMUS 2016. LNCS (LNAI), vol. 10051. Springer, Cham (2017). https://doi.org/10.1007/978-3-319-51957-9

21. de Dios Ortúzar, J., Willumsen, L.G.: Modelling Transport, 3rd edn. Wiley, Chichester (2001)

22. Rezaei, M., Noori, H., Rahbari, D., Nickray, M.: ReFOCUS: a hybrid fog-cloud based intelligent traffic re-routing system. In: 2017 IEEE 4th International Conference on Knowledge-Based Engineering and Innovation (KBEI), pp. 0992–0998, December 2017. https://doi.org/10.1109/KBEI.2017.8324943. bibtex*[number=] ISSN:

23. Sagara, H., Tanimoto, J.: A study on social diffusive impacts of a novel car-navigation-system sharing individual information in Urban traffic systems, IEEE Xplore, pp. 836–842 (2007). https://doi.org/10.1109/CEC.2007.4424557

24. Sarker, A., Shen, H., Stankovic, J.A.: MORP: data-driven multi-objective route planning and optimization for electric vehicles. In: Proceedings of the ACM on Interactive, Mobile, Wearable and Ubiquitous Technologies, vol. 1, pp. 1–35 (2018). https://doi.org/10.1145/3161408

25. Varga, L.: On intention-propagation-based prediction in autonomously self-adapting navigation. In: Proceedings - 2014 IEEE 8th International Conference on Self-Adaptive and Self-Organizing Systems Workshops, SASOW 2014, vol. 16, pp. 38–43 (2015). https://doi.org/10.1109/SASOW.2014.17

26. Weerdt, M., Stein, S., Gerding, E., Robu, V., Jennings, N.R.: Intention-aware routing of electric vehicles. IEEE Trans. Intell. Transp. Syst. **17**, 1–11 (2015). https://doi.org/10.1109/TITS.2015.2506900

27. Cong, Z., De Schutter, B., Burger, M., Babuska, R.: Monitoring of traffic networks using mobile sensors. In: 17th International IEEE Conference on Intelligent Transportation Systems (ITSC), pp. 792–797. IEEE, Qingdao, October 2014. https://doi.org/10.1109/ITSC.2014.6957786. http://ieeexplore.ieee.org/document/6957786/

28. Zheng, Y., Capra, L., Wolfson, O., Yang, H.: Urban computing. ACM Trans. Intell. Syst. Technol. **5**, 1–55 (2014). https://doi.org/10.1145/2629592

Financial Market Data Simulation Using Deep Intelligence Agents

Natraj Raman[1(✉)] and Jochen L. Leidner[2]

[1] S&P Global, 20 Canada Square, London, UK
natraj.raman@spglobal.com
[2] Refinitiv, 30 South Colonnade, London, UK
jochen.leidner@refinitiv.com

Abstract. Trading strategies are often assessed against historical financial data in an effort to predict the profits and losses a strategy would generate in future. However, using only data from the past ignores the evolution of market microstructure and does not account for market conditions outside historical bounds. Simulations provide an effective supplement. We present an agent-based model to simulate financial market prices both under steady-state conditions and stress situations. Our new class of agents utilize recent advances in deep learning to make trading decisions and employ different trading objectives to ensure diversity in outcomes. The model supports various what-if scenarios such as sudden price crash, bearish or bullish market sentiment and shock contagion. We conduct evaluations on multiple asset classes including portfolio of assets and illustrate that the proposed agent decision mechanism outperforms other techniques. Our simulation model also successfully replicates the empirical stylized facts of financial markets.

Keywords: Agent based modeling · Deep learning · What-if scenarios

1 Introduction

Financial traders typically backtest their investment strategies on historical market prices in order to predict how a strategy would perform in the future. However, relying solely on past market data to gain insight into the effectiveness of a trading strategy in the future is inappropriate for a number of reasons. Firstly, past market data will often not resemble closely the behaviour of a future market due to the noisy and non-ergodic nature of financial timeseries. Secondly, the changes that occur to market microstructure over time limits the actual data available for testing to recent past and the dearth of data makes it challenging to train complex strategies. Finally, historical data can never capture every possible market situation and therefore may not account for unforeseen

---

N. Raman—Work conducted when author was working at Thomson Reuters.
Refinitiv—The Financial and Risk business of Thomson Reuters is now Refinitiv.

Y. Demazeau et al. (Eds.): PAAMS 2019, LNAI 11523, pp. 200–211, 2019.
https://doi.org/10.1007/978-3-030-24209-1_17

extreme market events. Hence there is a compelling opportunity to augment historical prices with synthetic prices generated using simulations. Such simulated market data has practical applications when evaluating trading strategies.

Agent-Based Models (ABMs) [1] provide an effective technique to realistically simulate data from complex systems such as financial markets. ABMs exploit the collective behaviour that emerges through the interactions between a large number of heterogeneous agents to perform simulations. ABMs of financial markets represent the traders who place buy and sell orders as individual agents endowed with varying degrees of intelligence ranging from random decision making [2] to a trend following strategy [3]. In this paper, we introduce a new class of agents that make trading decisions using deep learning models [4]. Our conjecture is these trading agents empowered with deep intelligence behave in an adaptive manner leading to more robust decision making. Two key questions need to be answered when using such sophisticated agents: (i) Does the use of deep learning lead to better decision making of an agent? and (ii) Are the decisions diverse enough to ensure agent heterogenity? By employing a state-of-the-art multi-layer Recurrent Neural Network with attention mechanism [5] and using an enriched form of the raw market data as input, we empirically illustrate that the proposed solution outperforms other decision making techniques. In order to ensure diversity in trading outcomes, we utilize a number of models that are trained for different trading objectives such as short term vs long term gains and small vs large asset returns.

Simulations enable the exploration of different market conditions and modelling cataclysmic events that the market might not have encountered before. Our ABM supports various *what-if* scenarios such as sudden sharp drop in prices, sustained pessimistic or optimistic market sentiment and propagation of exogeneous shocks. Performing such *what-if* analysis would allow traders to assess how different scenarios might impact the results of their strategy.

It is important to validate that the simulations generated by an ABM are representative of the characteristics observed in financial markets. Our extensive experiments reveal that the proposed model replicates the main stylized facts [6] such as fat-tailed returns distribution, zero autocorrelation of returns and volatility clustering. We evaluate our model on four different asset classes across various time intervals and also consider a portfolio of assets. The model is calibrated based on real world market prices.

Our main contributions include exploiting the latest advances in deep learning for agent decision making, demonstrating heterogenity in agent decisions, measuring market reaction under different scenarios and support for portfolio of assets. To the best of our knowledge, this is the first study that combines deep learning with ABM for simulating financial markets under different scenarios.

The paper is organized as follows: Sect. 2 briefly reviews the literature, Sect. 3 describes the agents behaviour and the deep learning network structure, Sect. 4 provides empirical evidence and Sect. 5 summarizes our findings.

2   Related Work

Our naming "Deep Intelligence" agents refers to the expressive power of an agent when making decisions. Traditionally, there have been many levels of intelligence associated with individual trading agents. These include agents without any strategy (Zero Intelligence) [2], agents that bid based on profit margins (Zero Intelligence Plus) [7], agents that only take into account their budget constraints (Limited Intelligence) [8], agents that follow trend (Chartist) and agents that have a mean reverting phenomenon (Fundamentalist) [3]. We introduce here a new type of agent whose intelligence is based on deep learning methods. While there have been a few proposals [9–11] that highlighted the benefits of combining machine learning or deep learning with agent based modelling, to our knowledge, no previous work has conducted experiments that assess the viability of this concept. There is a rich body of literature [12] on stress testing financial markets. In contrast to classical methods, we use agent based simulations. Although agent based computations have been used before [13–15] for studying market dynamics under different conditions, our work differs from these by the types of scenarios we explore and our support for a variety of asset classes.

3   Methodology

We first specify the structure and behaviour of the agents. We then detail how an agent uses a deep learning classifier to decide whether to sell, hold or buy an asset based on the prevailing market conditions. An overview of the agents and their interactions within the model is illustrated in Fig. 1.

3.1   Agent Specification

The agent based model comprises of a number of trading agents who trade an asset by placing limit or market orders to an artificial stock market. The market maintains a Limit Order Book (LOB) that tracks the direction (i.e. buy or sell), quantity and price of each order over a time period T. At each trading session t, the market matches the orders according to the prices and publishes market data such as the open, low, high, close and volume along with the best bid and ask prices at the top of the book.

There are a number of deep learning classifiers with each classifier being trained for a different trading objective (e.g. returns threshold, temporal window etc.). A classifier provides probabilistic outcomes $\phi = [\phi_s, \phi_h, \phi_b]$ of the sell, hold and buy actions as described in Sect. 3.2. The ith deep intelligence agent determines the direction of an order $D_{i,t}$ at time t by sampling from the discrete probability distribution of a classifier outcome. In the event of an outcome being buy or sell, a limit order is placed with the price and quantity computed stochastically as follows:

$$P_{i,t} = \bar{P}_{t-1}(1 + \delta)(1 + \nu_{i,t}) \qquad \nu_{i,t} \sim \mathcal{N}(0, \sigma^2) \qquad (1)$$
$$Q_{i,t} = \eta_{i,t}(1 + \omega) \qquad \eta_{i,t} \sim \mathbb{U}[Q_{min}, Q_{max}] \qquad (2)$$

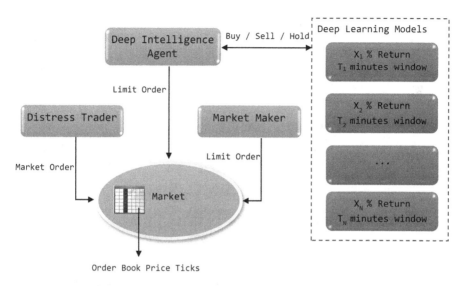

Fig. 1. Agent types and interactions.

Here $\bar{P}$ is the closing price, σ and δ are parameters that control the price drift, ω is the strength of the direction signal and Q_{min} and Q_{max} are the lower and upper bound for the order size. In addition to the deep intelligence agents, there is also a single market maker agent that provides liquidity by placing limit orders that are randomly priced κ ticks away from the best bid and ask. The agents can cancel their order after γ sessions.

The model supports performing various *what-if* scenario analyses. For example, to simulate a sudden drop in the prices it is possible to activate a distress trading agent that places aggressive sell market orders. These orders with no price limits generates an asset price shock that causes other agents to react negatively to the asset. This contagion effect causes the prices to drop sharply within a short duration. The distress trader is parameterized by the activation time point, the quantity to sell and the duration it takes to liquidate the asset. It is also possible to simulate the prices under bearish and bullish market conditions. This is achieved by adding a bias probability vector $\xi = [\xi_s, \xi_h, \xi_b]$ to the classifier outcome ϕ. For example, to reflect a bearish market sentiment we can set $\xi_s > 0$ and similarly specify $\xi_b > 0$ to capture a bullish market sentiment.

A simple extension to the model allows multiple assets organized as a group to trade together. The assets do not share the classifiers. However, when deciding a trading direction for an asset, the probability distribution of trading directions of other assets in the group are considered. Formally, let $\{A^1, ..., A^M\}$ be a set of assets, ϕ^m be the classifier outcome for the mth asset and β be a strength parameter that controls the importance of group level information. The trading direction for asset m is sampled as follows:

$$D_{i,t}^m \sim \beta\phi^m + (1-\beta)\frac{\sum_{j\neq m} \phi^j}{\sum_{j\neq m} \|\phi^j\|_1} \tag{3}$$

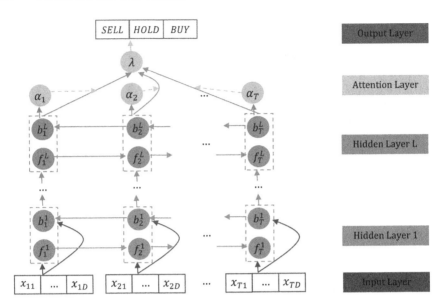

Fig. 2. Network architecture of the deep BD-LSTM with attention mechanism.

3.2   Deep Learning Classifier

Let $D = \{(x^n, y^n)\}_{n=1}^N$ be training set pairs where each $x^n = (x_1, ..., x_t, ...x_T)$ is an input sequence that represents the current market prices over a time period T and each $y^n \in \{Sell, Hold, Buy\}$ is an output action label. The inputs are embedded in a rich feature space as detailed in Sect. 4 and each $x_t \in \mathbb{R}^D$. We use a Recurrent Neural Network (RNN) composed of Long Short-Term Memory (LSTM) cells to train a sequence classifier.

An LSTM [16] uses input, forget and output gates to determine the cell states at each time step. In order to incorporate information from both the past and future of an input sequence, we propose to use a bi-directional LSTM (BD-LSTM) [17]. Consequently, there are now two sets of LSTM states: $(f_1, ..., f_t, ...f_T)$ for the forward direction that reads the input sequence from x_1 to x_T and $(b_1, ..., b_t, ...b_T)$ for the backward direction that reads in reverse from x_T to x_1. Here $f_t, b_t \in \mathbb{R}^K$ where K is the number of hidden neurons. A combined hidden state at time t is produced by concatenating the forward and backward state i.e. $h_t = [f_t, b_t]$. To produce a deep model, we introduce L hidden layers in the network with h_t^l being the hidden state at depth level l.

Instead of the traditional approach where the last hidden state h_T^L is used to determine the output class, we pursue an adaptive technique that searches the entire sequence $(h_1^L...h_T^L)$ in order to effectively capture the patterns in the data. This attention mechanism [5] is formulated as follows:

$$u_t = tanh(W_u h_t^L + b_u) \qquad \alpha_t = \frac{exp(u_t^T c)}{\sum_t exp(u_t^T c)}$$

$$\lambda = \sum_t \alpha_t h_t^L \qquad\qquad p(y) = softmax(W_y \lambda + b_y) \tag{4}$$

First, the hidden state h_t^L is projected into a representation u_t, which in turn is used to obtain a normalized weight α_t that measures the importance of the information at a particular time step. Finally, the weighted sum of hidden states λ is used for determining the classifier output. The vectors W, b and c are learnt during the training process. Figure 2 presents the network structure.

4   Evaluation

In this section we assess in detail the properties of our model. As a first step in the analysis, the performance of the proposed deep learning algorithm is compared with various baseline methods. Synthetic price ticks generated via extensive Monte-Carlo simulations are then presented. Finally, the ability of our model to reproduce well-known stylized facts of the financial market is investigated.

Data. The Thomson Reuters Knowledge Direct API [18] is used to retrieve the timeseries of intraday prices such as open, high, low, close and volume. The market prices are collected for a two month time-period between 25th September and 25th November 2018 at frequency intervals 1, 5 and 30 min respectively. Technical analysis is performed on the price sequence using the following standard quantitive indicators [19]: Rate of Change, Simple and Exponential Moving Average, RSI, Momentum indicator, Chaikin Money Flow, Chaikin Accumuation/Distribution, Close Location Value, Commodity Channel Index, Williams RSI, Money Flow Index, Aroon indicator, Moving Variance Ratios, Moving Average Convergence Divergence and Bollinger Bands. With the use of different time period parameters, the prices are embedded in a 62 dimensional feature space. We consider four different asset classes namely Equities, Exchange Traded Funds, Currencies and Commodities. For equities, we use five companies from the financial sector: i. Wells Fargo & Co (*WFC.N*), ii. US Bancorp (*USB.N*), iii. CIT Group (*CIT.N*), iv. American International Group (*AIG.N*) and v. Stifel Financial Corp (*SF.N*). The largest exchange traded fund in the world SPDR S&P 500 Trust (*SPY*) that tracks the popular S&P 500 stock market index is also considered. This instrument offers ample liquidity with extremely high trading volume. The foreign exchange rate of Euro/US Dollar (*EUR=*) is used for evaluating the model in currencies market. Transactions contributed by different electronic brokering systems around-the-clock are averaged to deduce the indicative spot exchange rate. For commodities, we consider the Brent Crude Oil (*LCOc1*) future prices traded at Intercontinental Exchange (ICE) between 01:00 and 23:00 GMT.

4.1 Classification Results

Is the deep learning algorithm really necessary to determine the sell, hold or buy trade direction? In order to answer this question, we compare the classification results of standard algorithms with the proposed deep learning algorithm. We also justify the architecture presented here by conducting evaluations of simpler neural network structures.

Settings. The evaluations are performed on a real world dataset constructed from 1 min interval market prices of the SPY instrument for a six week period between 1st October and 9th November 2018. The price timeseries was split into 15 min dense overlapping windows with a total of 11,610 sequences. A price return threshold of 0.02% was used, with a value less than the threshold being *sell* class of a sequence, greater than the threshold being *buy* class and *hold* class otherwise. This particular threshold provided a good balance in the samples between the various classes. The dataset was split into 80% train and 20% test with the deep learning algorithms using 20% of the training data as a validation set. For all the classification algorithms, a coarse to fine parameter search was performed in order to determine the value of hyper-parameters. The best parameter combination had a batch size of 32, a learning rate of 0.001, a learning decay rate of 0.9 and a drop out of 0.5. The number of hidden neurons K was set to 128.

Comparison. Table 1 shows the Precision, Recall and F1-Score results for various classification algorithms on the test dataset. A chartist baseline method that simply relies on the price trend to predict the direction of the trade does not produce good results. Furthermore, the results are abysmal when the feature space is constructed naively just by using the market prices directly from the order book. Hence it is important to enrich the feature space with technical indicators as suggested here. It is evident that traditional classifiers such as Support Vector Machines (SVM) and ensemble classifiers such as Random Forests and Gradient Boosting Trees do not perform as well as the LSTM based algorithms. This signifies the importance of employing a sequential pattern recognition technique such as an RNN. The inclusion of multiple hidden layers and a bi-directional layout improves the classification performance by at least 3%. This justifies the use of a deep network architecture. Finally, the benefits of the attention mechanism is highlighted by an increase of 5% in F1-Score. The confusion matrix of the results for the attention mechanism is presented in Fig. 3. Re-assuringly, almost all classification errors are between buy vs hold and sell vs hold.

4.2 Simulation Results

Synthetically generated prices for four different asset classes are presented in Fig. 4. The top left section displays the real and simulated prices for the Exchange Traded Fund SPY, with each tick representing a 1 min interval. The blue line shows the prices averaged from 10 iterations for 300 ticks. The light blue background depicts the range of prices in all the simulation runs. Note that the prices

Table 1. Classification results comparison for intrinsic validation.

Classifier	Technical indicators	Precision	Recall	F1-Score
Chartist	No	0.18	0.30	0.21
Gradient Boosting	No	0.30	0.42	0.28
LSTM (1 layer)	No	0.29	0.41	0.34
Random Forest	Yes	0.54	0.55	0.54
SVM	Yes	0.57	0.57	0.57
Gradient Boosting	Yes	0.59	0.59	0.59
LSTM (1 layer)	Yes	0.70	0.70	0.70
BD-LSTM (5 layers)	Yes	0.73	0.73	0.73
BD-LSTM (5 layers + Attention)	Yes	0.78	0.78	0.78

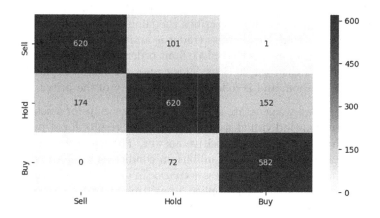

Fig. 3. Confusion matrix for the 5 layer deep BD-LSTM using attention mechanism.

are computed from the mean of the best bid and ask prices published by the market at each tick. The red line shows the observed market prices for 5 h between 15:00 and 20:00 GMT on 7th November 2018. This real world price timeseries is used to calibrate the free parameters of the model. In the above simulation run, 300 agents were used with γ being 1, σ being 0.0005 and δ being close to 0. The deep learning classifiers were trained for different combinations of returns threshold (0.02%, 0.05%) and time windows (10 min, 15 min, 30 min).

The real and simulated prices for the Euro/US Dollar currency pair ($EUR=$) is shown in the top right section of Fig. 4. Here each tick corresponds to a 5 min interval, with the 250 ticks representing 20 h worth of data. While the blue line is the average price as before, the light blue lines are some samples from the simulation runs. The red line displays the exchange rates on 13th November 2018, based on which the model is calibrated. The bottom left section plots the real and simulated prices for commodity $LCOc1$ over a 3 day period between 26th and 28th

September 2018. A tick frequency of 30 min is used here. Finally, the intraday prices for equity *WFC.N* is shown in the bottom right section. The model was calibrated against one minute interval trading data on 23rd November 2018. The above results demonstrate the ability of the simulation model to handle a diverse set of assets, a variety of time intervals and calibration against both past and future dates relative to the period in which the deep learning models were trained.

What-if Scenarios. Our model is also successful in generating synthetic prices for *what-if* scenarios. Figure 5 shows the simulated prices under different market conditions for *SPY*. While the blue line represents the synthetic prices under steady state conditions, the green and red line projects the potential prices under bullish and bearish market conditions, respectively. In order to simulate the bullish condition, a bias probability of 0.15 was set to the buy action. Similarly, a bias probability of 0.2 was set to the sell action. By using different values of these bias probabilities, the extent of the particular market condition can be influenced. The maroon line describes the simulated prices under a sudden price drop scenario. Here the distress trader is activated near the 100th tick. In contrast with the other agents that place limit orders, the distress agent places a sell market order for the next 20 ticks. This causes a 2% drop in the asset prices within a short duration, and is followed by a recovery of the prices.

Asset Groups. Can we generate synthetic data for groups of assets that trade together rather than individual assets? Simulation results for a portfolio of 5 stocks shown in Fig. 6 provide a positive answer. The left section of this figure shows the simulated prices under equilibirium conditions while the right section displays the simulations under a stress scenario. In order to model the disorderly condition, an exogeneous shock is applied for a 50 min duration to assets *WFC.N*, *CIT.N* and *SF.N* by setting the bias probability of sell action to 0.8 and β to be 0.5. This evidently causes the prices of these assets to drop between the 60th and 110th tick. What makes the scenario interesting is the impact of this shock on the other two assets in the group. It can be seen that the prices of both *USB.N* and *AIG.N* fall during this period even though they were not explicitly subjected to the shock.

Stylized Facts. Finally, we provide evidence that our model replicates the main statistical properties of financial markets. A timeseries of log returns for *SPY* is calculated from the price paths of individual simulation runs. The histogram of these log returns pooled over all the runs is plotted in the top left section of Fig. 7. This distribution is clearly leptokurtic and has an excess positive kurtosis of nearly 2, revealing its fat-tailed nature. Furthermore, the Q-Q plot in the top right section of this figure confirms that the distribution of the simulated log returns is different from the normal distribution. We also find that the autocorrelation values of the simulated price returns do not have any significant pattern and are close to zero as illustrated in the bottom left section. Additionally, as shown in the bottom right section, the autocorrelation of absolute returns decay towards zero providing evidence for volatility clustering.

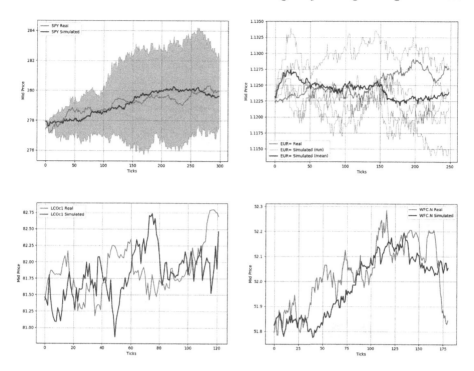

Fig. 4. Real and simulated prices for different asset classes. *top-left*: Exchange Traded Fund *top-right*: Foreign Exchange *bottom-left*: Commodity *bottom-right*: Equity. (Color figure online)

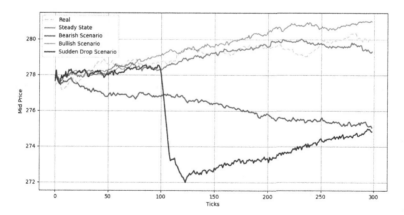

Fig. 5. Simulated prices for various what-if scenarios. (Color figure online)

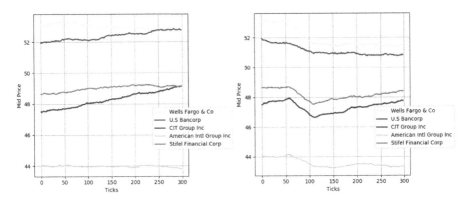

Fig. 6. Assets traded in a group. *left*: Steady State Scenario. *right*: Stress Scenario.

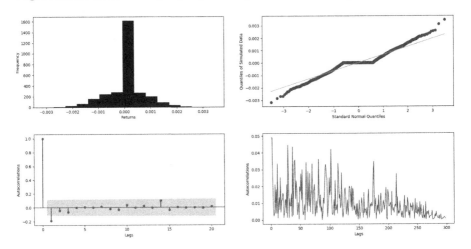

Fig. 7. Extrinsic validation using stylized facts. *top-left*: Histogram of log returns. *top-right*: Q-Q plot. *bottom-left*: Autocorrelation of returns. *bottom-right*: Autocorrelation of absolute returns.

5   Conclusion

We presented an agent based model to simulate financial market data for various assets under different market conditions. Unlike traditional agents that make trading decisions based on rules, heuristics or simple learners, our new class of deep intelligence agents exploit the latest advances in artificial intelligence for decision making. Our experimental results confirmed that the proposed method is superior to classical techniques and that the simulations exhibit properties of real world market. The simulated market prices are practically useful when backtesting trading strategies. In the future we intend to automatically learn the correlation between assets and define new financial risk scenarios.

References

1. Turrell, A.: Agent-based models: understanding the economy from the bottom up. Bank Engl. Q. Bull. **56**(4), 173–188 (2016)
2. Ladley, D.: Zero intelligence in economics and finance. Knowl. Eng. Rev. **27**(2), 273–286 (2012)
3. Leal, S.J., Napoletano, M., Roventini, A., Fagiolo, G.: Rock around the clock: an agent-based model of low-and high-frequency trading. J. Evol. Econ. **26**(1), 49–76 (2016)
4. Hinton, G.E., Osindero, S., Teh, Y.W.: A fast learning algorithm for deep belief nets. Neural Comput. **18**(7), 1527–1554 (2006)
5. Bahdanau, D., Cho, K., Bengio, Y.: Neural machine translation by jointly learning to align and translate (2014). arXiv preprint arXiv:1409.0473
6. Cont, R.: Empirical properties of asset returns: stylized facts and statistical issues. Quantitiative Finance **1**, 223–236 (2001)
7. Palit, I., Phelps, S., Ng, W.L.: Can a zero-intelligence plus model explain the stylized facts of financial time series data? In: Autonomous Agents and Multiagent Systems, vol. 2, pp. 653–660 (2012)
8. Panayi, E., Harman, M., Wetherilt, A.: Agent-based modelling of stock markets using existing order book data. In: International Workshop on Multi-Agent Systems and Agent-Based Simulation, pp. 101–114 (2012)
9. Rand, W.: Machine learning meets agent-based modeling: when not to go to a bar. In: The Proceedings of Agent (2006)
10. Tozicka, J., Rovatsos, M., Pechoucek, M: A framework for agent-based distributed machine learning and data mining. In: Autonomous Agents and Multiagent Systems, ACM (2007)
11. van der Hoog, S.: Deep Learning in agent-based models: a prospectus. Technical report, Bielefeld University (2016)
12. Alexander, C.: Market Risk Analysis, Value at Risk Models. Wiley, Chichester (2009)
13. Braun-Munzinger, K., Liu, Z., Turrell, A.: An agent-based model of dynamics in corporate bond trading. Bank of England Working Paper No. 592 (2016)
14. Paddrik, M., Hayes, R., Todd, A., Yang, S., Beling, P., Scherer, W.: An agent based model of the E-Mini S&P 500 applied to Flash Crash analysis. In: Computational Intelligence for Financial Engineering & Economics, pp. 1–8 (2012)
15. Mathieu, P., Gaciarz, M.: Improving classifier agents with order book information. In: International Conference on Practical Applications of Agents and Multi-Agent Systems, pp. 204–215 (2013)
16. Hochreiter, S., Schmidhuber, J.: Long short-term memory. Neural Comput. **9**(8), 1735–1780 (1997)
17. Schuster, M., Paliwal, K.: Bidirectional recurrent neural networks. IEEE Trans. Signal Process. **45**(11), 2673–2681 (1997)
18. Thomson Reuters Knowledge Direct API. https://developers.thomsonreuters. com/thomson-reuters-knowledge-direct-trkd/thomson-reuters-knowledge-direct-api-trkd-api. Accessed 1 Dec 2018
19. Rechenthin, M.: Machine-learning classification techniques for the analysis and prediction of high-frequency stock direction. The University of Iowa (2014)

Smart Farming – Open Multi-agent Platform and Eco-System of Smart Services for Precision Farming

Petr Skobelev[1]([⊠])[iD], Vladimir Larukchin[1][iD], Igor Mayorov[2][iD],
Elena Simonova[3][iD], and Olga Yalovenko[4][iD]

[1] Samara State Technical University,
Molodogvardeyskaya Str., 244, 443100 Samara, Russia
{skobelev, vl}@kg.ru
[2] Institute for the Control of Complex Systems of Russian Academy of Sciences,
Sadovaya Str., 61, 443020 Samara, Russia
imayorov@kg.ru
[3] Samara National Research University,
Moskovskoye Shosse, 34, 443086 Samara, Russia
simonova@kg.ru
[4] Peschanokopskaya Agrarian Laboratory, Rostov Region,
Peschanokopskiy District, Razvilnoe Village, Usadba SKhT Str.,
Building 3, Office 12, 347561 Rostov-on-Don, Russia
olyayalovenko@gmail.com

Abstract. The paper is addressing new challenges in agriculture, which are becoming nowadays critical for many countries, including climate changes, exhausted soils, aged farmers, etc. One of the new trends is associated with a step from Agriculture–4.0 focused on automation of physical processes for precision farming – to Agriculture–5.0 based on Artificial Intelligence (AI) for digitalization of domain knowledge and automation of farmer decision-making processes. A brief overview of existing IT systems for precision farming is given, key limitations are discussed and business requirements for developing AI solutions are formulated. The concept of digital eco-system of smart services for precision farming is proposed based on AI-technologies. The paper presents functionality and architecture of multi-agent platform and eco-system and identifies vitally important smart services for everyday operations of farmers. The structure and content of ontology-driven knowledge base for precision agriculture is considered, aimed at formalizing specifications of modern types of crops, agro- and bio-technologies, etc. The virtual "round table" is proposed as a generic framework for forming well-balanced recommendations for farmers with the use of ontology-based model of agricultural enterprise, which forms a specification of situation for automatic decision-making. Finally, the first case studies of the industrial prototype of the solution development are discussed.

Keywords: Precision farming · Multi-agent platform · Digital eco-system · Smart services · Multi-agent technologies · Ontology · Knowledge base · Decision making

© Springer Nature Switzerland AG 2019
Y. Demazeau et al. (Eds.): PAAMS 2019, LNAI 11523, pp. 212–224, 2019.
https://doi.org/10.1007/978-3-030-24209-1_18

1   Introduction

Many countries in the world are now facing significant challenges in agriculture: climate changes, exhausted soils, aged farmers, growing demand for high-quality and safe food and ecology-clean technology of farming, low productivity and efficiency, shift to small farms, etc. One of the steps to address these challenges was Agriculture–4.0 focused on automation of physical processes, integrating in-field sensors, GPS control of machine positions, satellite image processing, etc. [1–3].

However, the growing complexity and dynamics in agriculture form the new trend of Agriculture–5.0 focused on Artificial Intelligence (AI) for automation of decision-making for farmers. New classes of AI solutions need to be supported by Knowledge Bases on products and modern agro- and bio-technologies, insects, pesticides and fertilizers, etc. It can also include a variety of AI-based technologies for adaptive planning and scheduling, pattern recognition, neuron networks and machine learning models and methods, big data and predictive analytics.

The objective of Smart Farming project is to provide open multi-agent platform and eco-system of smart services for development and application of new AI models, methods and tools for digitalization of knowledge and automation of decision-making processes in agriculture.

In this paper, we are developing the concept of open multi-agent platform and eco-system of smart services for precision farming, present the main functionality and architecture of smarts services that are now in progress, as well as results of the first case studies on solution delivery.

The expected result of developments is climate-oriented, ecologically friendly and economically efficient precision farming for worldwide applications.

2   Key Market Requirements

Food production in Russia [4] is a major export item (6%), its volume in 2017 rose to a record of $20.7 billion (+21% compared with 2016). In 2017, grain exports from Russia also increased in this volume, and reached a record of 43 million tons. In the goods structure of grain supplies, wheat accounts for 74%, barley – 13%, corn – 12%, and other types – 1% (according to 2014 data). Russian grain is supplied to dozens of countries in the world with main consumers in North Africa and the Middle East.

However, more than 70% of Russia's agricultural lands is at risk: droughts, frosts, hail, freezing out of winter crops, strong wind and rain, waterlogged soil, etc. There is a steady increase in damage from dangerous weather phenomena: their number in Russia has increased by more than 2.5 times in the last 10 years.

In this regard, it is necessary to create climate-optimized, environmentally friendly and cost-effective crop production, which requires considerable financial investments, advanced knowledge and skills, training of specialists, etc. Another important task is reduction of losses in the chain of finished products: from purchasing and supply - to consumers (up to 25–40%).

Thus, a vitally important task is creation of smart systems to support decision-making by farmers with the following aims:

- assisting farms in introducing methods of precision farming and increasing productivity and efficiency of crop production;
- reducing costs along the whole chain of production, processing and storage of products by creating an e-market, eliminating intermediaries, etc.

To solve these problems, we propose development of methods and tools of artificial intelligence (AI), which support digitalization of knowledge and decision-making processes in daily operations of farmers at plant cultivating enterprises.

3 Overview of Existing IT Products for Precision Farming

Currently, the market has a wide range of information systems designed to solve various problems in precision farming [5–10].

The Russian company Agro-Soft, which is the distributor of the German company Land-Data Eurosoft, is engaged in implementation of precision farming using traditional information and space technologies [5]. Products of the Russian company GEOMIR are designed to create basic e-maps of fields, determine the actual boundaries of the field, generate yield maps, and keep statistics on harvesting [6].

The Canadian company Farm-At-Hand provides systems for monitoring the progress of field work: sowing, fertilizers and plant protection products, harvesting, and others. Information on the existing agricultural equipment (model, serial number, purchase price, maintenance) is stored in a smartphone. The system provides assessment of the state of the machine park, and monitoring of all purchases [7]. The Android MachineryGuide application, developed by Afflield Ltd., a Hungarian company, is a navigation software for even and precise sowing or field spraying. The application provides a visual field management, including cases of poor visibility and collection of statistics on results of operations performed [8].

The British company Hands Free Hectare has implemented full automation of all crop growing processes: from sowing - to harvesting. Machines are managed by technical staff from the control room. Drones with on-board multispectral sensors are applied [9]. In the Online farm management system of the American company Exact Farming the following functions are implemented: recording the history of using fields and monitoring their condition (field mapping, field card, vegetation index and NDVI maps, real-time control of the situation), and basic accounting functions controlling expenses for fields [10].

It can be seen, that all these systems are collecting huge amounts of data and help farmers to visualize the situation on the fields but no one of these systems is focused on digitalization on knowledge and automation of farmers decision making.

In last period of time, a number of new studies have been recognized focused on the use of ontologies and multi-agent technology in agriculture [11–13]. The mentioned developments present the first prototypes designed mainly for research objectives and helped to prove of concepts. Some of the systems aimed to provide recommendation services but no one can provide advice-based scheduling. In any case, even these first prototypes are showcasing the key benefits of ontologies and multi-agent technology for solving complex problems in agriculture by using domain knowledge, negotiations and self-organization of agents with conflicting interests.

Analysis of these systems leads to the following conclusions:

- the created multi-agent systems are mainly the first prototypes, which require further development for large-scale practical use;
- the described industrial IT systems are "closed" for accessing internal information and connecting new services;
- all discusses industrial systems are mainly informational, aimed primarily to collect data and provide routine functions with cost accounting;
- these systems provide data, but do not contain knowledge bases which are required for decision-making support;
- there are no models, methods and decision support tools for farmers which affect adaptive re-scheduling of resources;
- it is not possible to connect other services that will support the agro-chain and allow purchases, logistics, storage, etc.;
- there is no built-in market for products and services.

At the same time, the existing global information platforms, such as those of the Moncanta company, are not only closed, but also designed for use of only their own seeds, fertilizers, chemicals, etc.

4 Digital Platform and Eco-System of Smart Services

One of the key innovations of the proposed solution is the use of ontology-driven knowledge base for digitalization and formalizing of domain-specific knowledge and automatic decision-making based on the previously developed multi-agent technology for trucks and factories, supply chains, mobile teams, etc. [14–16]. Multi-agent platform provides the conceptual framework [17] for developing Smart Services (as a kind of "Internet of Everything") for agriculture – where agents of services play the role of autonomous "digital twins" of fields, crops, fertilizers, insects, etc.

In the presented example (Fig. 1), the Agent of Satellite2 has recognized Event1 - problematic situation on Field3 (in red). Agent of Field3 has negotiated with Agent of Drone2 and Agent of Drone3 has requested for detailed inspections. As a result of inspection, Agent of Machine1 and Agent of Machine3 are allocated and scheduled for implementing precision farming technology for Field3 – for example, to bring more fertilizers and pesticides. These agents are designed as state-full software services, which can compete and cooperate on the virtual market of the agricultural enterprise and may differ by quality of services, availability in time and prices, etc. Two different satellites or three different fertilizers can compete for one field. Each smart service here can be represented by a decision-making machine with a container of all the necessary information and can work asynchronically with all other services.

The discussed concept of smart services is in match with the definition of digital eco-systems [18]: "A digital ecosystem is a distributed, adaptive, open socio-technical system with properties of self-organization, scalability and sustainability inspired from

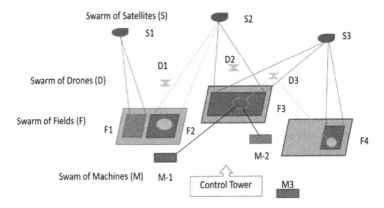

Fig. 1. The concept of multi-agent precision farming. (Color figure online)

natural ecosystems. Digital ecosystem models are informed by knowledge of natural ecosystems, especially for aspects related to competition and collaboration among diverse entities".

With the use of multi-agent platform, the digital eco-system for precision farming can be organized not as a traditional fully centralized, hierarchical, monolithic and deterministic solution, but as an open cloud-based environment available for any authorized third party developers: buyers of crops, providers of pesticides and fertilizers, universities, consulting and hi-tech companies, start-ups, associations of farmers, etc. The benefits of decentralized organization of decision-making systems are discussed in [15].

The developed eco-system will contain the following parts:

1. **Open Digital Platform for Eco-System support** – cloud-based software environment, in which software services are organized as "agents" – autonomous software objects, which are able to react to events, perform planning and control execution of plans but also coordinate their decisions by protocols of negotiations. The main parts of the platform will be memory storage for secure saving of big data and applying real-time analytics and forecasting, sessions of negotiations, enterprise service bus, etc.
2. **Knowledge Base on Precision Farming** – contains useful information on modern technologies of precision farming, specifics of soil, types of crops, required machines, fertilizers, insects, illnesses and receipts of treatment, pesticides, etc. The domain knowledge will be formalized with the use of agricultural ontologies based on semantic networks [19] for automatic decision-making processes by software agents and farmers, which can help specify the problem and find well-balanced solutions for farmers.
3. **Smart Fields, Smart Crops, Smart Fertilizers, Smart Soil, Smart Pesticides, etc**. – a number of software agents organized as smart services, which will monitor the state of their "owners", make plans and generate recommendations, negotiate results with other services and users.

4. **Service of "Round Table"** – agents of smart services are organized in a virtual "Round Table" for coordinated decision-making support and consulting for farmers. New unpredictable events trigger affected agents, which need to reach a new consensus by re-balancing their plans and coming to a conclusion on what to do in a new situation, consulting from the Knowledge Base of precision farming. Agents of services can compete and cooperate, suggesting different reactions for use of bio-technologies, fertilizers, pesticides, etc.

5. **Smart Agent of Farmer in Mobile Phone** – work as the farmer's agent (assistant) helping to provide adequate reaction to events, making planning and adaptive re-planning of agricultural operations, reminding about important stages of crop cultivation, advising on problems with the use of tablets or mobiles.

The objective of the digital platform and eco-system of smart services is to help farmers and agricultural enterprises improve everyday operations through recognition of problem situations and adaptive management of their resources, making next steps towards digitalization of their knowledge and all operations and direct communication with customers, providers of fertilizers and pesticides, machines, etc.

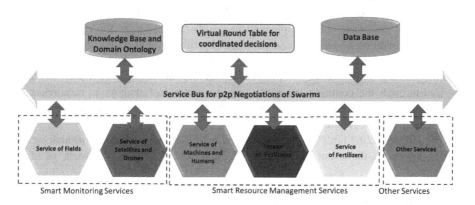

Fig. 2. Digital platform and eco-system of smart services.

As a result of the first developments, the following list of the most important smart services has been identified (Fig. 2):

– *Data Base on Farmers Fields* – supports full list of farmer fields with digital information on the history of all operations, boundaries and 3D-model of the profile of landscape, bio-chemical characteristics of soil, weather conditions, accumulated water and minerals, fertilizers and pesticides;

– *Smart Strategic Planning for Crop Rotation* – provides adaptive strategic planning of crop rotation for the new season, starting with sowing of crops and finishing with harvest of crops under conditions of weather forecast, available resources, etc.;

– *Smart Monitoring* – takes hyper-spectrum images of fields by satellites and drones and will try to recognize types of problems, including non-seeding, insect attacks, etc.;

- *Smart Operational Scheduler* – provides adaptive resource allocation, scheduling, optimization and control in real time, including machines and workers, mobile teams of agronomists and trucks, pesticides and fertilizers;
- *Smart Finance* – will compute planned and actual farmer budgets:
- *Smart Maintenance* – planning of machine repairing.

Agent of farmer could be connected with Institutions of Agriculture and Associations of farmers for individual consultancy and observing results and plans. It can also directly communicate with other farmers, receive consulting from them and to share knowledge and best practices across the community of farmers.

5   Virtual Round Table of Agents Representing Smart Services

A digital eco-system of smart services is created to work with the ontological model of each plant-growing enterprise, integrating data on the fields, their processing history, planted crops, available machinery, state of warehouses, etc.

The main idea of the digital eco-system is to enable services to compete for the customer and cooperate, i.e. complement each other. Users have the opportunity to choose configuration of services and pay for it by subscription. Each smart service is represented by an autonomously operating software agent, capable of reading and recording data in the ontological enterprise model and interacting with agents of other services through the common enterprise bus. As a result of analysis of requirements and business processes of the plant-growing enterprise, the following set of agent types has been developed (Table 1).

The virtual "round table" is a set of regulations for coordinated decision-making by service agents in the event of problem situations that simulates the work of farm specialists.

Design of the eco-system of smart services includes the following components in order to implement the concept of a virtual "round table":

- Knowledge base for forming and making coordinated decisions;
- Digital platform for launching services and their communication, including data transfer bus;
- The Moderator Agent managing the course of negotiations, from setting a problem situation - to fixing the result of negotiations;
- Agents of smart services that can read scene data or record their results, as well as interact with each other according to protocols;
- Task panel, where smart services record tasks for solving and choose tasks for themselves;
- The scene with the formalized model of the problem situation, together with the developed action plan and the expected result;
- Business radars to assess the decisions made;
- Agent negotiation log that helps audit the decisions made.

Table 1. Agent classes at the "round table"

Agent type	Functions and goals
Field Agent	Determines the choice of the most appropriate crop for achieving field efficiency, taking into account preceding crops, soil types, relief and other factors
Crop Agent	Determines the choice of the most appropriate field for the plant variety and then - the order of operations for cultivation and control of process technical maps. The crop agent also generates tasks for agents of machinery, brigades, and monitoring
Plant protection product (PPP) Agent	Determines the type of plant protection products to be applied in the field. Plans technological operations for PPP application. Minimizes the amount of applied pesticides
Fertilizer Agent	Plans tasks from agronomist by types, order and timing of fertilizer application. Minimizes the amount of applied fertilizer in accordance with the technical process
Monitoring Agent	Determines the choice of satellites or drones for processing requests and possible delivery times for images, provides data on field surveys, determines field indices, identifies inhomogeneities in the fields
Agent of Pests (Insects) or Diseases	Based on the identified inhomogeneities in the fields and related parameters (weather conditions, calendar of disease development, proximity to a forest area, etc.), the agent tries to determine the most likely pests or possible plant diseases, determines the possible PPP type for treatment or insect control
Agronomist Agent (AA)	Plans crop rotation and determines crops for sowing in fields, controls the state of fields, determines technological operations for each field and plant
Brigade Agent	Forms, coordinates and monitors plan implementation for crop processing (plan for shift-daily tasks)
Machinery Agent	Generates the field processing plan, sets maintenance requirements, selects machine operators and machinery by specialization type, minimizes downtime
Machine Operator Agent	Plans working hours, and employment calendar as agreed with the Agronomist Agent
Staff Agent (Moderator)	Moderates the "round table", controls indicators set by the agronomist and supports the process of plan coordination by agents

Service agents solve their tasks based on their own target functions and functions of bonuses and fines, which reflect the degree of achieving the specified indicators in the virtual system market. Each agent, having reached certain values of indicators, receives or gives virtual currency. The system can impose fines on the agent and offer it some bonuses, as well as lend to the agent, allocating funds to it in order to improve its condition. The virtual "round table" (VRT) of service agents is created in the event of any problem situation arising from a significant deviation from the expected result. In the course of work, VRT can be replenished with agents of those services that are affected by the changes. Description of the situation in the form of a scene is available to all agents of VRT. Under control of the moderator agent, each agent analyzes the situation and makes its own proposal, which is recorded in the scene.

For this event, the next participant is activated according to the specified rules. Solution proposed by the agent and presented in the scene is analyzed by other agents, and the process is either continued with control transferred to the next agent, or a conflict occurs, understood as a contradiction between the goals, preferences and limitations of agents, for example, going beyond the season budget. In this case, the agent-moderator stops the process, identifies the agent that made the greatest contribution to the result, and asks it to "adjust" the proposal, for example, finding a different fertilizer that would be close in quality but cheaper. If there is a new solution and the conflict is resolved, the process continues. As a result, direct negotiations between agents provide conflict resolution by mutual concessions based on satisfaction functions and functions of bonuses and fines. Concessions can be made both by individual agents, and agents of the enterprise as a whole, when concessions of several individual agents give a general increase in the target function of the whole system. After resolution of one local conflict, new conflicts may emerge - such "movement" at VRT continues until all conflicts are resolved or, if there are no more options to solve the problem, control is transferred to the user of the corresponding agent. As a result, the problem solution that is coordinated with all agents and users is formed at the virtual "round table".

One of the possible agent interaction protocols of the virtual "round table" is shown in Fig. 3. The main idea of the method is to find an agent that provides a minimum value but requires maximum investments, and improve its position in a step-by-step way.

The proposed model of the virtual "round table" makes it possible to create and apply various AI methods and tools for elaborating and making coordinated solutions using tools of resource planning, big data analytics, forecasting, etc.

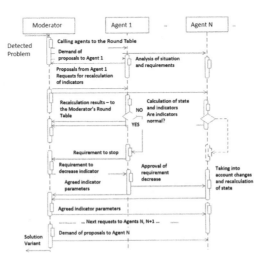

Fig. 3. Protocol of the virtual "round table".

6 Ontology-Driven Knowledge Base for Precision Farming

Benefits of using ontologies as a tool for knowledge digitalization and formalization in computer-readable format are well-known [20]. Agents receive from ontology the necessary domain knowledge and rules for decision making. The main reason of using ontologies in the considered solution is to digitalize and formalize required knowledge for automatic decision-making and separating domain knowledge from the source code of the solution [19]. The detailed overview of existing ontologies for agriculture can be found in [21]. The issue is that all these ontologies are not fully applicable for modelling of agricultural enterprise with the use of available resources – but it is critical for planning and scheduling.

The developed ontology of precision farming for wheat production is more focused on specifying the following main classes of concepts and relations:

- characteristics of climate zone and related sorts of crops;
- sorts of wheat and some other crops usually combined with wheat;
- types of precision farming technologies (No-Till for saving water, etc.);
- types of pesticides and fertilizers;
- types of illnesses and diseases, plant treatment;
- types of insects and their damages; when they appear, how to protect plants;
- sorts of soil, balance of minerals, agro-chemical attributes;
- classes of machines and technical tools and equipment;
- classes of farmers and their competencies;
- classes of spare parts, required fuel, other materials.

A fragment of the developed ontology for precision farming is given in Fig. 4, which defines the concept of "Task" – as the most important for scheduling tasks dynamically. With the use of ontology it becomes possible to create ontological model of the enterprise and specify available resources, problem situations, plans and schedules for everyday operations based on the formally defined concept of "Task".

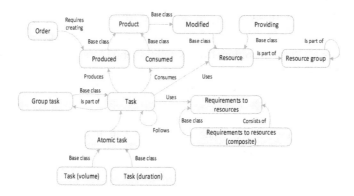

Fig. 4. Basic ontology of planning.

The proposed model of the virtual "round table" makes it possible to create and apply various AI methods and tools for elaborating and making coordinated solutions in resource planning, big data analytics, forecasting, etc.

7 Example of Work

Let us briefly consider an example of decision-making at the virtual "round table" in the created eco-system of smart services:

– The Satellite Agent identifies that one of the fields of the enterprise is problematic, with a new inhomogeneity.
– The Field Agent initiates task formulation to determine causes of the problem and develop action plans for its countering.
– The Drone Agent offers its service, preliminarily planning shooting.
– The agronomist receives the offer he can agree to. Next, drones with a hyperspectral camera perform remote survey of the problem area. The result is recorded in the Field Database - a data repository about the field.
– New images area initiate the task of recognizing the problem type.
– Plant Disease and Pest Agents are activated, which compete in their inputs.
– Let the pests be determined as the most likely reason of the problem situation.
– The Agronomist Agent schedules the agronomist's visit to the field for making decisions on the spot.
– When the agronomist visits the field, he discovers that the cause of the problem situation is different - under-feeding of plants.
– When the agronomist enters this information into the system, the Fertilizer Agent starts planning fertilization, taking into account available fertilizers.
– Agents of Machinery and Machine Operators reschedule their work.
– Machine operators receive new daily tasks on their tablets.
– The Field Agent records the event of finding the causes of the problem and working out measures of influence.
– The Field Agent sets the field for further monitoring and control in order to track changes and confirm the result.

Decisions on operational adjustment of field visits plans, made on the basis of remote analysis of crop condition from satellites or UAVs, are transmitted to the agronomist through a mobile application (Fig. 5), which allows him to view the field map in real time, as well as up-to-date information about fields and performed work, obtained from the knowledge base. The agronomist can also make marks and track changes via the event feed. The application has a client-server architecture, can work offline, locally saving the changes made, and upload them to the knowledge base when connecting to the network. Similar mobile applications are available for foremen and machine operators.

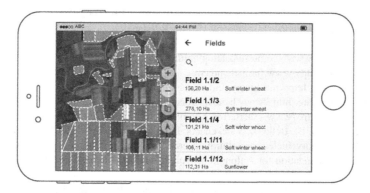

Fig. 5. Prototype of agronomist's mobile application.

8 Conclusion

The first prototype of Smart Farming platform and eco-system was developed and applied for one of the best wheat producers in Russia – Peschanokopskaya Agro Group (Rostov region) which includes three farming enterprises with about 30 000 Ha in total configured in 350 mosaic fields. The smart services for planning can help farmers develop plans for seasonal crop rotation and share limited resources across farm fields. As a result, efficiency of all operations has increased by up to 10% within the last 2 years. Productivity achieved in 2016 was 59,6 centner per Ha and in 2017 the growth was up to 64 centner per Ha, which is the best result for Rostov region.

The key innovations of the proposed platform and eco-system are based on the use of knowledge base and multi-agent technology for solving complex problems of adaptive resource management.

The next step in solution development will be to establish Smart Market-Place where key participants of agriculture industry can directly sell their products and services with the use of smart contacts, crypto-currency and block-chain technology.

Acknowledgements. The work was supported by the Ministry of Education and Science of the Russian Federation in the framework of contract agreement № 14.574.21.0183 – the unique ID number is RFMEFI57417X0183.

References

1. Zarco-Tejada, P.J., Hubbard, N., Loudjani, P.: Precision agriculture – An opportunity for EU farmers – Potential support with the CAP 2014–2020. Joint Research Centre (JRC) of the EU, Monitoring Agriculture Resources (2014)
2. Banu, S.: Precision agriculture: tomorrow's technology for today's farmer. J. Food Process. Technol. **6**, 8 (2015). https://doi.org/10.4172/2157-7110.1000468
3. Sfiligo, E., Heacox, L.: Top 10 Technologies in Precision Agriculture Right Now, 12 August 2016. http://www.precisionag.com/systems-management/top-10/

4. Bulletin: The main indicators of agriculture in Russia in 2017. http://www.gks.ru/wps/wcm/connect/rosstat_main/doc_1140096652250. (in Russian)

5. Agro-Soft. http://agro-soft.ru

6. GEOMIR. http://www.geomir.ru/catalog9.html

7. Farm at Hand. http://www.farmathand.com

8. MachineryGuide. http://machineryguideapp.com/en

9. Hands Free Hectare. http://www.handsfreehectare.com/

10. ExactFarming. http://www.exactfarming.com/en

11. Ali, O., Germain, B., Belle, J., Valckenaers, P., et al.: Multi-agent coordination and control system for multi-vehicle agricultural operations. In: Proceedings of AAMAS 2010, International Foundation for Autonomous Agents and Multiagent Systems, pp. 1621–1622 (2010)

12. Min, Z., Bei, W., Chunyuan, G., Zhao qian, S.: Application study of precision agriculture based on ontology in the internet of things environment. In: Zhang, J. (ed.) ICAIC 2011. CCIS, vol. 227, pp. 374–380. Springer, Heidelberg (2011). https://doi.org/10.1007/978-3-642-23226-8_49

13. Pudumalar, S., Ramanujam, E., Harine Rajashree, R., et al.: Crop recommendation system for precision agriculture. IEEE (2017). https://doi.org/10.1109/icoac.2017.7951740

14. Müller, Jörg P., Fischer, K.: Application impact of multi-agent systems and technologies: a survey. In: Shehory, O., Sturm, A. (eds.) Agent-Oriented Software Engineering, pp. 27–53. Springer, Heidelberg (2014). https://doi.org/10.1007/978-3-642-54432-3_3

15. Rzevski, G., Skobelev, P.: Managing Complexity. WIT Press, London (2014)

16. Skobelev, P.: Towards autonomous ai systems for resource management: applications in industry and lessons learned. In: Demazeau, Y., An, B., Bajo, J., Fernández-Caballero, A. (eds.) PAAMS 2018. LNCS (LNAI), vol. 10978, pp. 12–25. Springer, Cham (2018). https://doi.org/10.1007/978-3-319-94580-4_2

17. Budaev, D., Lada, A., Simonova, E., Skobelev, P., et al.: Conceptual design of smart farming solution for precise agriculture. Int. J. Des. Nat. Ecodyn. 13(3), 307–314 (2018)

18. Digital ecosystem. http://en.wikipedia.org/wiki/Digital_ecosystem

19. Skobelev, P.: Ontologies activities for situational management of enterprise real-time. Ontol. Designing 1(3), 26–48 (2012)

20. Ontology Summit 2017 Communiqué. http://s3.amazonaws.com/ontologforum/Ontology Summit2017/Communique_v8.pdf

21. Skobelev, P., Simonova, E., Smirnov, S., et al.: Development of knowledge base in the "Smart Farming" system for agricultural enterprise management. Procedia Comput. Sci. 150, 154–161 (2019)

Demo Papers

SMACH: Multi-agent Simulation of Human Activity in the Household

Jérémy Albouys[1,2,3,5(✉)], Nicolas Sabouret[3,4], Yvon Haradji[5],
Mathieu Schumann[5], and Christian Inard[1,2]

[1] Laboratoire des sciences de l'ingénieur pour l'environnement,
La Rochelle, France
[2] Université de La Rochelle, La Rochelle, France
{jeremy.albouys1,christian.inard}@univ-lr.fr
[3] Laboratoire d'informatique pour la mécanique
et les sciences de l'ingénieur CNRS, Orsay, France
nicolas.sabouret@limsi.fr
[4] Université Paris Sud, Orsay, France
[5] EDF R&D, Paris, France
{yvon.haradji,mathieu.schumann}@edf.fr

Abstract. The SMACH platform is a multi-agent based simulator supporting the study of human activity at the scale of a household, and its impact on the electricity consumption. It generates both activity diagrams and load curves for every electrical appliance in the household. Three different user interfaces can be used to manipulate the simulator: a participatory simulation interface, an educational interface and a technical interface for energy experts. This demonstration for PAAMS presents all three interfaces and the features offered by the SMACH platform.

Keywords: Agent-based simulation · Energy consumption ·
Simulation of human activity

1 Introduction

In the context of energy consumption reduction, studying and understanding the residential sector appears as a key factor. Indeed, according to the EIA[1], this sector is the first electricity consumer in the United States. Moreover, 57% of the final energy consumption in Europe is used for space heating [6]. However, the residential sector is characterized by a high variability due to the impact of human activity [1]. Predicting human activities and energy loads of buildings are thus of crucial important to predict energy consumption.

Today, two kinds of models exist to simulate such household consumption. The first model are based on stochastic models [5], to simulate "average" human

---

[1] https://www.eia.gov/energyexplained/print.php?page=electricity_use.

© Springer Nature Switzerland AG 2019
Y. Demazeau et al. (Eds.): PAAMS 2019, LNAI 11523, pp. 227–231, 2019.
https://doi.org/10.1007/978-3-030-24209-1_19

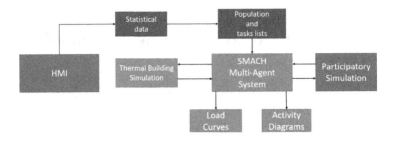

Fig. 1. SMACH general architecture

activity. One limitation is that the simulated behaviors do not correspond to real life situations and lack variability. The second approach relies on multi-agent simulations (MAS) [2]. Such models allow a fine-grained simulation of the human activity. The SMACH platform, developed in collaboration between EDF and several academic partners, is one of them.

2   Main Purpose

SMACH aims at simulating household activity and electrical consumption. It is based on two main components. The first one is a multi-agent system simulating human activity in households. It uses statistical data based on time-use surveys [4] to produce varied and realistic lists of daily tasks for each inhabitant of the household. Based on this information, the agents of the SMACH platform select the activity to perform at every time step, using control parameters such as the current activity of other inhabitants, the price of the energy, their previous activities and the parameters of the tasks. Each task can be associated with the use of electrical appliances that consume electricity.

The second component is a multi-zone thermal model of the household that simulates indoor temperature and the energy consumption for room heating [3].

The SMACH engine is thus able to generate load curves coupled with activity diagrams. It is used at EDF for research purposes, to understand the electrical energy consumption in existing households, to study the impact of new households configuration or public policies and to anticipate future situations like collective self-consumption at the scale of a neighborhood or electrical vehicles.

3   Demonstration

Our demonstration will illustrate the possibilities of the SMACH multi-agent simulation through three different user interfaces. Figure 1 illustrates the connection between these interfaces and the platform.

3.1   Technical Interface

While it is possible to manually configure all the details of the household (number of inhabitants, list of tasks with their duration parameters, list of electrical appliances, etc), the SMACH platform can generate these parameters automatically from statistical data. With this expert interface, the household generation is configured by selecting several parameters including the number of households, their geographical area, the characteristics of the building and appliances, and the inhabitants policies related to energy use. The system then generate as many households as asked (often thousands for large scale studies), which are then individually simulated by SMACH, producing one load curve and one activity diagram for each household. In the demonstration we will generate a city population then produce the activity diagram and the load curves for all of them. The user interface is used by energy experts to study a large variety of configurations and scales.

3.2   Dedicated Interface for Load Curves Generation by Energy Experts

Participatory Simulation bridges the gap between simulated and real inhabitants.

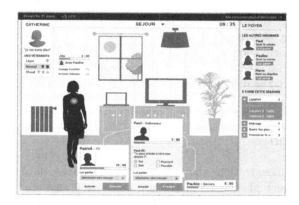

Fig. 2. Participatory simulation interface

The dedicated interface (Fig. 2) allows modellers to demonstrate to people the simulation of their own household in real time. The participants can interact with the simulation and change the behavior of each member of the family during the simulation. In the demonstration, we will show how people can interact with the platform to modify the behavior of the agents. This interface has been used to validate the SMACH model and the realism of the produced simulation.

3.3 Educational Interface

EDF developed an Educational Interface for SMACH, with the purpose of increasing awareness of general audience about the impact of occupant activities on the building's energy consumption.

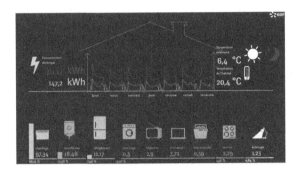

Fig. 3. Educational simulation

Thanks to this interface, the user can easily configure a household and set up consumption habits and general policies such as the setpoint temperature for room heating. It can then see how minimal changes on such parameters impact the energy consumption. The demonstration will present the creation of a household and will show a result in which the user will observe the difference between a base case scenario and a modified scenario with changes to the initial configuration, and the distribution of the energy consumption of each electrical appliance (Fig. 3).

4   Conclusion

The present demonstration showed various interfaces developed with the SMACH multiagent platform and the use cases they answered to. We discuss their operation and results for professional use and for general audience.

References

1. Bahaj, A.S., James, P.A.B.: Urban energy generation: the added value of photovoltaics in social housing. Renew. Sustain. Energy Rev. **11**(9), 2121–2136 (2006). https://doi.org/10.1016/j.rser.2006.03.007
2. Ferreri, E., Salotti, J.M., Favier, P.A.: Prediction of electrical consumptions using a bio-inspired behavioral model (2017). http://www.ibpsa.org/proceedings/bausimPapers/2014/p1183_final.pdf
3. Plessis, G., Kaemmerlen, A., Lindsay, A.: BuildSysPro: a Modelica library for modelling buildings and energy systems (2014). https://doi.org/10.3384/ECP140961161. http://www.ep.liu.se/ecp/096/122/ecp14096122.pdf

4. Reynaud, Q., Haradji, Y., Sempé, F., Sabouret, N.: Using time-use surveys in multi agent based simulations of human activity. In: Proceedings of the 9th International Conference on Agents and Artificial Intelligence, ICAART (Icaart), vol. 1, pp. 67–77 (2017). https://doi.org/10.5220/0006189100670077

5. Widén, J., Wäckelgård, E.: A high-resolution stochastic model of domestic activity patterns and electricity demand. Appl. Energy **87**(6), 1880–1892 (2010). https://doi.org/10.1016/J.APENERGY.2009.11.006. https://www.sciencedirect.com/science/article/pii/S0306261909004930

6. Zimmermann, J., Griggs, M., King, J., Harding, L., Roberts, P., Evans, C.: Household electricity survey a study of domestic electrical product usage. Report, RAND Corporation (2012)

Giving Camel to Artifacts for Industry 4.0 Integration Challenges

Cleber Jorge Amaral[1,3](✉) ⓘ, Stephen Cranefield[2] ⓘ, Jomi Fred Hübner[3] ⓘ, and Mario Lucio Roloff[4] ⓘ

[1] Federal Institute of Santa Catarina (IFSC),
Florianópolis, Brazil
cleber.amaral@ifsc.edu.br
[2] University of Otago, Dunedin, New Zealand
stephen.cranefield@otago.ac.nz
[3] Federal University of Santa Catarina (UFSC), Florianópolis, Brazil
jomi.hubner@ufsc.br
[4] Instituto Federal Catarinense (IFC), Blumenau, Brazil
mario.roloff@ifc.edu.br

Abstract. Interoperability is a key factor of Cyber-Physical System (CPS) concept. Based on studies that use Multi-Agent System (MAS) as the core of a CPS, we are proposing to model many resources of the factories following the well-known Agents and Artifacts model for integrating agents and their environment. To enhance the interoperability of this system, we use the Apache Camel framework, a middleware to define routes to integrate a wide range of endpoints using different protocols. In this paper, we are demonstrating our camel component for artifacts in the context of Industry 4.0.

Keywords: Cyber-Physical System · Smart factory · Industry 4.0 ·
Internet of Things · Industrial internet · 4th industrial revolution

1 Introduction

The wide use and diversity of resources bring challenges when it is necessary to integrate industrial resources as required by *smart factories* of Industry 4.0 concept. In this sense, interoperability, which means that the Cyber-Physical System (CPS) and all sorts of resources can communicate with each other, is a key factor [3]. Multi-Agent System (MAS) is being the CPS in many studies. However, these applications are becoming very complex and computationally heavy especially due to indiscriminately *agentification* of entities.

This paper demonstrates *CamelArtifact*, our Apache Camel component for artifacts. The artifact is a non-autonomous entity which takes advantage of the separation of concerns of a MAS in dimensions [1] which is being proved as a

Supported by IFSC - Propicie, Petrobras - AG-BR, UFSC and University of Otago.

Y. Demazeau et al. (Eds.): PAAMS 2019, LNAI 11523, pp. 232–236, 2019.
https://doi.org/10.1007/978-3-030-24209-1_20

better approach to apply in some dynamic and complex scenarios. In order to address interoperability, we are using Camel infrastructure to create routes of communication with many available protocols and endpoints.

2   Main Purpose

In Agents and Artifacts approach (A&A), there is the agents' dimension for proactive entities which encapsulate autonomous execution in some activities, and the environmental dimension which includes *artifacts*, as passive components, simpler entities that can be manipulated and shared by agents. Artifacts are used by the agent through its interface which provides operations to achieve the services it offers. Typically, artifacts' implementation is computationally lighter than agents since they are passive entities [4].

The Apache Camel framework is a lightweight Java-based message routing and mediation engine [2]. Camel can achieve high-performance processes since it handles multiple messages concurrently and provides functions such as routing, exception handling and testing, that allows the creation of complex routes. The complexity of the protocol of each supported technology is embedded in a component, which works as a bridge to Camel routes.

With *CamelArtifact*, different device protocols and networking technologies can be integrated to a MAS similarly, using Camel as routing and mediation engine. In this sense, the developed component is responsible for linking artifacts and external resources. Each *CamelArtifact* may contain route definitions using specific endpoints for each resource. The endpoints are encapsulating the communication protocol complexity.

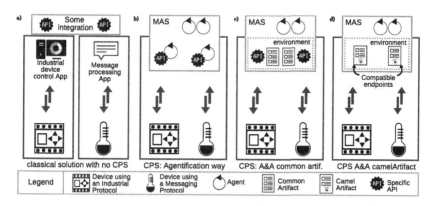

Fig. 1. Factory automation with two devices. (a) Integration among applications needs ad hoc solutions. (b) Integration using MAS *agentification* approach. (c) MAS using common artifacts integrated by APIs. (d) MAS using CamelArtifact and endpoints.

In fact, Factory's automation is evolving from low integration level (Fig. 1a) towards Cyber-Physical Systems (CPS) concept, which is integrating virtual and physical processes. CPS has a standardised abstraction and architecture integration in a broad sense. This concept is central to the so-called *smart factory* of Industry 4.0. MAS is playing the central part of CPS virtualising entities allowing decentralised control and interoperability in many research. However, studies [3] opted to represent almost any factory entity as agents (Fig. 1b), which increases complexity and brings synchronisation challenges.

Virtual representations of the plant, including software entities as well as the physical world, may be reached at A&A approach using *artifacts* and *workspaces* (Fig. 1c) what was already being explored by [5]. However, this study was limited to OPC devices by an API. Actually, without a mediation tool like Camel the usual solution to integrate artifacts and each technology is by APIs, what increases development efforts. Using our proposition (Fig. 1d), interoperability is facilitated using Camel and its several available components for different protocols.

3   Demonstration

The component *CamelArtifact* is demonstrated by implementing a MAS in the Industry 4.0 context (Fig. 2). The application has implemented communication routes between artifacts and industrial devices. For each device usually two routes are created: (i) to send data from the artifact to the device, and (ii) another route to the other way around. There are five different devices and protocols in this illustration: a shop-floor industrial device using OPC protocol (e.g. a Programmable Logical Controller); an Enterprise Resource Planning software (ERP) using REST; e-mail endpoint using SMTP protocol; an Internet of Things (IoT) device using MQTT protocol (e.g. a sensor); and, Telegram, a messaging application.

For each kind of device, it was added an instance of *CamelArtifact* with related routes. Messages that are arriving or being sent can be transformed. The transformation is used to make compatible both sides of the route depending on the application. The artifact may have route definitions on itself or it may receive and send messages through other *CamelArtifact*, which may forward messages. The use of forwarding function may save computer memory, on the other hand, each artifact as a *CamelArtifact* has his own thread taking computer parallelism advantages.

The MAS was designed with Jason agents. One of them is in charge to write and read the OPC item and then apply on ERP the updated data. Another agent is responsible for a Call For Freight Proposals, choosing the best offer and sending an e-mail to hire the winner. Finally, an agent is responsible to track the truck until it is close to the target destination and then send a message to the customer through Telegram.

In short, this implementation illustrates that *CamelArtifact* can help in some situations in the context of Industry 4.0:

- Heterogeneous integration (e.g. OPC, REST, e-mail, MQTT, and Telegram);
- Adaptation of the system in case of a change of endpoint technology;

– Message routing for other artifacts and external devices;
– Transforming messages for endpoints compliance;
– Balancing between scalability and the use of computational resources.

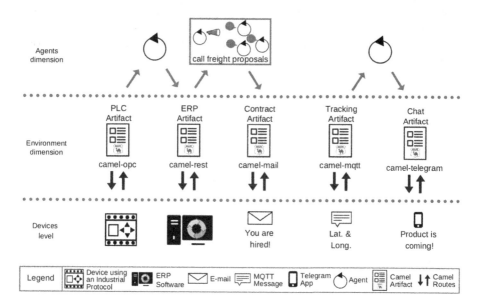

Fig. 2. An automated product delivery example: packaging, updating ERP software, contracting the best offer for freight, tracking and chatting with the customer.

4   Conclusion

In this paper, we have shown a *smart factory* scenario using Agents and Artifacts (A&A) approach modelling non-autonomous entities as artifacts which can later be shared by agents. External applications and devices are integrated in our system and perceived by the agents as artifacts and not as agents, as usual in other approaches. This is special suitable when the external applications do not have properties of agents. We illustrated a MAS connected to heterogeneous devices in an industrial context using a new camel component for artifacts. These common applications, with multiple resources and potentially multiple protocols show that, with our Apache Camel component, the MAS is empowered to communicate to heterogeneous devices.

References

1. Boissier, O., Bordini, R.H., Hübner, J.F., Ricci, A.: Dimensions in programming multi-agent systems. Knowl. Eng. Rev. **34**, e2 (2019)

2. Ibsen, C., Anstey, J.: Camel in Action, 1st edn. Manning Publications, Greenwich (2010)
3. Leitão, P., Karnouskos, S., Ribeiro, L., Lee, J., Strasser, T., Colombo, A.W.: Smart agents in industrial cyber physical systems. In: Proceedings of the IEEE (2016)
4. Ricci, A., Piunti, M., Viroli, M.: Environment programming in multi-agent systems: an artifact-based perspective. Auton. Agent Multi-Agent Syst. **23**, 158–192 (2011)
5. Roloff, M., Amaral, C., Stivanello, M., Stemmer, M.: MAS4SSP: a multi-agent reference architecture for the configuration and monitoring of small series production lines. In: INDUSCON (2016)

AncientS-ABM: A Novel Tool for Simulating Ancient Societies

Angelos Chliaoutakis[✉] and Georgios Chalkiadakis

Technical University of Crete, Kounoupidiana Campus, 73100 Chania, Greece
{angelos,gehalk}@intelligence.tuc.gr

Abstract. In this paper we demonstrate a tool that can be employed to build agent-based models (ABMs) for use in social archaeology. Specifically, our tool is based on the NetLogo modeling environment, and enables the creation of agent-based models of ancient societies, based on archaeological input. The models created by our tool can be used to obtain a better understanding of ancient societies, and assist archaeologists in testing the validity of existing or novel hypotheses and theories. We note that apart from assisting archaeologists in their work, the demonstrated tool can serve educational or recreational purposes as well: the ABMs created with the tool can, for instance, constitute the "backbone" of interactive platforms for use in schools or museums; and can conceivably be employed in history-focused digital strategic game environments.

Keywords: Agent-based model · Self-organization · Social archaeology

1 Introduction

Social archaeology seeks to understand the social organization of past societies at many different points in time [9]. For instance, do the main social units, individuals or groups, participate on a more-or-less equal basis, or do prominent differences in status or rank within the society (or perhaps even different social classes) exist? Answering these questions is very hard when exploring prehistoric communities, as written records in early societies are scant. The variety of methods used and the inherent uncertainty of the domain gives rise to a rich space of hypotheses regarding the social organization of early societies.

Over the past two decades, social and computational archaeology has utilized agent-based modeling for simulating ancient societies, in an attempt to answer such questions [5,7,8]. This is due to an ABMs' ability to represent individuals or societies, and encompass uncertainty inherent in archaeological theories. Moreover, incorporating ideas from multiagent systems (MAS) research in ABMs can enhance agent sophistication, and contribute on the application of strategic principles for selecting among agent behaviours [10].

© Springer Nature Switzerland AG 2019
Y. Demazeau et al. (Eds.): PAAMS 2019, LNAI 11523, pp. 237–241, 2019.
https://doi.org/10.1007/978-3-030-24209-1_21

Against this background, here we present *AncientS-ABM*, a NetLogo-based tool that serves the following purposes: *(a)* it can be employed for the study of practically any society of choice, and can easily incorporate and help test any theories proposed by archaeologists; and *(b)* it showcases how MAS-originating concepts, techniques, and algorithms can be incorporated in archaeology ABMs. Unlike most existing ABM approaches in archaeology, which employ a simple reactive agent architecture, AncientS-ABM can be and has already been used to populate its models with *utility-based* agents. Our agents act autonomously towards utility maximization, and can build and maintain complex social structures. Furthermore, our models can (demonstrably) incorporate a number of different social organization paradigms and various technologies. Indeed, using agent-based models that were built on knowledge derived from archaeological research, but do not attempt to fit their results to a specific material culture, allows for the emergence of dynamics for different types of societies in different types of landscapes, and can help derive knowledge of socio-economic and socio-ecological systems applicable beyond a specific case study.

2 Main Purpose

We now describe the main purpose and present the basic functionality offered by *AncientS-ABM*. For interest, we describe briefly how we have employed the tool to create and study an artificial ancient society of autonomous agents residing at the *Malia* area of the island of Crete during the Early Bronze Age [2–4].

To begin, the tool was developed using the NetLogo modeling environment[1], which is a free, open source and cross-platform system that runs on the Java virtual machine and it is fully programmable using an extended Logo dialect to support agents. Model parameters values correspond to estimates found in archaeological studies and currently offered by the interface (Fig. 1): *number of agents per settlement's cell, agricultural strategy* (intensive or extensive), *level and distribution of resources, number of settlements* per scenario, *agent migration radius, proximity of a new location to an aquifer* or not, *resources amount stored* by an agent per year and agent decision-making based on different *social organization paradigms*: independent, sharing, egalitarian, self-organized and hierarchical (static). The modeler is able to visualize environmental information on-the-fly such as elevation, slope, aquifer density and level of resources, as well as river and spring features and locations of known archaeological sites.

In AncientS-ABM, an agent can correspond to either an individual, a household, or a settlement. For instance, in our research focusing on the Minoan society [2–4], *households* are utility-based autonomous agents who they can settle (or occasionally resettle) and cultivate in a specific environmental location. They also possess a knowledge of their environment that allows them to choose their forage sites, gain experience, and even plan future movements. Several agents may live and interact in a specific area. The tool allows their world to be a

---

[1] https://ccl.northwestern.edu/netlogo.

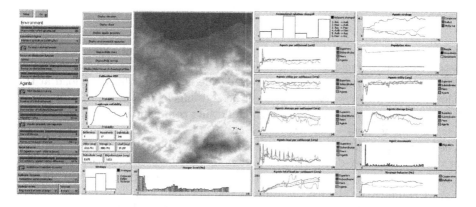

Fig. 1. AncientS-ABM interface and parameters.

precise recreation of the landscape, using environmental information built from available archaeological and topographical data.

AncientS-ABM allows us to assess the influence of different *social organization paradigms* on land use patterns and population growth. Interestingly, AncientS-ABM incorporates a social paradigm of agents *self-organizing* into a "stratified" social structure, and continuously re-adapting the emergent structure, if required [2]. Moreover, in order to model societal transformation accurately, agent behaviour has to be analysed from a *strategic* perspective as well. AncientS-ABM provides the modeler with the ability of performing a "game-theoretic" study of the agents' society. This allows us to study the evolution and adaptation of strategic behaviours of individuals operating in the artificial ancient community, and the effect these have on the society as a whole [3].

AncientS-ABM has allowed us to obtain important intuitions regarding the evolution of early Minoan societies. Our simulation results [2,3] demonstrate that self-organizing agent populations are the most successful. The success of this social organization paradigm that gives rise to stratified, *non-egalitarian societies*, provides support for so-called *"managerial"* archaeological theories: these assume the existence of different social strata in Neolithic/Early Bronze Age Crete, and consider this early stratification a pre-requisite for the emergence of the *Minoan Palaces*, and the hierarchical social structure evident in later periods [1]. In many scenarios, populations converge to adopting cooperative strategies; in line with the view that, though complex societies emerge to a large extent due to conflict and competition, these social conditions seldom exist without cooperative agreements, alliances and cooperation networks [6].

Furthermore, in [4] we studied the extent by which the cataclysmic volcanic eruption of Thera (Santorini) impacted the Minoan social evolution. Our results support archaeological theories suggesting that the Theran eruption led to a gradual (and not immediate) breakdown of the Minoan socio-economic system.

3 Demonstration

The tool is based on the NetLogo (6) modeling environment. NetLogo runs on the Java Virtual Machine, so it works on all major platforms. Java 8 runime or later is required. "AncientS-ABM" source code is available for download at the following link: http://www.intelligence.tuc.gr/~angelos/PAAMS19_96.zip. After download, extract content and run the following command:[2]

```
# java -jar AncientS-ABM.jar
```

When the "AncientS-ABM" user interface is available on the screen, you may set the available user-defined model parameters as you prefer or leave the default ones. Press the "setup" button to initialize the model and then the "Go" button to start running the simulation. Finally, you may find a demonstration video of the ABM at the following link: https://youtu.be/Aa6mEsDqGfg.

4 Conclusions

In this work we intertwined MAS and EGT techniques to build a generic ABM for simulating complex social systems interacting within a spatial environment. Our model uses existing archaeological evidence and it can readily incorporate any archaeological theory or historical data offered, in order to explore alternative hypotheses regarding the social organization of ancient societies.

References

1. Cherry, J.: Polities and palaces: some problems in Minoan state formation. In: Peer Polity Interaction and Socio-Political Change, pp. 19–45. Cambridge University Press (1986)
2. Chliaoutakis, A., Chalkiadakis, G.: Agent-based modeling of ancient societies and their organization structure. Auton. Agent. Multi-Agent Syst. **30**(6), 1072–1116 (2016)
3. Chliaoutakis, A., Chalkiadakis, G.: Evolutionary game-theoretic modeling of past societies' social organization. In: The 2018 Conference on Artificial Life: A Hybrid of the European Conference on Artificial Life (ECAL) and the International Conference on the Synthesis and Simulation of Living Systems (ALIFE), pp. 98–105 (2017)
4. Chliaoutakis, A., Chalkiadakis, G., Sarris, A.: Employing agent-based modeling to study the impact of the Theran eruption on Minoan society. In: Proceedings of the 3rd Conference on Computer Applications and Quantitative Methods in Archaeology - Creece (2019, in press)
5. Crabtree, S.A., Bocinsky, R.K., Hooper, P.L., Ryan, S.C., Kohler, T.A.: How to make a polity (in the central mesa verde region). Am. Antiq. **82**(1), 71–95 (2017)
6. Gumerman, G.J.: The role of competition and cooperation in the evolution of island societies. In: The Evolution of Island Societies, pp. 42–49 (1986)
7. Heckbert, S.: Mayasim: an agent-based model of the ancient maya social-ecological system. J. Artif. Soc. Soc. Simul. **16**(4), 11 (2013)

---

[2] Make sure there is no space or special characters on your path (pwd).

8. Janssen, M.A.: Population aggregation in ancient arid environments. Ecol. Soc. **15**, 19 (2010)
9. Renfrew, C., Bahn, P.: Archaeology: Theories, Methods, and Practice, 1st edn. Thames and Hudson (1991)
10. Wellman, M.P.: Putting the agent in agent-based modeling. Auton. Agent Multi-Agent Syst. **30**, 1175–1189 (2016)

A Demonstration of Generative Policy Models in Coalition Environments

Daniel Cunnington[1(✉)], Graham White[1], Mark Law[2], and Geeth de Mel[1]

[1] IBM Research, Winchester, UK
{dancunnington,gwhite,geeth.demel}@uk.ibm.com
[2] Imperial College London, London, UK
mark.law09@imperial.ac.uk

Abstract. Autonomous systems are expected to have a major impact in future coalition operations to assist humans in achieving complex tasks. Policies are typically used by systems to define their behavior and constraints and often these policies are manually configured and managed by humans. This paper presents a demonstration of a recent Generative Policy-based Model (GPM) approach applied to generating coalition policies for asset serviceability. This demonstrates the flexibility of the approach for generating policies in a distributed coalition environment to facilitate effective collaboration between coalition partners.

Keywords: Generative policy models · Generated policies ·
Symbolic learning · Coalition environments

1 Introduction

In the future battlespace, coalition systems and devices will be required to operate in challenging environments that impose certain constraints such as lack of or low-bandwidth connectivity to back-end services, rapidly changing environmental conditions and the requirement to abide by legal regulations and mission directives [5]. Therefore, coalition systems and devices require the capability to adapt and evolve such that they can behave autonomously 'at the edge' in previously unseen contexts. Crucially, systems need to understand the bounds in which they can operate based on their own (and that of other systems) capability, constraints of the environment and safety requirements. According to Bertino et al. [1], policies can be seen as directives given by a managing party to one or more managed parties in order to guide their behavior in coalition missions and collaborative activities. Policies are usually expressed as technology independent rules aiming to enhance the hard-coded functionality of the managed parties by the introduction of an interpreted logic that can be dynamically changed without modifying the underlying implementation. Policy-based management therefore significantly increases the self-managing aspects of coalition operations. However, conventional approaches to policy-based management that are typically based

© Springer Nature Switzerland AG 2019
Y. Demazeau et al. (Eds.): PAAMS 2019, LNAI 11523, pp. 242–245, 2019.
https://doi.org/10.1007/978-3-030-24209-1_22

on a top-down approach by which policies are specified through multiple refinement steps by a centralised policy administrator do not transfer effectively to the military environment. This is especially true of distributed, coalition scenarios where centralized policy management may not be possible due to environmental constraints. This paper presents a demonstration of recent work in GPM architectures showcasing their applicability to generating policies in a distributed, coalition environment. The paper is structured as follows. In Sect. 2 we outline the main purpose of our work, in Sect. 3 we present the associated demonstration and finally we conclude in Sect. 4.

2   Main Purpose

The main purpose of our work is to develop a flexible, secure and scalable generative policy architecture that is capable of meeting the complex requirements of distributed coalition environments. Within the International Technology Alliance for Distributed Analytics and Information Sciences (DAIS-ITA), we have proposed the notion of Generative Policy-based Models (GPMs) [7], where managed parties are provided with an initial policy specification. Each managed party can dynamically generate its own policies from the initial specification and possibly evolve its policies over time based on a change in operating context. As part of our work we have explored using a symbolic approach for learning policy models [2,3], utilising state-of-the-art Answer Set Grammars (ASGs) [6].

Within a coalition environment, coalition partners are required to work together which may involve sharing assets with one another. An asset could be a physical device such as a surveillance camera, an autonomous system such as an Unmanned Aerial Vehicle (UAV) or an asset could be a virtual service such as a database or a specific type of machine learning model such as a face recognizer or weaponry detector. Given the constantly evolving context and potentially dynamic asset pool caused by coalition partners frequently bringing assets online/offline during a mission, local and global serviceability policies that define the type of requests that an asset or coalition partner can service will be constantly in flux and it wont be possible for a human operator to generate all of these policies for all assets in all possible contexts in a timely manner. Also, given the distributed nature of a partners assets, the coalition partner as a whole requires means to keep track of the serviceability of its asset pool through a generated policy and also is responsible for communicating this updated policy in a distributed manner to its assets.

3   Demonstration

For the purposes of demonstration, we have utilised an agile knowledge representation framework alongside synthetic ground truth generation [4] in order to create a dataset of annotated asset requests, which is released online[1]. This approach enables customised annotations of ground truth data to facilitate complex

---

[1] https://github.com/dais-ita/coalition-data/.

evaluations of GPMs. In our demonstration, the United Kingdom (UK) is working alongside the United States (US) and a fictitious third party 'Kish' as part of a coalition undertaking a particular mission. Other assets currently present in the environment have learned to accept or reject serviceability requests from other coalition parties and each asset stores a log of annotated request examples, with respect to a given context and its own capabilities and constraints. Initially these annotations could be captured by monitoring human behaviour or configured by a managing party. The UK then introduces a new autonomous UAV into the environment and in order to enable the UAV to function as part of the coalition, the UAV is required to learn a GPM such that it can generate policies that govern its behaviour in varying contexts, i.e. autonomously decide whether or not to service a request from another coalition party. Firstly, the UAV communicates with nearby assets to obtain annotated serviceability request logs. The UAV then constructs and solves an ASG that represents a GPM which can be used to generate a set of valid behaviours, i.e. requests that can be serviced within a given context. The demonstration shows the interaction with and querying of the generated policy in natural language whilst also explaining how the GPM can be used to generate a new set of valid behaviours given a different contextual environment. Figure 1 shows the UAV rejecting a serviceability request due to a no-fly zone, as indicated by its generated policy in this context. Having learned a GPM, the coalition can operate in a distributed manner, where assets can behave autonomously to service requests for various capabilities. Also, this can be extended to make use of a Software Defined

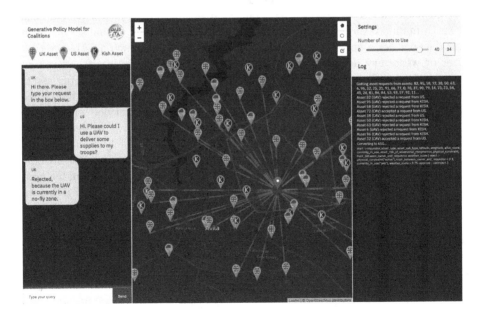

Fig. 1. Requesting use of a coalition partner's asset

Network to generate a coalition-wide policy that defines how different requests can be serviced by different coalition devices, without using a centralised asset management system.

4   Conclusions

This demonstration paper has presented a symbolic, ASG-based GPM applied to distributed coalition environments. The demonstration shows how real-time constraints that occur in the operating context such as adverse weather conditions, restricted operating capability and evolving trust relationships between coalition partners can be learned in order to generate policies for coalition devices to collaborate effectively in distributed environments.

Acknowledgments. This research was sponsored by the U.S. Army Research Laboratory and the U.K. Ministry of Defence under Agreement Number W911NF-16-3-0001. The views and conclusions contained in this document are those of the authors and should not be interpreted as representing the official policies, either expressed or implied, of the U.S. Army Research Laboratory, the U.S. Government, the U.K. Ministry of Defence or the U.K. Government. The U.S. and U.K. Governments are authorized to reproduce and distribute reprints for Government purposes notwithstanding any copyright notation hereon.

References

1. Bertino, E., Calo, S., Touma, M., Verma, D., Williams, C., Rivera, B.: A cognitive policy framework for next-generation distributed federated systems: concepts and research directions. In: The IEEE 37th International Conference on Distributed Computing Systems (ICDCS), pp. 1876–1886, June 2017. https://doi.org/10.1109/ICDCS.2017.78
2. Calo, S., Manotas, I., Verma, D., Bertino, E., Law, M., Russo, A.: AGENP: an ASGrammar-based GENerative policy framework. In: Calo, S., Bertino, E., Verma, D. (eds.) 2nd International Workshop on Policy-based Autonomic Data Governance, pp. 3–20. Springer, Cham (2018). https://doi.org/10.1007/978-3-030-17277-0_1
3. Cunnington, D., et al.: An answer set grammar-based generative policy model for connected and autonomous vehicles (2019, submitted for publication)
4. Cunnington, D., White, G., de Mel, G.: Synthetic ground truth for evaluating generative policy models. Submitted for review at International Conference on Smart Computing, DAIS Workshop 2019 (2019)
5. Defence, M.: Future operating environment 2035, December 2015. https://www.gov.uk/government/publications/future-operating-environment-2035
6. Law, M., Russo, A., Elisa, B., Krysia, B., Jorge, L.: Representing and learning grammars in answer set programming. In: The Thirty-Third AAAI Conference on Artificial Intelligence (AAAI-2019) (2019)
7. Verma, D., et al.: Generative policy model for autonomic management. In: IEEE SmartWorld, Ubiquitous Intelligence Computing, Advanced Trusted Computed, Scalable Computing Communications, Cloud Big Data Computing, Internet of People and Smart City Innovation, pp. 1–6 (2017)

An Agent-Swarm Simulator for Dynamic Vehicle Routing Problem Empirical Analysis

Nicola Falcionelli[✉], Paolo Sernani, Dagmawi Neway Mekuria,
and Aldo Franco Dragoni

Università Politecnica delle Marche, Ancona, Italy
{n.falcionelli,d.n.mekuria}@pm.univpm.it
{p.sernani,a.f.dragoni}@univpm.it

Abstract. This demo shows an empirical analysis of the Dynamic Vehicle Routing Problem in multiple configurations, within a agent-swarm optimization scenario. With the purpose of statistically evaluating how solutions to this problem evolve when varying gobal system parameters, an agent-swarm simulator has been implemented within the Netlogo framework, and used to extract experimental data.

Keywords: Vehicle Routing Problem · Optimization · Ant Colony · Meta heuristic · Simulator · Netlogo · Robots · Swarm robotics · Agents

1 Introduction

The Vehicle Routing Problem (VRP) is a class of problems in operations research, widely used in logistics for fleet management. In its most general configuration, it consists of minimizing the cost (e.g. time or distance) of serving one or more customers by one or more vehicles. Each vehicle has a limited capacity, and refers to one or more depot for replenishment. When the position of the customers nodes is not fixed, and not known a priori by the vehicles, the problem becomes known as the Dynamic Vehicle Routing Problem (DVRP) [4].

Finding global optimal solutions for (D)VRPs under realistic circumstances is usually intractable, having a NP-Hard complexity [6]. This opens the field to a whole research field of sub-optimal search strategies and heuristics that rely on constraint relaxation, simulated annealing, gradient descent variants and swarm intelligence. As opposed to intelligent agents capable of advanced reasoning [2,3], swarm intelligence harnesses the intelligent behaviour that emerges from the interaction of many, very simple agents. One of the most notable examples is the Ant Colony Optimization strategy [1], a nature-inspired meta-heuristic for finding optimal paths in graphs.

© Springer Nature Switzerland AG 2019
Y. Demazeau et al. (Eds.): PAAMS 2019, LNAI 11523, pp. 246–250, 2019.
https://doi.org/10.1007/978-3-030-24209-1_23

2   Main Purpose

In this setup of agent-based optimization, this demo introduces a simulator developed within the Netlogo framework [5] for analyzing the behaviour of an agent-swarm designed for solving a DVRP. Given the practical impossibility of doing so in a closed or in a globally optimal form, the main use of this simulator is to empirically show how changes in the overall system's parameters (e.g. the number of agents in the swarm) affect global fitness metrics. Differently from classical optimization problems, the simulator does not use graphs for data representation. Instead, it is based on a discrete 2-dimensional space, where traveling agents (TA) can freely move to serve as many customers as they can, until they run out of resources and have to go back to a depot for replenishment. Every TA can decide autonomously, in a completely distributed fashion, which customer it should target and where it should move, based on its own knowledge of the surroundings. It is important to highlight that the TAs do not interact with each other in any way, for example, not agreeing in advance who is going to serve which customer. Instead, the customers' positions are discovered dynamically as the TAs explore the 2-dimensional environment. If one or more customers happen to be inside a TA's field of view, and the TA has not yet run out of resources, it will follow the greedy policy of going towards the nearest customer. As soon as they run out of resources, the TA will point towards the depot, and start searching for new customers again. Then, when all the customers have been served, three overall fitness metrics can be computed:

- d, the distance covered by all TAs;
- t, the time needed for all the customers to be served;
- An overall cost $c = \alpha d + \beta t$, a linear combination of the previous metrics, where α and β are two normalization and weight constants.

By varying the system's parameters, the simulations allow to experimentally determine which are the most convienient configurations, and thereby, effectively enhance existing real-case fleets or help in making fleet management choices (i.e. how many vehicles, vehicles capacity, how many depots, etc.).

3   Demonstration

The entry point of the demo is the simulator's graphical user interface (see Fig. 1), from which a certain configuration can be setup by manually specifying the values for the set of parameters, together with other general settings (visualization, simulation speed, etc.). Once done with the parameters initialization, a simulation can be launched, and the graphical components representing the 2-dimensional space, the physical entities (i.e. TAs, obstacles, depots) and abstract features (i.e. TA's remaining resources and field of view) will be displayed/updated accordingly. The customizable aspects of the system have been organized in two main groups:

- *Physical features*, that include the total number of TAs, the TA's loading capacity and the number of depots;
- *Smart features*, which comprehend TA's angle of vision, depth of vision, and the ability to keep memory of previously encountered customers (that they could not serve) over the 2-dimensional space.

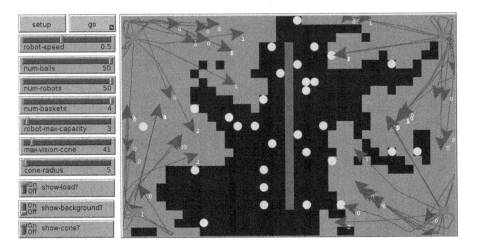

Fig. 1. Simulator GUI showing tunable parameters and graphical counterparts of TAs (arrows), customers (circles), viewed cells (green), obstacles (red), load (white numbers) and depots (grey boxes). (Color figure online)

The setup and running phases can also be performed automatically, by exploiting the Netlogo BehaviourSpace functionality. It allowed to effectively script the simulations, define parameter ranges, and to obtain an extensive configuration-space analysis. From an experimental point of view, Smart and Physical features have been treated as two independent sets of discrete variables. This led to the definition of two separate experiments, in which global metrics have been measured after separately varying Physical or Smart features values. This assumption of variable independence was indeed necessary in order to make the results both more graphically readable and to avoid combinatorial explosion of possible configurations (due to the cartesian product of the parameters' ranges). Results of the configuration-space analysis are shown in heatmaps (see Figs. 2 and 3): every point represents the average of a fitness metric across 10 repetitions with a particular parameter's combination.

4   Conclusion

This demo introduced an agent-swarm simulator for solving and analyzing the DVRP within different configurations. After defining such configurations in

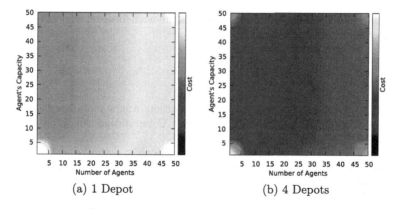

(a) 1 Depot   (b) 4 Depots

Fig. 2. Physical Features tests. The other parameters are kept constant.

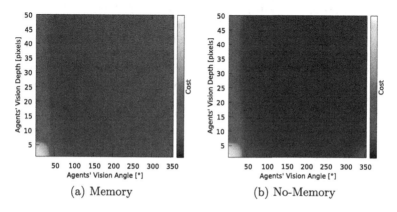

(a) Memory   (b) No-Memory

Fig. 3. Smart features tests. The other parameters are kept constant.

terms of parameters, and proposing fitness metrics, experimental data have been extracted and used to have an understanding of how the agent-swarm behaves.

More precisely, heathmaps in Fig. 2 show how the cost metric c changes with respect to variations on the number of TAs, the TAs' capacity and the number of depots. As expected, the case with 4 depots show overall better performance than the other, and how TAs do not need a big capacity in order to obtain good solutions. In this case, the fact of having many TAs is more important than a large storage capacity. Anyway, the number of TAs cannot be arbitrarily large, as the global distance d (which is part of the overall cost metric c) will grow as well. In the case of 1 depot, the best configuration turned out to be a single TA with the largest capacity.

Heatmaps in Fig. 3 show the effects of changing vision and memory features. They both highlight how the vision angle is predominant over the vision depth, and good performance can be obtained with relatively low vision capabilities. It is surprising to see that the memory feature does not always have a significant impact, but turns out to be more useful with limited vision capabilities (especially with low vision angles).

References

1. Dorigo, M., Di Caro, G.: Ant colony optimization: a new meta-heuristic. In: Proceedings of the 1999 Congress on Evolutionary Computation, vol. 2, pp. 1470–1477. IEEE (1999)
2. Falcionelli, N., et al.: Indexing the event calculus: towards practical human-readable personal health systems. Artif. Intell. Med. **96**, 154–166 (2019). https://doi.org/10.1016/j.artmed.2018.10.003. http://www.sciencedirect.com/science/article/pii/S0933365717305948
3. Mekuria, D.N., Sernani, P., Falcionelli, N., Dragoni, A.F.: Reasoning in multi-agent based smart homes: a systematic literature review. In: Leone, A., Caroppo, A., Rescio, G., Diraco, G., Siciliano, P. (eds.) ForItAAL 2018. LNEE, vol. 544, pp. 161–179. Springer, Cham (2019). https://doi.org/10.1007/978-3-030-05921-7_13
4. Pillac, V., Gendreau, M., Guret, C., Medaglia, A.L.: A review of dynamic vehicle routing problems. Eur. J. Oper. Res. **225**(1), 1–11 (2013)
5. Tisue, S., Wilensky, U.: Netlogo: a simple environment for modeling complexity. In: International Conference on Complex Systems, vol. 21, pp. 16–21, Boston, MA (2004)
6. Toth, P., Vigo, D.: The vehicle routing problem. In: SIAM (2002)

Heráclito: Intelligent Tutoring System for Logic

Fabiane Flores Penteado Galafassi[✉], Cristiano Galafassi,
Rosa Maria Vicari, and João Carlos Gluz

Federal University of Rio Grande do Sul, Porto Alegre, RS, Brazil
fabiane.penteado@gmail.com,
cristianogalafassi@gmail.com, rosa@inf.urfgs.br,
jcgluz@gmail.com

Abstract. The present article aims to present the Heraclito environment that has in the Logical Studies and Exercises Logic (LOGOS) an important tool. The Heraclito environment assists students in solving various types of Logic exercises and provides the LOGOS Electronic Notebook to create and edit formulas, truth tables and proofs of Propositional Logic. The LOGOS Electronic Notebook is compatible with tablets, smartphones and PCs. It is currently being used with 1st and 2nd year undergraduate students in curricula in the scientific and technological areas. In addition, the Heraclito environment has an Intelligent Tutor System based on Multiagent Systems that identifies the individual knowledge of each student in the context of Natural Deduction in Propositional Logic.

Keywords: Intelligent Tutor System · Propositional Logic · Formula Editor · Test editor and true tables

1 Introduction

The discipline of Formal Logic is of great importance for the curriculum of the scientific and technological areas (generally grouped under the English acronym STEM - Science, Technology, Engineering, and Mathematics) and is usually offered between the 1st and 2nd semester of the graduation. Considered fundamental in the training of students, it enables the development of the skills of logical analysis, formalization and problem solving. These skills, which in turn are necessary for understanding the various contents and activities found in this curriculum.

Empirical studies indicate serious difficulties encountered by students in assimilating the concepts of this discipline. These studies point to high rates in terms of disappointments and mainly dropouts, leading to higher than expected student retention. These dropouts, in particular, tend to occur at the beginning of the discipline, especially when the contents of Natural Deduction began to be approached in the context of Propositional Logic [1]. In practice, the difficulties begin when concepts like formula, rule of deduction and formal proof begin to be presented. In order to contribute to the improvement of these indexes, the dialectical methodology of teaching (socio-historical approach used in the classroom) was associated to a computer mediation model, modeled on an ITS, which was called Environment Heráclito.

© Springer Nature Switzerland AG 2019
Y. Demazeau et al. (Eds.): PAAMS 2019, LNAI 11523, pp. 251–254, 2019.
https://doi.org/10.1007/978-3-030-24209-1_24

In this sense, the Electronic Notebook LOGOS made available by the Heráclito environment is composed of two editors: the Formula Editor and Truth Tables Editor and the Proof Logic Editor. The editors also have the support of a tutor (online) in this exercise resolution process. The environment stands out from other Logic teaching environments in three fundamental aspects: (a) a complete adherence to Dialectic and Historical Partners principles in the implementation of mediation and mentoring processes; (b) an adaptive and flexible student model; (c) a complete support for the teaching of the formal concepts of Propositional Logic.

2 Main Purpose

The Heraclito Environment was made possible through the OBAAMILOS project and consists of an STI focused on the teaching of Logic. Its development was based on a study carried out through tools to support the teaching of logic, including theorem provers, verifiers/editors of formal tests and tutors' systems found in the literature. Its main objective is to help students solve exercises that need to calculate the logical value of a formula, through truth table exercises and argumentation exercises through the rules of Natural Deduction. In order to do so, it provides the Logical Electronic Exercise Logbook - LOGOS which, besides providing two editors, also counts on the pedagogical support of a tutor in the accompaniment and development of the exercises (step-by-step).

The Heraclito environment was developed through the use of agent technology for pedagogical purposes. These agents are responsible for the interaction of the student/tutor/environment assisting in the development of the resolution of the exercises indicating correct, incorrect and not recommended paths during the course of the test. The tutorial service aims to help the student in the step-by-step of solving the exercises, playing the role of the teacher. All interaction of the student/tutor/environment is monitored, and the actions recorded serve to determine the actions of the tutoring service. This service uses a set of learning strategies, built specifically for Logic, based on classroom experiences. If the student is unable to advance in a test, for example, he has the option to use the help button to ask for tips, examples or what the next step is to take. This Help option can be triggered at any point in the exercise.

3 Demonstration

The LOGOS Electronic Notebook of the Heráclito environment can be used in online mode, with the support of the tutoring service, or in offline mode, as a visiting user, but without the tutoring. For online mode you need to log in to the environment. On the home page you can register and log in (in a few steps, which are "name", "last name", "email" and "password"). After login or access as a visitor to the environment, the electronic notebook LOGOS and its editors are presented. The Logic studies and exercises notebook offers the user the Formulas and Truths Editor and the Propositional Logic Proof Editor. Also, the environment also provides Sects. 1 and 2 in the E-book format of Introduction to Propositional Logic of teachers Gluz and Py [7] (Fig. 1).

Fig. 1. LOGOS.

The Proposed Logic Proof Editor has the main functionality of assisting in the elaboration of proofs of formal arguments through the rules of Natural Deduction (DNLP). The edition of the tests offers two types of options for resolution of the exercise (see Fig. 2).

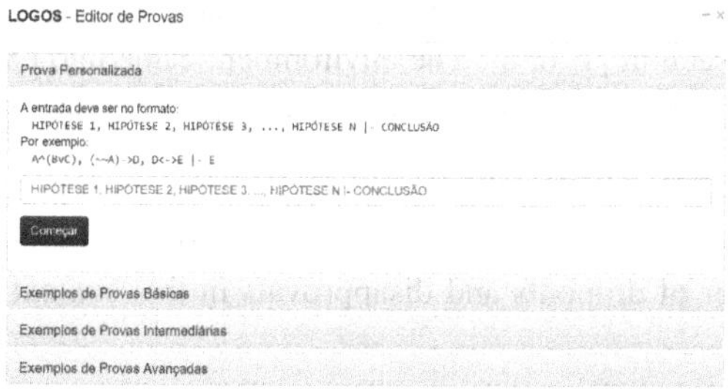

Fig. 2. Proposed logical proofreader interface.

In Personalized Test the student can enter his hypothesis and conclusion and start the exercise. In the interface of the proof editor the argument should be typed as shown in the example above HYPOTHESIS1, HYPOTHESIS 2, HYPOTHESIS 3, … HYPOTHESIS N | - CONCLUSION in the data entry field for the new test and click Begin. The following is Fig. 3 that present the insertions of the hypotheses and the edition of the rules of deduction.

Fig. 3. Interfaces of insertion of hypotheses and edition of rules of deduction in Propositional Logic.

The second option is to choose an exercise sample from the list with pre-selected tests that are sorted by difficulty levels: Basic Tests, Intermediate Tests and Advanced Tests. The application and operation of each rule of inference are best described and detailed in the user guide of the LOGOS (manual) notebook. The guide can also be accessed through the environment when logged in [9].

4 Conclusions

The Electronic Notebook LOGOS of the teaching environment Heráclito, presented in this article aims to help students learn concepts of Propositional Logic. Empirical experiments conducted with this environment show that the possibility of aid is real and that, in addition, the environment is being well accepted by students. The results of these experiments, as well as other productions related to this environment and its components can be seen in [1, 6, 8]. The environment came into experimental use and can be accessed and used by any student at: http://labsim.unipampa.edu.br:8080/ heraclito/ [9].

In developing and adapting the Heraclito environment, it is hoped to contribute not only to a better understanding of the contents covered in the Logic discipline, but also to reduce the number of dropouts and disapprovals in this context.

References

1. Galafassi, F.F.P.: Agente Pedagógico para Mediação do Processo de Ensino-Aprendizagem da Dedução Natural na Lógica Proposicional. Master Thesis. UNISINOS (2012)
2. FIPA-ACL. "FIPA ACL Message Structure Specification". Foundation for Intelligent Physical Agents. Disponível em. http://www.fipa.org/specs/fipa00061/SC00061G.html. Accessed 30 Mar 2019
3. Bellifemine, F., Caire, G., Greenwood, D.: Developing multi-agent systems with JADE. In: Wooldridge, M. (ed.) Wiley Series in Agent Technology, Liverpool University, UK (2007)
4. Bordini, R.H., Hübner, J.F., Wooldridge, M.: Programming Multi-Agent Systems in Agent Speak using Jason, vol. 8. Wiley, Hoboken (2007)
5. Galafassi, P.F.F., Santos, A.V., Peres, R.K., Vicari, R.M., Gluz, J.C.: Multi-plataform interface to an ITS of proposicional logic teaching. In: 13 International Conference on Practical Applications of Agents and Multi-Agent Systems, 2015, Salamanca. Highlights of Practical Applications of Agents, Multi-Agent Systems, and Sustainability - The PAAMS Collection, vol. 524, pp. 309–319 (2015)
6. Gluz, J.C., Bueno, R., Peres, R.K., Galafassi, P.F.F.: Tutoria Inteligente Completa para os Conceitos Formais da Lógica Proposicional: Experimentos e Resultados. VI Congresso Brasileiro de Informática na Educação (CBIE 2017). In: Proceedings of the XXVIII Brazilian Symposium of Informatics in Education (2017)
7. Gluz, J.C., Py, M.: Lógica para Computação. Coleção EAD. Editora Unisinos (2010)
8. ISELab - Laboratório de Engenharia de Softwares Inteligentes. Projeto Heráclito: Ambiente Inteligente de Ensino de Lógica. http://obaa.unisinos.br/drupal7/?q=node/25. Accessed 30 Mar 2019
9. AMBIENTE HERÁCLITO. http://labsim.unipampa.edu.br:8080/heraclito/. Accessed 30 Mar 2019

Demonstration of Multiagent Reinforcement Learning Applied to Traffic Light Signal Control

Carolina Higuera[1(✉)] , Fernando Lozano[2] , Edgar Camilo Camacho[1] ,
and Carlos Hernando Higuera[3]

[1] Universidad Santo Tomás, Bogotá, Colombia
{carolinahiguera,edgarcamacho}@usantotomas.edu.co
[2] Universidad de los Andes, Bogotá, Colombia
flozano@uniandes.edu.co
[3] Universidad Pedagógica y Tecnológica de Colombia, Tunja, Colombia
carlos.higuera@uptc.edu.co

Abstract. We present a demonstration of two coordination methods for the application of multiagent reinforcement learning to the problem of traffic light signal control to decrease travel time. The first approach that we tested exploits the fact that the reward function can be splitted into contributions per agent. The second method computes the best response for a two player game with each member of its neighborhood. We apply both learning methods through SUMO traffic simulator, using data from the Transit Department of Bogotá, Colombia.

Keywords: Adaptive traffic light signal control · Best response · Coordination graphs · Multiagent reinforcement learning

1 Introduction

In this work, we test solutions to decrease travel times based on multiagent reinforcement learning, modeling the problem as a multiagent Markov Decision Process (MDP). A collection of agents learns to minimize vehicle queuing delays and queue lengths at all junctions. Coordination between agents is done in two different ways. In the first approach (Q-VE) agents are modeled as vertices in a coordination graph and the joint action is found with the variable elimination algorithm. The second method (Q-BR) computes the action for an agent as the best response of a two player game with each member of its neighborhood.

2 Main Purpose

Multiagent RL for traffic light control allows to split the global function Q into a linear combination for each agent. However, decisions made at the individual

© Springer Nature Switzerland AG 2019
Y. Demazeau et al. (Eds.): PAAMS 2019, LNAI 11523, pp. 255–258, 2019.
https://doi.org/10.1007/978-3-030-24209-1_25

level must be optimal for the group. Hence, the problem of coordination is to find at each step the joint action:

$$\mathbf{a}^* = \underset{\mathbf{a}' \in \mathcal{A}}{\operatorname{argmax}} Q(\mathbf{s}^k, \mathbf{a}') \tag{1}$$

2.1 Coordination Graphs - (Q-VE)

In a coordination graph, $G = (\mathcal{V}, \mathcal{E})$ agent $i \in \mathcal{V}$ needs to coordinate its actions with its neighbors $\Gamma(i) = \{j : (i, j) \in \mathcal{E}\}$. Given the action $\mathbf{a}^*$ and joint state s_{ij}^k, we update the factors Q_{ij} for each edge $(i, j) \in \mathcal{E}$ with:

$$Q_{ij}(s_{ij}^{k-1}, a_{ij}^{k-1}) := (1 - \alpha)Q_{ij}(s_{ij}^{k-1}, a_{ij}^{k-1})$$
$$+ \alpha \left[\frac{r_i^k}{|\Gamma(i)|} + \frac{r_j^k}{|\Gamma(j)|} + \gamma Q_{ij}(s_{ij}^{\ k}, a_{ij}^{\ *}) \right]$$

To find the optimal joint action $\mathbf{a}^*$ in (1), we use the variable elimination algorithm (VE) proposed by Gaustrin *et al.* [3].

2.2 Best Response from Game Theory - (Q-BR)

We follow the work done by El-Tantawy *et al.* in [2], in which each agent participates in a two player game with its neighborhood $\Gamma(i)$. Agent i creates and updates a model θ that estimates the likelihood of action selection for each neighbor $j \in \Gamma(i)$.

To find the best joint action, $\mathbf{a}^*$, each agents computes its best response, which is the action that maximizes the Q factor at their neighborhood level, regardless of the policies of other members:

$$a_i^* = \underset{a_i \in \mathcal{A}_i}{\operatorname{argmax}} \left[\sum_{j \in \Gamma(i)} \sum_{a_j \in \mathcal{A}_j} Q_{ij}\left(s_{ij}^k, a_{ij}\right) \times \theta_{ij}\left(s_{ij}^k, a_j\right) \right] \tag{2}$$

2.3 Learning Parameters

The state vector for each agent has the hour to include temporal dynamic; the maximum queue length (in vehicles) in all edges, and the queuing delay (in minutes) of stopped vehicles in every edge. Regarding the actions, all agents have two phases. Finally, the reward function encourages short queue lengths and waiting time experienced by the vehicles throughout the road.

$$r_i = - \sum_{k=1}^{edges} \beta_q (q_k)^{\theta_q} + \beta_w (w_k)^{\theta_w} \quad \forall i \in \mathcal{N} \tag{3}$$

Where, *edges* is the number of approaches of agent i. q_k and w_k are the maximum queue length and queuing delay in edge k. β_q and β_w are coefficients to set priority. θ_q and θ_w balance queue lengths and waiting times across approaches.

3   Demonstration

Both methods were simulated in a network of Bogotá, as shown in Fig. 1 through the SUMO simulator [4] and the TraCI environment. To compare Q-VE and Q-BR methods, we implement independent Q-learning as proposed by Camponogara *et al.* in [1] and, the coordination method proposed by Xu *et al.* in [5].

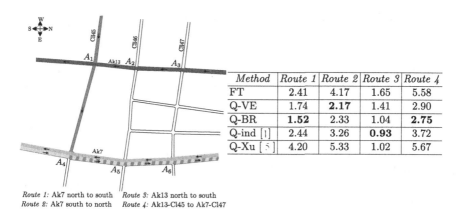

Method	Route 1	Route 2	Route 3	Route 4
FT	2.41	4.17	1.65	5.58
Q-VE	1.74	**2.17**	1.41	2.90
Q-BR	**1.52**	2.33	1.04	**2.75**
Q-ind [1]	2.44	3.26	**0.93**	3.72
Q-Xu [5]	4.20	5.33	1.02	5.67

Route 1: Ak7 north to south   *Route 3:* Ak13 north to south
Route 2: Ak7 south to north   *Route 4:* Ak13-Cl45 to Ak7-Cl47

Fig. 1. Test framework for multiagent traffic control

Q-VE and Q-BR achieve reductions of at least 14% and at most 48% with respect to Fixed Time. The largest reductions are obtained with Q-BR. We note that Q-BR policy generates green waves along arterials, as show in Fig. 2.

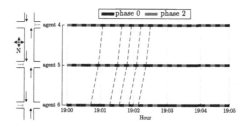

Fig. 2. Space-time diagram for route 1, Ak7 north to south, with Q-BR policy. At some intervals, agents 4, 5 and 6 coordinate their actions to generate a platoon.

In Fig. 3 we found that the reward evolution with independent learning is very similar to the one obtained by the coordinated method Q-BR. Nonetheless, the policy learned by Q-BR positively influence other variables that are not included in the reward function.

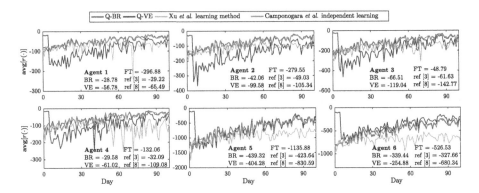

Fig. 3. Agents learning curves. With Q-VE and Q-BR it was achieved a better reward in comparison with FT control.

4   Conclusions

Distributing the reward function into contribution per agent simplifies the problem, since the Q factors can be splitted into dependencies between agents. This is represented by the coordination graphs, which are favorable for the application of the VE algorithm. This method allows an exact solution to the joint action selection problem. However, as the algorithm eliminates agents, neighborhoods change and may include ones that are not adjacent, thus, may not have direct communication. The method would require an estimation of the Q factors for nonadjacent agents.

On the other hand, the coordination strategy based on BR presents good scalability, due to communication between agents is known a priori. However, policies in the neighborhood are not shared knowledge, so a greater transmission of information is required to estimate and model the behavior of neighbors.

References

1. Camponogara, E., Kraus Jr., W.: Distributed learning agents in urban traffic control. In: Pires, F.M., Abreu, S. (eds.) EPIA 2003. LNCS (LNAI), vol. 2902, pp. 324–335. Springer, Heidelberg (2003). https://doi.org/10.1007/978-3-540-24580-3_38
2. El-Tantawy, S., Abdulhai, B., Abdelgawad, H.: Multiagent reinforcement learning for integrated network of adaptive traffic signal controllers (MARLIN-ATSC): methodology and large-scale application on downtown toronto. IEEE Trans. Intell. Transp. Syst. **14**(3), 1140–1150 (2013). https://doi.org/10.1109/TITS.2013.2255286
3. Guestrin, C., Koller, D., Parr, R.: Multiagent planning with factored MDPs. In: NIPS-14, pp. 1523–1530. The MIT Press (2001)
4. Krajzewicz, D., Erdmann, J., Behrisch, M., Bieker, L.: Recent development and applications of SUMO - Simulation of Urban MObility. Int. J. Adv. Syst. Measure. **5**(3&4), 128–138 (2012)
5. Xu, L.H., Xia, X.H., Luo, Q.: The study of reinforcement learning for traffic self-adaptive control under multiagent Markov game environment. Math. Probl. Eng. **2013**, e962869 (2013). https://doi.org/10.1155/2013/962869

Modular and Self-organized Conveyor System Using Multi-agent Systems

Paulo Leitão and José Barbosa[✉]

Research Centre in Digitalization and Intelligent Robotics (CeDRI),
Instituto Politécnico de Bragança,
Campus de Santa Apolónia, 5300-253 Bragança, Portugal
{pleitao,jbarbosa}@ipb.pt

Abstract. This paper describes the implementation of a modular, flexible and self-organized cyber-physical conveyor system build up with different individual modular and intelligent transfer modules. For this purpose, multi-agent systems (MAS) is used to distribute intelligence among transfer modules supporting plugability and modularity, complemented with self-organization capabilities to achieve a truly self-reconfigurable system.

Keywords: Multi-agent systems · Cyber-physical systems ·
Self-organization

1 Introduction

Cyber-physical systems constitute the backbone to implement the Industry 4.0 principles. CPS is emergent approach that focuses on the integration of computational applications with physical devices, being designed as a network of interacting cyber and physical counterparts to form a large system [3]. Multi-agent systems (MAS), based on its inherent capabilities to distributed intelligence and adapt to emergence without external intervention, is suitable to implement such industrial CPS. In particular, MAS distributes the intelligence among cloud and edge nodes to allow achieving more reactive and self-organized systems facing the condition change and reconfiguration.

The objective of this paper is to describe the implementation of a modular and self-organized conveyor system that uses MAS, enhanced with self-organization techniques, as enabler for its operation and reconfiguration. This system demonstrates the potential benefits of using distributed artificial intelligence methods in the development of modular, flexible, adaptive and reconfigured industrial solutions.

The rest of the paper is organized as follows. Section 2 describes the main purpose of the MAS demonstration work and Sect. 3 presents the demonstration itself, namely referring the development of a modular CPS conveyor system using MAS technology, the enhanced of the agent-based system with self-organization

© Springer Nature Switzerland AG 2019
Y. Demazeau et al. (Eds.): PAAMS 2019, LNAI 11523, pp. 259–263, 2019.
https://doi.org/10.1007/978-3-030-24209-1_26

capabilities to face the on-the-fly reconfiguration, and the modular and self-organized conveyor system working in practice. Finally Sect. 4 rounds up the paper with the conclusions.

2   Main Purpose

The problem considered in this work is related to a conveyor transfer system comprising a sequence of modular conveyors, where each individual one comprises 1 motor and 2 light sensors (to detect parts in the input and output positions), as illustrated in Fig. 1.

Fig. 1. Requirements of the modular conveyor transfer system

The parts are transferred among the conveyor modules from the input location (at the first module) to the output location (at the last module). The transfer between two consecutive transfer modules is performed in the following manner (see Fig. 1): (i) conveyor C1 only stops its motor when the part arrives to the sensor S1, and (ii) conveyor C2 starts its motor when the part arrives to sensor S0. This modus operanti establishes interdependencies between transfer modules that increases the complexity of the problem since it is necessary to know the sequence of transfer modules. The question is how to implement the control system for such modular and reconfigurable transfer system?

The traditional approach is to use a centralized logical control based on an IEC 61131-3 program running in a PLC (Programmable Logic Controller). This solution is simple to program and is industrial adopted. However, it presents limitation in terms of scalability and reconfigurability, and the existing interdependencies among conveyors increase the development complexity. Particularly, what happen if we need to swap the order of the conveyors or add a new conveyor?

Having this in mind, an alternative design approach to support the easy and on-the-fly reconfiguration of the conveyor system should be considered. The use of MAS principles allows to create a CPS based on several modular Cyber-Physical Components (CPC) that can reach the plugability and reconfigurability on-the-fly if enhanced with self-organization techniques.

3   Demonstration

3.1   Building a Modular CPS Conveyor System

Each individual conveyor module is composed by the physical conveyor, a mini computer capable of running agents, particularly a Raspberry Pi, and an interface board which goal is to make the voltage logical conversion between the conveyor and the mini-computer operation levels.

The control logic of the module is achieved by the internal behaviour of the intelligent software agent, which is continuously acquiring the signals from the physical conveyor, i.e. its sensors, and is controlling the motor action. The aggregation of agent with the mini-computer and the physical device constitutes a CPC, as depicted in Fig. 2, which posteriorly form a cyber-physical conveyor system by the emergence of several CPCs. At this stage, the work presented in [1] has been developed in the sense that all the logical functions and approach were kept but the system power supply was re-designed into a battery power module, increasing the mobility and pluggability of each module.

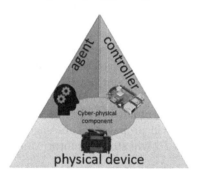

Fig. 2. Cyber-physical conveyor component

The agents running locally in the Raspberry Pis were developed by using the JADE framework [2]. Since the several conveyor modules have the same behaviour, all instantiated agents are from the same class type and execute the same logical behaviour, simplifying the deployment into different modules batch sizes. Agents are communicating using the well-known FIPA-ACL standard and messages are being exchanged using the WiFi capability of the Raspberry Pi.

3.2   Enhancing Self-organization Capabilities

In such modular conveyor transfer systems, where there is not a predefined sequence of modules, the agents need to determine, individually, its position in the sequence for a proper transfer operation. This is more important when a change in the conveyor system occurs, e.g., addition, removal or swap of modules. The MAS technology allows to implement a modular cyber-physical conveyor system, but a step further is required to reach a completely adaptiveness and reconfigurability.

For this purpose, self-organization techniques were embedded into the agents' behaviour. Self-organization can be described as the ability of an entity or system to adapt its behaviour to external changing conditions without any central entity interference. Several examples of such mechanisms can be found, in nature, offering inspiration to adapt and deploy into the present situation, e.g. ants or bees food foraging behaviour.

In the present work, a simple but efficient self-organization mechanism was developed and deployed, consisting in the transmission of tokens among the agents, similarly to the token passage mechanism in a $4 \times 100\,\mathrm{m}$ relay run.

3.3   Self-organized Conveyor System Working in Practice

Briefly, each cyber-physical conveyor is initiated without the knowledge of its position. Whenever a part reaches a conveyor input sensor, the agent will initiate the conveyor movement by starting the electrical motor. If the agent associated with the conveyor has no previous knowledge of its position, i.e. doesn't have a *position ID*, it will assume that it is the first of the system, assigning itself the first *position ID*. After this, whenever the conveyed part reaches the output sensor, the agent will propagate a message with its *position ID* to the other agents, i.e. it will pass the *token*. The conveyor which *position ID* equals the *token + 1* will start its motor to receive the part. In case that a given conveyor does not know its position, i.e. does not have a *position ID*, it will also start its motor in order to detect if it is the next conveyor in the system. Also, each time a part reaches the input sensor of a cyber-physical conveyor, besides to start the electrical motor, the agent will propagate a message with its *position ID*. The agent that has the *previous ID* will stop its motor, similarly to release the token to the next runner.

A video showing the system operation is located at http://youtu.be/HMG2_tTGk20. Here it is possible to observe all the aforementioned features with the capability to support the addition, removal and swap of the conveyor order on-the-fly.

Fig. 3. Cyber-physical conveyor system running in practice.

The presented approach shows how the use of multi-agent systems, enhanced with self-organization capabilities, allows to design and deploy industrial complex large-scale systems, exhibiting plugability and reconfigurability on-the-fly.

4 Conclusions

MAS is an enabler to develop industrial CPS due to its capability to distribute intelligence by a society of autonomous control nodes. The combination of MAS and self-organization techniques allow the development of industrial modular and reconfigurable solutions, aligned with the Industry 4.0 principles. This paper describes the implementation of a modular and self-organized conveyor system that uses MAS, enhanced with self-organization techniques, as enabler for its operation and reconfiguration.

References

1. Barbosa, J., Leitão, P., Teixeira, J.: Empowering a cyber-physical system for a modular conveyor system with self-organization. In: Borangiu, T., Trentesaux, D., Thomas, A., Cardin, O. (eds.) Service Orientation in Holonic and Multi-Agent Manufacturing. SCI, vol. 762, pp. 157–170. Springer, Cham (2018). https://doi.org/10.1007/978-3-319-73751-5_12
2. Bellifemine, F., Caire, G., Greenwood, D.: Developing Multi-agent Systems with JADE. Wiley, Hoboken (2007)
3. Leitão, P., Karnouskos, S., Colombo, A.: Industrial automation based on cyber-physical systems technologies: prototype implementations and challenges. Comput. Ind. **81**, 11–25 (2016)

Multi-agent Coordination for Data Gathering with Periodic Requests and Deliveries

Yaroslav Marchukov$^{(\boxtimes)}$ and Luis Montano$^{(\boxtimes)}$

Instituto de Investigación en Ingeniería de Aragon (I3A),
University of Zaragoza, C/Mariano Esquillor, s/n, 50018 Zaragoza, Spain
{yamar,montano}@unizar.es

Abstract. In this demo work we develop a method to plan and coordinate a multi-agent team to gather information on demand. The data is periodically requested by a static Operation Center (OC) from changeable goals locations. The mission of the team is to reach these locations, taking measurements and delivering the data to the OC. Due to the limited communication range as well as signal attenuation because of the obstacles, the agents must travel to the OC, to upload the data. The agents can play two roles: ones as workers gathering data, the others as collectors traveling invariant paths for collecting the data of the workers to re-transmit it to the OC. The refreshing time of the delivered information depends on the number of available agents as well as of the scenario. The proposed algorithm finds out the best balance between the number of collectors-workers and the partition of the scenario into working areas in the planning phase, which provides the minimum refreshing time and will be the one executed by the agents.

Keywords: Multi-agent system · Data gathering · Connectivity constraints

1 Main Purpose

Data gathering and delivering by multi-agent systems using collectors have been dealt with in the literature. In [1] the collectors are permanently connected to the central server, they do not need to go to a depot point. In patrolling missions [4], the agents restrict the motion to some locations or areas, or moving the collectors to pre-fixed rendezvous points as in [3]. In this new proposal, we make more flexible the movement of the workers towards their goals, which change in every cycle, and to the collectors. Likewise, the workers establish their meeting area to synchronize with the collectors, dynamically computed, according to the amount of data to share.

© Springer Nature Switzerland AG 2019
Y. Demazeau et al. (Eds.): PAAMS 2019, LNAI 11523, pp. 264–268, 2019.
https://doi.org/10.1007/978-3-030-24209-1_27

2   Demonstration

This demo work describes in an illustrative manner the operation of our algorithm proposed in [2], using a team of 20 agents. All the agents are initially located near to the OC, having connectivity with it. The algorithm proceeds in two steps:

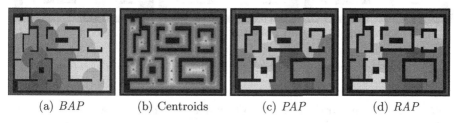

(a) *BAP*   (b) Centroids   (c) *PAP*   (d) *RAP*

Fig. 1. Segmentation procedures. (b) depicts the centroids initialization for *PAP-RAP*

1. Planning the deployment: (1) splitting the scenario into working areas for the workers, finding out the best balance of collectors-workers, Fig. 1; (2) computing the trajectories of the collectors and associating the workers to share their data, Fig. 2. It is a decentralized algorithm that can be executed by the OC or by some of the agents. It is executed offline, previously to deploy the team. The information of the deployment mission is shared between the agents. The first batch of goals are assigned to the workers.
2. Executing the best plan: the trajectories of the workers are planed and executed to visit the goals of their segments, to synchronize with the OC or with a collector in movement, Fig. 4(a). They start the mission going to their respective segments. Then, the plan is executed online by the workers when they visit their assigned goals each gathering cycle.

Fast Marching Method (FMM) [5] is used in different parts of the algorithm, solving the scenario segmentation and path planning for workers and collectors.

2.1   Planning the Deployment

The best ratio collectors-workers is computed for the scenario. The algorithm plans the mission in two steps for each collectors-workers balance.

Scenario Segmentation. First, the scenario is divided into N_w working areas for the same number of workers. The algorithm tests different partitions using three different segmentation algorithms based on FMM method, depicted in Fig. 1: Balanced Area Partition (*BAP*), Polygonal Area Partition (*PAP*), and Room-like Area Partition (*RAP*). *BAP* method uses FMM, extending N_w wavefront until cover all the free space. *PAP* and *RAP* routines consist of two phases: initialization of N_w centroids in areas distant from obstacles, Fig. 1(b), and then moving these centroids, balancing the distances between them. In the case of *RAP* the wavefront is expanded in such a way that the resulting segments fit better the shape of the rooms.

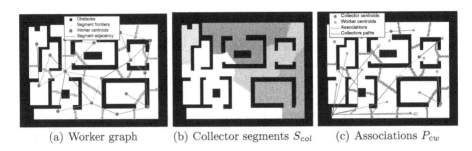

(a) Worker graph   (b) Collector segments S_{col} (c) Associations P_{cw}

Fig. 2. Collectors' computation 20 agents, 4 collectors and 16 workers, using PAP.

Collectors' Paths and Associations with Workers. The collectors paths and the associations to communicate with the workers are depicted in Fig. 2. Firstly, the algorithm obtains the adjacency graph for the centroids of the segments, Fig. 2(a). Secondly, an iterative procedure groups the working segments to compute the segments of the collectors for workers-collectors association, taking into account the shape of the worker's segments, Fig. 2(b). Third, the paths of the collectors from the OC are obtained, balancing the time of the collectors and of the workers estimated trajectories, Fig. 2(c).

2.2   Executing the Plan

The time devoted by each worker in its associated segment during the execution of the plan depends on the goals to be visited and on the cycle time of its collector. That time is computed to maximize the number of goals to be delivered to the collector or to the OC in the current cycle, Fig. 4(a). The workers' trajectories and the area in which they have to synchronize with the collector in movement are computed every cycle according to that objective.

2.3   Selecting the Best Solution

The method selects in the planning phase the best configuration represented by the kind of segmentation (BAP,PAP,RAP) and the ratio collectors-workers by means of a Utility function U. It balances the number of delivered goals and their refreshing time at the OC. It is computed as $U = \alpha(1-T_{refresh})+\beta N_{goals}$, being $T_{refresh}$ and N_{goals} normalized values. The weighting factors have been set to $\alpha = \beta = 0.5$, giving the same priority to both terms. The refreshing times Fig. 3(a), the delivered goals Fig. 3(b), and the utilities combining both Fig. 3(c), have been computed for $N = 20$ agents and for 0 to 8 collectors. In the planning phase, U is estimated to obtain the best configuration to be executed afterwards. In the figures bands between minimum and maximum values are also shown for several real executions, in order to analyze how well the estimated values had been computed. Figure 4(a) depicts the evolution of the trajectories and synchronization of a worker and a collector during the mission. A snapshot

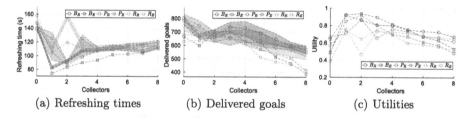

(a) Refreshing times   (b) Delivered goals   (c) Utilities

Fig. 3. Values estimated by the planner (E) and in the real executions (R). The letters B, P, R in the legends refer to BAP, PAP, RAP methods respectively.

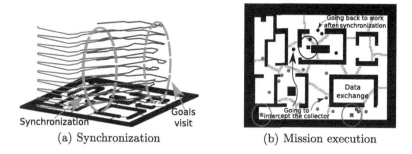

(a) Synchronization   (b) Mission execution

Fig. 4. Mission execution. In (a), blue and red lines are a worker and its collector trajectories, respectively. (b) shows a snapshot of a mission execution for PAP and 2 collectors (blue and black squares), the red square OC, and the circular workers associated to each of them (the same colour as the corresponding collector). (Color figure online)

of the execution for the best obtained plan is represented in Fig. 4(b) and a simulation can be found in the link[1].

3 Conclusions

This work allows to conclude that using some agents in the role of collectors for uploading the information at OC is more efficient that directly moving all the agents to the OC, considering the balance between the refreshing time and the number of delivered goals. The best number of collectors is found within a range 1–4, being the BAP and PAP segmentation methods the best ones depending on the scenario characteristics (see [2] for details). The Room-like partition RAP, which is extensively used for SLAM problems, appears as the worst solution for solving the stated deployment problem.

Acknowledgments. This research has been funded by project DPI2016-76676-R-AEI/FEDER-UE and by research grant BES-2013-067405 of MINECO-FEDER, and by project Grupo DGA-T45-17R/FSE.

---

[1] http://robots.unizar.es/data/videos/paams19yamar/demo.mp4.

References

1. Guo, M., Zavlanos, M.M.: Distributed data gathering with buffer constraints and intermittent communication. In: IEEE International Conference on Robotics and Automation (ICRA), pp. 279–284, May 2017
2. Marchukov, Y., Montano, L.: Multi-agent coordination for on-demand data gathering with periodic information upload. In: 17th International Conference on Practical Applications of Agents and Multi-Agent Systems, 26–28 June 2019
3. Meghjani, M., Manjanna, S., Dudek, G.: Fast and efficient rendezvous in street networks. In: IEEE/RSJ International Conference on Intelligent Robots and Systems (IROS), pp. 1887–1893, October 2016
4. Portugal, D., Rocha, R.: MSP algorithm: multi-robot patrolling based on territory allocation using balanced graph partitioning. In: Proceedings of the 2010 ACM Symposium on Applied Computing, SAC 2010, pp. 1271–1276. ACM (2010)
5. Sethian, J.A.: A fast marching level set method for monotonically advancing fronts. In: Proceedings of the National Academy of Sciences of USA, vol. 93, no. 4, pp. 1591–1595, December 1996

Finding Fair Negotiation Algorithms to Reduce Peak Electricity Consumption in Micro Grids

Simon T. Powers[1(✉)], Oscar Meanwell[1], and Zuansi Cai[2]

[1] School of Computing, Edinburgh Napier University,
Edinburgh EH10 5DT, UK
S.Powers@napier.ac.uk
[2] School of Engineering and the Built Environment,
Edinburgh Napier University, Edinburgh EH10 5DT, UK
Z.Cai@napier.ac.uk

Abstract. Reducing peak electricity consumption is important to maximise use of renewable energy sources, and reduce the total amount of capacity required on a grid. Most approaches use a centralised optimisation algorithm run by a utility company. Here we develop a decentralised approach, where agents represent the interests of a household, and negotiate over when to run various appliances. We have developed an experimental framework that allows users' perceived fairness of different negotiation algorithms to be evaluated.

Keywords: Smart grid · Resource allocation · Load balancing

1 Introduction

With the increasing affordability of renewable energy sources such as solar panels and wind turbines, more and more households and communities are starting to become prosumers that produce their own electricity as well as consuming it from the national grid. Groups of households and organizations that jointly invest in renewable sources are known as community energy systems [1]. A community energy system establishes its own micro grid – the electricity that it produces is distributed amongst its members, reducing the amount that they have to buy in from external energy suppliers. Financially, it is advantageous for members to use as much of the energy that the system produces as they can, because the price they get for selling it to the national grid is much lower than the cost of buying in energy to meet their demand.

A key problem that community energy systems then face is load balancing. If every household uses their appliances (e.g. electric heaters, dishwashers) at the same time, then the energy the community produces will be unable to meet this demand, and they will be forced to buy in a large amount from the national grid, possibly supplied by non-renewable sources. A solution to this problem lies in reducing peak consumption by spreading usage out throughout the day. In principle, this can flatten consumption if every household's usage is spaced out to match production from the renewable source. However, each household also has their own preferences for when they would like to use their appliances. This means that if households are going to be motivated to subject

Y. Demazeau et al. (Eds.): PAAMS 2019, LNAI 11523, pp. 269–272, 2019.
https://doi.org/10.1007/978-3-030-24209-1_28

their usage to load balancing, then they need to both see a reduction in peak consumption and hence cost to them, and perceive the load balancing process as treating them *fairly* [2].

To address this problem, we propose the use of a multi-agent system embedded in Home Area Networks. A Home Area Network connects smart appliances and control switches to a smart meter that can turn them on and off [3]. In our design, each household is represented by an agent. A household enters their preferences for the timeslots in which they would like to run various appliances. Their agent then negotiates with the agents representing other households in the system to produce a schedule for running their appliances, which is then sent to their smart meter. We are interested in which kinds of negotiation algorithms households perceive as treating them fairly.

2   Main Purpose

We assume that for a given day the total amount of energy that all households in the community energy system wish to consume is divided into hourly timeslots of equal Kilowatt hour capacities. In a more realistic setting, the size of each timeslot would be based on the predicted amount of energy that the renewable energy source would produce during that time period.

We are currently investigating users' perceptions of the allocations resulting from three negotiation algorithms. The first allocates timeslots randomly to users. The second involves running an English auction to allow households to bid for timeslots. Each household is allocated a number of virtual credits that they can use to bid for timeslots for the following day. In the initial version of the system all households are allocated the same amount of credits that they can use for bidding. However, it is possible to allocate different amounts of credits to households, for example based on their size, or the amount of money they have invested into the community energy system. These would represent fairness in the distribution of resources based on need or effort, respectively [2]. The bidding process could be done interactively by users themselves, or on their behalf by their agent, depending on the level of involvement that the household wishes to have.

The third algorithm, inspired by work on social capital in multi-agent systems [4], involves an initially random allocation of timeslots to households. Agents can then propose timeslot exchanges to other agents. In the base version, agents only accept a proposed exchange if that exchange will allow one of their own timeslot preferences to be satisfied. In a second version, agents gain reputation points by accepting an exchange that is not beneficial to them. These reputation points can be cashed in on the following days, by allowing the agent to exchange a certain number of reputation points for the guaranteed allocation of a particular timeslot. As with the auction mechanism, this algorithm could be fully automated by the agents, or could allow households to propose exchanges interactively.

3 Demonstration

We have developed a prototype of an application that allows users to enter their preferences for the timeslots in which they would like to run various appliances (Fig. 1), and take part in one of the three algorithms (Fig. 2). We then solicit feedback from the user about how satisfied they were with the allocations that they received from that algorithm (Fig. 3). The experimenter can choose the number of timeslots that users can allocate their appliances to on a day, the types of appliances that can be allocated, the negotiation algorithm that will be used, and the number of days that will be simulated. A number of users can then be invited into the laboratory. We record users' preferences, the resulting allocations, and users' satisfaction with the allocation. At the end of the experiment each user is shown the allocations that every other user received on each day along with their preferences, and are asked to rate the fairness of the series of allocations.

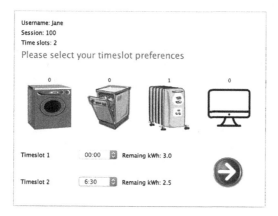

Fig. 1. Here the user has chosen 00:00–01:00 and 06:30–07:30 as slots in which they would like to run appliances that can be time delayed. Each slot has up to 4 kWh of electricity available for the user to distribute between various appliances as they choose. In this example, the user wishes to run their electric heater for 1 h at 06:30.

Fig. 2. The user then bids for their chosen timeslots if using the auction algorithm.

Fig. 3. Finally, the user is shown the resulting allocations from the negotiation algorithm and asked to rate their satisfaction.

4   Conclusions

Load balancing to reduce peak consumption is important to allow maximal use of renewable energy sources. It is also important for energy companies supplying through the national grid, who have to provide excess capacity to meet peak demand. In contrast to centralised optimisation processes run by a utility company, we have proposed a system based on decentralised optimisation, where each household is represented by an agent responsible for meeting its preferences, and that optimises by negotiating with other agents. In addition to monetary incentives, we focus on the perceived fairness of the load balancing algorithm. This is important given that behavioural economics experiments demonstrate that people have a preference for fairness in addition to monetary incentives [5].

References

1. van der Schoor, T., Scholtens, B.: Power to the people: local community initiatives and the transition to sustainable energy. Renew. Sustain. Energy Rev. **43**, 666–675 (2015)
2. Pitt, J., Schaumeier, J., Busquets, D., Macbeth, S.: Self-organising common-pool resource allocation and canons of distributive justice. In: 2012 IEEE Sixth International Conference on Self-Adaptive and Self-Organizing Systems, pp. 119–128. IEEE (2012)
3. Shao, S., Pipattanasomporn, M., Rahman, S.: An approach for demand response to alleviate power system stress conditions. In: 2011 IEEE Power and Energy Society General Meeting, pp. 1–7. IEEE (2011)
4. Petruzzi, P.E., Busquets, D., Pitt, J.: Self organising flexible demand for smart grid. In: 2013 IEEE 7th International Conference on Self-Adaptation and Self-Organizing Systems Workshops, pp. 21–22. IEEE (2013)
5. Fehr, E., Schmidt, K.M.: A theory of fairness, competition, and cooperation. Q. J. Econ. **114**, 817–868 (1999)

EMiR 2.0: A Cognitive Assistant Robot for Elderly

J. A. Rincon[1(✉)], J. Palanca[1(✉)], V. Botti[1(✉)], A. Costa[2(✉)], P. Novais[2(✉)],
V. Julian[1(✉)], and C. Carrascosa[1(✉)]

[1] D. Sistemas Informáticos y Computación,
Universitat Politècnica de València, Valencia, Spain
{jrincon,jpalanca,vbotti,vinglada,carrasco}@dsic.upv.es
[2] Centro ALGORITMI, Escola de Engenharia,
Universidade do Minho, Guimarães, Portugal
{acosta,pjon}@di.uminho.pt

Abstract. This paper presents the *EMiR* robot, which is based on the RobElf robotic platform. *EMiR* has been developed as a cognitive assistant robot which is able to detect and to classify the emotional state of the human with whom it interacts. Moreover, *EMiR* integrates a powerful recommendation module that allows the robot to suggest activities to be done by the humans taking into account the emotional states among other aspects.

Keywords: Assistant robot · Emotions · Elderly

1 Introduction

In recent years we have seen an increase in assistant robots, which are offered as companions for the family and as assistants for the care of the elderly. These robots incorporate different image and audio processing techniques, which facilitate interaction with the human being. However, the information obtained through these techniques need to be processed using image and audio processing techniques in order to eliminate the existing noise. The result obtained is then analyzed using artificial intelligence (AI) tools, which using the processed data is able to identify people and/or objects, transform voice into text and text into voice facilitating the interaction between the human and the robot. Some of these robots have locomotion mechanisms that allow them to move within the environment, others are table robots which behave like personal assistants.

One of the characteristics that these robots currently possess is the ability to classify the emotional state of the human with whom they interact. As well as the ability to express an emotional state of their own, depending on the information they obtain from the environment around them. This characteristic, added to the previous ones, allows the users to feel a certain affinity for the robot, as well as, to facilitate the interaction with it.

© Springer Nature Switzerland AG 2019
Y. Demazeau et al. (Eds.): PAAMS 2019, LNAI 11523, pp. 273–276, 2019.
https://doi.org/10.1007/978-3-030-24209-1_29

This article presents *EMiR*, an assistant robot capable of interacting with humans, using voice and emotion detection as communication elements. Likewise, *EMiR* uses powerful recommendation tools, which make it stand out from other robots in its class. These recommendation tools improve the way *EMiR* interacts with humans.

2   Related Work

Recently, it is observable the increase of interest in assistive robots and their development. Current sociological shift demands technological solutions that are able to interact with elderly people. Thus, the sudden increase of the number of robots available that have as goal solving this sociological issue. Furthermore, they are increasingly refined and advanced in terms of aspect and features, being more human-like in both fields.

In recent years, we have seen a growing interest in robots, many of which are available to people. These robots have nice looks, a powerful background of artificial intelligence, navigation in complex environments, artificial vision, etc. Some of them, such as Pepper [1] and Romeo [2] from *Aldebaran* or Aido [3] or Buddy [3] from *Frog Robotics*, are presented as a new generation of home robots. One of the main applications of these robots is to assist older people in their daily life. Usually, these robots are used as a form of therapy or health care. In therapy field, we can find the Paro robot [4]. The Paro robot is an advanced interactive robot developed by AIST, which offers the well-known benefits of animal therapy to be administered to patients in environments such as hospitals. This robot was built to be a companion to children and elderly, prompting a positive emotional response due to its visual aspect. In the healthcare field we can find the Mabu robot of Catalia Health[1], who learns over time about the personality, interests and therapeutic challenges of each patient. This allows Mabu to create conversations adapted to each patient. The structure of these conversations is based on well-known behavioral models of psychology to promote behavioral change.

From these projects we have observed that while the physical aspect, and its underlying impact (as displayed by PARO), is very advanced and the target of a careful development, they lack in terms of functionality. The actions that makes one human and their emotions are not explored by these projects and we believe that after the initial impact of the visual aspect it is what makes them really human-like. We, as humans, strive for human empathy, and is what our project aims for.

3   EMiR

EMiR is based on the RobElf[2] robotic platform. RobElf is a homemade robot focused mainly on accompanying and interacting with family members. RobElf

---

[1] http://www.cataliahealth.com/introducing-the-mabu-personal-healthcare-companion/.

[2] https://www.robelf.com.

is able to store and recognize people, tell stories for children and serve as a video surveillance tool. Although it is a good platform, RobElf does not have activity recommendation tools for family members. Although RobElf has the ability to smile and express emotions such as anger, sadness, happiness and surprise, he is not able to recognize them. Introducing these utilities would allow the robot a better way of interacting with family members. This would allow RobElf to integrate as one more member of the family.

However, the computational capacity of RobElf is very limited and the introduction of these two new utilities, it is necessary to use external services that can recommend and detect emotions. To detect emotions, *EMiR* uses deep learning as an artificial intelligence (AI) tool, allowing it to classify 7 emotions: afraid, angry, upset, happy, neutral, sad and surprised. *EMiR* uses this classification to recommend an activity that is according to the emotional state of the family member.

Figure 1 shows the *EMiR* operating diagram, which has been divided into three steps. The first is the step of interaction with the human, this step involves the identification of the person, the interaction by voice, identifies the emotional state and interacts with the human with simple dialogues. Step second, *EMiR* modifies his facial expression to represent a series of possible emotional states (Fig. 2). In step third, *EMiR* uses the acquired information (person identification and emotional state) to suggest some type of activity. Finally, all the information obtained and the recommendations generated by the system are represented on an LCD screen.

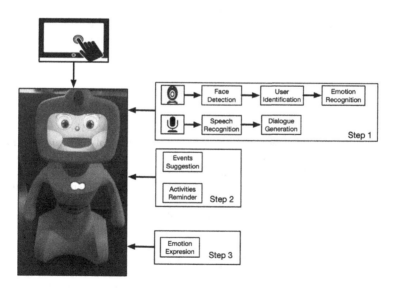

Fig. 1. Flow diagram of the *EMiR* robot operation.

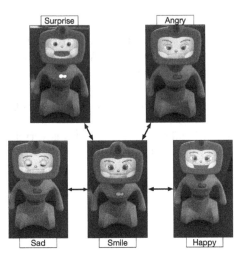

Fig. 2. Emotions expressed by *EMiR*.

4   Conclusions and Future Work

Robotics in the last decade have achieved a very important role in our society, which no longer perceives the robot as a tool used in industry. Robots are acquiring an important role in different scenarios and one of the most important is the assistance to elderly people. It is for this reason that in this article we have presented an approach of a commercial robot applied to the care of elderly people, to which we have added new capabilities for recognition of emotions and recommendation of activities.

References

1. Tanaka, F., Isshiki, K., Takahashi, F., Uekusa, M., Sei, R., Hayashi, K.: Pepper learns together with children: development of an educational application. In: IEEE-RAS International Conference on Humanoid Robots, pp. 270–275, December 2015
2. Claudio, G., Spindler, F., Chaumette, F.: Vision-based manipulation with the humanoid robot Romeo. In: IEEE-RAS 16th International Conference on Humanoid Robots (Humanoids), pp. 286–293. IEEE, November 2016
3. Martinez-Martin, E., del Pobil, A.P.: Personal robot assistants for elderly care: an overview. In: Costa, A., Julian, V., Novais, P. (eds.) Personal Assistants: Emerging Computational Technologies. Intelligent Systems Reference Library, vol. 132, pp. 77–91. Springer, Cham (2018). https://doi.org/10.1007/978-3-319-62530-0_5
4. Wada, K., Shibata, T., Saito, T., Tanie, K.: Effects of robot assisted activity to elderly people who stay at a health service facility for the aged. In: IEEE/RSJ International Conference on Intelligent Robots and Systems (IROS), vol. 3, pp. 2847–2852 (2003)

Agent Process Modelling

When Multiagent Systems Meet Process Models and Microservices

Thiago R. P. M. Rúbio$^{(\boxtimes)}$, Henrique Lopes Cardoso, and Eugénio Oliveira

LIACC/DEI, Faculdade de Engenharia, Universidade do Porto,
Rua Dr. Roberto Frias, 4200-465 Porto, Portugal
{reis.thiago,hlc,eco}@fe.up.pt

Abstract. In this paper we propose the adoption of Agent Process Modelling, a theoretical-practical framework for the orchestration of agent behaviours running process models. The agent model is revisited from a distributed, cloud-native perspective and agents' capabilities are externalized as microservices. Agent logic is represented in process models that orchestrate services execution by using a standard process notation, BPMN, increasing explainability and verification of agents decisions. As a preliminary work, we demonstrate a possible workflow to design and run agent-processes by instantiating the FIPA ContractNet protocol.

Keywords: Agent Process Modelling · Multiagent systems ·
Business Process Modelling · BPMN · Microservices

1 Introduction

Multiple efforts for bridging the gap between Multiagent Systems (MAS) and Business Process Models (BPM) have been presented in the last decades [1,4]. However, multiple challenges, such as processing requirements, explainability of autonomous decision-making or the huge gap between design and implementation discourage non-expert people from embracing the MAS paradigm. On the other hand, recent efforts both in academia and in industry have proposed process models as a way to organize and coordinate networked (web) services in a sustainable manner [3]. The synergy between agents and processes to leverage their benefits of both is still an open field of research.

This work presents the Agent Process Modelling (APM), a theoretical and practical framework for developing agent-process models: agents that are orchestrated with process models. APM goals are to provide a flexible cloud-native way of modeling agent-based systems (even non-technical stakeholders can design their own agents without requiring specific knowledge of MAS) and a scalable way for running virtually unlimited populations of agents, by delegating agents' capabilities to microservices [2].

© Springer Nature Switzerland AG 2019
Y. Demazeau et al. (Eds.): PAAMS 2019, LNAI 11523, pp. 277–280, 2019.
https://doi.org/10.1007/978-3-030-24209-1_30

2   Main Purpose

Literature covering both MAS and processes can be divided into two basic groups: (a) using business process models to generate agent code [3,8]; and (b) designing multiagent systems and agent interactions using process models [1], a perspective that addresses *inter-agent* processes. *Intra-agent* processes are still lacking attention, and yet, process models could represent a way to explain agent behavior, a major challenge of MAS. We believe that we can leverage the growth of microservices as the *de-facto* architecture and for agents-process capabilities and deploy scalable cloud-based applications.

Recent research highlight the advantages of using process models as a natural approach for microservices orchestration [5]. APM represents an externalization of the agents capabilities in a distributed manner using the concept of microservices. The agent's decision logic corresponds to a process model.

A very simple formalization can help us understand the agent-process model and its relationship with the practical application described in Sect. 3. An Agent Process Model system *APMs* is composed by a set of *Agents* and a set of *Processes*. Each *agent* must be associated with a known process model, *process* ∈ *Processes*. Agent *Knowledge* corresponds to a set of variables that can be updated in run-time, with *variable* = *key* × *value*. Finally, the agent's *Goals* give some information about its performance. A *goal* represent a logical operation between a variable's value and another variable or value.

$$APMs = \langle Agents, Processes \rangle$$
$$agent = \langle process, Knowledge, Goals \rangle$$
$$goal = \langle variable, operation, (variable|value) \rangle$$

3   Demonstration

APM combines process models and agent systems: from an agent perspective, it is composed by the agents capabilities in the multiple services they can reach, and the agent function is delegated to the process model execution. In order to demonstrate how to model and run APM we take the well-known FIPA Contract-Net[1] as an example. We show how to model the correspondent agent-processes, one for the initiator agent and the other for a participant.

3.1   Design, Run and Monitor Workflow

The APM workflow comprises three basic steps: (i) design process models; (ii) create agents by associating with existing processes and (iii) monitor agents:

i. Design Process Models. Figure 1 shows the initiator process model diagram, designed with the modeler service. The participant model would be very similar and is omitted by space limitations. The diagrams include decision points for each of the possible received messages.

---

[1] http://www.fipa.org/specs/fipa00029/SC00029H.html.

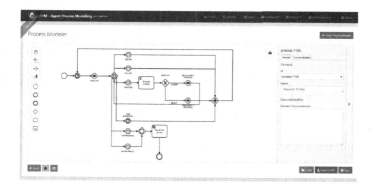

Fig. 1. Initiator process

ii. Create and Run Agent-Process Instances. To create an agent-process instance, we select one of the available process models and proceed with the configuration as in Fig. 2. Agent's knowledge is initially set with the process model variables (services to call and other information from the world) but can also be altered anytime. Therefore, goals can also be included for monitoring each individual agent.

Fig. 2. Agent-Process association

iii. Monitor Agent-Process Executions. Figure 3 shows a run-time visualization of the agent: we can see its properties, such as the process instance running and the current state of the process execution (the blue timer event) as well the evolution of the variables and the goals' performance evaluation.

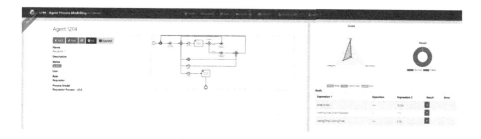

Fig. 3. Agent run-time monitoring: process execution, variables and goals

4   Conclusions

APM is a theoretical-practical framework for developing agent-process models which externalize agent capabilities to microservices and orchestrate agent logic with processes. APM represents a new strategy that adds flexibility to design, run and evaluate any kind of agent models from a cloud-native perspective, leading the adoption of multiagent systems even for non-technical people. Big agent populations are enabled by both the distributed scalability characteristics of the system and the easiness to create new agent instances from existing processes. APM can be applied to any application domain, including market-based scenarios [7] or Cyber-Physical Systems [6], simulated or real.

References

1. Coria, J.A.G., Castellanos-Garzón, J.A., Corchado, J.M.: Intelligent business processes composition based on multi-agent systems. Expert Syst. Appl. **41**(4), 1189–1205 (2014)
2. Dragoni, N., et al.: Microservices: yesterday, today, and tomorrow. Present and Ulterior Software Engineering, pp. 195–216. Springer, Cham (2017). https://doi.org/10.1007/978-3-319-67425-4_12
3. Dumas, M., La Rosa, M., Mendling, J., Reijers, H.A.: Process-aware information systems. Fundamentals of Business Process Management, pp. 341–369. Springer, Heidelberg (2018). https://doi.org/10.1007/978-3-662-56509-4_9
4. Endert, H., Küster, T., Hirsch, B.: Mapping BPMN to agents: an analysis. In: Agents. Web-Services, and Ontologies Integrated Methodologies, pp. 43–58 (2007)
5. Oberhauser, R.: Microflows: lightweight automated planning and enactment of workflows comprising semantically-annotated microservices. In: BMSD 2016 (2016)
6. Rúbio, T.R.P.M., Lopes Cardoso, H., Oliveira, E.: Adaptive multi-agent system for smart grid regulation with norms and incentives. In: Camarinha-Matos, L.M., Falcão, A.J., Vafaei, N., Najdi, S. (eds.) DoCEIS 2016. IAICT, vol. 470, pp. 315–322. Springer, Cham (2016). https://doi.org/10.1007/978-3-319-31165-4_31
7. Rúbio, T.R., Kokkinogenis, Z., Lopes Cardoso, H., Oliveira, E., Rossetti, R.J.: ResMAS-a conceptual MAS model for resource-based integrated markets. In: Bajo, J., et al. (eds.) International Conference on Practical Applications of Agents and Multi-Agent Systems, pp. 117–129. Springer, Cham (2017). https://doi.org/10.1007/978-3-319-60285-1_10
8. Wagner, G.: Information and process modeling for simulation-part i. J. Simul. Eng. **1**, 1 (2018)

Social Recommendations: Have We Done Something Wrong?

Alessandro Sapienza$^{(\boxtimes)}$ and Rino Falcone

Institute of Cognitive Sciences and Technologies,
ISTC-CNR, 00185 Rome, Italy
{alessandro.sapienza, rino.falcone}@istc.cnr.it

Abstract. In this Demo we wish to demonstrate that it is not possible to evaluate a recommender's ability on the basis of how good it is in carrying out the task we are interested in. On the contrary, a recommender should be evaluated as such. Although this mechanism is often used in literature, it unavoidably leads to incorrect results.

Keywords: Social recommendation · Trust · Multi-agent system

1 Introduction

Inside MASs, the role of recommenders/recommendations [5, 7] has largely been proved to be fundamental. They allow us to generalize knowledge, to extend our network of connections and to have access to new potential partners we could not even identify otherwise, without paying a high cost to evaluate them on our own.

For example, consider the case in which an agent X needs to select a partner to carry out a task τ for him. X may decide to choose his partner himself or to rely on one or more recommenders, such as in the event that he does not directly know any reliable agent able to satisfy his request.

For the sake of space, in this work we just focus on showing the experimental results, putting aside some important aspects. For a more detailed discussion, please refer to the work [2] of the same authors.

2 Main Purpose

The current literature has widely showed that the recommenders' evaluations cannot be considered as they are, but it is instead necessary to weigh them on the basis of the value of their informative contribution. In general, trust [1] seems to be a good approach to evaluate how much weight we should attach to these recommendations.

What we would like to prove in this work is that it is not just enough to introduce the trust dimension; we also need to use it properly.

For instance, if X needs to find a partner to carry out τ, and Z recommends Y to him, in turn Z should be evaluated, but on the basis of how good he is in providing

© Springer Nature Switzerland AG 2019
Y. Demazeau et al. (Eds.): PAAMS 2019, LNAI 11523, pp. 281–284, 2019.
https://doi.org/10.1007/978-3-030-24209-1_31

recommendations for the task τ, not for its ability in performing the task itself. Even if this second approach is very often used in literature, such as in trust propagation [3, 4], it just leads to erroneous results.

After all, should you need a dentist, if a friend of yours would suggest one to you, would its opinion less worthy because he is not a dentist himself? On the other hand, would you ever ask a good dentist to suggest you a good dentist? Beyond sounding weird, this may also imply issues of motivational nature: would this dentist be interested in suggesting me another one to do its job? Would he answer correctly or would he try to deceive me?

3 Demonstration

With the purpose of demonstrating that these two aspects need to be kept separated and considered as such, we developed an agent-based simulation through NetLogo [6].

In this experiment, we take into account the possibility that the recommenders may not faithfully report they information they have. In general, each agent possesses a partial and subjective knowledge of the network. He can however report it as it is to the trustor, or he may report a different result. We are not interested in analyzing the motivation beyond this action (which can be due to the aspect of competence or willingness), but we just consider this possibility in our framework.

In the simulation world, we decided to study a population of medium size, 200 agents. Each agent moves around the world and interacting with its peers, in order to collect information about how they perform.

At the beginning, these agents start knowing each other. For each shift, each of them interacts with a given percentage of the population, randomly selecting the agents and then asking them to perform the task τ. Thus, each requester evaluates the performances of the agents it meets, concerning the task τ, memorizing these performances. For the sake of simplicity, we suppose that the subjective perception of the performance coincides with the actual performance, i.e. there is no mistake in the evaluation process of a specific performance.

At the end of this phase, each agent will have a partial (because it has met just a random subset of the agents) and subjective (it evaluates how the other agents performed with it, but it does not know their objective performances) knowledge of the network. This knowledge depends on the duration of the setup phase (hence the number of interactions that each agent has with others). We have established a fixed duration of 100 ticks, in order to let them make enough experience.

In a next step, a further agent, the trustor, enters the simulative world and needs to select an agent to perform the task τ for it. It therefore addresses a percentage of agents in the world (ranging from 1% to 100%) and asks for a recommendation on a specific agent to perform the task.

The different contributions may be aggregated considering the ability of the recommender as such, or wrongly considering its ability in performing the task τ.

After that, the trustor selects the most recommended agent.

We compare the performance of our algorithmic mechanism with the EV (error of evaluation), which is the difference between the highest individual's trustworthiness

$tw_{highest}$ and the one identified by the individual's recommendation $tw_{selected}$. This value is defined in the interval [0,1]. The lower it is, the better the method is used. Ideally (for a perfect recommender and a perfect performer) it should be zero.

$$EV = tw_{highest} - tw_{selected}$$

Each measurement is averaged over 500 instances.
Experimental Setting:

1. World dimension: 33 × 33 patches, wrapping both horizontally and vertically
2. Number of agents: 200
3. Setup phase duration: 100 ticks
4. Percentage of interactions in the setup phase: 2%
5. Percentage of agents interviewed by the trustor: {1, 5, 10, 25, 50, 100}%

As shown in Fig. 1, the trustor's performance is subjected to an important decrease when it confuses the recommenders' abilities. On average, in the wrong assignment case (orange curve) the performance is even 30% worse than the other case.

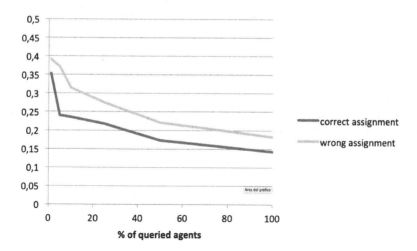

Fig. 1. EV variation when the trustor identifies correctly or wrongly the weights for recommendations

4   Conclusions

The main purpose of this demo was to prove that, even if the concept of trustworthiness is largely used to aggregate different recommendations and for trust propagation, this dimension needs to be used carefully and in the proper way. If we look for a potential partner to carry out the task τ and we ask for recommendations, we cannot take into account the ability of the recommender in performing τ: this would be erroneous and would led us to equally wrong results. On the contrary, we need to consider its ability as a recommender, which may be totally or partially unrelated.

In particular, in the case in question we have chosen to investigate what happens if these two trustworthiness values are totally unrelated. Actually, they could be related to each other, although different, so the difference in the EV could be less.

Acknowledgments. This work is partially supported by the project CLARA—CLoud plAtform and smart underground imaging for natural Risk Assessment, funded by the Italian Ministry of Education, University and Research (MIUR-PON).

References

1. Castelfranchi, C., Falcone, R.: Trust Theory: A Socio-Cognitive and Computational Model. John Wiley and Sons, Chichester (2010)
2. Falcone, R., Sapienza, A.: Selecting trustworthy partners by the means of untrustworthy recommenders in digitally empowered societies. In: Demazeau et al. (eds.) PAAMS 2019. LNAI, vol. 11523, pp. 55–65 (2019)
3. Guha, R., Kumar, R., Raghavan, P., Tomkins, A.: Propagation of trust and distrust. In: Proceedings of the 13th International Conference on World Wide Web, pp. 403–412. ACM, May 2004
4. Jamali, M., Ester, M.: A matrix factorization technique with trust propagation for recommendation in social networks. In: Proceedings of the Fourth ACM Conference on Recommender Systems, pp. 135–142. ACM, September 2010
5. Liang, Z., Shi, W.: Analysis of ratings on trust inference in open environments. Perform. Eval. **65**(2), 99–128 (2008)
6. Wilensky, U.: NetLogo. http://ccl.northwestern.edu/netlogo/. Center for Connected Learning and Computer-Based Modeling, Northwestern University, Evanston, IL (1999)
7. Yolum, P., Singh, M.P.: Emergent properties of referral systems. In: Proceedings of the Second International Joint Conference on Autonomous Agents and Multiagent Systems, pp. 592–599. ACM, July 2003

An Agent Based Technique for Improving Multi-stakeholder Optimisation Problems

Neil Urquhart[✉] and Simon T. Powers

Edinburgh Napier University, School of Computing,
10 Colinton Road, Edinburgh, UK
n.urquhart@napier.ac.uk

Abstract. We present an agent based framework for improving multi-stakeholder optimisation problems, which we define as optimisation problems where the solution is utilised by a number of stakeholders who have their own local preferences. We explore our ideas within the domain of the University Timetabling Problem, demonstrating how a solution created by traditional timetabling methods may be further improved from the perspective of individual stakeholders (students) by agent based methods. We also note that this approach lends itself to increasing the level of trust in such systems by potentially allowing the stakeholders to view the actions taken by agents on their behalf.

Keywords: Timetabling · Optimisation · Real-world · Explainability

1 Introduction

Many real-world optimisation problems exist within a problem domain that has many stakeholders, who each make use of the solution produced and have their own "local" opinions and preferences. Such problems are frequently solved using a centralised solver that produces a feasible solution that addresses the global problem constraints. Examples of such problems include University timetabling [2], Vehicle Routing Problems [1],mobile workforce scheduling [4] or crew scheduling problems [5], see Table 1.

In the domains listed in Table 1 there may be many stakeholders each of which will have a view as to how the solution should meet their requirements. For instance in timetabling a member of staff or a student may wish to avoid having classes at specific times, or within crew scheduling an individual may have a preference to work shifts that cover certain times or have a preference for specific types of work.

In this paper we suggest that the interests of stakeholders can be represented by a multi-agent system (MAS). We propose that existing optimisation techniques are used to produce a solution that satisfies the global hard and soft constraints of the problem. This initial solution is then passed to a multi-agent system for personalisation according to the needs of the stakeholders.

© Springer Nature Switzerland AG 2019
Y. Demazeau et al. (Eds.): PAAMS 2019, LNAI 11523, pp. 285–289, 2019.
https://doi.org/10.1007/978-3-030-24209-1_32

Table 1. Some optimisation problem domains and associated stakeholders

Problem domain	Stakeholders
Timetabling	Staff and students
Vehicle routing	Drivers and customers
Mobile healthcare scheduling	Employees and patients
Crew scheduling	Employees

Within the MAS there are two classes of agent: the *Problem Agent*, and a set of *Stakeholder Agents* (see Fig. 1 and Table 2). The Problem Agent maintains the solution and ensures that it remains valid (i.e. that it continues to satisfy the hard constraints of the problem). The Stakeholder agents each represent the views of one particular stakeholder and request changes to the solution in order to better meet the needs of the stakeholder.

Table 2. The goals and actions of the agents within the system.

Agent	Goal	Possible actions
Stakeholder agent	Achieve as many of the local objectives as possible	Request moves and swaps within the global timetable
Problem Agent	Maintain the integrity of the global solution	Allow request
	Action as many of the requests from stakeholders as possible	Deny request

In this study we will use the University Timetabling domain based on the authors' experiences at Edinburgh Napier University as a test-bed for our ideas.

2   Main Purpose

The University Timetabling problem domain is well known, [2] and many techniques exist to optimise timetables according specific criterion. In the case of Edinburgh Napier University, timetables for staff and students are created by a commercial software package used by University administrators. With an increasing emphasis on improving the student experience, producing timetables that are tailored towards the needs of students becomes more important.

The authors propose that the University's conventional software is used to produce a feasible timetable, which is then passed to our system for customisation. The role of the Problem Agent (as defined in Sect. 1) is undertaken by the Timetable Agent and the stakeholders by Student Agents.

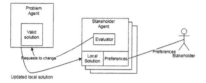

Fig. 1. The MAS architecture.

To facilitate communication between the Timetable Agent and the Student Agents a timetable ontology has been designed. Within the ontology a timetable is defined as a collection of 45 slots, each occupying 1 h (from 09:00 to 17:00 giving 45 slots over a 5 day week). Each slot may be occupied by an event, each event being associated with a module and having a type as lecture, practical or tutorial. Each event also takes place within a room, the size of which limits the numbers of attendees.

Each Student Agent is supplied with a copy of their timetable by the Timetable Agent. The Student Agent may then evaluate its timetable against criteria supplied by its stakeholder. This criteria takes the form of a list of slots that the stakeholder wishes to keep free. The Student Agent can now evaluate their timetable against this local criterion, highlighting events which occupy slots that the student wishes to keep free. A second ontology describes the requests which my be made by the Student Agent. Such requests are possible as many events (especially tutorials and practicals) are duplicated. A move request is suitable where a student wishes to move to an event that has space for an incoming student. Where an event is full, a swap must be arranged with another student making a reciprocal move between events. Where a swap has to be arranged, the student initiating the swap passes the swap request to all other students, who respond if they are able to make the swap.

A fundamental principle is the the Timetable Agent treats all requests as atomic - each request is fulfilled entirely or rejected. Any request that would breach a hard constraint within the timetable is rejected. In this way the Timetable Agent ensures the overall integrity of the timetable.

3 Demonstration

The authors have implemented the basic system in Java using the Java Agent Development Environment [3] for the agents, ontologys and message passing. The demonstrator can import data from the University timetabling system and can also be used with simpler test data.

Figure 2 shows a sample sequence of messages passing between 2 stakeholders and a timetable agent. In this simple example the agents can be seen requesting changes (moves) and being notified of the outcomes.

In order to allow the Student Agents to hold realistic criterion, students within the university were surveyed regarding their attitudes to timetabling.

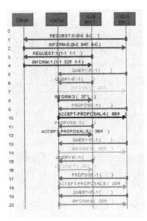

Fig. 2. A screen shot from the JADE sniffer demonstrating 2 stakeholders (student1 and student2) optimising their timetables by communicating with the timetable agent (oracle). Requests for changes are Proposals messages and the response (confirming or denying the change) is an Accept_Proposal. We can also see the agents requesting updated timetables (query_if) and being informed of the updated timetable (inform).

One of the questions within the survey required the student to highlight those slots which they wished to keep free. In this initial version that information was used to allow the Student Agents to evaluate their timetable. Each student agent is randomly allocated the survey results of a respondent. In a production system a student would advise their agent directly through a suitable interface.

4   Conclusions

We present a technique for using agents to improve University timetables. We believe that this framework could be applied to other multi-stakeholder optimisation problems (see Table 1).

A major development to be implemented is to allow a coalition of Student Agents to move an event (subject to timetable constraints). Also to be investigated is measuring the global and local utility of changes and whether that utility value can be used to encourage changes which result in the most effective improvements. We also believe that by allowing stakeholders to specify their own local criteria, and then explaining why the local agent was or was not able to have changes made to accommodate them, we can increase trust in such systems.

References

1. Adewumi, A.O., Adeleke, O.J.: A survey of recent advances in vehicle routing problems. Int. J. Syst. Assur. Eng. Manag. **9**(1), 155–172 (2018)
2. Babaei, H., Karimpour, J., Hadidi, A.: A survey of approaches for university course timetabling problem. Comput. Ind. Eng. **86**, 43–59 (2015). https://doi.org/10.1016/j.cie.2014.11.010

3. Bellifemine, F., Bergenti, F., Caire, G., Poggi, A.: Jade — A Java Agent Development Framework. In: Bordini, R.H., Dastani, M., Dix, J., El Fallah Seghrouchni, A. (eds.) Multi-Agent Programming. MSASSO, vol. 15, pp. 125–147. Springer, Boston, MA (2005). https://doi.org/10.1007/0-387-26350-0_5
4. Urquhart, N., Hart, E.: Optimisation and illumination of a real-world workforce scheduling and routing application (WSRP) via map-elites. In: Auger, A., Fonseca, C.M., Lourenço, N., Machado, P., Paquete, L., Whitley, D. (eds.) PPSN 2018. LNCS, vol. 11101, pp. 488–499. Springer, Cham (2018). https://doi.org/10.1007/978-3-319-99253-2_39
5. Yen, J.W., Birge, J.R.: A stochastic programming approach to the airline crew scheduling problem. Transp. Sci. **40**(1), 3–14 (2006). https://doi.org/10.1287/trsc.1050.0138

Author Index

Ahn, Yong-Yeol 3
Albouys, Jérémy 227
Amaral, Cleber Jorge 232
Amirat, Yacine 127
Atmani, Nawel 127

Barbosa, José 259
Blythe, Jim 3
Bollenbacher, John 3
Botti, V. 273

Cai, Zuansi 269
Calbimonte, Jean-Paul 16
Calvaresi, Davide 16
Camacho, Edgar Camilo 115, 255
Carrascosa, C. 273
Chalkiadakis, Georgios 237
Chemero, Anthony 168
Cherifi, Asma 127
Chhetri, Mohan Baruwal 103
Chibani, Abdelghani 127
Chliaoutakis, Angelos 237
Ciatto, Giovanni 29
Costa, A. 273
Cranefield, Stephen 232
Cunnington, Daniel 242

de Mel, Geeth 242
Dragoni, Aldo Franco 246
Dubosson, Fabien 16

Esmaeili, Ahmad 42

Falcionelli, Nicola 246
Falcone, Rino 55, 281
Ferrara, Emilio 3
Flammini, Alessandro 3
Fukuda, Munehiro 139

Galafassi, Cristiano 66, 251
Galafassi, Fabiane Flores Penteado 66, 251
Garcia Alvarado, Fernando 78
Garcia, Alvaro Paricio 188

Ghorrati, Zahra 90
Gluz, João Carlos 66, 251

Haradji, Yvon 227
Harold, Charles 103
Hart, Nathaniel 139
Higuera, Carlos Hernando 115, 255
Higuera, Carolina 115, 255
Huang, Di 3
Hübner, Jomi Fred 232
Hui, Pik-Mai 3

Inard, Christian 227

Jahed-Motlagh, Mohammad Reza 42
Julian, V. 273

Kallen, Rachel W. 168
Khanouche, Mohamed Essaid 127
Kosiachenko, Lisa 139
Kowalczyk, Ryszard 103
Krohn, Rachel 3

Larukchin, Vladimir 212
Law, Mark 242
Leidner, Jochen L. 200
Leitão, Paulo 259
Lerman, Kristina 3
Lopes Cardoso, Henrique 277
Lopez-Carmona, Miguel A. 188
Lozano, Fernando 115, 255

Maffi, Alfredo 29
Marchukov, Yaroslav 153, 264
Mariani, Stefano 29
Matos, Paulo 180
Matson, Eric T. 42, 90, 127
Mayorov, Igor 212
Meanwell, Oscar 269
Mekuria, Dagmawi Neway 246
Menczer, Filippo 3
Montano, Luis 153, 264

Mozayani, Nasser   42
Muric, Goran   3

Nalepka, Patrick   168
Novais, Paulo   180, 273

Oliveira, Eugénio   277
Oliveira, Pedro   180
Omicini, Andrea   29

Pacheco, Diogo   3
Palanca, J.   273
Powers, Simon T.   269, 285

Raman, Natraj   200
Richardson, Michael J.   168
Rincon, J. A.   273
Roloff, Mario Lucio   232
Rúbio, Thiago R. P. M.   277

Sabouret, Nicolas   227
Saltzman, Elliot   168
Sapienza, Alessandro   55, 281
Sapienza, Anna   3
Schumacher, Michael   16
Schumann, Mathieu   227
Sernani, Paolo   246
Simonova, Elena   212
Skobelev, Petr   212

Tregubov, Alexey   3

Urquhart, Neil   285

Vicari, Rosa Maria   66, 251

Weninger, Tim   3
White, Graham   242

Yalovenko, Olga   212

Printed in the United States
By Bookmasters